The Second Republic

The Second Republic

POLITICS IN ISRAEL

Asher Arian

CHATHAM HOUSE PUBLISHERS, INC.
Chatham, New Jersey

THE SECOND REPUBLIC
Politics in Israel

Chatham House Publishers, Inc.
Post Office Box One
Chatham, New Jersey 07928

PUBLISHER: Edward Artinian
COVER DESIGN: Lawrence Ratzkin
PRODUCTION SUPERVISOR: Katharine F. Miller
COMPOSITION: Bang, Motley, Olufsen
PRINTING AND BINDING: R.R. Donnelley & Sons Company

LIBRARY OF CONGRESS CATALOGING-IN-PUBLICATION DATA
Arian, Alan.
    The Second Republic : politics in Israel / Asher Arian.
        p.   cm.
    Includes bibliographical references and index.
    ISBN 1-56643-052-6
    1. Israel—Politics and government. 2. Political parties—Israel.
3. Political culture—Israel. I. Title.
JQ1830.A58A75   1998
306.2'095694—dc21   97-5247
                                                                  CIP
                                                                  r97

Manufactured in the United States of America
10 9 8 7 6 5 4 3 2 1

*It was my hope that, in addition
to other potential audiences,
my children would use this book
in their studies.*

LEOR (Dukie), AVIV, *and* SHELLY
were too fast for me and graduated.

*It is still a delight to dedicate this book
to them, and to*
SIGAL, MICHAL, ORI, MOR, TAL,
and
KEREN.

Contents

Figures

Tables

Acknowledgments

I am grateful to Ruth Amir, Miri Bitton, Avraham Brichta, Andre Eschet-Schwarz, Sandra Fine, Reuven Hazan, Fanny Itach, Rachel Lael, Dave Nachmias, Gidi Rahat, Michal Shamir, Neta Sher-Hadar, Rafael Ventura, Eran Vigoda, and Shevach Weiss for their guidance and assistance in preparing this volume.

It is a pleasure to acknowledge my appreciation to the following institutions for their support and encouragement: The Israel Democracy Institute, the Department of Political Science of the University of Haifa, and the Ph.D. Program in Political Science at the Graduate School and University Center of the City University of New York.

Thanks also to Edward Artinian, a good friend and publisher.

1. Introduction

A political system must be understood in terms of the people who live under it, their values and ideals, the resources at their disposal, the challenges that face the system, and the institutions developed to meet these challenges. Israel is a fascinating example of a complex system that has developed in a relatively short time (since the 1880s) into a dynamic country that has undertaken colossal commitments in the military, economic, and social fields. There seems to be never a dull moment, with Israel capturing an inordinately large share of the world's attention.

Israel has undergone tremendous changes over the decades, and none as momentous as those of the last decade of the twentieth century. These historical changes ushered in the second republic of Israel, a period in which accommodation among neighbors seemed possible; the former parliamentary system was replaced by one in which the Knesset (parliament) and the prime minister were separately and simultaneously elected; the highly centralized nature of the economic system began to be relaxed; and a very large wave of immigration of Jews arrived from the former Soviet Union.

Israel's political history can be divided into three periods: (1) the time of independence and state consolidation between 1948 and 1967; (2) the period encompassing the Six-Day War of 1967 and the ensuing twenty-five-year struggle to extricate the country from the fruits of that victory; and (3) the period starting in 1993, which began the process of seeking accommodation with the Palestinians. The Labor Party dominated the first period and competed with Likud in the second. The third period coincides with the emergence of Israel's second republic. New issues, new constitutional rules, new leadership.

A peace treaty has existed with Egypt since 1979, but it was with the signing of the mutual recognition agreements between Israel and the Palestine Liberation Organization in Washington in 1993 (also called the Oslo accord) that peace was recognized as a policy option in the war-torn Middle East. A peace treaty was signed with Jordan in 1994, and negotiations were begun with the Palestinians, Syrians, and Lebanese to end the long years of confrontation. The political system abandoned the smoke-filled rooms of the party bosses to the open air of the public arena with the advent of the direct election of the prime minister and the selection of the Knesset lists by the members of the major parties in primary elections. The economy continued its transformation from centralization and state monopoly to more openness and market orientation spurred by the partial lifting of the Arab boycott and by significant international investment. Another demographic revolution occurred with the arrival of more than a half million immigrants from the former Soviet Union.

Each of these expansions introduced a parallel contraction, however. The promise of peace was challenged by the specter of disunity and terror. A Jew assassinated the prime minister of Israel in November 1995, and Arab suicide terrorists killed sixty people in bus bombings and explosions in crowded shopping areas in February and March 1996 in order to stop the peace process.

With the decrease in power of the political bosses, the political parties had yet to find the appropriate mechanisms to fill their classic functions of aggregating interests and articulating demands. The parties were largely eclipsed as the politics of fleeting popularity based on television talk shows and opinion surveys emerged. Add to that a lessening of the power of the Knesset as a result of the direct election of the prime minister and the absence of meaningful parliamentary checks to balance the power of the prime minister. At the very moment of the decline of parties and parliament and the significant strengthening of the executive, the Supreme Court of Israel became more activist than ever before.

The booming economy occasioned an ever-widening gap between the rich and the poor in Israel, with many—half of them Arabs—below the poverty line. In addition, the relaxation of government control of various sectors of the economy has often meant the emergence of a few dominant actors active in many of these sectors, rather than a pattern of pluralistic competition.

The large immigration from the Soviet Union, as well as the much smaller one from Ethiopia, brought to the country many individuals whose classification as Jews was in doubt according to the Orthodox rabbinate charged to decide on such matters. The demographic transformation of the country, along with the fear of increased terror, resulted in the partial replacement of workers from the territories of the Palestinian Authority. These Palestinians had been squeezed out of the labor market by new immigrants, at least in some occupations and for a certain period of time, and by foreign laborers who were brought to the country in very large numbers.

As the state celebrates its fiftieth anniversary in 1998, other changes will make the state seem very different compared to its recent past. The strong sense of isolation that Israel experienced is receding. The collective ethos that once characterized the country has been replaced by individualism. While this individualism existed in the past, it was often denied; now it is celebrated. Choice and options in university education, travel, communications, and entertainment, to name a few, are more plentiful than before, and growing. Health care is now provided as a national service, with the attendant weakening of the major labor union, the Histadrut, whose membership base was once ensured because the Histadrut was once the major health care provider. Even the esteemed Israel Defense Forces (IDF) may no longer be the key mechanism of social integration in the country as it reconsiders its future needs and policies of recruitment in an age of changing military threat and technology of warfare. And there has been a parallel growth of both secularism and religion in the country, decreasing the spirit of coexistence and pluralism, and increasing the anxieties and fears of a "war of cultures"—or worse—among the Jews of Israel.

Since independence in 1948, Israel has changed enormously. From a population of 780,000, it increased by 1995 to 5.5 million. There were 130,000 students at independence, compared with 1.6 million in 1995. There were 700 university students before the war of independence (one-third were killed in that war), and in 1995 there were 100,000. Exports in 1950 amounted to $35 million, and to $64.3 billion in 1993. In 1948, less than 6 percent of the Jews of the world lived in Israel; in 1995 more than a third did. The percentage of the population with thirteen years or more of formal education jumped from 9 percent in 1960 to 27 percent in 1993. One percent of the population lived in housing with three or more persons per room in 1993, compared with 21 percent in 1960; 40 percent of the population lived in housing with one or fewer persons per room in 1993, compared with 7 percent in 1960. Israel's gross national product rose from $2.5 billion in 1960 to $64.3 billion in 1993. The number of tourists arriving jumped from 110,000 in 1960 to 1.8 million in 1993. Private cars in Israel increased in that same period from 24,000 to almost 1 million, telephone subscribers from 68,000 to 1.8 million, air passengers from 223,000 to 4.5 million.

Despite all these dramatic changes, Israel's political system has retained its democratic form, and that is a remarkable achievement on its own. Israel is unique, just as any other country is unique. And yet because of its record, it is tempting to declare Israel "truly unique." Merely by its membership in the exclusive club of democratic nations (in which parties compete for power in free elections), Israel is in a special category. In the 1970s and 1980s, when this club shrank until only a couple of dozen countries in the world met the criteria of democracy, Israel persisted. And this at a time when the defense burden on Israel was unparalleled in other countries, democratic or not. Other countries had large immigrant populations, but proportionate to its size none had absorbed so many immigrants in so short a time as had Israel. When the ranks of the world's democracies again swelled with the collapse of the Soviet Union, Israel was one of the older established democracies in the world.

Political scientists who compare political systems find difficulty in fitting Israel into their schema. Discussing political parties, Giovanni Sartori found the extended dominance of Mapai exceptional; Arend Lijphart, in his study of relations between major ethnic, religious, and language groups, left Israel outside his framework because of its uniqueness; when studying the relations between the military and civilian sectors, or the success in curbing runaway inflation without causing large-scale unemployment or political and social upheaval, Israel is often regarded as special; and discussions of political modernization point to Israel as falling outside many general patterns.[1] The system begun in 1996 of separately electing the parliament and the prime minister is certainly unique.

But we should resist the temptation of establishing a "truly unique" category for Israel. We should recognize special conditions and achievements but should strive at the same time to recognize the similarities and patterns that are familiar to students of other societies. For in other senses Israel's political and social experiences are similar to those of other countries.[2] The scarcity of local resources meant continual searching for foreign sources of import capital, and importing this capital gave the central authorities great sway not only over the economy of the country but over its politics as well. The large numbers of immigrants facilitated the development of machine politics, but the children of these immigrants provided the voters for the successful challenge to the dominant party. Politics in Israel tends to be party politics, and party politics tends to be hierarchical. Lacking a majority of one party in the system, smaller parties (usually religious ones in Israel) hold the balance of power in coalition formation.

As Israel enters its second half-century of statehood and moves well into its second century of development (independence was in 1948; modern Jewish settlement in Eretz Israel began in the early 1880s), it faces problems and issues that are neither new nor unique but will have a strong impact on the system. Through these issues, the politics of the second republic will be played out.

Legitimacy

Almost five decades after independence, the issue of legitimacy still poses a potential threat to the country. Political legitimacy refers to the basis on which the exercise of political authority is established. A system is legitimate when its decisions are generally and widely accepted as just and proper by major groups in the system.

The prestate years in Eretz Israel (the land of Israel) witnessed the development of a regime that had authority without sovereignty. That is, the population on the whole voluntarily undertook to obey the rules and laws set down by the leadership, including taxation and conscription. This was in addition to the rules set down by the mandatory power that held sovereignty. For our purposes, however, what is important is the perception of legitimacy on the part of the overwhelming majority of the population toward the organized decision-making bodies of the Yishuv (the prestate Jewish community).

The prestate period saw both secular and religious challenges to the legitimacy of the Yishuv's decisions. The Revisionists split from the organized Yishuv over issues of policy toward the British mandatory power, arguing that Yishuv institutions and their decisions were not binding on them; in a word, that they were illegitimate. David Ben-Gurion never forgave the Revisionists and their Herut successors for this withdrawal and attempted to deny them legitimacy when he placed them in the company of the communists, the other ostracized group of mainstream Israeli politics in the years following statehood, by declaring that all parties were candidates for his coalition government except the communists and Herut.

In the Yishuv era and for some even in the state period, the haredi ultra-Orthodox (especially the Neturai Karta group) adopted an anti-Zionist position that denied legitimacy to the laws of the state and the rules by which decisions are made. The basis of their opposition was theological and thus represented potentially a most dangerous challenge to the State of Israel. More recently, some elements in the ultranationalist fringes of the Zionist right have rejected government decisions regarding the peace process, even resulting in the assassination of the prime minister of Israel, on the same basis. The basis of their opposition is also theological and represents no less of a challenge. But whatever the basis of the opposition, when religious authorities (or others) declare that their divinely revealed law is superior to and in contradiction with man-made law, severe crisis is inevitable. The existence of competing bodies of law to which significant segments of society owe their allegiance is a prescription for disaster. This situation has been avoided to date in Israel because most religious groups accept the legitimacy of the laws of the state (see chapter 10), but the potential for crisis exists, especially if highly emotional issues emerge to divide the public. Most of the Jewish terrorist groups in the 1980s and 1990s have been religious and have justified their behavior on religious grounds.

The rules by which decisions are made must be perceived as legitimate, and so too must the decisions themselves. One may disagree with a decision yet concede that the decision-making process is legitimate and that those who participate in it have the legitimate right to do so. It is important to distinguish clearly between legitimacy and legality. The question is not only whether the decision makers have the legal right to make the decision but whether the decision is generally accepted. If the debate over the future of the post-1967 territories is between returning them and annexing them, it is likely that major groups in the country (military, press, politicians) hold that either or both options are legitimate. The crisis for the political system arises when people are asked to support or act on decisions they perceive to be illegitimate.

Legitimacy in Israel is by no means assured simply because the government has been duly elected and constituted. Sensitive issues have the potential for polarizing the body politic. The future of the territories taken in the Six-Day War was such an issue. But even then the matter must be broken down further: There was little real opposition to the transfer in 1995–96 to Palestinian control of the Gaza Strip and to cities on the West Bank of the Jordan (Bethlehem and Nablus, for instance); there was some opposition to the transfer of Hebron. There is likely to be strong opposition to a treaty that turns over the Golan Heights to Syria, and fierce opposition to an agreement understood as giving up sovereignty over part of Jerusalem.

The population was divided between those who felt strongly about retaining sovereignty over these territories and those who felt that annexing them would change the basic nature of the state and would hence be detrimental. This kind of basic issue holds great danger for a democratic society because a mere majority for either position will not assuage the intense feelings of the other group. In the light of intense feelings, Prime Minister Menachem Begin showed masterful political skill in calling on the Knesset to determine the issue of removing the Israeli settlements from Sinai as part of the peace treaty with Egypt in 1979. By involving the entire political system in the decision, and not just his governing coalition, he won an overwhelming vote supported more by the Alignment opposition than by his own Likud. The coalition of these two groups was more than enough to overcome the fervent opposition of those who wanted to stop the withdrawal from the Sinai.

Identity

Whether an individual has a clear concept of the nation-state and his or her place in it is an important question asked by political scientists.[3] The state is the most pervasive object of identification in modern political life, surpassing in importance the family, clan, village, movement, and political party. The Zionist idea was catalyzed into the Zionist movement at the end of the nineteenth century as nationalist ideas and movements were sweeping Europe; Israel was born at a time when many new states were emerging. But Israel calls itself a "Jewish state"; this notion has been expressed in legislative declarations and is fervently believed by most Israeli Jews. When asked, "Are we in Israel an inseparable part of the Jewish people or a separate people?" 85 percent chose the first option.

An overwhelming and growing majority of Jews in Israel identify themselves as both Jews and Israelis. More than two-thirds in 1965 and almost three-quarters in 1974 responded that being Jewish played an important part in their lives. When asked about the centrality of being Israeli, 90 percent of the same samples reported in both 1965 and 1974 that "Israeliness" plays an important part in their lives.[4]

In 1996, the overwhelming majority of Jews identified themselves as "Jewish" and "Israeli." Respondents were given four identities to rank: Jewish, Israeli, their ethnic classification (Ashkenazi or Sephardi), or religion (observant or secular). The results are presented in figure 1.1. More than 40 percent of the respondents chose each of "Jewish" and "Israeli" as both first and second choice. Ethnic and religious observance identities were left far behind.

There was a clear difference in ranking when the responses were broken down by the choice for prime minister in 1996, Binyamin Netanyahu of the right-wing Likud or Shimon Peres of the left-wing Labor Party (see figures 1.2 and 1.3). About 70 percent of Netanyahu supporters ranked "Jewish" first, and about 30 percent ranked "Israeli" first. The choices of Peres supporters were the reverse, but neither camp had a monopoly on either of these two identities, nor did many of their supporters choose the more particularistic ethnic or religious observance categories in the first or second places.

For most Jews in Israel, then, there is no discrepancy between being Israeli and being Jewish. Israel is "Jewish" in the sense that its language is Hebrew, its school curriculum is heavily laced with Bible and Jewish history, and its holy days are Jewish in origin and are set in accord with the Hebrew calendar (although important events such as summer vacation, payday, and even the date when winter uniforms are distributed in the army are determined by the Gregorian calendar).

Enormous efforts are expended in the educational system to promote both Jewish and Israeli identities. Politicians have developed a status quo agreement that supposedly freezes the religious issue as it was in the prestate era—in effect it is the basis for all further negotiations while claiming nothing has changed. Since the Second World War, the Jewish world has almost unanimously accepted Zionism and the security of Israel as the top priority on its agenda. It is not surprising, then, that few Israelis feel cross-pressured regarding these topics. To be sure, there have been expressions of support for one end of the continuum or the other. The Ca-

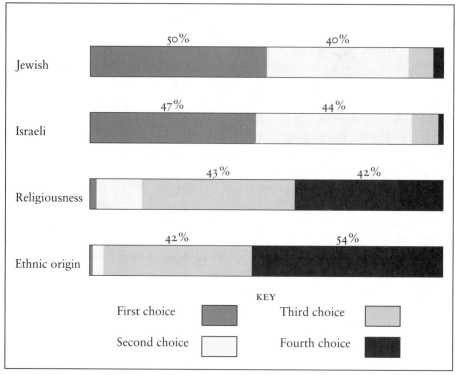

FIGURE I.I
SELF-IDENTIFICATION ("IDENTITY") AMONG JEWS, 1996

naanite movement of the 1950s held that the geographical expression of its identity as originating from the land of Canaan was more meaningful to its identity than the Jewish identity that included 2,000 years of Diaspora; this latter identity was adopted by the Zionist movement. At the other extreme are individuals who reject the national expression of Judaism—the State of Israel—and whose sole identification is with the Jewish religion. For some of them, such as the Neturai Karta group, citizenship in a Jewish state is a secular detail of no religious significance since the state was not wrought by divine decree. For others, it is outright blasphemy to support such a state, and hence it follows that obstructing it becomes laudable.

While the identity issue seems resolved for most Israeli Jews, the system is faced with three crucial issues. The first is the meaning of a Jewish state; the second is the role of the State of Israel for Jews who do not live in Israel. The third is the relation to the state of non-Jews living in Israel.

What does it mean to have a Jewish state? Is Israel a country of Jews or a country with Jewish content? How is this Jewish content to be institutionalized in the life of the state and who is to decide? What expression is

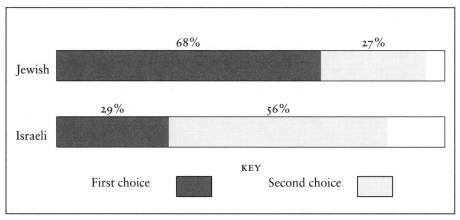

FIGURE I.2
SELF-IDENTIFICATION ("IDENTITY") AMONG JEWISH
NETANYAHU VOTERS, 1996

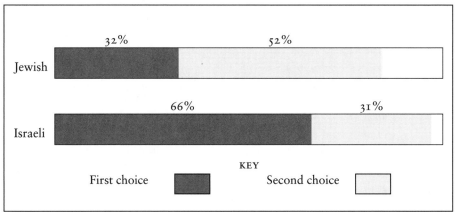

FIGURE I.3
SELF-IDENTIFICATION ("IDENTITY") AMONG JEWISH
PERES VOTERS, 1996

Judaism to have in the life of the state? More specifically, can both freedom of religion and freedom from religion be ensured? And what of pluralism of Jewish expression?

Israel has dealt with this problem up to this point in two ways: it has promised the retention of the status quo in synagogue-state affairs (meaning that arrangements in effect during the prestate period regarding religion and religious practice would be extended into the state period), and it has afforded monopoly status to Orthodox Judaism when the state provides a role for religion (as in personal law issues such as marriage and divorce) to the virtual exclusion of other forms, such as the Conservative and Reform movements. The implication of this practice is to limit certain personal liberties, such as for marriages in cases in which the Orthodox rabbis have deemed it forbidden, to limit access of organizations and individuals to funding provided by the government for religious affairs, and to institutionalize limits on the role of women in communal religious life.

This state of affairs is a constant problem in a population that is not particularly observant. The estimates are that about a quarter of Israeli Jews are observant in an Orthodox sense or even beyond that, including 6 to 10 percent haredi, or ultra-Orthodox; that about 40 percent are determinedly secular; and that the rest are somewhere between those poles. While many are tolerant and even sympathetic to a religious way of life, many are not, and a sizable minority would resist the imposition of a religious lifestyle.

The irony of the situation is that as Israel becomes more secular, the perception persists of the growth of the power of the Orthodox religious parties. In 1996 they won a record 23 seats of the 120-member Knesset. These Orthodox parties can tolerate the seculars and try to educate them; they abhor the Conservatives and Reform, feeling that they have usurped the titles, prayers, and ceremonies of Judaism. As Orthodoxy becomes more influential in Israel, the power of the other denominations of Judaism is increasing in other Jewish communities around the world.

Second is the role of the State of Israel for Jews who do not live in Israel. Conceiving itself as a Jewish state has been translated in practice to a policy that makes every Jew a citizen of Israel virtually for the asking. The Law of Return is the concrete expression of the prophetic vision of the "ingathering of the exiles." The statistical fact is that more than a third of the world's Jews live in Israel, but the boundaries of Israel's political system are hard to set because the spiritual and material influence of Jews who are not Israelis is often felt. Many Israelis see their national undertaking as providing a refuge for the world's Jews; and many Jews in the world show pride, concern, and anxiety (or other emotions) toward Israel in a manner unusual for citizens of foreign countries. Regardless of the distribution of opinion regarding Israel among the Jews of another country, the question of identity is always near the surface. Sometimes it is asked by Jews themselves and sometimes by those who wish to question the loyalty of the Jews. It is not a new question. If Jews were persecuted in the Middle Ages for having a distinct religion, in modern times this dilemma is compounded by the existence of the State of Israel and the difficulties this raises regarding both religious and national loyalties.

The third issue is the difficult dilemma faced by non-Jewish citizens of Israel. For most, the experience raises fundamental conflicts of identity. Let us begin by noting that the Arab population in Israel (in the boundaries preceding the 1967 war) is referred to as the "minorities." What a wonderful example of a Hebrew expression laden with ideological meaning! The Arabs are a minority (some 18 percent at this time) in the formal sense, but this does not accurately reflect the demography of Eretz Israel or the Middle East, nor does it take into account Arab sensibilities. Called on to support a Jewish state in a period of intense Arab nationalism and when other forces are calling for the establishment of a Palestinian state is a difficult position to be in. Israeli Arabs are not called on to serve in the army (the Druze are), and this can be seen as a measure of semicitizenship because army service is so important in determining the pecking order of Israeli political and bureaucratic life.

The way this group identifies itself is a crucial challenge to the system and a heavy burden on the members of the group. Almost 80 percent of them voted in the 1996 election. A representative sample was presented with the parallel question asked of the Jews in 1996, with the response options being Arab, their religion (Moslem, Christian, Druze), Palestinian, or Israeli, with the results presented in figure 1.4. Their choice pattern was much more complex than that of the Jews. On the whole, Israeli Arabs have demonstrated prudence in their dilemma; but it would be shortsighted not to recognize the strains they are under as a potential source of crisis for the system.

Integration

Over a hundred years ago, modern Jewish settlement in Eretz Israel began. The first hundred years were dominated by eastern European immigrants and their children. Positions of power, institutions, the culture, the economy, and the educational system were in their hands. But a great historical asymmetry occurred. The Zionist movement—based on secular, nationalist European ideas—was not particularly successful among secular European Jews. While most were ready to subscribe to its ideology, fewer were actually willing to live in Israel. In a sense, the Zionist movement generated a leadership but failed to attract its natural followers.

After independence, large-scale immigration of Jews from Arab countries began. The people who arrived tended to be more traditional than their European counterparts who came to Israel or their cousins from Arab lands who did not. They proved to be much more loyal to the Zionist cause as a group. Only 10 percent of the world's Ashkenazi (European) Jews live in Israel compared with two-thirds of the Sephardim (generally from Asian and African countries). The progress of the Sephardim in terms

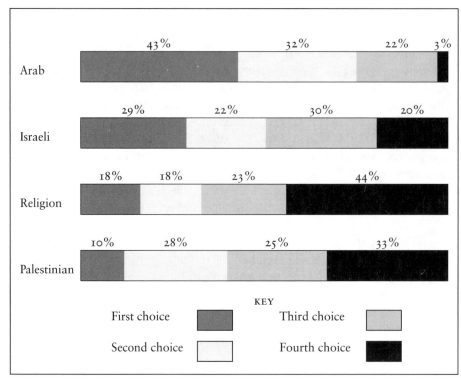

FIGURE I.4
SELF-IDENTIFICATION ("IDENTITY") AMONG NON-JEWS, 1996

of education and occupation was swift; undergoing extremely rapid development, they were also faced with negative aspects of modernity such as the breakdown of the patriarchal family and soaring crime rates. In the early 1980s, as the Israeli-born sons and daughters of Sephardi immigrants became a vocal and numerous factor in Israeli elections, the issue of their integration into the system emerged in a boisterous and sometimes violent manner. On the whole, extreme positions have not been taken, although there have been visible exponents of these. Undoubtedly the Sephardim have lately achieved higher levels of influence and power than they had in the past; they have made substantial gains in the political arena and have advanced socially and economically as well, but not nearly as much as the Ashkenazim. The majority position of the Sephardim among the Jews of Israel did not last long; most of the immigrants in the mass wave from the former Soviet Union were Ashkenazim. The issue of the integration of the Sephardim into Israel's political and social life will remain a tender one for years to come.

It is clear that the demographic and sociological changes that the Israeli population is experiencing will profoundly affect the political system. A century of Ashkenazi dominance has passed, but it does not follow that we are entering a century of Sephardi dominance. What is more likely is the emergence of a native-born leadership that is more Israeli than Ashkenazi or Sephardi. The children of Israel wandered in the desert forty years before they entered the land of Israel, before a new generation emerged to take on the burdens of nationhood. Israel's fortieth birthday came and went, and the election of Netanyahu in 1996 marked the emergence of a young, Israeli-born leadership. In fact, Netanyahu was born after the state was founded.

A problem of integration in another sense is posed by Arabs living in the territories that resulted from the 1967 war. Many of those Arabs now live under the Palestine Authority, but in terms of security and foreign policies they are still under Israel's control. The vast majority of them have known no other form of government than autonomy or occupation by the Israel Defense Forces. The issue of their future will loom large in the coming years, and the Israeli political system will be tested as the permanent status agreement with the Palestinians is worked out. Should they have their own state or not? Can a sovereign state commit to permanent demilitarization? And if it does, how meaningful is that commitment? What is to be done with the Jewish settlers and settlements in the territories? Should Jews not have the right to live anywhere in Eretz Israel? The dilemmas will be stark, the answers complex.

Political Culture

As change occurs in Israel's relations with its neighbors and in its position in the world, the character of the issues that dominate domestic politics is likely to shift. The topics of security and foreign policy will likely remain central in public awareness, but the nature of the debate and the domestic implications are likely to change. In the past, maintaining security and continuing the welfare state were dealt with as consensual issues. Maintaining strong defenses will still be the overriding concern of all Israeli governments, and many policies will still be cast in the name of defense. The welfare state will still be sanctioned because of the importance of providing citizens with minimum standards so that the youth will be fit for army life. But in the second republic it is likely that these topics will be more divisive and that the debate will spill over into the political system more openly than in the past. What type of army is best suited to the changing conditions, a broad-based conscription army as in the past, or a much smaller, professional volunteer army with high levels of technological capability? What are the implications of these choices for the defense of the country, and what is the likelihood that an officer class will emerge that sees itself different from but better than the elected leaders? Can the imperatives of international economic competition allow a full-fledged welfare state? Are the rewards of national economic success to be shared, or should the successful be allowed to enjoy the fruits of their effort, while many others live at a much lower economic level?

If the country becomes less entangled with issues of the territories and of the Palestinians, will it then be able to come to grips with the real questions of Zionism, including the meaning of a Jewish democratic state? What is the meaning of a Jewish state? A state full of Jews, or a state filled with Jewish content? And who is to define Jewish content? For that matter, who is to define who is a Jew? In a postwar period, one could imagine public concentration on issues such as these, and possibly even a Labor-Likud coalition of secular Zionist parties defining the relations with the Jewish religious and with the Arab parties.

Even in the second republic, various other characteristics are likely to remain. Politics in Israel has always been party politics, and party politics has been elite politics. These basic patterns are likely to remain, even though changes occur. For example, the party system has undergone a shift from dominance to competitiveness, and the major political parties have become much more electorate oriented, as seen clearly in the legislation to elect the prime minister directly and in the introduction of primaries by party members to select the lists.

The dominant party from the 1930s until 1977 was the Labor Party. Herut (Likud), the party once declared illegitimate by the dominant party's leaders, was the largest vote getter in the 1981 elections. At these elections the two parties took 95 of the 120 Knesset seats, with the Likud only one seat stronger than Labor. After the 1988 elections, the Likud was still one Knesset seat stronger than Labor, but by then the total number of seats won by the two parties had dropped to 79, with Likud winning 40, Labor 39. By 1996, Labor had a two-seat advantage, except that the total number of seats for both Labor and Likud was only 66. But by the 1996 elections, the prime minister was directly elected, and Netanyahu won control of the government by getting 30,000 votes more than Peres did out of the 3 million votes cast. Competitiveness flourished, but the rule for forming a coalition that could control a majority of the Knesset changed.

The fall of the share of the two big parties coincided with the emergence of a new electoral system that allowed the voter two opportunities to express his or her preference, once for the prime minister and once for the Knesset. Sectarian groups—the religious, the Arabs, the new immigrants —achieved very high levels of representation and found avenues of expression outside the large parties. Membership in parties rose slightly, but the role of parties in government became less clear. Legislative activity increased because of the activity of individual legislators; the Knesset as an institution became the weakest of the three branches of Israel's government, mostly because the political parties had lost their cohesiveness and focus.

Responsiveness to the public has grown over the years, yet Israel's political system retains features of centralization and hierarchy. Party members now select the leaders of the two major parties and the electorate votes for the prime minister. But the prime minister is afforded enormous power with few checks or balances on his behavior. His power includes the ability to control both the Knesset majority and the major ministries. It is hierarchical in the sense that a party, a politician, and a citizen all tend to know their place in the power structure and rarely overreach themselves. The opposition accepts its relatively powerless role just as a junior coalition power accepts its relatively subordinate role in the calculus of power. Eyes tend to focus on the leader, waiting for the cue. Individuals and groups fit into this structure, and political parties tend to be collections of factions, or nuclei, around leaders, jockeying for position in the pyramid of power. The hierarchical nature of the structure is facilitated because subordinate groups and individuals are likely to be dependent on decisions made at higher levels of the hierarchy regarding appropriations and appointments.

All this fits in nicely with Israel's bureaucratic public life. The centralized economy encourages dependency, with the government controlling about half of the economy's activity and directly influencing much of the country's economic life. These figures register enormous economic influence and hint at enormous political power. Add to that the fact that almost two-thirds of those employed work in services and that three-quarters of the employed are salaried, and the impact of the control of the centralized economy is clear.

Just as the role of political party and the centralized nature of the economy are likely to retain importance in the second republic, so too with ideology. The style of Israeli politics is ideological. The use of symbols, rhetoric, and coded phrases has always been evident in the Israeli political experience and is not likely to diminish soon. What is also true is that Israeli politicians can be very pragmatic and can review long-expressed ideological formulations if their understanding of political reality so demands. The population on the whole tends to be less ideological, but shows high degrees of deference to the ideological phrases of politicians, just as it does to the decisions of the leadership.

Israel's political culture demonstrates a fascinating mix of ideology and pragmatism.[5] The socialist ethic that ruled for decades has withered, although it is still found in preserves such as ideological meetings of the Histadrut (federation of trade unions), in some kibbutzim and moshavim, and in a few youth groups. But the element of nationalism has retained its intensity, if not strengthened. The materialism of many Israelis has been observed often, and it seems to have become the norm; despite very high levels of taxation, the ethos developed is one of seeking creature comforts in the present tense. This materialism does not blunt, and indeed perhaps enhances, high levels of identification with the system by most Jews and a willingness to sacrifice for its preservation and maintenance.

The most enduring feature of the system is likely to be the politician. Israeli politicians tend to be dependent on the party and its institutions for their influence and livelihood. But all of them, except for two or three at the apex of the pyramid, share a generally low level of prestige. In the late 1970s, "Knesset member" was sixty-fourth out of ninety preferred occupations ranked by a national sample.[6] A taste of the orientation of the public is gleaned from the story of the Haifa-area resident arrested for attacking his neighbor with a knife. In explaining his behavior, he claimed that his neighbor had called him a politician.[7]

The politician and the political system have three distinct spheres of activity, each with its own rhythm and rules. These are electoral politics, coalition politics, and bureaucratic politics. The politician divides his time among the three, but the nature of his investment and his hope of profit are different in each sphere. Electoral politics may be the most important formally because the election of the prime minister and the allocation of Knesset seats as determined by voters on election day establish the division of political power. Electoral politics is limited to the campaign period, though the press and public (and perhaps politicians as well) think of political life as an unending campaign.

Coalition politics can come up at any time, but usually involves a handful of actors. But since the coalition is necessary to rule, the payoff of the coalition game is high. Coalition politics determines who will control important government ministries, Knesset committees, policies, and budgets. Crisis in the coalition is an effective way of pressuring for more, but there is also a danger that power already achieved will be lost if the coalition crumbles.

Bureaucratic politics is likely to be the major investment of the politician. He must retain or enhance his position within his organization if he is to continue his career. He may well assume that others covet his position; if he is the representative of a group, he may assume that others in the group would like to see him rotate out of office; within his party there are other groups that feel deprived as they are denied representation because of one group's success in achieving positions of influence; certainly, outside his party, members of other parties have set their goal to replace him and his party. He must keep the politics of his constituency organization, his party, and the country clearly in mind as he meets, speaks, maneuvers, and negotiates to retain power for himself, his group, and his party. This in-group fighting is the kind of politics that is most hidden from the public eye but the one that probably takes up most of the energies of the politician.

The world of Israeli politics often seems confusing to the uninitiated. One reason is that names of parties and alignments change, and that can be confusing. The basic uniformities are strong, however, and concentrating on major issues and patterns shows that the system often follows a few basic rules. For readers familiar only with Anglo-American politics, a word of advice: Try not to transfer your understanding of politics and its terminology to the Israeli system without adjustment. Terms such as left-right, checks and balances, and even democracy are widely used in Israeli politics. But it would be misleading to accept them in the same way they are used in other systems. Israel is much more understandable to someone who knows political systems in continental Europe. The forms and usages are more directly traceable there. Even then, Israel poses special problems, for its history is unique, and its politics must be understood in that light.[8]

The dilemmas faced by Israeli democracy are similar to those faced at the turn of the century by other advanced democracies. The details depend on the unique historical developments of various countries, but the complexity and confounding nature of the perplexities are familiar. These themes recur in the following chapters:

- ☐ Can the rule of law be maintained when many have intense and conflicting views of the appropriate sources of legitimacy in the system?
- ☐ Can pluralism and tolerance be fostered when religious and nationalist passions well up?
- ☐ How do you forge into a single nation citizens from various ethnic backgrounds and belonging to different religions?
- ☐ What is the meaning of participatory democracy when technological innovations atomize society and individualism is rampant?
- ☐ How are the branches of government to be balanced so that abuses of power will be checked and individual liberty maintained?
- ☐ What is the meaning of parliamentary democracy when political parties are in serious decline?
- ☐ How can you promote a sense of responsiveness and accountability for a political system perceived by a cynical electorate to be peopled by manipulating politicians?

☐ How can public needs by met by a profit-driven media?

☐ What is the role of the nation-state, and the responsibility of the welfare state, in a period of globalization and open borders and markets?

2. People of Israel

A key element in the development of any country, and certainly in Israel, is its population—its size, quality, and morale.[1] It is fitting to focus on the people of Israel for many reasons, not the least of which is the fact that the Zionist movement's overt goal was to change the place of residence of the world's Jews from the Diaspora to Zion. In that sense the Zionist movement has been quite successful. In 1882, there were 24,000 Jews in Eretz Israel, or .31 percent of the world's Jews. By 1996, Israel's 4.55 million Jews constituted 35 percent of the 13 million world Jewish population.[2]

Population is an important hint to politics and public policy. It is well worth keeping in mind that of Israel's 5.5 million population in 1995, about 82 percent were Jews, 14 percent Moslems, and 3 percent Christians. More than 90 percent lived in cities, 4 percent in villages, 3 percent in cooperative moshavim, and 2.5 percent in collective kibbutzim. Of the Jews, the continent of origin of 55 percent was Europe, 20 percent Africa, 16 percent Asia, and 8 percent America and Oceania.

Mass immigration of Jews to Israel continues to enjoy wide support on an abstract level from Jews in Israel and abroad, but the fact is that most Jews do not live in Israel. Any understanding of Israeli politics must rely heavily on an appreciation of who came and who did not, when they came, why some left, and how those who stayed became part of the system. We must take into account the relations between the Jews of Israel and the Jews of the world during this 110 years and the impact of the relatively large growth of the Jewish population in Israel on the Arab population of the country.

The bottom line of the immigration balance sheet is determined by a large number of forces including developments taking place abroad, the attitude of the ruling power, and the psychological predispositions of the immigrating population. These in turn affect the likelihood of successful absorption and the effect of immigration on the political institutions of the country. In general, the following points should be kept in mind:

1. There is no easy explanation for immigration. It is convenient to think of "pull" factors making a country attractive and "push" factors making the country from which one emigrates unattractive. Often these forces work in tandem. Usually there is no similar experience in a normal adult's life parallel to the dependency encountered after immigration to a foreign country. If the "pull" factors outweigh the "push" factors, absorp-

tion is likely to be easier. If one is imbued with ideological passion or religious vision, making *aliyah* ("coming up") to Israel will be managed even more successfully. Also, the social context is important. An individual coming alone is likely to have a much harder time than if he belongs to a group, be it a family, village, or political group. It is no accident that *landsmenschaft* develop after every substantial immigration. They answer a very basic need of community, roots, and ties to the familiar—things that are usually initially denied the immigrant.

2. While Zionism provided a ready ideology for immigration to Eretz Israel, most Jews who moved and who had other options chose not to come. That was especially true of the mass migration from Russia and Poland to the United States at the beginning of the twentieth century, and it is equally true of those Jews allowed to leave the Soviet Union near the end of the century. Note, however, that Jews of North African and Middle Eastern extraction came to Israel in higher percentages when they left their countries.

3. Much immigration is caused by external factors. Large numbers of Polish Jews arrived in Eretz Israel in the mid-1920s because of the double pressures of a general boycott having been declared on Jewish industry and commerce in their country of origin and a simultaneous legislation of quotas formulated in the Johnson-Lodge Immigration Act of 1924 in the United States, which limited access to a desirable country of destination. A record high number of 66,000 immigrants arrived in 1935, about a quarter of them from Germany, as conditions in pre–World War II Europe deteriorated. In 1957 a substantial number of immigrants from Morocco arrived, reflecting anxieties felt by Moroccan Jews as nationalism in North African countries began to emerge. Mass immigration from the Soviet Union toward the end of the century could be undertaken only when Soviet authorities granted exit visas; it is even more understandable in the light of immigration restrictions put in place by the U.S. government, thereby depriving access to the country of first choice for many Soviet émigrés.

4. Every immigration has its emigration. Some, especially if they are physically and financially able, are likely to return to their country of origin or to immigrate to another destination. In the massive immigration of many nationalities to the United States between 1908 and 1924, for every 100 immigrants there were 34 emigrants. During the second *aliyah* (1904–14) Ben-Gurion estimated that only one in ten remained (the figure is probably closer to three in ten).[3] Over time, about 10 to 15 percent of Israelis have left Israel.[4] For historians, sociologists, and demographers, this is a natural and well-known phenomenon. To the Zionist it is saddening, since one who believes in the ideological correctness of his cause sees immigration to Zion as a key element in its platform.[5]

5. Earlier waves of immigrants are advantaged compared with those who come later. This tends to be true for both groups and their leadership. By introducing a new group at the bottom of the absorption ladder, the group with longer tenure is "pushed up." The new group generally finds it harder to acclimate itself to the new country than those who preceded it. Especially regarding jobs, housing, and political power, the old-timers are likely to be very jealous of their privileges and suspicious of the demands of new groups. The groups that perceive themselves as deprived are likely to call for a reallocation of resources to alleviate their deprivation rather than invest large sums on absorbing new immigrants.

Periods of Immigration

For our purposes, the period between 1882 and 1996 can be divided into five categories. Each witnessed an expansion of the Jewish population in Israel, and each had an effect on the politics of the country.

THE FORMATIVE PERIOD: 1882–1924

The formative period saw the smallest immigration numerically but was the most significant politically. The very limited and select immigration of rather homogeneous populations was the time of the initial emergence of the political leadership that was to dominate Israel's years of creation.[6]

Before 1880, fewer than 25,000 Jews lived in Eretz Israel. They were concentrated in the four holy cities of Jerusalem, Hebron, Tiberias, and Safed and spent their time largely in study and prayer. Sustained by moneys collected from Jewish communities outside Eretz Israel, they prayed for the redemption of the land and the coming of the Messiah. Their reception of secular settlers who came to fulfill their prayers without divine help was notably cool.

The settlers of the first *aliyah* (1882–1903), numbering between 20,000 and 30,000, came in reaction to the growing anti-Semitism in Russia. Whereas most of their fellow Jewish immigrants went to the United States, this handful (compared with the 2.5 million Jews who left eastern Europe between 1880 and 1924) responded to the nationalist awakening among Jews and immigrated to Eretz Israel. Many of them had received ideological instruction in the first organized nationalist Jewish groups known as Hovevei Zion, but were dramatically lacking in funds and agricultural skills. Religious Jewish settlers were especially hostile, seeing the newcomers not only as religious offenders but as competitors for the limited charity sent from abroad. The immigrants were relatively educated, from urban backgrounds, and totally unprepared for the barren wastelands they encountered in Eretz Israel. This brave beginning was rescued from ignominious failure by "import capital," money sent from abroad, a feature of Israeli life that would persist. The efforts of Baron Edmond de Rothschild, a noted Jewish philanthropist, rescued the settlers but installed Rothschild agents as overseers; soon the settlers became accustomed to turning to Paris for help and even sent their children to France to school. Many of them did not return.

The second *aliyah* (1904–14) came out of the ferment of the unsuccessful Russian revolution of 1905 with its attendant ideas of social equality and freedom. Of the 35,000 who came during this period, almost all were from Russia, a few thousand from Romania, and 2,000 from Yemen. About 10,000 were pioneers in the sense of abandoning the easy life and comforts of home in order to participate in the Zionist revolution. Reports of malaria and other tribulations received from members of the first *aliyah* did not daunt them, but many proved unable to meet the challenge and left. This is the most important of the original *aliyot* in two senses: (1) three top leaders of the formative period in Israel's history—David Ben-Gurion, Yitzhak Ben-Zvi, and Yosef Shprinzak, Israel's first prime minister, second president, and first chairman of the Knesset, respectively—arrived then; and (2) the political organizations they founded would have the greatest impact on the future of the country.

Largely young, single, dedicated socialists, the members of the second *aliyah* proved more innovative than their counterparts in the first. Of course, they had a firmer base on which to work, thanks to their predecessors' efforts. The newcomers were successful in developing new kinds of agricultural settlements and industry and in promoting Jewish cultural activities. During this period political parties emerged, and the Histadrut was later created by them. These developments occurred naturally in response to challenges and problems faced in everyday living and not as a result of an ideological blueprint.

The interests of members of the first and second *aliyot* soon clashed. The young pioneers wanted to work at physical labor but found themselves shut out of businesses of their natural employers, the members of the first *aliyah,* because indigenous Arab labor was cheaper, more plentiful, and more experienced. Both sides used national-interest arguments, the landowners arguing that they were building a viable economy, the laborers pointing out that Jewish labor was an essential of a viable economy and that in its absence sizable immigration would not be possible. The battle over the "conquest of labor" was begun, and the laborers were successful in winning to their side the World Zionist Organization.[7] They set the tone for Jewish settlement and would ultimately emerge as national leaders. They also won the undying enmity of the plantation and orchard owners, an antagonism passed on from generation to generation in Israeli politics.

The success of the labor leaders was not in their ability to organize the workers or increase immigration substantially. In fact, most of the laborers were not organized in either of the two labor parties of the day, nor did they work predominantly in agricultural occupations. But they set a course and developed a commonality of cause and internal cohesion, which are preconditions of any politically successful organization.[8]

The years of the First World War saw a cessation of immigration and the ultimate liberation of Palestine from the Ottoman Empire by the British and Allied armies. In 1917, British Secretary of State for Foreign Affairs Arthur James Balfour sent Lord Rothschild his famous declaration announcing the support of the British government for Zionist aspirations in Palestine. And in the 1922 League of Nations Mandate for Palestine, Article 6 stated that "the Administration of Palestine, while ensuring that the rights and position of other sections of the population are not prejudiced, shall facilitate Jewish immigration under suitable conditions."

Immigration to Eretz Israel picked up again at the beginning of the 1920s with the end of the First World War and during the convulsions that swept over Russia in its revolution and attendant civil war. Most of the 35,000 members of the third *aliyah* (1919–23) came from Russia, 15,000 of them identifying themselves as pioneers. This influx of Jews brought the population in 1922 to 85,000, the same as it had been in 1914, counterbalancing those who had left.[9]

The third *aliyah* comprised mostly young, single males from Poland and Russia who had been prepared for their immigration by participation in agricultural training programs in Europe organized by Zionist organizations. They entered a more structured environment than had the members of the first and second *aliyot,* and strong ideological motivation was prevalent among them. Their experiences in Europe taught them the importance of political organization and control, and their nationalism brought them to Eretz Israel rather than America or other destinations. They accepted the authority of leaders already living in Israel (who were only a few years older than they) but pressured for their own goals. Many of them were members of groups, which afforded internal cohesion to their efforts and magnified their influence in the system. They and their predecessors of the second *aliyah* formed the generation of Israel's founding fathers.

We have seen how immigration was shaped by international developments as well as by the motivation of the immigrants. A third factor was the policy of the ruling authorities to immigration. The Turks opposed immigration but because of the system of capitulations under which Europeans enjoyed extraterritorial privileges throughout the Turkish Empire, and because of the ineffectiveness of the officers of the Ottoman administration to police immigration, about 80,000 Jews arrived in Eretz Israel between

1880 and 1914.[10] The British were conscious of Arab sensitivities to the growing Jewish population and were more aggressive in attempting to establish a policy of immigration during their Mandate.

The formula developed by the British was "economic absorptive capacity," and the immigration ordinance of 1920 tried to implement the formula by allowing in Jews of independent means, those with religious occupations, and dependents of residents. Beyond that, only "subsidized immigrants" (that is, those whose maintenance was guaranteed by the World Zionist Organization for one year, later to be redefined as those who had a definite prospect of employment) were admitted, and then only up to the quota set by the authorities. The subsidized immigrant category was specified in the labor schedule that the department of immigration of the Jewish Agency prepared; when approved by the British high commissioner, labor schedule certificates were issued to the World Zionist Executive, which distributed them according to a party key with each party receiving certificates in rough proportion to its political strength in the country.

1925–48

The years from 1925 to 1948 are the years of the Mandate, the struggle against the British, the struggle against the Nazis, the struggle for immigration, and ultimately independence.

Quotas were also being set in the United States to restrict the inflow of immigrants in the 1920s, and so when conditions in Poland provided a "push" for many Jews to leave that country, and as the economic depression in Europe worsened, the fourth *aliyah* (1924–30) arrived. Eighty-two thousand Jews arrived in this period, 35,000 in 1925 alone.[11] If the third *aliyah* was Russian and ideological, the fourth was Polish and middle class. Unlike the penniless socialists of the earlier *aliyot*, many of the Poles had some independent means, and their capitalism flourished. But in 1927 there was a severe economic crisis, and the economic foundations of the Yishuv, concentrated in agriculture, could not absorb large numbers of urban-oriented migrants. Unemployment was very high, and starting in late 1926, Jewish emigration gained momentum. Some 23,000 of 80,000 immigrants of the fourth *aliyah* are estimated to have left the country. In 1927 emigration exceeded immigration.

The fifth *aliyah* (1932–38) reacted to the spread of anti-Jewish activities in central and eastern Europe, especially the rise of Hitler in 1933. This was a huge immigration by local standards, numbering some 200,000. In 1935 alone a record 66,000 Jews arrived. The Jewish population of the country more than doubled in five years. The fifth *aliyah,* while often called the "German *aliyah,*" in fact comprised only a quarter of German and Austrian Jews. The biggest group numerically was from Poland, which did, after all, have the largest concentration of Jews in the world at that time; the biggest decline was from the USSR because restrictions on emigration were enforced. These central European Jews brought with them capital for investment and, along with their middle-class backgrounds, urban lifestyles and organizational skills.

In the aftermath of the mass immigration of the 1920s and 1930s the local Arab population reacted violently with demonstrations, strikes, and attacks. By 1939 the Jews, who had made up 4 percent of the population in 1882, had become 30 percent through immigration (see table 2.1). Economic difficulties fed Arab resentment. The British reaction was to limit the immigration of Jews severely. In 1933 and 1934 the Jewish Agency requested 60,000 labor certificates; the British allocated less than 18,000. In 1936, 10,695 were requested, but only 1,800 were approved. The problem could not be overcome easily. In seventeen years the Arab population had increased by 50 percent, the Jewish population by 500 percent.

The British introduced political criteria, as opposed to economic criteria, in setting the quota of Jewish immigrants, and they determined that 12,000 Jews per year would be the "political high level," or upper limit. This figure was more or less achieved for the years between 1936 and 1938, the figure jumping to 30,000 in 1939. Most of the immigrants came from Germany and Austria. As the clouds of war gathered, international immigration slowed to a trickle, but for the first time, Eretz Israel became the major migration destination of world Jewry.

The British White Paper of 1939 limited Jewish immigration to 75,000 for the next five-year period, making the Jews a third of the population and then terminating immigration. By the date the White Paper had immigration ending, only about 50,000 Jews had immigrated. Illegal immigration had existed throughout the Mandate, and since 1934 illegal immigrants were deducted from the quota of Jews permitted to enter Eretz Israel (if the number of illegals could be determined). After World War II, tens of thousands attempted to enter illegally, and many were successful. But after mid-1946, most of these Jewish survivors of European persecution were intercepted and 56,000 of them were imprisoned on Cyprus. Between 1945 and mid-1948 about 75,000 Jews came, most of them illegally.

The organizational efforts required to sustain illegal immigration, preparing the Yishuv for armed conflict with the Arabs or the British by manufacturing or procuring weapons, raising and training an effective fighting force—all this alongside the legal activities of absorbing immigrants, strengthening the economy, and developing a social infrastructure—were enormous. The busyness of the period swept up groups and individuals and generated national enthusiasm and levels of self-sacrifice the loss of which were sometimes bemoaned by later generations, who wished

TABLE 2.1

POPULATION OF JEWS IN ISRAEL AND THE WORLD,

1882–1996

Year	Size of population (in thousands)	Number of Jews in Israel (in thousands)	Percentage of Jews in Israel	Number of Jews in world (in millions)	Percentage of world's Jews in Israel
1882	600	24	4.0	7.7	0.3
1922	752	84	11.2	8.0	1.1
1939	1,545	464	30.0	16.6	2.8
1948	806	650	80.6	11.5	5.7
1954	1,718	1,526	88.6	11.9	12.8
1967	2,777	2,384	85.8	13.6	17.5
1986	4,331	3,561	82.2	13.0	27.4
1996	5,619	4,550	81.0	13.0	35.0
Including the territories					
1967	3,744	2,384	63.7		
1986	5,712	3,561	62.3		
1996	7,489	4,550	60.8		

SOURCES: Dov Friedlander and Calvin Goldscheider, *The Population of Israel* (New York: Columbia University Press, 1979); Dan Horowitz and Moshe Lissak, *The Origins of the Israeli Polity: Palestine under the Mandate* (Chicago: University of Chicago Press, 1978); and various volumes of *Statistical Abstract* and the *American Jewish Yearbook*.

NOTE: Population figures up to 1939 are for Eretz Israel. Figures for 1948 through 1996 in the upper rows relate to the pre-1967 borders; figures in the bottom three rows include the territories.

to return to "basic values." But on the verge of the symbolic victory of national independence there occurred the greatest modern tragedy to befall the Jewish people—the Holocaust. David Ben-Gurion's political wisdom in navigating these difficult straits raised him to a peak of popularity and general acceptance both in Israel and abroad. It was during this period of the multiplicity of tasks confronting the Yishuv that lieutenants were recognized for their organizational and leadership abilities, and careers in the public sector were begun.

The 1948 Declaration of Independence stated that "the State of Israel is open to Jewish immigration and the ingathering of Exiles." The first order enacted by the provisional government abolished the British restrictions on immigration and defined as legal those residents who had been "illegals" under British rule. Two years later, in 1950, after hundreds of thousands of Jews had come to the country, the Knesset passed the Law of Return, which grants to every Jew in the world the right to immigrate to Israel.

1948–54

In 1948 the remnants of the European Jewish society immigrated, but soon after the founding of the state, communities of Jews born in Asia and Africa made up the bulk of the new immigrants. The large number of these immigrants doubled the Jewish population of the country within these years and heightened the already difficult economic conditions faced by the new country. Between 1948 and 1951, 700,000 immigrants were added to the 650,000 Jews already in Israel. Despite the enormous demographic change, the political leadership successfully adapted and remained in power. The Arabs again protested, this time through force of arms, with neighboring Arab states attacking the new state in an attempt to abort its birth. Many local Arabs left, thinking that this was a temporary exodus until the fighting halted, and they became the crux of the Palestinian refugee problem still festering in the region. The reaction of the refugees is familiar: many German Jews in the 1930s believed that they had left "temporarily" until the Hitler nightmare passed, just as many Iranian Jews fifty years later set up temporary homes in Israel, France, or the United States, convinced that the Khomeini revolution would be short-lived.

After the establishment of the state, waves of immigration came at a fast and furious pace. First came the European immigrants imprisoned on Cyprus and in camps in Europe. Soon after, Jews from Bulgaria, Yugoslavia, Yemen, Aden, and Algeria arrived. In early 1949 there came Jews from Turkey and Libya and the entire community of 35,000 Jews in Yemen. Toward the end of 1949 the doors of Poland and Romania were opened, and the Jews streamed out, followed the next year by Iraqis and many more Romanians. The government was hard pressed to absorb, feed, and house the new immigrants. A war was being fought, and resources were scarce. Rationing of foodstuffs was introduced, and demands were made by leaders of the United Jewish Appeal in the United States to slow down immigration for six months in order to balance the budget. Ben-Gurion rejected all such pleas, arguing "economic conditions should be adjusted to immigration volume rather than the reverse."[12] The highest monthly immigration rate was recorded during the first seven months of 1951 when some 20,000 immigrants a month arrived in the country, mostly from Romania and Iraq. This monthly rate was almost as large as the entire first *aliyah*.

1954–89

In 1951 the Jewish Agency announced "rules of selection," hoping to reduce the number of people sponsored by the agency who were chronically ill, nonproductive laborers, or unwilling to settle in agricultural areas. The major realistic sources of potential immigration in the mid-1950s were Turkey and Iran with about 130,000 Jews still living there, and North Africa with half a million. Western countries did not seem a likely source, and the 3 million Jews in eastern Europe and the Soviet Union were prevented from leaving. Before the restrictions were set, only about 30,000 came to Israel from North African countries, with many of the middle and upper classes making their way to France. It is not clear whether the restrictions prevented larger immigration; what is clear is that after the Israeli economy started to pick up again, after the German reparations began, and especially after the victory of the Sinai campaign of 1956, immigration from North Africa, especially Morocco, began to pick up. After reaching a low annual figure of 18,000 immigrants between 1952 and 1954, the figure reached 70,000 in 1957, with Jews arriving mostly from Morocco, Poland, and Egypt.

The matter of quotas for North African immigrants reached a peak in the mid-1950s, and Prime Minister Moshe Sharett raised the quotas from 2,000 per month to 3,000. The reasoning behind the government decision was that the economy could absorb no more. The similarity between this and the original 1922 British position is striking. When Ben-Gurion returned to office in 1955 as prime minister, the policy was nevertheless unchanged. The Herut movement consistently opposed all immigration restrictions during these years, while others regarded them as unfortunate but necessary. Herut's ideological stance was not put to the test for most of its period in office (1977–92), for Israel's major problem was generally a lack of immigration and a growing *yerida* (emigration, or "going down"). It was challenged with the beginning of the mass immigration from the former Soviet Union in 1989.

Immigration between 1961 and 1965 reached 230,000, coming mainly from Morocco and Romania, with some from Argentina as well. By the Six-Day War in 1967 the sources of potential immigration had changed. Eastern European and North African reservoirs were largely dried up, leaving Western countries and the Soviet Union. Of the 250,000 Jews given exit visas from the Soviet Union in the 1970s, only 160,000 came to Israel.[13]

The task of dealing with immigration was complicated by the emergence of two competing bureaucracies: the Jewish Agency and the government Ministry of Immigrant Absorption. The fact that politicians and bureaucrats dealing with the complex issue of immigration were often from different factions or parties made the competition for resources and control of immigration more intense.

1989 TO THE PRESENT

The end of the Soviet Union saw a resurgence of Jewish immigration to Israel. Between 1989 and 1995, more Jews came to Israel than were in the country at the time of independence in 1948. Most of the 700,000 immigrants came from the Soviet Union, with 50,000 of them coming from Ethiopia. The differences between the two communities were stark. Not only did they come in great numbers, they came at once. In 1990, 185,200 Jews arrived from the former Soviet Union and in 1991, an additional 147,800. Of the Ethiopians, 14,200 came in 1991 alone, as a result of the airlift named Operation Solomon.

The government was completely unprepared for the task of absorbing such large numbers of immigrants, despite the pressure it had tried to exert over the years to force the Soviets to "let my people go." In the past most immigrant absorption activities had been hands-on projects by government ministries, the Jewish Agency, and philanthropic organizations. This time the decision was made to provide grants to the immigrants and to let them fend for themselves. The Likud government declared a policy of "self-absorption," which basically meant giving cash to the immigrants and hoping for the best. Perhaps because there was no other choice, perhaps because it was in the era of similar ideologies of small government in Thatcher's Britain and Reagan's United States, perhaps because the Likud was in power, the government wanted the market to deal with the problems and potentials of such a large influx of people. The ambition and ingenuity of many of the immigrants, and the upturn of the economy as a result of the 1993 peace accords, prevented disaster. After very difficult beginnings, many of the Soviet immigrants found employment and housing. The Ethiopians were much less successful. They were deemed unable to cope and were absorbed by government bureaucrats in a manner familiar to many who had immigrated earlier, with all the attendant resentments.[14]

Most of the 609,900 immigrants from the former Soviet Union between 1989 and 1995 were Ashkenazim, well educated, secular, and steeped in Western and Russian culture. They came because the Soviet Union was crumbling, the political and economic future was very uncertain, and they were concerned about anti-Semitism. Most of them discovered Zionism in Israel, not in the Soviet Union.[15] Many of their brothers, sisters, and cousins went to the United States and other Western countries during the same period, and many of these immigrants would have joined them if they could. But because of the familiar combination of a desire to leave and the unavailability of alternative destinations, many arrived in Israel. Israeli authorities tried to convince other governments, especially the United States, to limit the number of immigrants from these countries so that Israel would get more of them.

They came from various parts of the Soviet Union: about 30 percent each from Russia and the Ukraine; 21 percent from the central Russian republics of Kafkaz, Azerbaijan, and Georgia; 9 percent from Belorussia; 6

percent from Moldavia; and 3 percent from the Baltic republics of Estonia, Latvia, and Lithuania.[16] Almost 80 percent of the immigrants were Ashkenazim; Sephardi Jews were concentrated in the central republics. They came to a country with many familiar (if inferior, in their opinion) features, and with many persons who traced their ancestry to those same lands. They recognized the bureaucratic system with which they had to deal; many learned the language quickly and adapted to the new environment through a combination of personal, group, and communal efforts.

The major feature of this immigration was their high level of education. Sixty percent were professionals—compared to 28 percent for the Jewish population already in the country. In the 1989–95 period, 68,000 engineers arrived, making up 11.2 percent of the total immigrant group. Doctors and dentists made up another 5 percent (almost 10,000 doctors arrived in 1990–91 alone), and another 5 percent were teachers. More than 40 percent had thirteen years of education or more, compared to 24.2 percent in the general population.

The Ethiopian immigrants, by contrast, came to a country that was very different from the one they had left and one that had very few former immigrants like them. There were only 24,000 Ethiopians in the country when the Jews of Operation Solomon arrived. They came from an underdeveloped African country and were literally picked out of their country overnight. Tracing their Judaism back to King Solomon and Bat Sheba, their traditions had developed separately from the rest of the Jewish world. Ashkenazi and Sephardi Jews shared the development of the Talmud and the rabbinical oral tradition that the Ethiopians lacked. Accordingly, in addition to their economic and cultural "backwardness," in a religious sense they were seen as lacking as well.

Immigrants from the United States form a very small but important group in Israeli politics and society.[17] They are very visible in the settlers' movement in the territories and in civil rights and peace movements. In 1994 there were about 85,000 U.S.-born immigrants in Israel, less than 2 percent of the population. Compared to the general American Jewish population, these immigrants tended to be younger and more educated, a telltale sign of a pull, not push, immigration.

Some came before the Six-Day War, but the two largest groups came afterward, with 30,000 immigrants arriving between 1967 and 1973, and approximately 50,000 after 1973. Of the post-1973 group, about two-thirds were Orthodox. Many of the Orthodox immigrants chose to settle in Judea and Samaria; the town of Efrat, for example, is composed of 9 percent Americans. More than a third of those who came to Israel as immigrants eventually gave up and left the country; the rate for the Orthodox was about half that.

Emigration

In Israel every new immigrant is viewed as an important contribution toward the goal of the ingathering of Jews. As a general estimate, about 10 to 15 percent of Israelis have left Israel over time. It is very hard to give an exact number because records are not kept on emigrants. The definition of "emigrant" presents difficulties because Israelis living abroad, when asked, often insist that they are planning to return. In the 1980s, official figures reported that more than 300,000 Israeli citizens resided abroad.[18]

The early 1950s witnessed the highest rate of outflow in Israeli history. The proportion of emigrants to immigrants was higher (although the absolute number was lower) in the 1950s than in the late 1970s, a period in which problems of emigration concerned the public.[19] Many of those who left in the 1950s spent a few months or a couple of years in Israel after the Holocaust and then left for other countries. For those never involved ideologically with Zionism, Israel was a safe haven in a very long nightmare. For others, living conditions in Israel were too hard. A government plan to reverse this flow by encouraging residents to return seems to have been partially successful; those who have come back under this plan increased from 8,000 in 1991 to 14,000 residents in 1995.

Jews are known as a wandering people. The Zionist vision was that with a national homeland, certain of the "negative" features of the Diaspora would be expunged from the Jew, including his wanderlust. This has obviously not happened. Not only have most of the Jews not returned to Zion, but many continue in their mobile patterns. This was so even in the time of the second commonwealth, when the Jews made up 10 percent of the Roman Empire.[20] We also know that today, at every educational and income level, American Jews travel more than non-Jews. Every indication points to the fact that the wandering will continue in the future.

Nevertheless, the stigma attached to emigration has decreased considerably over the years. One result of Israel's becoming a more open and competitive society is a growing acceptance of the fact that where one lives is a private decision as well as a public one. When asked whether they were considering emigration, about 14 percent of the adult Jewish population in Israel and about a quarter of those in their twenties reported that they were.[21] Patterns of acceptability of this behavior seem stable, indicating that it is likely to continue into the future.[22] The other side of this acceptability is the decline of feeling that *aliyah* is essential to the country's future. In the 1970s, 85 to 90 percent agreed with that statement; in the 1986 and 1990 surveys the number fell to 82 percent; in 1992 to 71 percent, and in the 1994 and 1995 surveys to 64 and 67 percent.[23]

Sephardim-Ashkenazim

Demographic developments within the Jewish community are very important in understanding the politics of the State of Israel. In a population
coming from a variety of backgrounds, it is no wonder that communal and
institutional differences became a major resource in structuring the political landscape of the country.[24]

In Israeli politics one of the dominant criteria is ethnicity, not the
Jewish and non-Jewish distinction, but intra-Jewish ethnicity. The subject
is a complex one, but the major distinction among Jews is between Ashkenazim, who came to Israel from Europe and America, and Sephardim, who
immigrated from countries of Asia and Africa. While the terms are commonly used in contemporary Israeli politics, they obscure as much as they
reveal because they are borrowed from other spheres. They have their origins in the medieval period of sojourning in the Diaspora of the various
communities following different expulsions throughout history.[25] More ap-
propriately, three divisions should be used, consisting of an Oriental (eastern) community of Jews who never left Asia and Africa; the Sephardim,
whose language (Ladino) and ethnic culture originated in Spain before the
expulsion of 1492; and the Ashkenazim (referring to Germany), whose hy-
brid language was Yiddish. Sometimes language is suggested as a base of
distinction, but today both Ladino and Yiddish are vanishing languages,
and in any case they did not penetrate everywhere.[26] Hebrew is widely
spoken in Israel and not the other languages; Jews around the world are
likely to be more exposed to Hebrew than to Yiddish or to Ladino, so the
earlier language distinction is failing.

The terms themselves are related to different ritual practices and usage adopted by scattered Jewish communities. The Ashkenazi-Sephardi
terms are very problematic and imprecise. Thus, for example, many Jewish
communities of southern Europe were Sephardim, while communities in
the eastern Mediterranean, India, Yemen, and Ethiopia could not appro-
priately be put in either category. Especially in the last half of the twentieth
century, flourishing Sephardi communities have been established in the
Americas and especially in France. On the other hand, Ashkenazim lived in
Egypt and China. Regardless of the misleading inaccuracies incorporated
in the terms, this Sephardi-Ashkenazi nomenclature became part of the political reality of Israel and has emerged as a major theme in Israeli politics.

The theme, however, while still important, has changed. To begin
with, the proportions of the groups in the electorate have changed over
time. In 1977, the majority of the electorate was Ashkenazim (53 percent),
43 percent were Sephardim, and 4 percent were Israeli-born with fathers
also born in Israel. In the 1988 election, for the first time, the Jews of
Sephardi background outnumbered the Jews of Ashkenazi background in

the electorate. In 1992, with the mass immigration from the former Soviet Union, most of which was of Ashkenazi origin, the proportions were 48 percent Ashkenazim, 44 percent Sephardim, and 8 percent Israeli-born whose fathers were also born in Israel.[27]

As a larger percentage of Israeli Jews were native-born, this cleavage became more distant. As indicators, consider that a majority of Israeli Jewish voters and 90 percent of Jewish children in elementary schools at the beginning of the 1990s were native-born. They were exposed to a culture that downplayed—if it did not successfully alleviate the disparities—of these ethnic distinctions. The rate at which a member of one group married a member of the other group was a high and constant 20 percent. The number of children from these "mixed marriages" grew, and the blurring of the term's clear meaning was heightened. In response to a question about whether the respondent is Ashkenazi or Sephardi, about a third of the sample responds "neither" in survey after survey.

Beyond the label is the question of social and political meaning. Although fading, the labels are still of enormous importance. The major political parties vie to recruit politicians who could be presented as authentic leaders of these groups, and by 1996 the lists of both Labor and the Likud featured impressive and almost equal numbers of Sephardi politicians. And yet, in spite of significant headway achieved by Sephardim in and through politics, equality in terms of actual power was not achieved.

Keeping in mind that we are compressing too much into the popularly used dichotomy of Sephardim and Ashkenazim, we shall also rely on the usage of the government's Central Bureau of Statistics, which reports place of birth and father's place of birth (see tables 2.2 and 2.3). There is a very high correlation between the European- or American-born and Ashkenazim, and the Asian- or African-born and Sephardim, and hence we shall use the terms interchangeably. We should remember, though, that differences between Iraqi and Moroccan Jews (both called Sephardim here) are as great or greater than differences between Russian and German Jews (both Ashkenazim). The more recent interaction of these Jews with their host countries varied their common heritage as Sephardim or Ashkenazim just as a more distant history varied the common heritage shared by all Jews as they were developing the rituals, traditions, and language shared only by Ashkenazim or Sephardim.

Of the 13 million Jews in the world, about 85 percent are Ashkenazim and 15 percent Sephardim. About 10 percent of the world's Ashkenazim live in Israel, compared with about two-thirds of the Sephardim. Ashkenazim today make up about 55 percent of Israel's Jewish population, the Sephardim about 45 percent. The number of Israeli-born whose fathers were born in Europe and America was more than 640,000, whereas the

TABLE 2.2

JEWISH POPULATION IN ISRAEL BY CONTINENT OF BIRTH,
1948–95 (IN PERCENTAGES)

	1948	1954	1968	1976	1983	1995
Israel	35.4	31.4	44.0	50.9	58.1	61.1
Asia	8.1	19.0	12.8	10.4	8.8	5.8
Africa	1.7	7.9	14.8	11.7	9.8	7.5
Europe and America	54.8	41.7	28.8	27.0	23.3	25.7
Total	716,678	1,526,009	2,434,832	2,959,400	3,350,000	4,441,100

SOURCE: *Statistical Abstract, 1995, 98.*

Israeli-born of Asian- or African-born fathers numbered almost 985,000. An additional 1.1 million were born in Israel of fathers who were also born in Israel. In the past, most of this group was Ashkenazim, reflecting their earlier arrival in the country; today the group is divided more evenly among Ashkenazim and Sephardim.

The reproduction rates of the various ethnic groups are also different, although less so over time. The fertility rate of Jewish mothers born in Asia or Africa was 5.40 in the 1955–59 period, compared with 3.40 in 1975–79 and 3.26 in 1994. For European- or American-born Jewish mothers, it was 2.53 in 1955–59, 2.80 in 1975–79, and 2.18 in 1994. The rate for Israeli-born mothers has changed least, from 2.79 in 1955–59, to 2.91 in 1975–79, and 2.71 in 1994.[28] Because the age structure and growth rates of the groups differ, the impact on the political system through the composition of the electorate is not identical (see table 2.3). European- or American-born voters and their Israeli-born children constituted a majority of the electorate in 1969, but by 1988 they and the Asian and African voters and their Israeli-born voting children had the potential of electing the same number of Knesset members—forty-nine for each group. The latter group constituted a majority of the Jewish population in Israel, and their growth rates were higher than the Europeans. The large Ashkenazi base was evident in their potential in the 1969 elections: fifty-nine seats for the Ashkenazim, forty-three for the Sephardim. In 1996, their potential was augmented by the very large immigration from the former Soviet Union, mostly Ashkenazi. By 1996, the European- and American-born and their children could account for fifty seats, compared to forty-three seats for those of Sephardi background. The voting reserve as measured by children who have not yet reached voting age also favors the Ashkenazim after being a resource for the Sephardim for many years. This potential will be

TABLE 2.3
VOTING POTENTIAL OF THE JEWISH POPULATION IN ISRAEL, 1969, 1981, 1988, AND 1996

	Percentage in population				Percentage under 18				Knesset seats[a]			
	1967	1981	1988	1995	1967	1981	1988	1995	1969	1981	1988	1996
Israeli-born; father Israeli-born	6.51	13.2	19.5	24.4	62.3	70.7	74.7	66.1	4	6	8	13
Israeli-born, father Asian or African born	18.7	25.7	25.7	22.2	81.6	53.7	47.6	26.0	5	18	22	24
Israeli-born; father European- or American-born	16.4	16.4	16.2	14.4	49.1	35.8	37.1	27.9	13	16	16	16
Asian- or African-born	27.8	20.0	17.2	13.3	11.5	1.7	2.4	3.4	38	30	27	19
European- or American-born	30.6	25.1	21.4	25.7	3.6	5.4	5.8	10.5	46	36	33	34
Total number and percent	2,344,887	3,218,400	3,561,400	4,441,100	31.6	30.5	34.1	29.1	106	106	106	106

SOURCES: *Statistical Abstract, 1969,* 42–43; *Statistical Abstract, 1981,* 56–57; *Statistical Abstract, 1987,* 73–75; *Statistical Abstract, 1995,* 96–98.
a. Assuming 80 percent participation; 12,000 votes per seat in 1969, 17,000 votes per seat in 1981, 17,600 votes per seat in 1988, and 24,500 votes per seat in 1996.

realized when children who are under voting age (29.4 percent for the Asian and African children, 38.4 percent for the European and American children) begin voting. The future, however, belongs to the Israeli-born and to their children. Two-thirds of that group are yet to reach voting age.

The shifting mosaic of Israel's Jewish population is likely to persist. That its composition can detemine Israel's strength and vitality goes without saying. A country that invests in young people in school, army, and university only to see them set up families in distant lands has an important problem to face. External events and internal conditions in Israel will influence the rate and composition of immigration. While facing the challenges of the next hundred years, the achievements of the first hundred, with their dilemmas and lessons, must be kept in mind.

Non-Jews, Arabs, and Palestinians

The Jewish-Arab conflict is more than a century old and began when Zionists began settling Palestine. The origins of the Israeli-Palestinian conflict are much more recent: one prominent turning point was 29 November 1947, the day that the United Nations decided on the partition of mandatory Palestine between the two peoples living in the territory—the Jews and the Arabs. The leadership of the Yishuv, representing the Jewish community, accepted this decision, but the Higher Arab Committee rejected it.

On 14 May 1948, the day the British Mandate ended, Israel's independence was proclaimed. The Arabs did not accept this development, and the armies of Egypt, Jordan, Lebanon, Syria, and Iraq attempted to prevent the establishment of Israel by force. The conflict that simmered for years between two indigenous groups in a colonial territory escalated to the more visible status of armed conflict among nation-states. The war ended with an Israeli victory; the territory of the new country after the war was about 50 percent larger than that approved by the United Nations. Under the partition plan Israel was to be some 5,200 square miles in area, and after the war, it annexed an additional 2,500 square miles, making the postwar country about the size of the state of New Jersey. The territory west of the Jordan River held by the Kingdom of Jordan (the "West Bank") was annexed by Jordan in 1950; the Gaza Strip was controlled by Egypt, although never annexed by it.[29]

According to the original UN scheme, Jerusalem was to be an international city; as the cease-fire went into effect, the army of Jordan controlled the Old City and the eastern sections of it, the Israeli army the western neighborhoods. The city was divided. The Palestine refugee problem originated during this 1948–49 war. About 700,000 Arabs who lived in mandatory Palestine left, some voluntarily, some at the insistence of the

Arab armies who promised they would be allowed to return after the hostilities, and some at the hand of the Israelis during the war.[30] Some 60 percent of them found their way to Jordan, about 20 percent to the Gaza Strip, and another 20 percent to Syria and Lebanon. The solution of the refugee problem will be one of the more difficult issues to be tackled by Israel and the Palestinians in working on the permanent status arrangement.

The Six-Day War of 1967 was a major turning point in the conflict. Israel won an amazing victory, unified Jerusalem, added another million Arabs to those already under its rule, and conquered lands claimed by Egypt, Jordan, and Syria. During the Six-Day War, many of the refugees from the war of independence in 1948–49 again came under Israeli jurisdiction.[31] In the 1979 peace treaty with Egypt, Israel agreed to return the largely uninhabited Sinai Peninsula.

Despite the impression sometimes given by discussions of its strategic importance and military might, Israel is not a big country. The total area of the state and the territories under its control is comparatively small. At about 10,500 square miles (after the Sinai was returned), it was about the size of the state of Maryland, yet smaller than Armenia, Albania, or Belgium.

Israeli authorities have historically conceived of the conflict in the region as being between nation-states. Once Israel was established, the question was if, when, and on what terms Arab states would recognize Israel. Arabs living in Israel were granted citizenship but were treated with circumspection; in fact, they lived under military government for the first twenty years of statehood. Israelis have historically rejected the notion of a Palestinian state; some, such as Golda Meir in the 1970s, and Binyamin Netanyahu in the 1990s, argued that there was no such thing as a Palestinian nation and hence no Palestinian state was possible. Others added that the Arabs already had twenty-plus states and that an additional one was not needed for the relatively small Palestinian population; they could make Jordan the Palestinian state.

The Jewish State of Israel has a sizable population of non-Jews. Table 2.1 clearly indicates that the picture is not static. The complement of the percentage of Jews in Israel is made up of non-Jews. Before the establishment of the state, non-Jews were a large majority. With statehood in 1948 the relative weight of the non-Jewish population fell because the pre-1967-war boundaries excluded most of them. By 1954, after the Jewish population had more than doubled as a result of immigration, the concentration of Jews was at its highest, almost 90 percent. After that, the relative weight of non-Jewish Israelis grew steadily in spite of continued Jewish immigration because the non-Jewish rate of reproduction was higher than that of Jews. In 1994 the non-Jewish community comprised some 1.03 million people, of whom 782,000 were Moslems, 157,300 Christians, and 91,700 Druze. The gross reproduction rates were 2.23 for Moslems, .99 for Christians, and 1.73 for Druze, compared with 1.26 for Jews.[32] If the Arabs of the territories are added to these calculations, Jews make up a smaller majority of the Eretz Israel population (see table 2.1).

A very sharp distinction must be made between Arabs who are citizens of Israel and those who were under its military jurisdiction. The Arab citizens of Israel are those who remained after the 1948 war. They are full citizens in the sense that they organize politically, they vote, and they are elected to the Knesset. Psychologically, however, their position is much more complex. They live in a Jewish country whose symbols, flag, and anthem are Zionist. They are not called to serve in the army, one of the important rites of passage for Israeli youth and a key to advancement in the world of adults. Not being veterans, they are precluded from some of the benefits of Israel's welfare state. They make up less than 20 percent of the population but account for half of those under the poverty line. Only 2 percent of the budget of the Ministry for Religious Affairs is devoted to the needs of their community.[33]

But it is important to realize that Israeli Arabs have been, on the whole, law-abiding citizens. They are conflicted; they are cross-pressured.[34] Most identify with their Arab background, with their Palestinian roots and their refugee cousins, but also many identify themselves as Israelis. In fact, when asked in a preelection poll in 1996 to list the identity that best defined them, the ranking was 43 percent Arab, 29 percent Israeli, 18 percent according to their religion (Moslem, Christian, etc.), and 10 percent Palestinian. As a community they have conflicting identities; moreover, both Jews and non-Israeli Palestinians are unclear about where their loyalties lie (see table 1.4).[35]

Between the 1967 war and the 1993 Oslo agreement, the policy of Israeli governments was to avoid changing the legal status of the territories, except for Jerusalem and the Golan Heights, while supporting (with varying enthusiasm) Jewish settlements in the territories. The city of Jerusalem and much of the countryside around it were annexed by Israel soon after the 1967 war; Israeli law was applied to the Golan Heights (which belonged to Syria) in 1982. Applying Israeli law is less than annexation but leaves little doubt regarding the intentions of the ruling power. The decision to return territories for peace was consistently the platform of the Labor Party and became the policy of the government of Israel after 1993.[36] The Likud did not accept the principle, and the dilemma of the Netanyahu government was to remain loyal to the traditional hard-line Likud platform while conforming to international agreements based on the land for peace principle entered into by previous Israeli governments.

A sense of "creeping annexation" was prevalent among Palestinians because of the persistent policy of all Israeli governments to expropriate land for Jewish settlements. This expropriated land, added to land taken over by the Israeli authorities after the retreat of the Jordanian army in 1967 and the properties purchased by Israelis from Arab owners, brought the total holding by Israel on the West Bank to about a third. This development was deemed most dangerous by Palestinian nationalists.[37]

The Labor government headed by Levi Eshkol proceeded with settlement soon after the 1967 war, especially along the Jordan River and around Jerusalem. The beginning of Jewish settlement in territories with a large Arab population also began under Labor. This was in 1974, when Yitzhak Rabin and Shimon Peres, both of Labor, were prime minister and defense minister, respectively. They capitulated to the symbolic pressures of potential Jewish settlers living in temporary camps on lands central to the biblical past of Israel, and the political pressure of the rightist parties demanding government sanction and support for this policy of settlement. Under Labor leadership, the policy was begun that led to large-scale settlement in the territories.[38]

The big leap came during the Likud years between 1977 and 1992. In 1976, there were a little more than 3,000 Jewish settlers on the West Bank (Judea and Samaria). By 1988, the number had increased more than twenty-fold, with about 70,000 Jews living there. In May 1977 there were 34 settlements in the West Bank; in 1984, the number climbed to 114. In 1985, only one additional settlement was added. During the periods of the national unity governments, the pace of settlement represented a compromise between the desires of the Likud to go faster and the wishes of Labor to go more cautiously, although neither of the big parties opposed continued settling. The 1984 National Unity Government agreement limited new settlements to five or six new settlements annually, and the agreement that established the 1988 National Unity Government set eight settlements a year as its target, assuming that funds were available.

The 1990–92 Likud government made settlement a high priority. The Shamir government refused to halt settlement in 1992 in order to receive $10-billion loan guarantees from the United States to absorb immigrants from the former Soviet Union. This rift with the Bush administration (along with the Likud's other problems) led to the 1992–96 Labor government, which froze new settlements. Still, by 1996 there were 140,000 Jewish settlers, providing every new government with a promise or a problem, depending on its ideology. Not all the settlers were ideologues. Residing in the territories became a popular alternative for young Israeli-born Jews seeking reasonably priced housing in the suburbs of Jerusalem and Tel Aviv.

The Palestine Liberation Organization (PLO), generally considered to represent the Palestinians, was established in 1964. It had a very checkered political and diplomatic career trying to achieve the visibility and legitimacy needed to reach its ultimate goal of achieving national independence for the Palestinians. The PLO was often associated in the public mind of the West with terror and terrorism, accusations to which it sometimes admitted. The inhabitants of the territories achieved high levels of national solidarity, even though they were cut off from the PLO leadership. The inhabitants experienced the frustrations, inconveniences, and even humiliations of living under military occupation. Although Israel prided itself on its democratic forms, the Arabs in the territories were deprived of political and civil rights.[39]

The refusal by the Palestinians to accept the status of Israeli occupation erupted in the Intifada, the uprising of Arabs in the territories, which began in December 1987. A year later, the U.S. government agreed to enter into discussions with the PLO. The role of the PLO and its legitimacy were at a high point. Gradually, the portion of Israelis prepared to enter into negotiations with the PLO grew, although both major parties, the Likud and Labor, rejected the notion.[40] Some Israelis feared that the Palestinians' attitude went beyond refusal of occupation and that ultimately they wanted to dismantle the State of Israel. Therefore, tough policies—even distasteful ones—were a matter of continued survival. Others felt that solutions could be reached only by political, not by military, means. Caution, strength, and vigilance were needed, they felt, but so was a solution that would allow all sides to live in peace.

In Washington in September 1993, with a handshake between Rabin and Arafat, the Oslo agreement (formally known as the Declaration of Principles on Interim Self-Government Arrangements) was signed between Israel and the PLO. It included provisions for Palestinian self-rule in Gaza and Jericho and the transfer of specific government functions on the West Bank to the Palestinians. Two years later, in September 1995, the Oslo 2 agreement was signed.[41] It created three zones on the West Bank: (1) Area A, to be controlled solely by the Palestinians, included the cities of Bethlehem, Jenin, Nablus, Qalqilya, Ramallah, and Tulkarem, and parts of Hebron; (2) Area B, including many towns and villages, in which activities of the Palestinian Authority would be coordinated and confirmed with Israel; and (3) Area C, consisting mainly of unpopulated areas of strategic importance to Israel, and Jewish settlements, to remain under sole Israeli control. Oslo 2 included, among other things, a timetable for the redeployment of the IDF, elections to the Palestinian national council, and the beginning of negotiations regarding the permanent status between the negotiating sides.

The appropriate degree of interaction between the two societies has always been a hot political issue. Closure of the territories was often used as a form of defense after terrorist incidents, but it also had the effect of punishing the many Palestinians who worked in Israel. They could not get to their jobs, and the territories could not provide alternative employment. But separating the territories raised the possibility of two separate entities, a development that might make an independent Palestinian state more likely. In parallel, Palestinians began to work out for themselves what their society should be like.[42]

They had their work cut out for them. Although their living standard might be high compared with Arabs in other countries or with the 2 million Palestinians in Jordan and among the other 2 million scattered around the world, still it was much lower than that enjoyed by Israeli Arabs, not to mention Israeli Jews. While most homes had electricity, only 7 percent of that electricity was produced locally, the rest in Israel. While most Palestinian households, including those in refugee camps, had acquired television sets and refrigerators in the past twenty years, much of it was the result of dumping of used Israeli appliances on the Palestinian market; only 10 percent of these items were bought new. Moreover, only 2 percent of communities in the territories had proper sewerage, and 70 percent did not have telephones; two-thirds of the phone system predated the Israel takeover in 1967.

The Palestinian National Council met in Gaza City on 24 April 1996 (ironically enough, the forty-eighth anniversary of Israeli Independence Day according to the Hebrew calendar) and agreed to revise the Charter of the Palestine Liberation Organization, which had called for the destruction of the State of Israel. Israelis saw great symbolic importance to the charter, and Arafat had promised Rabin and Peres that the offensive articles would be annulled. By a vote of 504 to 54 (with 14 abstentions), Arafat kept his promise. Prime Minister Peres had agreed to admit sworn enemies of Israel and known terrorists into the territory controlled by the Palestine Authority (still controlled in terms of foreign and security policy by Israel) for the vote, since the charter could be amended only by a two-thirds vote of its 669 members. Beforehand, Arafat had co-opted elected members of the parliament of the Palestine Authority into the council, thus weakening the power of those living outside the land. Rather than amend the charter or vote on a new charter, a committee was empowered to report back to the council in six months, well after the Israeli elections, and while the negotiations for a permanent settlement were under way. The slow progress of finding a way for people to live in Israel crept forward.

3. Political Economy

The form of economy in Israel is a mixture of government activity and state planning, along with free enterprise. During the past decade there has been a marked shift toward consumerism and an atmosphere more friendly toward initiative, especially investment. Increasingly, the rhetoric of the country's economic ideology, regardless of the party in power, favors competition and market forces along with an activist welfare state; in practice, there is still a high degree of concentration of economic might at the centers of power and a growing gap between rich and poor.

The relative poverty of the country in resources and the tremendous expenses of defense and immigration absorption have created a highly centralized, overstretched economy. But defense has also provided an arena for technological innovation and creativity, and the mass immigration from the Soviet Union has introduced a talented pool of engineers, doctors, and computer specialists. Israel's economy benefits from the infusion of funds from abroad, but it is very competitive in many fields, and the standard of living of its population has reached European standards. The gap between rich and poor has grown, but the country's dedication to minimum standards for its population perpetuates a highly institutionalized network of organizations and bureaucracies.

The economy illustrates many of the major features of Israeli public life.[1] The economy is very centralized and is characterized by a high level of government influence. It provides the Jewish people living outside Israel with a tangible link with the country and its development. The economy has increasingly encouraged enterprise and initiative, yet is still dominated by a small number of actors, most of whom are well connected with government leaders. Repayment of past debt is a major burden for the economy, which has been dependent on loans and grants from foreign countries, especially the United States.

Costs of the defense effort make up the single largest expenditure and influence the structure of the entire government budget. The economy is a major political resource, and politicians have not hesitated to derive political and organizational benefits from its manipulation. Subsidizing basic consumer goods and public transportation has been characteristic of the policies of both Labor and the Likud, but this has recently declined. Unemployment is relatively low, but the rate of inflation is a constant worry.

Decisions that appease growing consumer demand and simultaneously continue expensive government projects have led to the mortgaging of future generations to the standards of today. Trade imbalances are huge and lead to indulging in loans in foreign and local currencies. The economy usually skews in favor of the salaried class immediately before elections. Attempts to reform the economy are difficult because of the vested interests that protect existing structures and the political unpopularity of such moves.

Prime Movers

Israel's political economy can be understood only in terms of the historical developments that produced the system. Imagine an economy with few if any raw materials; with great needs for funds to finance political and social projects; with connections to individuals, institutions, and governments abroad interested in aiding it; and with an administrative elite intensely loyal to the overriding goals of the economy yet flexible and ambitious enough to attempt an enterprise that is theoretically not promising. Add to this the need for secrecy, and the result may be something resembling the Israeli economy. These generalizations have held for the entire period of modern Jewish settlement in Eretz Israel, although many of the details have changed. The need for secrecy, for example, was originally intended to prevent the British mandatory power from discovering clandestine efforts at absorbing illegal immigrants. Secrecy was often justified because of a project's connection with national security needs or, later, to allow Israel to deal with firms or countries that did not want these dealings to become public knowledge. Today, the habit remains long after the need has vanished.

There have been three prime movers in the Israeli economy: the World Zionist Organization, the Histadrut, and the Israeli government. These prime movers were responsible for fashioning the Israeli economy and for developing it. At different points in the development of the economy of Eretz Israel since the 1920s, economic power has been distributed differently among the three. In the prestate era, the World Zionist Organization and the Histadrut reigned; after the establishment of the state, the Histadrut, and the government wielded enormous influence; in the 1980s the role of the Histadrut changed drastically, and economic power became even more centralized in the hands of the Israeli government.

NATIONAL INSTITUTIONS

The most important prime mover of the prestate period was the World Zionist Organization (WZO). After World War I, development of the economy was spurred by immigrants coming with capital of their own, but mostly it came about because of the activities of the WZO and the moneys it collected abroad and expended in Eretz Israel. The WZO, founded by Theodor Herzl in 1897, now meets once every four years based on elections held by Jews all over the world. Since statehood, the results of the Knesset elections determine Israel's representations to the Zionist Congress. Since 1959, Israel has had 38 percent of the delegates, the United States 29 percent, and all other countries together 33 percent.

The structure of the WZO is pyramidal; above the broad base of the Zionist Congress is the 518-member Assembly, and above that the executive committee with 192 members, and a smaller directorate. Israeli parties are dominant, and the payoffs and politics of the WZO are often a direct extension of party politics in Israel. In addition, representatives of Maccabi, WIZO, Bnei Brith, the Sephardic Federation, and the Orthodox, Conservative, and Reform movements in Jewry are members. Power tends to be shared, although important functions are kept for the major party if possible.

The aim of the Jewish Agency was to assist and encourage Jews throughout the world to help in the development and settlement of Eretz Israel. When the League of Nations established a Mandate for Palestine in 1922, it provided that "an appropriate Jewish agency" be set up to cooperate with Britain, the mandatory power. The Jewish Agency thus derived its name. The Executive of the Jewish Agency was the chief decision-making body in Eretz Israel and became the "state in the making."

It was natural upon achieving independence for the chairman of the Agency Executive (Ben-Gurion) to become prime minister and the head of the political department (Sharett) to become foreign minister. The political importance of the Agency far exceeded that of local institutions such as Knesset Israel, the Elector's Council (Asefat Nivharim), and the National Committee (Vaad Leumi). It was the Agency that had close working contacts with the mandatory power, and by 1930, as the outlook for the future of European Jewry darkened, it became even more important. By 1935 the Mapai party had won control of the Agency Executive, and Ben-Gurion had become its chairman. Such control was important symbolically because the fight over control of the Zionist movement between Jews living in Eretz Israel and those living abroad had gone on for a long time. Even more important were the political implications, for the ascent of Mapai shifted control of the moneys collected from abroad to Eretz Israel and from nonsocialist parties to socialist ones.

Relations between the State of Israel and the WZO and the Jewish Agency were formalized in 1952. This in effect froze the situation that then existed and recognized the WZO's and the Jewish Agency's continued activity in the fields of settlement, immigration, and education. After independence, the Agency was very active in the economy, owning Raasco, a construction company that had set up forty settlements, and Bank Leumi, the country's largest bank. In addition the Agency had partial ownership and control of Mekorot and Tahal, which developed water projects; Amidar, which provided and managed moderately priced housing developments; El Al, Israel's national airline; Zim, Israel's major shipping line; and the Israel Museum in Jerusalem. This partial list, along with a series of affiliated corporations, indicates the wide scope of the Agency's activities and its role in the economy.

Two other organizations of the WZO that were important in the pre-state period still exist, although their functions have largely been eclipsed by the state. The first is the United Jewish Appeal (Keren Hayesod/Magbit), which is the money-raising arm of the Zionist movement. Since it is often less problematic for Jews throughout the world to contribute to a Jewish philanthropic organization than directly to the State of Israel, the organization serves important functions, although its efforts are closely coordinated by the finance minister and the government. The ideology of the appeals is that Jews around the world have a responsibility to support Israel and therefore should contribute to it through a worldwide organization. As Israel prospered and the Jewish diasporas were challenged by assimilation or by oppression, a debate emerged about what share of the moneys raised by the UJA should be transferred to Israel and what share should be used for the needs of Jewish communities outside Israel.

The second important organization is the Keren Kayemet (Jewish National Fund), which was charged with purchasing and reclaiming the land. When the state was formed, many of its functions passed naturally to state authorities. The Israel Lands Administration is caretaker of nationalized land, which comprises more than 90 percent of pre-1967 Israel. The Administration has been located at various times in a number of ministries, its control of the real estate of the country making it a very valuable asset. When the Ministry of National Infrastructure was set up in 1996, headed by Arik Sharon, the Administration was one of the key building blocks.

In 1971, the Jewish Agency was reconstituted in name, becoming a partnership between the Zionist movement, controlled by the dominant Israeli political parties, and the leaders of Diaspora Jews, generally identified as "non-Zionists." In reality, Israeli parties continued to control the Jewish Agency's governance, structure, policies, budget priorities, and senior staff appointments. Differing agendas clearly drove the two groups of leaders. In 1995, Avraham Burg was elected chairman of the Jewish Agency and World Zionist Organization. At age forty, he was the youngest person ever to serve in that position, and he also happened to be a Labor leader, a dove, and an Orthodox Jew in favor of religious pluralism. Burg became very popular before the 1992 elections by sponsoring and winning approval in the Labor Party center a resolution that called for the separation of synagogue and state. Party leaders were so anxious that the resolution would hinder their future coalition-building plans with the religious parties that they called a special session to overturn the decision at the next meeting.

Funded mainly by Diaspora donations, the WZO and the Jewish Agency bring immigrants to Israel and help them start their new life in the country, and provide Jewish and Zionist education in the Diaspora. But they suffer from an aura of stagnation and occasional petty corruption. Fifty years ago, most money raised by the UJA in Jewish communities worldwide went to Israel. Concerned about the 52 percent intermarriage rate among American Jews, about the fact that three-fourths of U.S. Jews have never visited Israel, and about their alienation from Judaism in Israel, Burg proposed spending half the $500 million raised in Israel, the other half in the Jewish communities in which the money was raised. WZO leaders from the Diaspora rejected Burg's plan, demanding to keep a larger portion in their home communities. This debate occurred as some of the main American federations announced that they would reduce their allocations to the Jewish Agency from 39 percent to 37.5 percent of the funds raised by the UJA.

The WZO–Jewish Agency organization is faced with a disputed agenda, a shrinking staff (cut in half from its 3,200 employees level in 1990), and friction with ministries in Israel that have overlapping mandates. The WZO and the Jewish Agency are active in encouraging *aliyah*, in youth and educational work, in settlement, and in welfare work, and all these functions are also filled by government ministries. Compromises are worked out, such as the division of labor regarding immigrant absorption, by which the Jewish Agency deals with potential immigrants outside Israel, and the government's ministry of immigrant absorption handles immigrants in Israel, but personal, bureaucratic, and political interests keep getting in the way.

The WZO and the Jewish Agency provide alternative sources of income for social projects in Israel, thus freeing the government's budget for other purposes. Also, the continued existence of these organizations allows for activity and involvement by many non-Israeli Jews. As for settlements in the territories, different policy preferences have been expressed by senior bureaucrats of opposing parties. The result is conflicting bureaucratic initiatives with personal and organizational interests at stake.[2] The WZO and the Jewish Agency have been downsized considerably, but they still have important symbolic value and continue to be active in the economy. Controlling them provides patronage and activity, and although the size of the workforce and the range of activities have been reduced over the years, they still remain attractive political plums in Israeli politics.

THE HISTADRUT

The clearest organizational expression of political and economic power in the prestate period was the Histadrut. Formed in 1920 by socialist parties to further the economic, social, and cultural interests of the Jewish worker in Eretz Israel, it became an important power base for socialist parties.[3] Apart from representing workers in the negotiation of contracts with employers, it also incorporated the important collectivist enterprises of the country, including the collective kibbutz and the cooperative moshav. In addition the Histadrut was a major employer in its own right, supplying social welfare and economic services including education, health, housing, construction, manufacturing, culture, banking, insurance, and sport.

Cooperation between the Histadrut and WZO, and later with the state, allowed a pooling of resources. Bank Hapoalim, for instance, was set up by the Histadrut with the help of the WZO. Through the first four decades of statehood, the government Ministry of Finance allowed the Histadrut's pension funds to be invested in Hevrat Ovdim, the Histadrut's holding company, giving it a sure source of capital. With the dramatic changes of the 1980s and 1990s, featuring the takeover by the government of Bank Hapoalim, the collapse of Hevrat Ovdim, and government regulation of pension plan investments, those days were over.

The structure of the Histadrut changed little between its founding in 1920 and its streamlining (some called it gutting) in 1994. Through the years, many activities that formed the backbone of the Histadrut were transferred to or transformed by the state. The Histadrut holds elections among its members every four years, using a list system, in which most of the political parties of Israel compete. Until 1994, the Labor list (Mapai, or the Alignment, or whatever name is used at the time) always won an absolute majority in Histadrut elections and thus completely controlled this important source of power and patronage.

In the May 1994 elections, Labor was challenged by one of its own, Chaim Ramon, who was the minister of health in the Rabin government at the time. He split with Labor because it refused to support his proposed national health scheme. This topic was especially sensitive since one of the Histadrut's remaining bastions of power was Kupat Holim, its system of health clinics and hospitals. Ramon's list won 46.2 percent of the vote, running against the Histadrut secretary-general, Chaim Haberfeld, who headed the lackluster Labor list and won only 32.5 percent. Although Ramon won control of the Histadrut convention, Labor retained control of the labor councils, leading to low-level conflict between the two groups. If conceived of as two factions from the same camp, they did very well, but upstart Ramon's success was a cruel rebuke to the Histadrut's establishment and to those who had opposed Ramon in the Labor Party.[4]

At the conclusion of the Histadrut membership drive in October 1995, there were 650,423 members of the Histadrut,[5] 84 percent salaried, and about 9 percent pensioners. In 1993, 42 percent of salaried workers in the economy were members of the Histadrut,[6] placing Israel in a category of countries with similar rates such as Germany, Italy, and Canada, well ahead of the United States, Japan, or France, but far behind the Scandinavian countries.[7] This was in contrast to the reported number of 1.8 million members in 1994. The reason that the drop in membership was so severe was that one no longer needed to be a Histadrut member to get health insurance. The national health insurance law that went into effect in 1995 (see chapter 11) declared that applicants for insurance could not be turned down by a plan and that acceptance could not be made conditional on membership in another organization. In the past, many workers had suffered their membership in the Histadrut because of the health insurance coverage.[8] Even if we assume that the previous numbers were accurate and not bloated, membership had been falling at a rate of about 2 percent per year even before the law was enacted.

By winning the election and control of the Histadrut, and by decreasing the operations of this colossus, Ramon became a power to be reckoned with. He and his colleagues never left Labor and remained members in its Knesset delegation. His return to Labor's ranks after the Rabin assassination left him with his own party in the Histadrut (called Ram) in coalition with the Labor Party, of which he was a leader. The situation set him up as a contender for the head of his party and for the position of prime minister.

The Histadrut's economic activities were historically significant because it was willing to pioneer in sectors that would not attract a capitalist investor. Since the ideology was developing the economic base of the homeland and creating a class of Jewish workers in Eretz Israel, its economic behavior was often prone to risk taking.[9] Its historic role in the economy can be divided into four categories.

First, there was the administration, which involved bureaucrats and functionaries of the central administration; the executive committee, workers' councils, trade unions, Kupat Holim (the sick fund), pension plans, social welfare funds, *Davar* (the Histadrut's newspaper), and the *Jerusalem Post* (the English-language newspaper that until 1989 was jointly owned with the Jewish Agency). The most important of these was Kupat Holim, which employed almost 30,000 in the 1980s and was a major consumer of medical supplies and other commodities.

Second were the economic enterprises, which included Koor, Shikun Ovdim, Hasneh, and Bank Hapoalim, leaders in industry, building, insurance, and banking, respectively. Each was a leader in its field, and each had an important impact on the economy. In the mid-1980s, many of these enterprises felt the impact of the slick management practices that had characterized their operations. Historically their role in the economy had been very significant, but facing enormous deficits and a reduced labor force, they also had to curtail their bloated bureaucracies and their patronage. Becoming efficient in an economic sense was a serious departure from past practices.

In order to raise the capital to see them through the crisis, some of these enterprises sought government loans or guarantees; in the past, with the Finance Ministry controlled by the Labor Party, this type of appeal was natural. But under the Likud administrations of the 1980s, the government was less forthcoming. It made governmental support conditional on administrative reform of the enterprises. For example, in 1980, Finance Minister Yigael Horowitz reversed the policy that allowed Hevrat Ovdim to take unlinked loans from the pension funds run by the Histadrut. When Shimon Peres was prime minister in the mid-1980s, and when he became finance minister in 1988, he continued policies like this, hoping to recruit the Histadrut's support in curbing inflation. The unintended consequence was the ending of practices that had been extremely beneficial to the Histadrut. The economic crisis has also raised ideological issues. There were suggestions that the needed capital be raised by turning to private investors. This would indicate much more than economic trouble for the working-class Histadrut; it would also signify an important deviation from the socialist principle of class or national ownership of the means of production.

The crises could not be denied—but neither could the important role of the Histadrut in Israel's economy. For example, 27 percent of the country's 1986 industrial product was generated by Histadrut firms. Koor had more than 100 industrial firms, some 100 commercial firms, and 50 administrative and financial firms, including pension funds whose moneys financed many other projects. It was listed in *Fortune* magazine's list of the 500 largest companies in the world.[10] Koor was the country's largest industrial exporter and in 1986 employed 30,000 workers. The details can be expanded, but the point remains the same: the Histadrut was a key economic and political force of power in the country.

Third were the cooperative organizations set up to facilitate cooperative marketing for members. This included Hamashbir Hamerkazi department stores, Tnuva, and supermarkets. Tnuva is the country's largest supplier of fresh produce; in 1980 it supplied two-thirds of the country's fresh agricultural produce.

Fourth was the cooperative economy, which encompasses the kibbutz, the moshav, and other cooperative ventures. Some 21,000 workers were employed in this area, but less than 10,000 of them were members of the cooperatives. Difficult ideological problems were faced because the norm was against exploiting hired labor. Egged and Dan, for example, transportation cooperatives that accounted for 80 percent of the country's passenger movement, were periodically plagued with tensions between drivers who were cooperative members and drivers who were salaried employees. Another example is the eleven regional enterprises set up by the major kibbutz movement; of the 6,000 workers, 1,200 were kibbutz members. The perceived exploitation by these enterprises of the surrounding (largely Sephardi) population in development towns became symbolic in the ethnically charged elections of the 1980s.[11]

The kibbutz and moshav are prime examples of Israeli inventiveness and adaptation. They continue to perform agricultural miracles and have become active in industrial enterprises, which now account for half their product. But during the prestate and early state years these agricultural settlements, especially the kibbutz, were the focus of political and ideological power as well as economic success. This role of moral leadership has been eclipsed, and the decline of the kibbutz in the public mind is both cause and effect of the decline of Labor. But its economic achievements stand.

The roof organization of the settlement movements is the Agricultural Center. It represents 401 moshavim and 243 kibbutzim. They are dominant in most fields of agricultural endeavor, and in some fields (such as milk or flowers) they control almost all production. Cooperatives produce most of Israel's produce and some 80 percent of its agricultural exports, involving about two-thirds of those working in agriculture.

The economic power of the Histadrut was a major factor in the Israeli economy. When it and the government were controlled by the same party, the potential political and economic power was awesome—and that was the case between 1948 and 1977. Even with the ascent of the Likud, the Histadrut continued to play a major role in the economy, but the rules changed.

In each of the four areas, the Histadrut has changed dramatically.[12] And with it has gone the organizational basis, the patronage, and the power enjoyed by the Labor Party for seventy-five years. The reformers believed that the behavior of Labor regarding the old Histadrut was like that of a "suicidal whale," in Ramon's unforgettable phrase, while the New Histadrut (they actually changed its name) would allow for the reemergence of the labor movement as a vibrant leader of Israel in the future. The new leadership decided to focus on the trade union aspect of the Histadrut.

The New Histadrut moved its headquarters to Jerusalem from Tel

Aviv, sold many of its property holdings, reorganized the regional and local workers' councils, and retired or did away with the jobs of many of its activists. The Histadrut newspaper, *Davar*, was sold to the paper's employees, as were other publishing and cultural enterprises. After several false starts and partial Histadrut participation, *Davar* published its last issue in 1996. The role of the Histadrut in supporting competitive sports, and especially its *Hapoel* teams, was severely restricted.

The economic base of the New Histadrut was far different from the old Histadrut in terms of both scope and influence. The National Health Insurance Law of 1995 redefined the role of the Histadrut as an actor in health delivery; Kupat Holim was confined to providing facilities, with the collection of dues and the funding of expenses regulated and conducted by the National Insurance Institute and the Ministry of Health. Most important, the law abolished the condition of Histadrut membership for those insured by the Histadrut's Kupat Holim. Government legislation regulating pension plans effectively took a major source of capital out of the control of the Histadrut in exchange for covering the commitments of plans that were not actuarially sound because of growing life expectancy, lowered investment rates, and poor management.[13]

The Histadrut's share of Koor was sold to the California-based Shamrock Holdings, which paid $252 million for controlling 22.5 percent. Bank Hapoalim, which had been taken over by the government after the shares-manipulation scandal of 1983, was up for sale, although most of it was already outside the control of the Histadrut.[14] Even the special tax added to Histadrut membership since 1970, distributed in accordance with the Histadrut election results, was in question and subject to future legislation. Although only about a third of the Histadrut's members were actually identified with a political party, the dues became an important source of supplemental income for the parties.

THE GOVERNMENT OF ISRAEL

The government is by far the largest actor in the Israeli economy, and its role is growing. The public sector can be divided into three categories: units that provide governmental services, business enterprises of the state, and state-owned corporations.

The first category, units that provide governmental services, is the most extensive of the three. Activities are undertaken by governmental ministries or special units set up by the Knesset and financed by the public treasury. The category includes defense; ministries concerned with promoting certain aspects of the economy (energy, agriculture, atomic energy, transportation, industry and commerce, tourism, communication) or activities important to the economy (subsidizing credit and supporting public transportation); ministries concerned with the social welfare (education, health, labor, immigrant absorption, religious affairs, building, and housing) and activities related to public welfare (aid to the broadcasting authority, subsidizing basic food articles, and agricultural production); services of a general or administrative nature (the president, the Knesset, the prime minister's office, the ministries of finance, interior, police, justice, foreign affairs, the state controller, financing political parties); and municipal and local government arrangements for firefighting, water, and sewage.[15]

The second category is the business enterprises of the state, such as railroads, lands administration, the port of Jaffa, the government printer, and the arms industry. These sell services and goods and finance their operations largely by these sales. Another area of government activity is the statutory authority, established by law, which overlaps with activities already mentioned. They include the commissions for production and marketing in the various agricultural areas (vegetables, tobacco, milk products), Magen David Adom (the Israeli Red Cross), Yad Vashem (the Holocaust memorial organization), the National Insurance Institute, local authorities, the Bank of Israel, the council for higher education, the employment service, the ports authority, the airports authority, religious councils, the broadcasting authority, and the national sport lottery. This list does not have to be exhaustive to underscore the point that the government is very active in many facets of the Israeli society.

Government corporations, the third category, operate in areas such as natural resources, development, and tourism. The Government Corporations Law identifies a government company as one with at least 50 percent government ownership or 50 percent participation in its direction. Using this definition there were 119 such corporations in mid-1995, down from 189 in 1987. In 1994, 68,181 people were employed by government corporations, down from 72,655 in 1992, but still almost 5 percent of the workforce.[16] The reduction in number occurred because the government sold its share in small corporations; the big ones were yet to be released. If we add the subsidiaries of these companies and joint ventures between government and private owners and the more than 120 corporations set up by municipalities, the real scope of the activity becomes clearer. Some of Israel's most important government corporations include El Al, the aircraft industry (with 11,000 employees), and Bezek (with 10,600 employees).

Government corporations allow the government more flexibility of action in the marketplace than is usually the case with units under strict public scrutiny and financed by the treasury. But these corporations may become empires unto themselves, either not responsive to public demands or too dependent on the politicians who set up the corporations. In Israel each corporation is responsible to a minister, but the diversity and complexity of the corporation demand unusual talents to direct them effectively.

The picture of the Israeli economy painted in the preceding pages heavily emphasizes the structures created by public institutions both before and after the founding of the state. While the public sector is undoubtedly very influential, the private sector must not be ignored. With all its centralization and the influence of the government on its economy, Israel has encouraged private investment and economic activity. Many of these undertakings have proven beneficial to the investor and the economy alike. Corporations such as Klal or Hevra Leisrael were set up under very favorable terms in order to attract investment by Jews abroad.

As in most market economies, the watchword of the 1990s is privatization.[17] For Israel, in addition to the usual questions regarding privatization, the defense issue looms large. What activities should be recognized as monopolies? Does it make sense to replace concentration of economic control in government with concentration in the hands of a few individuals? What are the motivations of the buyers? Are there crucial or sensitive spheres the transfer of which to private hands could endanger national security?

The motivation of most investors seems to have been profit, rather than control of Israeli politics or economic life. Three examples of recent active investors:

1. The purchaser of a 24.9 percent controlling share of Israel Chemicals (for $230 million) was a group headed by billionaire Shaul Eisenberg, who already had extensive holding in Zim shipping line and Israel Oil Refineries, through his Hevra Leisrael. Eisenberg was also one the purchasers (with the Azorim real-estate firm and the Renaissance Fund) of Shikun Ufituah, the government housing firm sold for $283.5 million.
2. The Renaissance Fund, which included Charles Bronfman's Claridge Israel Investment Company as well as other investors, also bought control of Paz, one of the largest fuel distribution firms.
3. Businessmen Yuli Ofer and Muzi Wertheim got Bank Mizrahi for $110 million. Ofer had extensive real-estate and shipping holdings; Wertheim headed the Coca-Cola franchise.

The debate regarding privatization continues, although Prime Minister Netanyahu made it a top priority in his 1996 campaign. A moderate view sees it as beneficial only when there is competition or when changed market conditions demand efficiency and better management. Regarding national assets, such as the mineral resources controlled by Israel Chemicals, or the possibility of El Al being in private hands, the government holds a "golden share," through which it retains some measure of control and protects the national interest.

One of the most dramatic changes to take place in the daily life of Israelis has been the marked improvement of telephone and postal services. Long operating as government ministries, both functions were transferred in the mid-1980s to the status of government corporations. This allowed management greater flexibility in terms of planning and the workers a heightened motivation. One incentive to workers was more flexibility in the wage structure. Like all Israeli salaried employees, they were involved in the popular Israeli sport of comparing salaries and wanting to be "linked" to the wages of other groups. The government wanted the change to remove entrenched anomalies in these service areas; the workers were counting on higher wages. The results were very impressive.

Bezek, the telecommunications corporation, began in the 1980s wholly owned by the government. In the 1990s, 25 percent of its shares were offered on the open market, with 10 percent of the offering going to the concern's workers. Bezek created a revolution in its sphere of activity. One representative indication was that in 1984 a quarter-million households were waiting to have telephones installed, and half of them had already been waiting for three years. By 1993, there was a waiting list of 20,000 homes, which would be provided service soon.

The story of the National Railways has yet to end happily. An independent unit in a government ministry, in 1988 the railways were put under the jurisdiction of the Israel Ports Authority, a government corporation since 1961. The Ports Authority had a reputation of good management and a strong financial standing. The railways, with a weak political and financial position, were added to the Ports Authority by the government to make use of the surplus funds that had been accumulated by the Authority. This lowered the budget demands on the government and transferred the problems associated with a troubled and weak unit.[18]

Performance and Government Activity

Israel's economic achievements are impressive. Israel attained the highest gross domestic product (GDP) growth rate among Western (OECD) economies in 1991 (6.2 percent) and 1992 (6.7 percent) and one of the highest in 1993 (3.5 percent). The country's GDP was up 4.3 percent to $13,750, still barely half the U.S. level, but climbing. In 1993 its per capita GDP placed it twenty-first among 200 countries in the world. A 1994 World Bank report of the standard of living of the nations of the world listed Israel in eighteenth place.[19] Although a small country with a population of

TABLE 3.1

ECONOMIC INDICATORS IN SELECTED COUNTRIES

Country	GDP per capita 1993	Product growth 1995	Surplus (% of product) 1995	Average inflation 1992–95	Unemployment 1995	Public debt (% of product)
Japan	33.6	0.3	2.3	1.0	3.1	45
United States	24.6	3.3	−2.4	4.2	5.6	51
Germany	21.3	2.1	−0.8	3.1	9.3	31
Great Britain	16.3	2.7	−1.1	3.4	8.4	34
Israel	12.4	7.1	−4.7	10.8	6.3	92
Spain	12.2	3.2	0.0	5.4	22.7	41
Greece	7.1	1.9	−2.1	14.1	9.8	113

SOURCE: *Haaretz,* 30 June 1996, A2.

5.5 million, Israel's international position in some areas of industrial and agricultural production capacity and exports is remarkable. Free Trade Agreements with Europe (the EU and EFTA) and the United States facilitate Israel's exports and participation in international business enterprises, affecting its anticipated growth during the 1990s (see table 3.1).

Israel's GNP was larger than that of the neighboring Arab nations combined. In 1994, the GNP was $74 billion, up 6.8 percent. Between 1950 and 1976 the GNP increased by nearly 9 percent a year in constant prices and by 4.7 percent a year on a per capita basis. After that, growth stagnated (as it did in the rest of the world), GNP increasing by 2 percent in constant prices in 1975 and by only 1 pecent in the late 1970s. When calculated on a per capita basis, this gave Israel a standard of living higher than that of Italy. On an absolute basis, Israel's gross national product was higher than that of Egypt's, although Egypt had a population more than ten times the size of Israel's. This fact is even more impressive when we take into account that the Israeli economy was about 40 percent that of Egypt's GNP after independence in 1948.

The government has played a very active role in the Israeli economy. Its control of the budget, the rate of exchange, the money supply (nominally controlled by the Bank of Israel), and the granting of licenses, loans, and grants make it the single most important actor in the Israeli economy, affecting as much as 90 percent of the economy's performance. Almost any subject discussed finds government presence: the government is the country's biggest employer and its largest customer. It controls important economic resources: land, money, raw materials, water, and the right to grant or deny the use of these and related potential sources of income. The government determines subsidies, wages, and taxes, and in effect determines the standard of living for the bulk of the population.

Most imported foodstuffs are imported by the government or by government license, while food production is regulated by public commissions on which the government has major representation. Many raw materials are imported by government monopolies. Wage guidelines are set for salaried workers in consultation with the government; cost-of-living increases, so important in a country that has experienced three-digit (or more) inflation, are also determined after government consultation. Prices can be fixed by the appropriate ministry on goods deemed vital or on goods that enjoy the status of monopolistic commodities. Capital formation, investment programs, and the licensing of banks are other areas of government influence and activity.

The key ingredient in the government's influence over the economy is that for all practical purposes it has monopolized the capital market. Israelis save at a very high rate, mostly through retirement funds partially financed by employers, through investment plans, and through the stock market. Most of this activity is supervised by the Finance Ministry by way of issuing licenses to banks, or financial institutions under the control of the banks, that conduct such investments. Although this supervision is ostensibly to protect the public, in effect it allows the ministry tremendous leverage on the economy; the ministry controls the investment activity of the banks and financial institutions. In practice, most of these moneys are channeled into projects in tune with the priorities and goals of the government budget. For example, the finance minister, with the approval of the finance committee of the Knesset, can approve bond issues with tax reductions that obviously have a great influence on how the public invests its money. Other bonds are issued for institutional investments, thus creating a mechanism to absorb the very large amounts of money in pension funds. To privatize and encourage competition, the politicians must relinquish their control of this source of power.

One legacy of Israel's unique history was the expectation that any problem worthy of solving would be financed by the government or one of its agencies. Also, most projects could be presented in a way that would appeal to leaders anxious to implement Israel's priorities of security, economic development, social justice, and full employment. Loans would have to be guaranteed to attract industry; settlements would have to be built to enhance security; communication and transportation could be important in time of emergency; scientific and technological excellence must be pursued; housing must be provided; health services and hospitals must be improved; and so on. Few activities were outside the scope of government.

There were political consequences to these economic activities. Regardless of the motivations of the leaders who initiated the projects, they led to a tremendous concentration of power and resources in the hands of a very small number of politicians and civil servants. And when new immigrants widely perceived that their promotions and even their jobs depended on retaining the present bosses in power (as was the case through the 1950s and perhaps later as well), these perceptions could be translated into electoral victories and power perpetuation.

The key to Israel's political economy is dependence and influence, rather than outright control and direction. With its power to control prices and provide licenses, with its near monopolization of the capital market, and with its subsidizing of foodstuffs, transportation, land, and housing (in certain areas), most actors in the Israeli economy are influenced by and many are dependent on government policies. This dependency makes the economy highly sensitive to changes in personnel and policy. It also makes the positions of leadership of the Finance Ministry potentially powerful. But this dependency lowers the likelihood of change in the system because radical change breaks the dependency relations that are so important to both sides. It is easy, for instance, to raise wages before elections; it is extremely difficult to cut them back afterward.

The ministries that deal with economic matters are aided by the Knesset's penchant for delegating to the appropriate minister many of the details of legislation. This transfer of legislative activity to the executive branch allows the Knesset to deal in principle while the ministries deal with details, but in reality it means that enormous economic and political power is concentrated in the economic ministries. What is even more notable from a political point of view is that economic decision making in Israel ultimately leads to the government, and within the government to the Finance Ministry, especially to the minister and the director of the budget. Enormous power rests in these positions in the Israeli system, the Finance Ministry usually having an "agent" participating in key deliberations throughout the public sector *before* budgetary decisions are made. Having the information beforehand prevents the Finance Ministry from being surprised by an enterprising governmental unit and gives the ministry an effective veto for all plans and projects.

The use of the term "veto" is important because it would be incorrect to foster the impression that the Finance Ministry, its minister, or the budget director can easily bring about a revolution in the economic arrangements of Israel. The Israeli economy is simply too complex, and the interests and organizations at work are too many to be easily bent to the will or policy of determined men. For example, in 1980 Yigael Horowitz talked gloomily of the Israeli economy not being able to continue at its rate of government activity and expenditure, but he was forced to resign when the political calculations of the government brought in very different conclusions. It can be asserted, though, that when the top political leadership is united in attempting to achieve a goal, the chances of achieving it are greatly enhanced. This was most obvious in 1985 when Labor's Prime Minister Shimon Peres cooperated with the Likud's Finance Minister Yitzhak Modai in controlling an inflation rate that exceeded 400 percent yearly. Peres used the influence he had with the Histadrut, headed by Labor's Israel Kaisar. The Likud and Labor, both members of the National Unity Government, cooperated in holding back rampant inflation by agreeing to hold down prices, wages, and taxes, without causing undue inflation or social unrest.[20]

Except for very unusual circumstances, the political-economic leadership has more power preventing developments they see as negative or unnecessary than making drastic changes in the regular order of things. Most change that can be effected is incremental in nature. The system is simply too enmeshed, the interests too variegated, and the force of habit too great to allow for sweeping change. Furthermore, sweeping change demands much more political and bureaucratic clout than most political-economic leaders have had or have wanted to expend. The rule of thumb gleaned from Israeli political history is that finance ministers have usually been left to do their own thing, the prime minister being either too unknowledgeable or too preoccupied with other issues to involve himself in the economy. Nevertheless, other ministers quickly become spokesmen for ministries they are charged to lead and fiercely resist cuts in their budgets or perceived infringement on their turf. The high degree of concentration of Israel's economy should not be misunderstood to mean that structural changes can be brought about overnight. Almost all enterprises in the Israeli system see in the Finance Ministry the source of support or funds for expansion in good times or salvation in bad ones. And these, of course, are political and not exclusively economic issues.

An extremely important source of power for the finance minister and his advisers is their ability to determine the appointment of key figures in the economy. Many industries and economic units are directly tied in with government, and others are dependent on it. If the politicians who head the Finance Ministry desire to do so, they can influence the composition of a board of directors in the public sector by placing people loyal to them or by placing party activists in key positions throughout the economy. This practice stems from their power or their perceived power. More than that, their influence is not always needed; often appointments will be made in anticipation that they will find favor in the eyes of government leaders. This is the sure test of power because anticipatory behavior is a sign of a very large measure of influence and control.

It is little wonder that the finance minister is considered to be one of the most powerful persons in Israeli politics. In the twenty-nine years of Alignment rule, finance was one of the few ministries never to be held by anyone but a Mapai member. Even the Defense Ministry was given to Rafi after 1967 (first to Moshe Dayan and then to Shimon Peres), but the powerful leaders who served as finance ministers (Eliezer Kaplan, Levi Eshkol, Pinhas Sapir) were all Mapai leaders, as were two weaker personalities but important Mapai functionaries (Zeev Sharf and Yehoshua Rabinowitz), who also held the post. It was natural for the Likud in 1977 to give its top post to Prime Minister Begin and the role of finance minister to Simha Ehrlich, the leader of the Liberals, the other major party of the Likud. He was followed by Yigael Horowitz of a smaller Likud Party, then by Yoram Aridor, and later by Yigael Cohen-Orgad, both dedicated Herut members. In the National Unity Government of 1984, the finance minister was Yitzhak Modai of the Liberal Party, followed by Moshe Nissim, also of that party. With the advent of the 1988 National Unity Government, Shimon Peres became finance minister. Avraham Shochat, an ally of Rabin in the Labor Party, was finance minister between 1992 and 1996, followed by the Likud's Dan Meridor in 1996.

For certain financial decision-making cases, such as the setting of salaries for Knesset members, ministers, and judges, or the amount to be paid to political parties for financing their activities or the activities of government corporations or special allocations, the approval of the Knesset Finance Committee is also needed. This committee reflects the composition of the governing coalition and usually presents no problem (see chapter 9). The cooperation of the chairman of the Finance Committee is essential, making him one of the most powerful people in Israeli politics. Close cooperation between the finance minister and the chairman of the Finance Committee can mean an enormous concentration of power.

An idea of the direct involvement of the government can be gleaned by the development of the economy by sectors. While it is not easy to measure precisely, the relative size of the government sector in the economy is growing. It was customary to speak of three sectors of the Israeli economy: the private sector, the government sector, and the Histadrut sector. During the first fifteen years of statehood, the public sector and the Histadrut sector accounted for about 20 percent each (excluding the Jewish Agency) of the net domestic product, with the government sector share in net product growing since 1953.[21] For 1969, based on employment figures, the public sector employed 33.6 percent of salaried workers, the Histadrut sector 18.1 percent, and the private sector 48.3 percent.[22] Using economic figures of the early 1980s (not employment statistics), the estimate was that the private sector accounted for about 40 percent of economic activity in the country, the Histadrut 20 percent, and the government 40 percent. Since the retreat of the New Histadrut from economic activity, the share of both the private and government sectors has risen.

Political leaders at times undertake economic risks because they fear that not taking the risks will expose them to even larger political dangers. Two examples are the bank shares crash of 1983 and the issue of the kibbutz debt, and they are related.

The banks ensured persistent upward demand for their shares by regulating their price through schemes such as having bank subsidiaries post demand for their shares. While illegal, the process was undertaken with the full knowledge of the government, the Knesset, and the Bank of Israel. The regulation resulted in an average appreciation of the value of the banks' shares at a rate of 30 to 40 percent per annum in real terms. After a few years of such activity, the shares of the banks were grossly overvalued in terms of their economic value. In October 1983 the prices of bank shares collapsed abruptly. The government came to the rescue of hurting shareholders and covered much of their loss. The government set a floor on the prices of the bank shares and agreed to purchase all the outstanding shares at a predetermined dollar price over a period of six years. The guaranteed prices were above market price so the government held the shares. The government obtained almost no voting rights, however, even though the shares constituted almost 100 percent of the banks' equity. Later legislation procured the voting shares for the government as of 1993. The banking industry was nationalized, not by intention, but because political considerations overrode economic ones.[23] While the heads of the major banks were tried and convicted of fraud for manipulating the price of their shares, the political leadership was never put on trial.

In the same period, eager to expand their farms and factories and tempted by unlinked, long-term bank loans at a time when three-digit inflation took the pain out of repayment, many kibbutzim (as well as many others) borrowed at the old values and planned to pay back at the new ones. Shimon Peres, as prime minister of the National Unity Government, desired to introduce a measure of discipline into the economy in 1985 by reducing inflation to double figures and raising interest rates. At that moment, the banks demanded their money back, and the kibbutzim could no longer afford to pay. The kibbutz movement faced a debt of $10 billion.

In 1989 the government and kibbutzim worked out an arrangement that canceled some of the debt, deferred payment on other parts, and forced some kibbutzim to liquidate their obligations by selling land to real-estate developers. In early 1992, the Likud government responded to skyrocketing urban housing prices and an insatiable hunger for building land, along with the pressure of the huge immigration from the former Soviet

Union. The government ordered the Israel Lands Administration, official caretaker of state land, to free some farmland for residential building, and a handful of kibbutzim and moshavim in the Tel Aviv and Jerusalem areas were paid handsomely by real-estate developers for land they had been leasing.

The largest part of the kibbutz debt was held by Bank Hapoalim, formerly owned by the Histadrut, and the second largest part by Bank Leumi, formerly owned by the Jewish Agency. The government was in the process of selling Bank Hapoalim and wanted to put Bank Leumi on the market soon afterward, but the unresolved question what the kibbutzim owed the banks was one of the major obstacles delaying finalization of the Hapoalim sale. Unless a buyer knew the value of the assets on the bank's books, it was impossible for a final price to be set. In the Finance Ministry and the central bank, reconsideration of the idea of selling the banks was under way, reflecting the close relationships between the government bureaucracy and former bureaucrats who held the top private banking jobs. The banks had substantial holdings in their investment companies, and control of Bank Hapoalim provided major stakes in Koor and Klal holding companies.

The role of the government in the economy of Israel is unprecedented among democratic regimes; the involvement of political actors in the economy is enormous and has increased over the years. Direct government activity is very high; the national budget's share of the gross national product (GNP) rose from 32.5 percent in 1950 to 95 percent in 1980. This would be unimaginable if it were not for sources of income outside the country. A time-series study of the relations between government consumption and GNP (without the Histadrut or the national institutions) revealed that the ratio was between .33 and .36 until the 1960s, then it contracted to about a quarter, and rose above 40 percent after 1967.[24]

The defense budget in Israel was 9.8 percent of the gross national product in 1995,[25] down from 25.5 percent of the GDP in 1982 and 12.8 percent in 1989. The world rate of military expenditure to GNP was 4.9 percent in 1989 and 6 percent in 1982; the world percent rates of military expenditure as a percentage of GNP for 1995, 1989, and 1982 were 4.9, 5.9, and 6 percent, respectively.[26] This decline expressed less military budget relative to a national budget burdened with many other pressures; it also could be lowered because of the growth in the size of the economy and the relative lessening of hostility levels of Israel's neighbors. But given the military threats Israel faced and the political risks it considered taking, it was not surprising that the downward slide of the military budget caused concern in many quarters. Comparable figures for the United States have defense at 21 percent of the national budget, 6.4 percent of GNP, and military expenditures per capita at $1,000. The Soviet Union before its breakup also spent $1,000 per capita for the military, and spent about 15 percent of its GNP on the military. For the United Kingdom, the figures were 14 percent of the budget, 5.3 percent of the GNP, and $450 per person, and for France they were 7 percent, 3.3 percent, and $370, respectively.

The government budget supposedly reflects the priorities of the government.[27] In Israel this is so only indirectly because much of the budget is based on moneys generated and spent abroad, and because activities supported by the government need not be directly financed by it (Jewish Agency activities, for example). Calculating the budget as a percentage of the GNP may be a misleading figure because transfer payments are not included in the gross national product. Thus, for example, when the National Insurance Institute supports a retired person or gives a family allowance, these payments are not incorporated in the GNP, although they play an important role in the nation's economic and social policy. Similarly, subsidies paid by the government are not calculated as part of the GNP. The sums involved are very large; transfer payments are as high as 40 percent of the GNP in Israel.

Lest we lose focus because of the details, it is important to remember that the structure and statutory arrangements of the economy provide the government in general and the finance minister in particular with large measures of responsibility regarding the national economy and tempting possibilities to utilize power to further economic and political ends. But the finance minister is not omnipotent. His major resource lies in his ability to direct, develop, suppress, or reduce the activities of the public and private sectors. But as the economy has developed, complete dependence on the government has been reduced; in the 1950s employment and housing were almost completely dependent on government activity, but this is not the case now. At the same time, powerful groups and institutions within the economy have emerged—largely thanks to government policy. Large unions within the Histadrut, important financial institutions, and major investors have the potential for opposing government policy in an effective manner.

Import Capital

Israel's achievements would not have been possible without the importation of capital. Just as other countries have imported foodstuffs, raw materials, or automobiles, Israel, in addition, has imported money. The most consistent sources of this money have been the Jews of the world, who have regularly contributed to Israel through donations, loans (Israel bonds), or investment. Between 1948 and 1978, collections (not including loans or investments in Israel) reached a level of more than $5.7 billion, nearly two-thirds of it from the United States.[28]

What has become even more important than the support of the Jews of the world is the support given Israel by other governments, especially West Germany and the United States. Reparations paid by the West German government to the government of Israel in the 1950s aided Israel in overcoming one of its earliest and most difficult economic periods. Food was rationed as hundreds of thousands of new immigrants continued to pour into the country. By 1978 over $4 billion had been received from the Bonn government, of which $836 million was reparation payments to the Israeli government for Nazi actions in World War II (these payments ended in the 1960s). In addition, personal restitution payments to Israeli citizens for acts against them during the Nazi rule continued; in 1980 restitution payments amounted to $468 million.[29]

Most of Israel's import capital in recent years has come from the government of the United States, about $3 billion a year since the early 1980s (some 60 percent in military aid and 40 percent for economic support). Most of this aid was given as grants; only a small portion was loans that had to be returned. Israel, however, still had very large payments to make on past debts. The dramatic nature of the rise of American aid is well illustrated by the fact that in 1970 U.S. aid to Israel totaled $71 million, of which $30 million was military aid and only $1 million of the total was in grants. In his speech to the U.S. Congress in 1996, newly elected Prime Minister Netanyahu said that Israel was planning to ask for a reduction in the economic support provided by Washington. But no timetable was given for such a request.

Foreign aid allows policymakers to avoid decisions regarding the country's priorities; since expenses need not be reduced, programs that otherwise would not be funded are continued. While the aid has continued to flow, Israel learned that not all its demands would be met. The government was forced to discontinue the development of the Lavi jet fighter in 1987 when it became clear that the United States would not continue to underwrite the project. In 1987 the gap between imports and exports (deficit in the balance of payments) was almost $3.5 billion, compared with about $450 million in 1967.[30]

Israel's total foreign debt at the end of 1994 reached $41.2 billion. More than half that sum were government liabilities payable in foreign currency, a result of the long-term independence and development bonds sold mostly to Jews abroad; an additional amount was owed by the government but payable in local currency. Developments regarding this topic are striking and unmistakable: a sharp rise in the public foreign debt and a lowering of the role of debts to Jews (bonds) in the equation. In 1955 the national debt payable in foreign currency was $491 million with the government owing $398 million of it; $198 million, or almost 50 percent, was owed to bondholders. By 1980, bondholders made up a little over a quarter of the total foreign debt of the government payable in foreign currency. This even while the size of the debt to bondholders increased 14.5 times in the twenty-five years between 1955 and 1980, while the total foreign debt of the government increased by double that rate, 28 times.

Israel's yearly debt, however, is greater than the support it receives from the United States. In 1982 Israel was pledged to repay $3.2 billion. About 14 percent of the GNP was expended on servicing the yearly debt! In 1982 about $1 billion was spent returning principle and servicing the interest on the first large loans given by the United States in 1973. In the 1995 government budget, 13 percent was earmarked as interest.[31] In the 1990s, the U.S. government guaranteed $10 billion in bank loans for Israel to aid in immigrant absorption.

As U.S. support jumped after 1973 and then stabilized, the proportion of Israel's needs supplied by the contributions of world Jewry shrank. The amount contributed by world Jewry was not large compared to the billions supplied by the American treasury. In the United States more than $500 million a year was donated by American Jews to the United Jewish Appeal, which must finance local activities as well as programs in Israel. The sale of Israel Bonds to the United States in the same period was more than half a billion dollars a year.[32]

Moreover, as Israel proved itself militarily strong, many Jewish communities began to rethink the tradition of putting Israel's needs before communal ones. Slowly a shift in priorities developed, and the share of contributions sent to Israel tended to decrease. The development coincided with the passing of the older generation of American Jewish community leaders whose formative years were spent while the Holocaust was raging and while the State of Israel was being formed. For the younger generation of leaders, Israel was a fact of life, and other needs of the Jewish community had also to be attended to. Some Jews outside Israel were critical of Israel in an unprecedented manner. The war in Lebanon, the Who is a Jew? issue, and the handling of the Arab uprising divided many of these Jewish communities (just as they divided Israeli Jews). This development decelerated the traditional rate of contributions to Israel. Jews continued to contribute, but their proportionate share in Israel's import capital was lower.

The relation between economics and politics is especially interesting from this perspective. This chapter has argued that because of the government's ability to influence much of the economy of Israel, it has a potent tool to increase its political power. Yet this does not seem to be the case with the influence of the Jewish fund raisers abroad in influencing the policies of the Israeli government or of the major government supporter of the Israeli economy, the United States. We must seek the explanation to this difference in the ideology of supporting Zionism on the one hand and the practicalities of trying to influence a sovereign power on the other.

Being dependent on someone else's money is not the best recipe for independence of action. The Jews of the world, while often politely listened to, were excluded from policy decisions in Israel. This folk wisdom followed Ben-Gurion's thinking that one who wants to influence Israeli policy should live in Israel. The strains that have resulted from the attempted division of labor, which has Jews outside Israel collecting the money and leaders within Israel deciding how to spend it, have existed for a long time.

In the 1920s the WZO tried to influence social and economic development within Eretz Israel from its headquarters abroad; this brought about a series of conflicts with the pioneers, especially socialists. When Mapai became the dominant force in the World Zionist Executive in 1933, it acted to consolidate its control over the inflow of moneys. Since then, tensions between donors and receivers have been mitigated by consultation and by passing out honorific titles without allowing economic power to be translated into political power by outsiders to Israeli politics.

The dependence of Israel on American funds has traditionally been cited by Arab states as proof of American complicity in Israeli policies. It is clear to them that economic power can be translated into political influence and, American protestations notwithstanding, the Americans are not serious in altering Israel's foreign policy course. The Americans have indeed used their economic weapon, usually in Israel's favor. They have generally been careful to avoid putting pressure on Israel by cutting off aid, although more subtle devices such as withholding a shipment of purchased material, failing to approve suggested increases in aid, or threatening not to guarantee loans given by others have been used. How a big power influences a smaller power is a complex and fascinating topic; what seems clear is that the options open to the big power are not unlimited. History has shown that short of cutting off aid completely, translating economic aid into political obedience is a difficult task. But there are intermediary steps, such as making the flow of money more difficult. One of the arrangements that advantages the United Jewish Appeal in the United States, for example, is that it is recognized by the authorities as a charitable organization and hence, according to U.S. tax law, contributions to it can be deducted from one's income tax. It is sometimes financially rewarding for Americans to donate to the UJA (or other charities) and thus put themselves in a lower tax bracket. Should these rules change, a different atmosphere, psychological and economic, might be revealed.

The most economically beneficial way to import capital is through export based on foreign investment. In the 1990s, Israel provided many foreign investors with an attractive option: the likelihood of a quiet and stable political environment, a well-trained workforce, and the strong probability of profit. The first was achieved by the partial lifting of the Arab boycott as a result of the Oslo accords with the PLO, the second because of the successful spinoff of technologies developed in military and defense-related industries along with the educated professionals who recently immigrated from the former Soviet Union, and the third through government subventions for investors. With its labor force, its strategic location between North America, Europe, and the Far East, and the free-trade pacts with both the United States and Europe, Israel has a potential as spectacular as Hong Kong or Singapore.[33]

In 1995, a total of $2.3 billion was invested in Israel, a twenty-fold increase from 1992, and this after being largely ignored by the investment world. Most opportunities were seen in high-tech industries where salary levels were relatively low by international standards, and quality was good. More important, the ratio of engineers to the general population was 135 per 10,000 people; in the United States it was 70 to 10,000. Venture capital in Israeli industry soared to $480 million in 1995 from $55 million in 1991.[34] Major high-tech companies became very active in Israel. Corporations such as Intel, IBM, Digital Equipment, Motorola, and National Semiconductor all created major research and development centers. The Intel Corporation, one of the world's major producers of integrated circuitry and chips for microprocessors, for example, accepted a Ministry of Industry and Trade offer of a $380 million grant, conditional on Israel being the site of a $1 billion Intel expansion project.

While import capital—loans, grants, contributions—has always been important in the Israeli economic equation, much of the burden has fallen on Israelis themselves. Israelis are very highly taxed. Like any other government, Israel has tried to finance its activities by absorbing capital from the Israeli public. By 1978 about 45 percent of the total government income came from domestic sources, with 55 percent collected abroad. Financing Israel's massive public consumption has required heavy taxation; in some years the Israeli citizen has borne the highest tax burden, relative to income, in the world. During the first decade, taxes equaled one-eighth of the GNP; in the 1960s, the proportion reached one-quarter, wavered between one-third and one-half in the 1970s, and peaked at 52 percent in 1986; since then, it has fallen again. At no time, however, has taxation covered more than two-thirds of the government budget.

Employment and Distribution

Because Israel's economy was so dependent on foreign capital and the defense budget so large, the government's role was central. The role of government is also important because Israel is a country of immigrants, and dependency relations developed easily. Lacking land, capital, and a profession (or the opportunity to work in their profession), many who came to Israel found themselves dependent on the various bureaucracies for all their needs. The kind of labor market that developed accelerated the economic concentration delineated earlier in the chapter.

Attempting to resolve the problems of economic scarcity, unemployment, security, and integration of the new immigrant groups led to governmental policies that structured the labor market. The logic behind labor absorption in the economy was political as well as economic, favoring services, especially in the public sector. The government, by virtue of its economic concentration and primary role in setting wages and price policies, had a major role in determining public welfare. Much of the workforce was salaried, and many worked in public-sector enterprises, making them financially dependent and within relatively easy grasp of the tax authorities. A very large majority of salaried people are directly affected by the wage policy of the government.

In 1995 there were 79,869 government employees excluding teachers and employees of government corporations.[35] About a third of the nation's employed people worked in jobs for which the government was either the direct or indirect employer, including the armed forces, teachers, employees of municipalities and local authorities, the Jewish Agency, workers of government corporations, Kupat Holim, and civil servants. This figure does not include workers in industries still under the control of the Histadrut, whose salaries are influenced by a national wage agreement that does not need the approval of the Finance Ministry, or the banks, which were taken over by the government after it rescued them from the bank-shares collapse. This makes the Israeli economy somewhat immune to the fluctuations and crises of the international economic system that affect most of the industrialized world, but dependent on the ability of its leaders to procure the budget needed to keep this service sector operating.

A second important feature of the labor market is that most of the employed work in the services sector. Of the 1.87 million employed persons in 1994, 3.3 percent worked in agriculture; 28.6 percent worked in industry including mining, manufacturing, electricity, water, and construction; and the remaining 68.1 percent worked in such service occupations as commerce, hotels, communication, finance, and business. About a third of the total, half of those working in services, were employed in public and community services.[36] These figures support the notion prevalent in Israel that working in industry does not provide the status or economic rewards that working in services does. But it also means that a great many jobs are dependent on government and public budgets, not on the productive capacity of the economy. When broken down by nationality and sex, the magnitude of the trends changes a bit. The non-Jews are more active relatively in agriculture and industry and Jews more in services. Women are also more concentrated in services.

It was difficult to construct a modern industrial society with a population whose largely middle-class backgrounds gave them inadequate preparation for such a task. Most important from a political point of view was the willingness of the leadership to provide employment by creating jobs even if some of them were redundant or unnecessary. One of the direct results of such high levels of government control and influence was that social and political goals (and not only economic ones) could sometimes guide decision makers in their deliberations. For example, industries might be located in developing areas for reasons of dispersing the population or to provide employment for people sent to inhabit these areas, even if the location made little economic sense. Much of the workforce is involved in compulsory army service, including reserve duty ranging from thirty to sixty days for many men until well into middle age. Israeli leaders, regardless of party, have tended to rank full employment very high on their list of policy goals. And on the whole they have been successful in preventing unemployment. Unemployment at about 6 percent remained low in the 1990s as the economy boomed. The low rate by international comparisons contrasted with the scores of millions unemployed in many industrialized nations. Some 100,000 Palestinians worked in the local economy; when they were not allowed in for security reasons for long periods of time, foreign workers were also used. By 1996, it was estimated that 110,000 legal foreign workers were in the country, along with an additional 100,000 illegals.[37]

The mechanism of setting wages underscores the central role of the government.[38] The process begins with negotiations between officials of the Finance Ministry, the Histadrut's trade union division, and the coordinating committee of the employers. The result of the negotiations is a national wage agreement. The government's role is usually one of arbitrator because the workers want more and employers want to pay less. The government is not only a major employer but is also elected by the largely salaried electorate and, no less important, is responsible for the national economy. After the guidelines have been set, attempts are made to reach specific agreements in the various economic sectors and later in individual plants. This long and extended process means that labor issues are almost always in the news, and many contracts are signed long after previous ones have expired. The Histadrut and the government are influenced by political and economic considerations; both are major employers, and the leadership of both must stand for reelection. When both the Histadrut and the government were headed by Labor, cooperation was the rule, although arguments, even heated ones, did occur. But their solution was generally achieved through intraparty committees or discussions. When the Likud headed the government and Labor controlled the Histadrut, an attempt was made by the government to limit the role of the Histadrut to economic matters and diminish the Histadrut's role in decisions with political importance.[39]

The point of major interest is that the wage policy of the country, not just of civil servants, is monitored by the center. Industrial enterprises are bound by general guidelines determined in wage negotiations, municipal workers are bound by the dependency of the municipalities on national budgets, and so on. The Civil Service Commission was relieved of its role in these wage negotiations in the mid-1980s, and power over this sensitive area was transferred to the controller of salaries, who is more closely under the control of the finance minister. According to the 1985 law, a unit that receives funding from the national budget may pay salaries, fix pensions, or provide other benefits only in accordance with the general guidelines of the controller of salaries of the Finance Ministry.

The finance ministers of Israel have used their power in this centralized wage structure for political benefit. The clearest proof of this is seen when we examine economic indicators and their relations to the elections. It is a well-documented fact that the relative growth rate of nondefense spending is largest in election years and that the largest increase in real wages occurs in election years. Data through 1973 convincingly show the growth of average annual per capita consumption in the year preceding elections compared to generally low levels in previous years.[40] Changes in real general income occur slowly, reaching a crescendo during election years. One analysis showed that in the first year after the election the average wage change was .9 percent, followed by 1.8 percent in the second year after the election, and 4.2 percent in the third.[41] The peak is reached in the fourth year, when the average wage change was 6.5 percent. Extra-economic factors are at work here. Using this kind of analysis, it was less surprising that Labor held power through eight elections and that the Likud could use its economic clout in 1981 to perpetuate its power. In a sense it is more surprising that the Alignment lost political power at the polls in 1977 than that it held it for so long.

The economy has generally not been a major political issue in elections because the government strives to make people feel as good as possible about the economy before elections. The most startling example of economic interference was Yoram Aridor's policy of decreasing excise taxes on goods such as color television sets before the 1981 elections. Aridor's policy came on the heels of Finance Minister Yigael Horowitz's resignation and his predictions of catastrophe for the Israeli economy. The subjective change in mood probably did as much as anything else to turn around the Likud's poor performance in the polls and get it moving in the "right direction"—their slogan for election day.

The turnover of 1977 can be partially understood by the policy of the Alignment in the mid-1970s to cut government nonmilitary spending and services and increase taxes, especially among that portion of the population with higher incomes. This was precisely the group that defected most from the Alignment (although not only because of the tax increase) and gave its votes to the DMC, in this way accelerating the ascent of the Likud. The Bank of Israel reported that real available income per capita dropped between 1973 and 1976 by 8 percent. For the lower classes this was but another reason to vote Likud and not Alignment, but for upper classes that wanted to vote for neither the Likud nor the Alignment, the available alternative was the DMC. To be sure, the economic downturn was related to the Yom Kippur War and the upswing for the Likud had begun earlier and had been associated with demographic changes within the population, but the inability of the Alignment to fashion an economic policy consistent with vote getting was another sign of its deterioration and another reason for the turnover.[42]

While the ethos of the country is egalitarian, in fact inequality and poverty are great by comparative standards and are growing (see table 3.2). The inequality index puts Israel ahead of the countries presented, including the United States. Not only did the index increase between 1990 and 1994, the percentage of the population below the poverty line grew from 16.9 to 18 percent in that same period.[43] Although less than 20 percent of the population, Arabs make up half of those in poverty. Inequality had been lower in the past, but its increase was steady over the years. Using the Gini coefficient as a measure, for which perfect equality is 0.0, in 1982 it was 0.222, and in 1985 it was 0.327.[44] In 1987, the income available for the highest decile to spend after meeting basic expenses was 7.6 times as large as was the available income for the lowest decile. National Insurance Institute figures showed that in 1988, the two highest deciles earned 49.7 percent of the gross national income, and the lowest two deciles earned only 2.2 percent. When welfare payments were added in, the share of the lower two deciles was 6.3 percent.[45]

The income data presented in table 3.3 by continent of birth make it clear that Ashkenazim have been favored. Israeli-born Jews had a gross income of 113.2 in 1994, with 100 being the rate for those born in Europe

TABLE 3.2
INEQUALITY AND POVERTY
IN SELECTED WESTERN COUNTRIES

Country	*Inequality index by net family income (Sweden = 100)*	*Percentage of population under poverty line*
Sweden	100	9.1
Germany	128	6.6
Great Britain	134	9.2
Netherlands	149	5.0
France	156	7.6
United States	161	17.7
Israel, 1990	165	16.9
Israel, 1994	175	18.0

SOURCE: Zvi Zussman, "Poverty and Economic Gaps," *Economic Challenges in the Next Four Years,* Caesaria Conference, Israel Democracy Institute, 16–17 July 1996.

TABLE 3.3
GROSS INCOME PER HOUSEHOLD
BY CONTINENT OF BIRTH

Base: Born in Europe or America = 100

	1965	1970	1975	1980	1985	1990	1994
Jews, total	90.1	90.0	94.2	91.5	92.2	92.5	108.8
Israeli-born Jews	108.6	103.3	102.5	93.8	95.4	90.8	113.2
Asian- or African-born Jews	71.7	73.9	82.2	80.1	80.7	88.2	112.5
European- or American-born Jews	100.0	100.0	100.0	100.0	100.0	100.0	100.0
Non-Jews	—	61.1	86.9	64.9	62.1	59.0	74.3

SOURCES: *Statistical Abstract, 1981,* 293–94; *Statistical Abstract, 1995,* 331.

and America. The fact that Asian- and African-born Jews did better than the European-born stems from the fact that most of the European-born were new immigrants from the former Soviet Union. It was the non-Jews who were consistently below all Jewish groups in income. Analyses by period of immigration and level of education, not displayed here, show that the longer one is in the country and the more education one has, the better the gross income, but that continent of birth and ethnic group still matter.

Inequality in the society is steadily growing and is at a higher level than the egalitarian expectations of the founders of Israel. Per capita income, for example, grew over the years, but income differentials between the veteran Ashkenazi and the newcomer Sephardi groups also widened. This increasing gap occurred because Ashkenazim tended to save more and to invest more, thus increasing the original disadvantage of the Sephardim in relative terms. The gap was also fostered by differing levels of education, by differences in knowing how to work the system by networking in the labor market (especially among employees), and because the Ashkenazim tended to dwell in the country's major cities as opposed to the outlying regions. Between 1969 and 1987, the number of noncitizen Arabs (from the territories) in the labor force tripled, from about 2.5 percent to about 8 percent. This process contributed to an improvement in the position of the Sephardi workers, but in relative terms the Ashkenazi groups gained even more. Among the self-employed, Sephardim have done well, and their average income was higher than those of the Ashkenazi group. Nonetheless, the Sephardim tended to fill lower prestige occupations and hence this "alternative route of social mobility" was partial at best.[46]

4. The Political Elite

Politics in Israel is party politics, and party politics is elite politics. The Italian political sociologist Gaetano Mosca, writing at the end of the nineteenth century, accurately described the situation in Israel a century later:

> In all societies ... two classes of people appear—a class that rules and a class that is ruled. The first class, always the less numerous, performs all political functions, monopolizes power and enjoys the advantages that power brings, whereas the second, the more numerous class, is directed and controlled by the first.[1]

The character of society and the direction it is taking can be understood in terms of the composition, structure, and conflicts of the ruling group.

Implicit in the unequal distribution of political power in a democracy is the realization that voting and elections are not the only avenue for expressing political preferences and getting them adopted. Instinctively we know that some individuals have more influence than others. In organizations the hierarchy of ranks clearly identifies those who have a higher likelihood of having their decisions implemented in general; a teacher has more power than a student, in the army an officer is more powerful, in a plant the manager determines what the worker will do, and in the home usually the parents decide what is to be done. In democratic situations equality is the rule. Each of us has considerable power because our vote is equal to everyone else's and, no less important, everyone else's vote is equal to ours.

But in reality, a ruling elite emerges. Even if we are able to change elites by voting in the opposition party at the next election, even if we are able to limit them by the constitution (written or unwritten) the country has developed, effective political power is never in the hands of the people. Moreover, an elite is not usually a collection of isolated individuals but is likely to be homogeneous, unified, and self-conscious. Individuals in the elite know one another well, have similar backgrounds, and share values, loyalties, and interests, although they may have differences of opinion on political issues and their personal ambitions may lead them to clash with one another.

It is important to appreciate that the preceding generalization regarding the unequal distribution of political power is a universal phenomenon. Only an extremely small proportion of the citizens of any country has any real chance of directly influencing national policy. Most people most of the time do not have the resources, access, or interest to involve themselves in policy decision making. In matters of curbing inflation (because the issue is so complex) as in matters of peace and war (because the issue is so sensitive), small groups of decision makers make decisions that affect all of us. This is true in all countries and at all times.

Participation and the Elite

Patterns of political stratification tend to be pyramidal in shape throughout the world;[2] it may well be that the Israeli political pyramid is higher than that found in some other democratic countries and its slope more sharp, but the general contours are the same. Most of the population does but one political act and that is to vote. This public is crucial to the politician, but as individuals the voters have very limited influence. Voters have one important collective political resource: numbers. In Israel the ranks of *nonparticipants* are very thin; voting participation is very high. Among Jews, those who fail to vote do so almost universally for technical reasons; there is more purposive abstention among non-Jewish Israelis, but even among this group a very large majority participates.

The *attentive public* is composed of those who have the skills and resources to become activists, who follow politics intently, but who take no active part other than voting. Data on very high levels of news consumption in Israel, as expressed by reading newspapers, listening to and watching news on radio and television, suggest that the size of the attentive public may be greater than in other countries (see chapter 12).

Activists may be party members, middle-level bureaucrats, or educators. They may be classified as those who take some active interest in politics by talking occasionally with a politician or writing a letter to a newspaper, but usually their action is limited to the issues to which they react.

The *influentials* are turned to by leaders and decision makers for advice. Their opinions and interests must be taken into account because their potential sanctions are feared. This stratum may include party officials, media personalities and journalists, university professors, army officers, labor union officials, high-level bureaucrats, industrialists, financiers, religious leaders, and officers of Jewish groups abroad. This group is even more limited in numbers but is likely to react to a broader spectrum of issues of public policy.

The second-highest stratum consists of the *proximate decision makers,* those individuals directly involved in policymaking, usually ministers and senior administrative officeholders. At the apex of the pyramid is the group of *top leaders,* which in Israel may consist of the prime minister and perhaps another two or three individuals. The symbiosis between the two highest strata is extremely important, for while the proximate decision makers provide support, legitimacy, and organization for top leaders, top leaders in their turn provide proximate decision makers with ideological direction, backing, and considerable status and power. People in the second stratum are anxious to sustain the top leadership because their own careers may depend on the continued success of the leadership and their own ambitions may be based on succeeding to the top leadership when the time comes.

At the apex of the pyramid, the top leaders have the final say if issues reach them. In Israel many issues of foreign and security policy are regularly brought for decision to the top leadership, while matters of internal and economic policy are not. In foreign affairs the top leadership tends to be the decision maker; in internal matters it tends to act as a final court of appeal if lower levels of decision makers cannot reach agreement among themselves.

The entire political system of Israel is stratified in terms of power, and so are the Knesset and the various political parties. The single member of the Knesset has relatively little power unless he is joined by many others, and this generally implies coalition support for his positions and support by the prime minister if possible. In turn, the government can almost always block unfavorable motions in the Knesset, and since it also has control of the government ministries, it controls the administration as well as the legislation of policy. Moreover, the individual Knesset member is almost always dependent on his political party for his reelection, whether his party features primaries or not, and so he is likely to gauge his behavior accordingly.

Crises of Succession

An indigenous Jewish political elite emerged in Eretz Israel only after the establishment of the British Mandate in the 1920s. Before then, political activity was circumscribed; Zionist politics, on the whole, was conducted in Europe. Herzl spent little time in Eretz Israel, Jabotinsky had his headquarters in Europe, and many leaders spent a good deal of their time abroad eliciting support and attending meetings.

With the second and third *aliyot,* the political organizations and the leaders of the country for the next generation and a half emerged. They were imbued with the ideals of socialism and collectivism that had become fashionable in the Russia they left after the unsuccessful Russian revolution of 1905. They were composed of two major groups: those born between 1885 and 1890 and those born at the turn of the century. These groups represented two distinct generational units in Israeli politics. The first group immigrated as part of the second *aliyah* between 1905 and 1912 and was instrumental in setting up the major political organizations of their day: the Ahdut Haavoda Party in 1919 and the Histadrut in 1920. These organizations were to dominate much of the political and economic activity of the Jewish community in mandated Palestine. The leader of this group, David Ben-Gurion, became Israel's first prime minister. He held the post, with brief interruptions, until 1963. The younger group arrived in the third *aliyah* (1919–23) and was greatly influenced by the Russian Revolution of 1917.[3]

Both groups came from Poland and Russia, both were highly motivated ideologically and politically, and both constituted a small fraction of the Jews who immigrated. These groups set up the important organizations in a political void. They were young, energetic, and self-sacrificing, and their successful efforts meant that they would be the leaders of the State of Israel when it was founded in 1948.

An implicit symbiosis developed between these two groups. Those in the older group were statesmen, making the grand decisions and setting policy. The younger group controlled the party machine, was faithful to the leadership, depended on it, and worked for it. The younger group thus ensured the perpetuation of the power of the older group because in the last analysis the leadership was also dependent on the party machine. With the acknowledged leadership fading from the scene in the 1970s, a crisis of succession loomed. The informal hierarchical relations that had been such an important part of the division of labor within the generational units of the party could not be easily transferred. The long years of shared experience and the generational solidarity that this produced prevented the flow of young, new leadership into the ranks.

A fascinating case in point is the political career of Moshe Dayan. After Dayan left the army as chief of staff in 1957, Ben-Gurion wanted to make him a government minister. The major objections came, as one might expect in a hierarchical system in which political apprenticeship is very long, from the second stratum of the ruling elite. Golda Meir and Zalman Aranne pointed out that Dayan should be trained as a politician in more humble surroundings than the government. By trying to bypass the third *aliyah* group of Mapai leaders, Ben-Gurion infuriated the party machine.

Ben-Gurion had no choice but to relinquish power to the third *aliyah* group, but on leaving office he became a bitter critic of this group and ultimately split with the Mapai Party he had founded. In 1965, Rafi was set up by Ben-Gurion along with some of the bright "young Turks" he had fostered in the defense establishment, such as Dayan and Peres. The new party appealed to many young Israeli-born supporters who resented the perceived fact that the party machine prevented adaptability to changing problems and blocked access to positions of power. Many, however, were torn between two long-standing allegiances: between the former leader of the party, Ben-Gurion, and the traditional leaders of the party machine.

The party machine was revitalized quickly by Pinhas Sapir, then minister of the treasury, before the 1965 elections. Sapir was younger than many in the leadership of the machine group, and as minister of finance was able to hold the machine together by setting policies that favored groups and individuals supportive of the party and its clients. As long as the structure of the party machine was hierarchically autonomous, career aspirations centered on the apex of the power pyramid. Now the key positions of the party machine were less attractive for ambitious politicians than were key posts in the national government. They strived to be in the Knesset or government ministers. The symmetrical relationship of the machine with the top leadership was broken. Machine leaders were suddenly dependent on the top leadership for career advancement. They could no longer trade off its support and activity for influence on ministers and policy. They were also less effective as brokers between the leadership and the followers. With the ascension of the third *aliyah* group to power, the party organization suffered, and it was eventually to be felt in the voting results.

The leadership attempted two methods of solving the crisis of succession. One was to ally themselves with other parties, thereby gaining depth of leadership. Before the 1965 elections they formed a joint list with Ahdut Haavoda, whose leaders had split from Mapai in 1944. Preceding the Six-Day War in 1967, Mapai exhibited a lack of leadership in foreign and security policies. They were, after all, areas in which Ben-Gurion had predominated. After some hesitation, Dayan was made defense minister and Rafi was included in the National Unity Government. In 1968 the Mapai leadership consolidated this process by forming, along with Rafi and Ahdut Haavoda, the Israel Labor Party.

The second method of solving the crisis of succession was by introducing new elements into the party leadership. Before the 1973 elections (and war), Sapir and his party decided to appoint former army heroes to positions of importance in the government, thus introducing an additional "social force." Gaetano Mosca writes that "as civilization grows, the number of the moral and material influences which are capable of becoming social forces increases. For example, property in money, as the fruit of industries and commerce, comes into being alongside of real property."[4] The social force in this case was that it became natural for those who had achieved success in the military field to play an active role in politics. Their backgrounds did not prepare them for party politics, however, let alone the intricacies of running a party machine.

Between 1973 and 1977, a fascinating process of differentiation began to develop in the ruling elite of the Labor Party. Cabinet members who had primary responsibility for security and foreign affairs (Yitzhak Rabin, Shimon Peres, Yigael Allon, Israel Galili, Aharon Yariv earlier) tended to be from a military background *and not* historically associated with Mapai, while some who dealt with internal matters were also those whose political careers *had been* dependent on the Mapai Party machine (Yehoshua Rabinowitz, Avraham Ofer, Aharon Yadlin, and Moshe Baram). A sense of common purpose never developed between the two groups. Rabin's leadership failed to bridge conflicting interests, styles, and backgrounds. The party's lack of accepted leadership was the backdrop against which the details of the political drama were played out: the competition between Rabin and Peres for the right to head the list (Rabin won), Rabin's resignation from the first on the list because of his wife's personal foreign currency problems, and Peres's ascension to first place a month before the election in 1977. It is little wonder that the military heroes were not successful in running their party. They were the victims, not the causes, of the crisis of leadership succession and the attendant passing of dominance from the Labor Party.

The emergence of the Democratic Movement for Change (DMC) reflected the crisis of succession discussed above. The DMC provided an alternative channel of upward mobility for leaders (political, military, economic, and university) who disdained the opportunity of competing for positions in the disreputed Alignment. The setting up of a new party reflected the disarray of the party system in 1977; both party leadership and electoral support was in flux. A bold move might create a party that would have a pivotal position in coalition calculations. While the DMC did not succeed in being pivotal (the Likud and the religious parties could rule without them), their achievement of winning fifteen seats was impressive in Israeli political terms.

Leaders change for many reasons; the only one that affects all of them is aging. When the political elite of the second and third *aliyot* faded from power, no successor generation was primed to take its place. Living in the shadow of giants can be a daunting experience for young, ambitious politicians. Rabin and Peres emerged as the successors, but they were plagued by lacking the qualities that make an elite work: a shared vision of the future and the willingness to work within the group to achieve political goals.

As the Rabin-Peres generation faded, Labor was again faced with the dilemma of leadership succession. There were many candidates. Whether there was an elite whose members saw themselves as a group and could act in that manner was a hard question to answer. A group of eight politicians, loosely allied with one another and moving quickly up the ranks, had the potential of being such a future elite. Members included Chaim Ramon, successful challenger of Labor in the Histadrut elections, Avraham Burg, the head of the Jewish Agency, Yossi Beilin, architect of the Oslo accords with the PLO, Yael Dayan (Moshe's daughter), and Amir Peretz, head of the Histadrut after Ramon resigned in the wake of the Rabin assassination. They were all active in politics for many years, they were young, and they shared a dovish viewpoint and a strong drive to power. They were Yuppie, reform-oriented Labor activists, all very ambitious, but their ties to the group were always an open question. For example, Ramon's run for the Histadrut was not supported by most of the others; Burg's run for the Jewish Agency, in contrast, was supported by the others after he was denied a cabinet position by Rabin.

Other potential leaders in Labor, not in this group of eight, include former IDF chief of staff Ehud Barak, and former Finance Minister Avraham Shochat. The Labor Party constitution requires that a primary be held for the head of the party within a year in the event of an electoral defeat. Peres held on to the leadership, but it was clear that he would eventually fade. There would certainly be a new head of party; it was harder to know whether a new ruling elite would emerge in Labor or whether a number of ambitious, talented individuals were competing with each other.

In the Likud, Begin's reign represented continuity with the Labor leadership in the sense that he was the last of the older generation still active in politics. His undisputed leadership of the Herut and the Likud was facilitated by the loyalty of his colleagues from the prestate underground years. The Liberal Party chose ministers to the Likud government, but none of them challenged the supreme leadership role of Herut's Begin. When Begin relinquished power in 1983 and was followed by Yitzhak Shamir, it was unclear if this was an interim premiership or if Shamir could win control of the Likud and the Herut movement. In fact, he controlled the party and the country for ten years, many of them in coalition with Labor in National Unity Governments.

The crisis of succession burst out in the Likud after the 1992 defeat and the decision by the defeated Shamir not to compete for the party leadership. The field was left to the next generation: Benny Begin, David Levy, Dan Meridor, Binyamin Netanyahu, Uzi Landau, Ehud Olmart, and the older Ariel Sharon. The next generation of political leadership included the "princes" of the movement, since the fathers of Begin, Landau, Meridor, Netanyahu, and Olmart had been prominent in the movement in the past. Netanyahu won control of the party—but not the admiration of his colleagues—in the Likud primary. The makings of a cohesive elite were available in the Likud because so many of the contenders were sons of the "fighting family," but Netanyahu's individualistic style thwarted this possibility. This once-young, now middle-aged successor generation, with decades of service already behind them, inevitably blocked access to a new group of young and ambitious party activists. As members of the founding generation left politics, some replacement took place, but newcomers found it difficult to penetrate because others were already in place. The veterans had an obvious advantage, especially in an age of primaries with hundreds of thousands of voters.

Following Mosca's analysis, the social forces in a society indicate the reservoir of potential talent to be tapped for the ruling elite. The young pioneers who set up the dominant political organizations in the 1920s were at the peak of their careers in the 1940s when their children came of age and began seeking their own way. Most of these children did not find politics an attractive career because the best jobs were filled by relatively young people. Moreover, a clear "social force" had emerged: defense. The army, the security establishment, the procuring of arms for the Jewish community, and service with the British armed forces in World War II—all these activities attracted the young men and women of the 1940s. By the 1960s two processes overlapped: the aging and retirement of the traditional political leadership and the retirement in their mid-forties of a generation of defense and army leaders due to the early retirement policy of the Israel Defense Force. The apex of the political pyramid was vacated just as the apex of the military pyramid was being rejuvenated. It was only natural for experienced army officers who had succeeded in a field that was clearly a "social force" to assume positions of responsibility and authority in politics.

This horizontal movement from the apex of one elite pyramid to the apex of another is called in Hebrew "parachuting." Instead of climbing to the top of the political hierarchy the way a foot soldier would, a general is parachuted in, bypassing the customary apprenticeship of years at the lower levels of the national party hierarchy. It is not surprising that the objections to bypassing traditional channels of advancement came from those who had been serving as second-stratum leaders waiting their turn to assume the role of top leaders.

The problem was that parties were crisis prone because there was no accepted way to replace a leader who had become entrenched in office. In the case of a Ben-Gurion or a Begin, this afforded the respective party years of sure leadership. When the crisis started, however, it was very intense. Recent legislation tried to redress this issue. The law for the direct election of the prime minister, which went into effect in 1996, provides that a person who has served seven consecutive years as prime minister cannot be a candidate in the next election. The major parties have also instituted rules for leadership succession. For example, in the Labor Party, the leader of the party is to be chosen in primaries by the party membership a year after the loss of a national election.

Both Labor and the Likud have experienced an influx of political leaders with army backgrounds who have vied for the top spot. In Herut, both Ezer Weizman and Ariel Sharon tried unsuccessfully to unseat Begin or at least to share power with him. Both men had impressive army careers before entering politics. Both figured prominently in the Likud's creation and victory in 1977, but Begin's role as top leader remained unchanged. In 1996, two ex-generals joined Likud and Labor respectively: Yitzhak Mordecai became defense minister after the 1996 Netanyahu victory; Ehud Barak was foreign minister in the Peres government formed after the Rabin assassination. Both of these men are likely to have prominent futures in Israeli politics.

The advent of direct elections may subvert the collective instinct of the group in politics and may advance a much more individualistic orientation. The early period of the Netanyahu regime certainly seemed to signal this development. Netanyahu's father had been active in the past, but he had worked with Jabotinsky and had been shunted aside when Begin took Herut over in the 1940s. To watch Netanyahu's insensitive treatment of his colleagues as he rushed to form his government after the 1996 election, one could not help but have the sense that Netanyahu was wreaking his father's wrath on the sons of the Herut leaders who had treated him so harshly fifty years before.

Religious parties were successful in passing political leadership to the second generation. The National Religious Party's (NRP) leadership struggles were mild compared to Labor and Likud, but, paradoxically, at the same time political power was slipping from its grasp. Zevulun Hammer's Youth Faction gained the status of party leader in 1977, along with the older group led by Yosef Burg (Avraham's father) by outmaneuvering the veteran political activist and head of the NRP machine, Yitzhak Rafael. By careful coalition building and adroit use of parliamentary procedure, Hammer's Youth Faction was able to prevent Rafael's inclusion on the party list. They also had Rabbi Chaim Druckman, identified with the Gush Emunim settlers' movement, placed second on the list. When Burg finally retired, Hammer was in place as leader.

But the picture clouded. One of the young leaders, Aharon Abu-Hatzeira, split from the NRP and set up Tami before the 1981 elections. Then Rabbi Druckman split from the NRP after the election and set up his own Knesset delegation. The ethnic issue raised by Tami and the nationalist issue raised by Gush Emunim plagued the NRP's ability to win votes. Thus, although the NRP (1) had impressive bases of power in the religious education system and the interior and religious affairs ministries, (2) had a platform of intense nationalism that tended to be in tune with the nation's mood, and (3) had determined their political succession, they were weak electorally, winning only four seats in 1984 compared to six seats in 1981 and twelve in 1977. The continued friction between Burg's group and the leaders of the Youth Faction weakened the party from within and prevented it from answering the challenges presented to it. In 1988, the NRP grew to five seats, after an intense battle for the lead position between Zevulun Hammer, on the one hand, and Avner Shaki, who represented the Sephardi hardliners, on the other. In the 1992 elections the NRP won six seats, and nine in 1996. The two "young" leaders had grown older competing with one another. On joining the government in 1996, Hammer remained the recognized leader, and Shaki was in the last place of the NRP's Knesset delegation.

Haredi leaders are appointed by the respective councils of rabbinical sages. Meir Porush's father, Menachem, was elected on the ultra-Orthodox Agudat Israel list for ten elections. In 1996, at age forty, Meir was head of the party. Arye Deri emerged as a shrewd national politician as head of Shas when he was still in his twenties. When Deri was indicted for misuse of public funds, and after the High Court ruled that he could not serve as minister while the trial was taking place, he left the government but retained his place in the centers of power. When Shas joined the 1996 government, it was represented by two unknown but loyal activists approved by Deri and the rabbis.

Knesset Members

Knesset members are an easily identified positional elite, a category often studied by political scientists. Israel held elections fourteen times between 1949 and 1996. On each of those occasions, 120 members were elected to the Knesset. In all, a total of 634 individuals have served as Knesset members through the 1996 elections.

About a third of each elected group is new (see figure 4.1); about two-thirds of Knesset members served more than one term. The average number of terms served through 1992 was 2.74, or about eleven years; the median was two terms, or about eight years. For the first elections, all members were necessarily new; for the July 1961 elections, held less than two years after the November 1959 elections, and decided upon months earlier, only nine new members entered. Besides those two unusual years, the range of new members in the 120-member Knesset was between 30 (1955) and 50 (1977); the average for those eleven elections (excluding 1949 and 1959) was 40.2 new Knesset members, and in 1996 it was 40 new Knesset members.

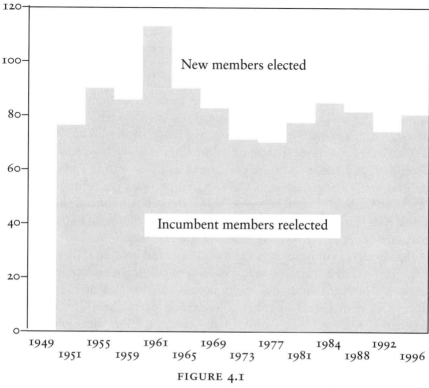

FIGURE 4.1

INCUMBENCY IN THE KNESSET, 1949–96

Almost 10 percent of the total number of people elected to the Knesset have served nonconsecutive terms in the Knesset. Mostly this was because after one term they achieved places in the list below the cutoff point the voters decreed for their parties in the next election. At a later election, they were more successful and were reelected. In 1996, two of the forty "new" members had previously been Knesset members.

The average age of Knesset members has varied a good deal. In the first twenty years of Israel's history the average age of Jewish members of the Knesset tended to become older and older, from 49.4 in 1949 to 54.3 in 1965; but this trend has moderated. In 1996, the average age was 50.1. The explanation for this is that many of the original Knesset members continued their parliamentary careers for a number of years, blocking entrance to the Knesset by younger members. As these older members faded, a more normal distribution was generated.

Even this pattern varied from party to party depending on size. A small party with a tight-knit leadership that perpetuated itself over the years (such as Agudat Israel) tended to have a higher average age from Knesset to Knesset. Menachem Porush of the ultra-Orthodox Agudat Israel was elected to the Knesset ten times; in 1996 the head of the Aguda list was his forty-year-old son, Meir.

Larger parties such as Labor and Likud could retain their leadership and introduce new blood at the same time. Consistent winners were Shimon Peres of Labor, elected eleven times (also elected on the Rafi and Mapai lists), and the Herut's (the major faction of the Likud) Menachem Begin, elected ten times. The aging of the Knesset is likely to be cyclical, especially if members pursue the parliament as a way of life and if the election results are relatively stable. Age-based parties have never won representation in the elections, however, although both pensioners' parties and a youth party have stood for election. The major parties are aware of the importance of appealing to these large age groups, but the general rule is that parliamentarians in Israel begin at middle age and hold on if they can.

The different rates of longevity reflect political developments in the country. The first two decades were decades of consolidation, and the political elite perpetuated its rule in hierarchical parties little affected by the demographic changes occurring in the country. Even the 1973 election, held soon after the traumatic Yom Kippur War, generated high levels of turnover, with the Labor Party doing less well than in the past, but retaining power.

The 1977 election saw the largest political upheavel in Israeli political history, with the dominant Labor Party losing its place of primacy to the Likud. These elections were influenced by the emergence of a reform-oriented party, the Democratic Movement for Change, which successfully siphoned off a considerable fraction of Labor's leadership and voters, partly because of scandals uncovered within the Labor Party.

No less important, however, was the coming of age of a generation of voters whose parents had immigrated from Asian and North African countries. Many of the parent immigrant generation had voted for the Labor Party and for related establishment parties, although they had suffered during their absorption into the country. The younger generation reacted against this establishment and catapulted the Likud to power.

After the 1977 elections, Israeli politics returned to a more stable basis, but turnover in Knesset membership became a familiar feature. The 1992 and 1996 elections represented other political swings, although the electoral shifts were smaller than in 1977. The rolls were swelled by the introduction of hundreds of thousands of new voters who had immigrated from the former Soviet Union. In 1992 the Likud engineered for itself an electoral loss of major proportions, much as Labor had done to itself in 1977.

The path to incumbency in Israel is simple.⁵ The first rule is to be high on the list; the second is to have your party win seats greater in number than your place on the list. If you are first, one seat will do, two is better, and so on; if you are tenth, ten would be the minimum number of seats needed by your party to ensure your incumbency, and so forth. Add to the general uncertainty of elections the fact that members of the big parties had to compete in 1996 for their places on the list in primary elections, and the picture of job insecurity is more complete.

Election results are obviously not known in advance, so the likelihood of being elected and reelected diminishes as one approaches the last place on the list that the party has usually won. Between 1973 and 1996, all Likud and Labor candidates above the thirty-ninth position on their respective lists were elected, with the following exceptions: for Labor in 1977 and the Likud in 1992 and 1996, thirty-two members were elected; the magic number for Labor in 1996 was thirty-four. But there has also been a cap on success: since 1973, neither party has elected more than fifty-one members. Those placed in the range of the forties in either party had every right to be anxious.

Candidates competing in the 1996 Likud primary were exposed to a previously unknown danger occasioned by the newly implemented law for the direct election of the prime minister. The law called for a second round of voting if no candidate got more than half the votes. That provision put enormous pressure on the candidates of the two big parties to prevent other candidates from their side of the political spectrum from running. In 1996, the pressure was on Netanyahu, since viable candidates from the right had announced their candidacy, and since there was a reasonable chance that Peres would win the needed majority on the first round. Netanyahu cut deals with David Levy's Gesher Party and with Rafael ("Raful") Eitan's Tzomet Party to present a joint Likud-Gesher-Tzomet list. These deals were negotiated just as the Likud was holding its primary for places on its list. Netanyahu assured Gesher and Tzomet seven seats each of the first forty places on the new joint list at the expense of Likud candidates. While the agreement was duly approved by the Likud center, the appropriate decision-making body, the effect of it was disastrous for ambitious Likud politicians. In the end, only the first thirty-two places on the Likud-Gesher-Tzomet list were elected to the Knesset in 1996, meaning only six each for Gesher and Tzomet and twenty places (instead of thirty-two) for Likud aspirants.

Being high on the list obviously increases the probability of being elected and reelected. Even for those not elected, the chance of becoming a Knesset member remains, since the next candidate on the list fills the place if a vacancy should occur. Some who entered the Knesset in this manner have had a chance for an important political future. For example, Ovadia Eli was tapped by Prime Minister-elect Netanyahu in 1996 to be Speaker of the Knesset. Unfortunately Eli had not been elected to the Knesset. The plan then devised was to delay his election as Speaker until the Knesset passed the law mandating the resignation of ministers from the Knesset and their replacement by the next person on their list (known in Hebrew as the Norwegian law). Then Eli would succeed to a vacant seat. A revolt in the Likud Knesset delegation prevented this development. Another example occurred when the Knesset elected Chaim Herzog in 1988 to be the president of the state; when he resigned from the Knesset, he was replaced by the next candidate on the Labor list who had not been elected, Chaim Ramon. Ramon, a young, ambitious politician, became the head of the Labor delegation in the Knesset, achieved a high place on the 1992 Labor list, was appointed minister of health in Rabin's government, and led a successful coup against his party in the Histadrut—all this even though he had almost not been elected to the Knesset four years earlier.

The sexual composition of the Knesset shows no tendency toward equality.[6] Women have never been numerous; the highest number was eleven members—less than 10 percent of the Knesset—achieved in 1992, 1973, 1955, 1951, and 1949.[7] In 1984 and 1961 there were ten women, nine in 1996, and eight in 1981 and 1977. Labor has always been careful to provide representation for women. Even though it dropped from fifty-two to thirty-two seats in 1977, the percentage of women in its delegations dropped only from 13.7 percent to 12.5 percent; seven in the outgoing Knesset, four in the incoming. In that transition, the increase for the National Religious Party was most impressive, from none to one. The Likud increased from one to two. All this indicates that women are still very far from achieving equality with men. In 1996, only three of the nine women were in parties that joined the ruling coalition (two in Likud and one in Israel b'Aliyah). Three of the others were in Labor, two in Meretz, and one in Hadash.

In the 1973 elections Marsha Friedman was elected to the Knesset on Shulamit Aloni's Civil Rights Movement list; at that time, Friedman was leader of the women's liberation movement. In 1977, 1981, and 1992, a women's list ran and failed to achieve representation. The woman who achieved greatest power in the system was Golda Meir, who was prime minister at the end of her colorful and eventful career. She was an important Labor Party leader who happened to be a woman. It would be historically inaccurate to characterize her as "representing" women in her many roles.

The political system of Israel was developed by new immigrants from eastern Europe during the first decades of the twentieth century. It was only natural for these politicians to continue dominating the political system during their lifetimes.[8] As the percentage of East European–born in the population diminished and the percentage of native-born increased, the incidence of native-born Israelis in the Knesset increased. But in an important sense this datum is misleading because the overwhelming tendency was for the second generation of Israeli Knesset members to be the sons of the East European–born first generation. The frequency distribution in the country of birth category may have changed, but the focus of political power and membership in the Knesset in the hands of those with European background was maintained. Sephardim were grossly underrepresented in the Knesset; the political power of the country was firmly in the hands of Europeans and their children.

As in any endeavor, those who are the founders—and especially if they are young—are likely to persist and dominate the endeavor for many years. This was the case with the Histadrut. When it was founded in 1920, many of its leaders were in their twenties.[9] The dominance of East Europeans is demonstrated dramatically when the place of birth of the thirty-seven signers of Israel's declaration of independence is analyzed. They were members of the National Committee and later the Provisional State Council that served up to the first general election of 1949. Of these "founding fathers," twenty-nine came from eastern Europe and six from the rest of Europe. One was born is Israel, one in Yemen. There was significant carry-over from this body to the first Knesset elected in 1949. Of the forty members of the expanded Provisional State Council, twenty-seven were elected to the first Knesset; twenty years later, in 1969, ten of them were still members of the Knesset.[10]

The number of Israeli-born Knesset members has continually increased, mostly as an artifact of the changing demographic composition of the population. European-born Knesset members made up more than 85 percent of the house as a result of the first three elections, 79 percent in the next two, and 68 percent in the sixth Knesset elected in 1965. By the seventh election the percentage of European-born members had fallen to 63 percent, then to 56 percent in the eighth and 38 percent in the ninth.[11] On the other hand, Israeli-born and Sephardi Knesset membership was increasing. The Israeli-born rose from 11 percent in the first Knesset to 14 percent in the fourth (1959) and to 24 percent by the seventh (1969), and to more than two-thirds in the thirteenth (1992) and fourteenth (1996). In 1973 they constituted 38 percent, 50 percent in 1977, and 60 percent in 1984. In 1996, twelve Knesset members were Arab or Druze, compared with seven elected in 1984 and five in 1988.

Knesset members of Asian and African birth have also increased steadily in number and now replicate more accurately their relative strength in the population. From 3 percent in the first Knesset to 8 percent in the fifth (1961), there were 12 percent in both the eighth and ninth (1973 and 1977), 25 percent in the tenth (1981), 20 percent in the eleventh (1984) and thirteenth (1992) Knessets, and 22 percent in the fourteenth (1996). The gradual increase of representation of the Sephardi community is clearer when those born in Asia and Africa are added to Sephardim born in Israel.

Both Labor and Likud, as well as many of the smaller lists, placed Sephardi candidates in prominent places on the list. In a major revision compared with past lists, Labor in 1988 fielded eleven candidates born in Asia or Africa among the first forty on its list. The parallel number for the Likud was six. Twenty of Labor's first forty in that year, and twenty-nine of the Likud's first forty, were born in Israel. Rabin and Netanyahu were born in Israel, but both Peres and Shamir were born in Poland. The composition of the Knesset delegations was coming more in line with the demographic changes taking place in the society.

The bias in favor of persons of European origin can be seen even more strongly in the composition of the governments in Israel. From independence until April 1974, fifty-eight of the seventy ministers were born in Europe, North America, and South Africa, compared with only four born in Asia and Africa. In the Likud government of 1977 as well, the vast majority of ministers were of European extraction. Of the nineteen ministers in 1981, three (Aharon Abu-Hatzeira, David Levy, and Moshe Nissim) were Sephardim. Of the less important category of deputy minister, three of the nine were Sephardim.

Apologists for the system explain that Sephardi Jews have not had the experience with democratic institutions and therefore have not been adequately prepared to take their proper role in the running of the country. Their day will come. Protesters argue that Sephardim have been consistently discriminated against in many spheres of life and that the political sphere is the most obvious area of this discrimination. Both sides point to the emergence of Sephardi political leaders in the politics of local government to prove their point. Apologists point to examples of successful politicians as proof that they are learning the rules and will ultimately emerge. Protesters respond that these leaders are already capable of much more important roles and are given busywork at the local level to harness their energies and co-opt them into the major party frameworks.

Politics as a Vocation

The emergence of a popular leader enhances any party's chances. But in addition to the top leader, a party must be endowed with strata of leaders and activists who will carry out the day-to-day tasks of running the party and the organizations it controls. Max Weber made the important distinction between those who see politics as a vocation and those who see it as an avocation: those who live off politics versus those who live for politics.[12]

Weber suggested that a system dominated by those who live off politics will tend to be conservative and static. A system dominated by those who live for politics has a better chance of generating innovative political leadership that will present new ideas and directions largely because they would be free of the party and its vested interests. This analysis applies well to Israel. After an initial period of ideological and organizational creativity, the political elite became conservative and its institutions static. In the popular idiom, the politician became more concerned with retaining his seat than with convincing others of his position.

The best way to understand this distinction is to contrast the *apparatchik* with the *cincinnatus,* as Zbigniew Brzezinski and Samuel Huntington did in their book *Political Power: USA/USSR.*[13] The *apparatchik* is the bureaucrat-politician commonly found in the former Soviet system. He has devoted his life to the party and has progressed from one bureaucratic post to another and from one agency to another. His socialization, his livelihood, and his career all depend on hierarchical relationships, on slowly climbing the bureaucratic ladder, on doing the job well but in the framework of the organization, its demands, and its ideology. The *cincinnatus,* in contrast, dominates the American political system. He is the "distinguished citizen who lays aside other responsibilities to devote himself temporarily to the public service." He is likely to be more independent in thought and action than his Soviet counterpart because he is less dependent on the party and its affiliated organizations for power, status, or livelihood. In fact, an American businessman, banker, or lawyer who agrees to go into politics or accepts an administrative appointment with the government usually takes a very substantial cut in salary. But he is likely to be on the job only a few years, lacking experience in government bureaucracy when he enters service and leaving with his experience when he exits.

The Israeli system has been dominated by the *apparatchik.* This was especially true between 1948 and 1977, when the Alignment parties dominated the government. Then, of Israel's seventy-seven ministers, fifty-two had spent most of their professional lives in bureaucracies. It is reasonable to suppose that their promotion stemmed from their success in learning to survive in that kind of organizational setting (including military and religious bureaucracies). The figures for the Likud governments between 1977 and 1981 show a more nearly even split between the two types. But the concentration of the *apparatchik* is especially great among those six ministers of the Likud period who also served during the Alignment (Menachem Begin, Moshe Dayan, Chaim Landau, Yosef Burg, Zevulun Hammer, and Ezer Weizman).[14]

Politics for many politicians in Israel is not only a way of life, it is also a way of earning a living. This point sheds important light on the mechanisms of control of the party over its political activists. With the gradual growth of activity on the part of the Jewish community in the prestate period, the number of offices expanded, as did the number of individuals for whom politics was the primary, if not exclusive, endeavor. The parties were able to attract talent not only because of their ideological appeal but also because public service was rewarded by a salary. Of the eighty-two political leaders of the prestate period, 42.5 percent earned their living from party-related activities.[15] When these findings are broken down by political party, a significant pattern emerges: leaders of the parties of the labor movement were much more likely to be on the party payroll than were leaders of the center and right parties. Of the prestate leaders, two-thirds of the left party leaders and one-third of the nonleft party leaders were salaried by party-sponsored organizations.

Yet another 20 percent of the labor movement leaders were members of kibbutzim. They could be assigned party work in order to fill ideological goals and political-economic interests of the kibbutz movement without any financial sacrifice or risk on their part. Their needs were provided for by the kibbutz, and they were free to devote themselves to public service. This was one of the important explanations for the overrepresentation of kibbutz members and kibbutz interests in Israeli politics.

The material dependence of politicians on political organizations did not cease with the establishment of the state. This dependence—with all that it implies regarding conformity, timidity, and loss of enterprise—continued to be the pattern in the large parties, especially those of the labor movement. The structure of these parties and their vast administrative networks, most clearly seen in the myriad activities of the Histadrut, provided a training ground for ambitious members to try to fill the ranks of the party leadership. When the occupations of the 374 Knesset members who served from 1949 through 1977 are analyzed (see table 4.1), it is seen that the distribution of Knesset members by source of livelihood was similar to the prestate period and that the parties of the left were much more likely to be represented by *apparatchiki* than were the parties of the right and center.[16] Activity in the movement and the party was seen as an expression of a commitment to a way of life. As public servants these politicians identified with the party and put themselves at its disposal. This was a great source of strength for the party, which could easily be reinforced, especially during the forty-odd years when the parties of the labor movement were in

TABLE 4.1

OCCUPATIONS OF KNESSET MEMBERS
BY MAJOR PARTIES, 1948–77

Party	Politician		Other		Total
	N	%	N	%	N
Mapai (including Rafi)	99	63	58	37	157
Ahdut Haavoda	15	94	1	6	16
Mapam	25	78	7	22	32
NRP	20	58	14	41	34
Agudat Israel	4	57	3	43	7
Poalei Agudat Israel	2	50	2	50	4
Herut	16	36	28	64	44
Progressives/Independent Liberals	7	50	7	50	14
General Zionists/Liberals	7	18	33	82	40
Communists	6	75	2	25	8
Others	4	22	14	78	18
Total	205	55	169	45	374

SOURCE: Emanuel Guttmann and Jacob Landau, "The Israeli Political Elite," in *The Israeli Political System*, ed. Moshe Lissak and Emanuel Guttmann, in Hebrew (Tel Aviv: Am Oved, 1977), 227.

control of the national institutions as well as the Histadrut. These psychological and economic dependencies accelerated oligarchical tendencies in these parties and assured support for the established leadership.

The center (*merkaz*) of Mapai, the legally constituted decision-making body, was dominated by people in the party's employ.[17] Most of the members had no independent means of support. As we go up the power pyramid, the higher the stratum, the higher the concentration of individuals dependent on the party.[18] This dependence on the party could be translated into political obedience if necessary. When engaged in battles with other parties or in gathering votes, the internal cohesiveness and esprit de corps were high. When faced with internal dilemmas, party bosses could usually count on the loyalty of party activists.

The Alignment parties were most likely to generate the *apparatchik* pattern. This was evident, for example, in the 1977 elections. Twenty of the Alignment's thirty-two Knesset members worked for the party as its representatives in the outgoing government, Knesset, or in party-related enterprises and local government. The forty-three member Likud delegation was much more varied in terms of the occupational structure of its members. Only six Likud members were primarily involved in political life. It is not surprising that the Likud had a much less intense organizational life, since it had been in opposition throughout most of its existence and never had control of the bureaucracies that the Alignment led. The DMC was the least *apparatchiki* of all. Of its fifteen members, only one reported that he was a party worker. Looking at this dimension only (while not ignoring the differences of ideology and personality that existed), it is not surprising that the DMC did not remain intact throughout the session of the ninth Knesset. The DMC leaders could "afford" to break up their organization, both in the sense that the organization was very young and had few vested interests and that the leadership had prestigious careers other than politics to which they could return.

The 1996 Netanyahu government was limited by the new law to eighteen members, including the prime minister. All had active public lives in their respective parties, had served in the Knesset before, or had developed their careers in the military; only one was not an elected Knesset member. Their average age (including Netanyahu) was 48.5. Seven were Sephardim and ten Ashkenazim; ten were born in Israel, five in Asian and African countries, and two in the former Soviet Union.

Prime Ministers and Presidents

Two roles in Israeli politics stand out as being at the head of the pyramid of power and prestige, that of prime minister and that of president. They are fundamentally different in nature. The prime minister's position is of supreme political importance, and the various networks of political struggle usually end up on his desk or close to it. The prime minister is directly elected by the public and is also the head of the executive branch and the cabinet, and as such, head of the coalition that rules the Knesset. As head of his party he also wields great political power, which enhances his powers as prime minister. In contrast, the president's role is largely honorific and symbolic, although he is formally head of state. Under the new law, the president must agree to the decision by the prime minister to disband the Knesset; under the old law, the president played a role in determining who would attempt to win a majority of the Knesset in support of his proposed government coalition.

Short biographies of the people who occupied these positions give an excellent indication of the structure of the Israeli political elite. Eleven of the sixteen were born in eastern Europe and four in Israel (two in Jerusalem and two in Tel Aviv). The parents of three of these four (the exception is Navon) had East European backgrounds and had been active in politics. Many of those who were born abroad came to Eretz Israel, left, and returned again, spending many years abroad in the interim. Most of them, whether of the socialist or the Revisionist camps, were trained as lawyers, a very bourgeois profession. This provided good training for politics and for dealing with the Turkish and British imperial bureaucracies; it also foreshadowed the formalistic, legal character of Israeli politics in both internal and foreign policies.

Ben-Gurion was the undisputed leader and Sharett a substitute prime minister. Only after Ben-Gurion's withdrawal from office did two of his close associates, Eshkol and Meir, achieve office. Rabin and Netanyahu were personifications of the second generation of Israeli politics: Israeli-born of European origin, military career, no significant political experience. Other candidates of Rabin's generation were denied by the Mapai Party leadership because they were associated with other factions of the labor movement: Dayan with Rafi, and Allon with Ahdut Haavoda. Rabin was selected, at least in part, because the others were rejected. Begin's victory in 1977 brought the last political leader of the founding generation to the prime ministry. Born in Poland, a Knesset member since the beginning, a lawyer by training, Begin twice led his party to electoral victory after eight unsuccessful attempts. Netanyahu symbolized the emergence of the candidate who can achieve office even if his colleagues are less than supportive of him: Netanyahu beat most of them in the race for the leadership of the Likud in the 1993 vote among the party's members, and then the prime ministry in 1996, with some of the other Likud leaders calling for his replacement.

Of Israel's nine prime ministers, six (with the exceptions of Begin, Shamir, and Netanyahu) were associated with the labor movement, seven (with the exceptions of Rabin and Netanyahu) achieved the prime ministry at an advanced age after long careers in party-related political work. Five of them (Sharett, Rabin, and Shamir are the exceptions) were also the heads of their political parties, and all of them could be considered professional politicians (or *apparatchiki*) in that none of them had a profession or means of support outside the bureaucratic structures of the party and the state.

The symbolic presidency, as we would expect, leaves more room for exceptions and deviation from the generalizations presented above. Three of the seven (Weizman, Ben-Zvi, Katzir) were intellectuals and academics. Navon was the only Sephardi among the sixteen. He was an active and effective Labor Party politician, although he was elected to the presidency after the election of 1977, which brought the Likud to power.

PRIME MINISTERS

David Ben-Gurion, first prime minister of Israel, was born in Poland in 1886. In 1906 he came to Eretz Israel as part of the second *aliyah* and as a leader of Poalei Zion. In 1908 he returned to Russia to join the army, and in 1912 he began studying law in Constantinople. With the outbreak of

World War I he returned to Eretz Israel, to be expelled by the Turks to Egypt. In 1919 he was one of the initiators of the establishment of Ahdut Haavoda. In 1920 he was active in setting up the Histadrut and the first assembly of the Jewish settlers in Eretz Israel, called Knesset Israel. Between 1921 and 1935 he served as the general secretary of the Histadrut. In 1930, when Mapai was founded, he was considered its leader. Between 1935 and 1948 he was the chairman of the Jewish Agency Executive. In 1948 he announced the establishment of the State of Israel and was its first prime minister and defense minister. He served in these capacities from 1948 to 1953 and from 1955 to 1963. By 1965 he left Mapai and founded Rafi to compete with his former party. After most of Rafi returned to Mapai in 1968 to form the Labor Party, Ben-Gurion set up the State List before the 1969 elections. Ben-Gurion retired from political life in 1970 and died in 1973.

Moshe Sharett, second prime minister of Israel, was born in the Ukraine in 1894. He immigrated to Eretz Israel with his parents when he was twelve. He studied law in Constantinople and served in the Turkish army in World War I. After the war he joined Ahdut Haavoda. In 1920 he went to London to study and became active in the World Zionist Organization. Between 1925 and 1931 he was editor of *Davar,* the Histadrut newspaper. In 1933 he was appointed head of the political department of the Jewish Agency in place of Chaim Arlozoroff (who had been murdered). Sharett retained this post until independence; in effect, he was the foreign minister of the state-in-the-making. When Ben-Gurion resigned in 1953, Sharett was chosen prime minister. He lacked the political and bureaucratic skills of Ben-Gurion, and in policy matters he tended to be more moderate and less activist than his predecessor. He set up Israel's diplomatic service and retained the post of foreign minister while he was prime minister. In 1955 Ben-Gurion became defense minister in place of Pinhas Lavon in Sharett's government, and before the 1955 elections he replaced Sharett as prime minister as well. In 1956, four months before the Sinai campaign, Sharett resigned from the government, objecting to Ben-Gurion's activist policies. Sharett remained active in public affairs until his death in 1965.

Levi Eshkol, Israel's third prime minister, was born in Russia in 1895. He immigrated to Eretz Israel in 1914 where he toiled as a worker and was one of the founders of Degania B, the kibbutz of which he was a member until his death. In the 1920s he was sent to procure arms in Europe and at the end of the 1930s he was a member of the national command of the Haganah (the Yishuv defense force). In 1937 he initiated the establishment of Mekorot, the Histadrut's water company. He was secretary of the Tel Aviv workers' council in the Histradrut; in the 1940s he managed the

Haganah's treasury. He was appointed by Ben-Gurion as the first director general of the defense ministry. From 1949 he was a member of the Jewish Agency Executive and head of its settlement department. In the early 1950s he was treasurer of the Jewish Agency and minister of agriculture and development. Between 1952 and 1963 he was minister of finance. By the 1950s he was a major figure within Mapai. In 1961 he formed the government that was headed by Ben-Gurion; later, Eshkol was Ben-Gurion's chief opponent in the Lavon Affair (see chapter 5). When Ben-Gurion resigned in 1963, Eshkol took over the posts of prime minister and defense minister. His conciliatory nature (and political considerations) led to an alignment between Mapai and Ahdut Haavoda before the 1965 elections, the formation of the National Unity Government before the Six-Day War in 1967, and the merger of Mapai, Ahdut Haavoda, and Rafi to form the Labor Party in 1968. He died in 1969.

Golda Meir, Israel's fourth prime minister, was born in Russia in 1898. When she was eight, her family moved to Milwaukee, Wisconsin. In 1921 she immigrated to Eretz Israel as part of the third *aliyah.* She was a member of kibbutz Merhavia until 1924. In 1925 she joined Ahdut Haavoda; in 1928 she was elected secretary of the women's workers' council; and in 1933 she became secretary of the Histadrut's executive committee. When many Mapai leaders were detained by the British on the "Black Sabbath" in June 1946, she ran the political section of the Jewish Agency. Before independence, Sharett ran the political section in the United States and at the United Nations, and Mrs. Meir ran the department in Jerusalem. In 1947 and 1948 she held secret talks with Jordan's King Abdullah. After independence, she served as head of Israel's first mission to the Soviet Union. She was minister of labor and national insurance (social security) between 1949 and 1956. Upon Sharett's resignation in 1956 she became foreign minister, a position she held until 1965. In the Lavon Affair she opposed Ben-Gurion. In 1966 she was appointed secretary of Mapai. She resigned from most of her positions in 1968, only to be called back to active political life in 1969 at age seventy-one, after Eshkol's death. She served as prime minister until 1974; during this period the Labor-Mapam Alignment won its biggest plurality (fifty-six seats in 1969), and the Yom Kippur War of 1973 shocked the country. In the aftermath of the war and criticism made of her and her government, she resigned in 1974. She died in 1978.

Yitzhak Rabin, the fifth person to be Israel's prime minister, served from 1974 to 1977 and from 1992 to 1995. He was born in Jerusalem in 1922. His parents came from eastern Europe and were active in the Histadrut and Mapai. He was a leading officer of the Palmach during the war of independence; by 1953 he was made a general, and between 1956 and 1959 he served as commander of the northern front. In 1964 he was appointed chief of staff and led the army during the Six-Day War. In 1968 he was appointed Israel's ambassador to Washington. He ran on the Alignment list in the 1973 Knesset elections, and in 1974 was appointed minister of labor in Golda Meir's last government. When Mrs. Meir resigned a month later, Rabin was earmarked for the prime ministry by the Mapai kingmaker, Finance Minister Pinhas Sapir; Rabin was chosen because of his past connections with the labor movement and his famous military record, and because he was not involved in the military mistakes of the Yom Kippur War. Rabin won the job after a close vote in the Labor Party center against Shimon Peres, the first time there was a contested election for the post in Labor Party history. Rabin was the first native-born prime minister and the first to lack a strong political background. For three months he led a minority government without the participation of the NRP in the coalition; by October 1974 the NRP reentered the coalition. In 1977 he again beat Peres for the leadership of the party, this time in the party convention. But in April 1977 foreign currency infractions by his wife were discovered, and Rabin removed himself from the first place on the Labor list and was placed in the twentieth spot. After the 1984 and 1988 elections, he became minister of defense. Rabin was chosen as head of the Labor list before the 1992 elections and was elected prime minister. The decision to recognize the PLO led to his being granted, along with Peres and Arafat, the Nobel Prize for Peace in 1994. In November 1995, Rabin was assassinated after a peace rally in Tel Aviv.

Menachem Begin, sixth prime minister of Israel, was born in Poland in 1913. Until he was thirteen he was a member of Mapam's youth group (Hashomer Hatzair). When he was sixteen he joined Beitar, the Revisionist youth group. In the 1930s he studied law and was active in the Revisionist movement. In 1939 Jabotinsky appointed him head of Beitar in Poland, the chief concentration of power of the movement. In 1940 he was arrested by the Soviets and sentenced to eight years' imprisonment for Zionist activities. He was sent to Siberia but released because he was a Polish citizen. After his release, he joined the Polish army and at the same time was appointed head of Beitar in Eretz Israel. He arrived in Eretz Israel in 1942 and became head of the Irgun in 1943; he led the Irgun until independence in 1948. A £10,000 bounty was offered by the British for his capture, but he evaded arrest. After the Irgun was disbanded and the Israel Defense Force was established, Begin was the natural candidate for leading Herut. He became the leader of the opposition, objecting strenuously to reparations from Germany and arms sales to Germany. In 1965 he ran at the head of the Gahal list, a joint list of Herut and the Liberal Party that was further expanded in 1973 and named the Likud. Between 1967 and 1970 Begin served as minister without portfolio in the National Unity Government. After eight unsuccessful attempts, Begin's Likud won a plurality of the votes in 1977 and 1981. Begin was the first Israeli prime minister to sign a treaty of peace with an Arab state, the 1979 treaty with Egypt; he was awarded the Nobel Prize for Peace, together with Anwar Sadat, in 1978. Begin resigned in 1983, evidently shaken by the results of the 1982 Israeli incursion into Lebanon and by the death of his wife. He died in seclusion in 1992.

Yitzhak Shamir, the seventh prime minister, was selected by the Herut faction of the Likud to succeed Prime Minister Begin in 1983 and served intermittently until 1992. Shamir was born in Poland in 1915 and came to Eretz Israel in 1935. He joined the underground movement fighting the British in defiance of the official Jewish policy of self-restraint. He joined the radical Lehi (Lohamei Herut Israel—the Israel Freedom Fighters), also known as the Stern Gang, and was widely considered to have played an active role in planning the assassinations of senior British officials. After statehood he worked for Mossad, Israel's intelligence agency, and later became a Herut member of the Knesset. He served as chairman of the Knesset after the Likud's ascension to power in 1977 and as foreign minister after Moshe Dayan resigned that post in 1980. In 1979 he opposed the peace treaty with Egypt, but since he was chairman of the Knesset at the time, he abstained rather than vote against it. In 1984, he became foreign minister in the National Unity Government headed by Shimon Peres and then rotated with Peres in 1986 and became prime minister again. After the 1988 elections, Shamir was successful in establishing another National Unity Government, which he headed. In 1992 he headed the Likud list in the election and lost to Labor's Yitzhak Rabin.

Shimon Peres, the eighth person to be prime minister, served in 1984–86 and 1995–96. He was born in Poland in 1923. He immigrated to Israel in 1934. When he was twenty, he was elected head of the youth group associated with Mapai. In 1947 he became active in the Haganah, procuring arms. During the war of independence he served in the Defense Ministry and after the war was the ministry's representative in the United States. Between 1953 and 1959 Peres served as director general of the Defense Ministry. He was elected to the Knesset on Mapai's list in 1959 and served as deputy defense minister until 1965. He was one of the architects of Israel's nuclear energy program and the cooperative efforts with France in military and political spheres. In 1965 he left Mapai and followed Ben-Gurion to form Rafi. He served as secretary general of Rafi but broke with Ben-Gurion when Rafi decided to form the Labor Party in 1968 along with Mapai and Ahdut Haavoda. Between 1969 and 1977 he served at various times as minister of immigration absorption, transportation, communication, information, and defense. In 1974, 1977, and 1992, he competed with

Yitzhak Rabin for the Labor Party's support for the role of prime minister but was defeated. In 1977, after Rabin removed himself from the top spot, Peres headed the Labor list in the election. Between 1977 and 1984 he headed the opposition to the Likud governments. He headed the National Unity Government from 1984 to 1986, at which time he rotated with Shamir. Peres became foreign minister and Shamir prime minister. In 1988, despite heavy opposition to his Labor Party, Peres led the party into the National Unity Government and became finance minister in Shamir's government. Before the 1992 elections he was defeated by Rabin in an election for the first position in the Labor Party held among the party's membership. After Rabin won the election, Peres served as foreign minister, bringing to fruition the Oslo accords with the PLO. Peres, Rabin, and Arafat shared the Nobel Prize for Peace in 1994. In 1995, after the assassination of Rabin, Peres assumed the prime ministry, only to be defeated by Netanyahu in the 1996 elections.

Binyamin Netanyahu, Israel's ninth and youngest prime minister, was the first to be directly elected. He was also the first prime minister to be born in Israel after the establishment of the state. He was born in Tel Aviv in 1949 and spent a number of years in the United States while growing up. He served as Israel's ambassador to the United Nations, and as deputy minister of foreign affairs. In that capacity he played a role in the 1991 Madrid Peace Conference. He won the leadership of the Likud in 1993 in an election among the party's members and was elected prime minister in 1996.

PRESIDENTS

Chaim Weizman, Israel's first president, was born in 1874 in Russia. He studied in Germany and Switzerland and received his doctorate in chemistry in 1899. In 1898 he participated in the second Zionist Congress, and before the fifth Congress in 1903 he was among the founders of the Democratic Party. In 1904 he accepted a position at Manchester University in England. In 1907 he visited Eretz Israel for the first time but decided not to settle there. In 1910 he became a British citizen. He emerged as a Zionist leader after World War I as a result of his connections with the British establishment. During the war he had aided the war cause through his scientific work, and in 1917 his diplomatic efforts brought about the Balfour Declaration promising the establishment of a Jewish national home in Eretz Israel. Weizman was then head of the Zionist Federation in England; with the Balfour Declaration, he achieved political stature throughout the Zionist movement. In 1919 he signed an agreement with King Feisal regarding cooperation between Arabs and Zionists. In 1921 he was elected president of the WZO and continued sporadically in that position, occasionally losing to the socialists, who often opposed him. In 1937 he settled in Rehovot in Eretz Israel. His pro-British policies were rejected by the Zionist Congress in 1946. In 1947 he settled in New York and was active in recruiting the support of President Truman to the Zionist cause. He was elected president of Israel in 1948; he continued in this post until he died in 1952.

Yitzhak Ben-Zvi, second president of Israel, was born in the Ukraine in 1884. In 1904 he came to Eretz Israel for a few months; in 1905 he began studying in Kiev. During the 1905 pogroms he was active in the Jewish self-defense movement. In 1907 he again came to Eretz Israel, this time as part of the second *aliyah.* He was active in socialist organizations. In 1910 he began studying law in Constantinople but was interrupted by World War I. He was arrested and expelled along with Ben-Gurion. He was a founding member of Ahdut Haavoda and a member of the secretariat of the Histadrut's executive committee. When the National Committee of the Yishuv was formed, he was elected to its directorate. In 1931 he was elected chairman of the National Committee's Executive and became president in 1945. The National Committee dealt mostly with local matters, leaving the important international matters to the Jewish Agency and the Histadrut. After independence, Ben-Zvi was elected to the Knesset but was never appointed a minister. In 1952 he was elected president, and he was reelected twice before his death in 1963. He was widely regarded as a historian and intellectual, dealing mainly with various Jewish ethnic groups.

Zalman Shazar, Israel's third president, was born in Russia in 1889. In 1912 he immigrated to Eretz Israel as part of the second *aliyah.* He studied in Europe until World War I and worked as a historian. In 1920 he returned to Eretz Israel as a member of a study mission and finally settled there in 1924. He became a member of the secretariat of the Histadrut's executive committee and a member of *Davar*'s editorial staff. He was given various missions for Ahdut Haavoda and later Mapai. He was a founding member of the Knesset and was appointed minister of education and culture in 1949. In 1951 he resigned from the government to head Israel's mission in Moscow, but the latter appointment did not materialize. In 1963, at the age of seventy-four, he was elected president. He continued in this post until his death in 1973.

Efraim Katzir, Israel's fourth president, was born in the Ukraine in 1916. When he was six, he immigrated to Eretz Israel with his parents. His studies were completed in Eretz Israel with the granting of his doctorate by the Hebrew University in 1941. In 1948, at President Weizman's invitation, Katzir joined the Weizman Institute for Science in Rehovot and headed its biophysics department. His career was academic and not political. He was elected president in 1973 and served until 1978.

Yitzhak Navon, Israel's fifth president, was born in Jerusalem in 1921 of a Sephardi family that had lived in Eretz Israel for generations. He studied Hebrew literature and Islamic culture at the Hebrew University and taught at a local high school. Between 1946 and 1948 he was head of the Arab section of the Haganah. From 1952 to 1963 he served as an aide to Ben-Gurion, and in 1965 he was a founder, along with Ben-Gurion, of Rafi. In 1965 he was elected to the Knesset on the Rafi list and was later elected on the Alignment list. In the eighth Knesset, he served as chairman of the foreign affairs and security committee. In 1978 Navon was elected president; he served until 1983. In 1984 and 1988 he became minister of education and culture in the National Unity Governments.

Chaim Herzog, Israel's sixth president, was born in Ireland in 1920. His father was the chief rabbi of Ireland. He immigrated to Eretz Israel in 1935 and studied law as well as attending the yeshiva in Hebron. He served in the British army during World War II. He served as head of intelligence in the Israeli army, as military attaché in Washington, and as Israeli ambassador to the United Nations. He was a member of Rafi and then of the Labor Party, and he was elected to the Knesset. In 1983 he was elected president; reelected in 1988, he served until 1993.

Ezer Weizman, the seventh president, was born in Tel Aviv in 1924. He served in the British Royal Air Force in World War II and as commander of the Israeli air force between 1958 and 1966, formulating the air force strategy that was successfully implemented in the Six-Day War. He retired from the IDF in 1969, after serving as deputy chief of staff, and joined the National Unity Government as minister of transport representing Gahal. After the Likud's ascension to power, he was appointed minister of defense and in that capacity he took part in the Camp David talks with Egypt. He resigned from the government in 1980, displeased with the pace of the peace process. He formed a list named Yaad in 1984 and was reelected to the Knesset; before the 1988 elections, Yaad negotiated for secure places on the Labor list. After both elections, Weizman served in the National Unity Governments between 1984 and 1990. He resigned from the Knesset in 1992 and was elected president in 1993.

A Sephardi for President

While political power has stayed firmly in the hands of East Europeans and their descendents, more Sephardim and others have achieved positions of prestige and influence over the years. Symbolically, the most important office in Israel is the presidency of the state. The president's role is nonpolitical with important moral, symbolic, ceremonial, and educational functions. He also has the power to grant pardons, which he usually does only after consultation with other authorities. The president symbolizes the sovereignty of the state, and ambassadors present credentials to him.

While the presidency wields some power, since the prime minister must get the president's approval to disband the Knesset (and formerly the president determined who would have the task of forming the government), the task is largely nonpolitical. Nevertheless, the decision of who will be president is certainly political.

The president is elected by the Knesset by secret ballot for a period of five years and may serve no more than two consecutive terms in office. The election is by majority vote after the candidates have been nominated by at least ten Knesset members, with the agreement of the candidates. On the first two ballots, an absolute majority of the Knesset (at least sixty-one votes) is needed for election; after that, a plurality is sufficient. The president may be removed from office if three-fourths of the Knesset members so vote.

In 1973, after the death of Zalman Shazar at the age of eighty-four, a popular candidate for the presidency was Yitzhak Navon. The son of an old Sephardi family in Jerusalem, he had a long career in public affairs, having served with Sharett and Ben-Gurion. The party machine, and especially Golda Meir, opposed Navon's candidacy for political rather than ethnic reasons. Navon had been disloyal to Mapai by aiding Ben-Gurion, Dayan, Peres, and others in forming Rafi in 1965. Many thought that Mrs. Meir's opposition was an act of anti-Sephardi discrimination when in fact it penetrated to the real heart of the matter—political loyalty. Mrs. Meir added another (nonethnic) dimension to the issue when she declared that she would find it inappropriate to have Ben-Gurion's aide ask her in his new capacity of president to form a government. Efraim Katzir was ultimately elected to the post. It was a blow to many Sephardim, since they were keen on Navon's election, but the Labor Party machine won the day and had a distinguished scientist as president.

When Katzir's term ended in 1978 and he declared that he would be unwilling to be reelected, Prime Minister Begin announced that it was his intention to elect a Sephardi as president and said that Yitzhak Navon of the Labor Party would be an appropriate candidate. What followed was a valuable lesson in how politics seeps into many areas of Israeli life: the election of the president, increased sensitivity to the growing Sephardi population, the desire to grant Sephardim representation at the highest symbolic levels of the state, and the inability of the Likud to elect its own candidate to the presidency. After the elections in 1977 (which brought the Likud to power after thirty years of opposition), its major factions could not agree on a candidate. In addition, and in a more general sense, the case points up the dilemma known as the Arrow Paradox of Voting.

The paradox, named after the economist Kenneth Arrow, occurs in a democratic setting when the voters (in a country or in a committee) have more than two alternatives and order their preferences in such a manner that no majority outcome is possible. The election of Navon in 1978 is a demonstration of the dilemma presented by the paradox. When Begin announced his support of Navon, he had not fully taken into account the reaction of the Liberal Party, which was anxious to elect Elimelech Rimalt, a long-time Liberal leader. Navon, supported by the Alignment and the DMC, was strongly opposed by the Liberals. Since Begin was adamant about the importance of electing a Sephardi as president, he proposed the candidacy of Yitzhak Shaveh, an obscure physicist, for the post. Begin's Herut supported the prime minister's candidate, as did La'am. The Alignment wanted Navon, but preferred Rimalt to Shaveh. The following situation developed: Shaveh had the support of forty-one Knesset members from Herut, La'am, and the NRP; Rimalt won the support of forty-seven Liberal and Alignment Knesset members; and Navon was supported by fifty-two members of the Alignment, DMC, and smaller parties. Equally important, the preferences of the groups differed:

(1) Alignment and others	(2) Liberals and others	(3) Herut and others
Navon	Rimalt	Shaveh
Rimalt	Shaveh	Navon
Shaveh	Navon	Rimalt

At a crucial moment Navon announced his unwillingness to continue as a candidate. It was clear that in the situation that developed, Rimalt would be the winner. As Shaveh would not be elected, he too withdrew his candidacy, and then Navon returned to the fray as an alternative to Rimalt. Begin's group preferred the Sephardi candidate, even though he was an Alignment politician, to the candidate of the Liberals. Despite the fact that Herut and the Liberals were the major factions in the victorious Likud, Herut joined the Alignment and the DMC in voting for Navon for president. Navon received eighty-six votes and was elected in April 1978.[19]

5. Political Parties

The basic division of the Israeli party system, easily understood in the light of the 1996 elections, is between Likud (the prime minister and 32 seats in the 120-seat Knesset) and Labor (34 seats). If we conceive of these two parties as the major building blocks of the system, the political spectrum becomes focused (see figure 5.1). Clustering around them are other parties of the left and the right, respectively; these other parties may have once been part of one of the bigger parties or might align with one of them in the future. Add to these two clusters the group of Jewish religious parties and the Arab parties, and the picture is complete except for loose odds and ends of some smaller parties.

In Israel's proportional representation system of elections, many lists and parties compete. The record was set in 1981 when thirty-one different lists ran; in 1996, twenty lists formally competed, although two announced

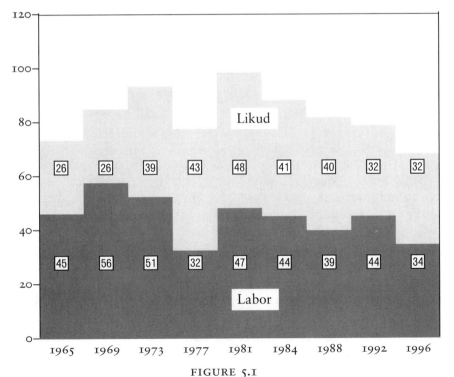

FIGURE 5.1
KNESSET RESULTS FOR LABOR AND LIKUD, 1965–96

their withdrawal before the election began. One reason for the decrease in the number of competing parties was that the minimum needed to win representation was increased from 1 percent to 1.5 percent before the 1992 election.

It is important to distinguish between lists and parties. A party is an ongoing institution that seeks power within the established rules of elections. A list is precisely what it says it is: a list of candidates prepared for the elections sponsored by a party or by a group of parties. Any registered party may run in the election. Setting up a party is easy: application by 100 citizens to the responsible official is all that is needed. A party may not oppose the existence of Israel as a Jewish and democratic state, it may not advocate racism, and it may not be a cover for illegal activity. Once the registrar determines that the party's platform and behavior are consistent with democracy, and that it keeps appropriate records of its accounts, the party is approved.[1]

Labor's list in 1996 was made up of one party; the Likud list was formally called Likud-Gesher-Tzomet and it was composed of the lists of three parties, the Likud, David Levy's Gesher, and Rafael (Raful) Eitan's Tzomet. In the past (as recently as 1984), the Labor and Mapam parties jointly set up a single list called the Labor-Mapam Alignment, and the Likud list was made up of two autonomous parties, Herut and the Liberals. In 1988, Labor and Mapam ran separate lists, and Herut and the Liberals merged into a single party called the Likud. By 1992, Mapam had joined with two other parties, the Citizens Rights Movement, and Shinui, to form a single list known as Meretz.

Concentration of the Vote

For a politician facing the challenge of forming a coalition in the Knesset or setting public policy, the size of the groups participating in the discussions and the interests they represent are crucial. Before the direct election of the prime minister, the first question for a politician was, how big was your own party; in other words, how far were you from a Knesset majority and how much would you have to pay others to help you form it? The next question would be, how big was the next biggest party; in other words, what chance would your opponent have to form a coalition if you failed to do so? These calculations changed after the adoption of the direct election of the prime minister law. The question now is, how much will you have to pay to win the support of other parties, since the issue of who will be the prime minister has already been settled? Under both systems, the point of departure is the size of the two large parties, Labor and Likud.

Another way of approaching Israeli politics is to consider the party system in terms of the distribution of power among the largest parties (see figure 5.2). This is based on the same election results as figure 5.1, except that it focuses on electoral size without distinguishing between political parties. Figure 5.2 clearly indicates two major periods in Israeli politics: one of dominance (by Labor), until 1977, and the other of competitiveness, between 1981 and 1996. Note that in addition to increasing competitiveness, the combined size of the two parties in 1996 was as low as it had been in the early years of statehood. This indicated the emergence of sectarian politics and fractionalization.

The two major policy breakthroughs (the Likud's 1978 peace with Egypt and Labor's 1993 accord with the PLO) came in each case a year after the election that increased the gap between the two parties. Members of the party in government that made each breakthrough had been big winners in the elections prior to the policy change, but winners only in a relative sense. They were able to shift policy not because they were relatively strong but because the second party was relatively weak.

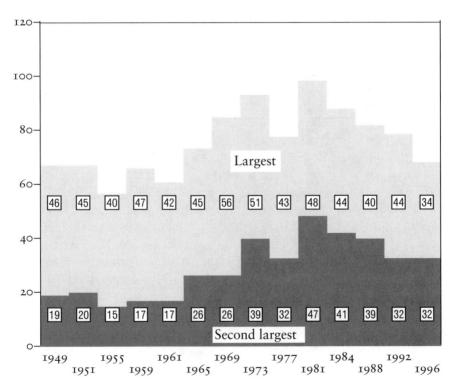

FIGURE 5.2

SEATS HELD BY THE TWO LARGEST PARTIES
IN THE 120-SEAT KNESSET, 1949–96

Labor's uninterrupted reign ended in 1977, after which the Likud and Labor competed for power. The Likud emerged as the largest party in 1977, grew more in 1981, and then began a downward trend. Labor peaked in 1969; its reemergence in 1992 was relative only to the poor showing of Likud that year. In the period of dominance the system was one-sided; the period of competition saw a heightening of the concentration of the vote at first and then the reemergence of smaller parties.

By 1981 the race between the Likud and the Alignment was very close; between them, they won almost 1.5 million of the almost 2 million votes cast, but only 10,405 votes separated them. Within the Jewish population the Likud was a bigger winner, since Arabs accounted for more than 40,000 of the Alignment total. The Likud continued its steady growth and added more than 100,000 votes to its 1977 total. The Alignment bounced back from its 1977 trauma and grew by 50 percent. But comparing the results of the elections between 1984 and 1996 to the Alignment's more glorious past leads to the inevitable conclusion that, despite the good 1981 showing, it remained a party in decline. The number of people who actually voted increased between 1969 and 1988 by almost 900,000. The difference between the Labor vote of 1988 (685,363) and the Alignment (Labor and Mapam) vote of 1969 (632,035) was only slightly more than 50,000 votes. (In 1988, Mapam ran alone and won 56,345 votes.) The Likud, on the other hand, added more than 370,000 votes, growing from 338,948 in 1969 to 709,305 in 1988.

The 1992 election that brought Labor back to power and allowed Rabin to reach an accord of mutual recognition with the PLO in Oslo was made possible more by the decline in the Likud vote than by a renewed Labor Party. Labor won forty-four seats, the same that it had in 1984.

The drop to thirty-four seats and thirty-two seats respectively in the 1996 election was a harsh blow to both Labor and Likud. Likud had thirty-two seats in 1992 also, except that in 1996 Gesher and Tzomet were partners in the joint list with Likud. Levy's Gesher had been part of the Likud until 1995, but Raful Eitan's Tzomet had independently won eight seats in the 1992 elections. Labor received 818,570 votes to the Likud-Gesher-Tzomet's 767,178 votes.

In the prime minister's race of 1996, the division between Netanyahu and Peres closely followed the Likud-Labor split of 1981. With almost 3 million votes cast, Netanyahu won 1,501,023 votes, Peres 1,471,566. The votes of the Likud-Gesher-Tzomet list were only 51.1 percent of those that Netanyahu won; Labor won only 54.5 percent of the Peres total.

The trend toward bigness began in 1965 with the emergence of the Mapai–Ahdut Haavoda Alignment and the Herut–Liberal Gahal, and it peaked in 1981 (ninety-five seats between Likud and Labor; see figure 5.1

and table 5.1). It is not an unrelated fact that growth of the two-parties' share of the vote coincided with the emergence of amalgamated parties, that is, lists set up by a combination of parties.[2] In 1965, in reaction to the split in Mapai caused by the setting up of Rafi by Ben-Gurion, Dayan, Peres, Navon, and others, old-time Mapai leaders formed an electoral coalition with Ahdut Haavoda in order to avoid political defeat. By 1968 Rafi, Mapai, and Ahdut Haavoda had formed the Labor Party, and in 1969 Labor joined Mapam in the Alignment. Meanwhile, the right Herut and center Liberals were founding an electoral bloc for the 1965 elections, expanded in 1973 under pressure from Ariel Sharon, with the acquiescence of Begin, to form the Likud.

This kind of arrangement afforded party activists many advantages. Their quota of parliamentary seats was fixed through negotiation with the

TABLE 5.1

SHARE OF 120-MEMBER KNESSET SEATS WON
BY TWO LARGEST PARTIES, 1949–96

	Biggest winner	Second-biggest winner	Total seats	Competi- tiveness ratio[a]
1949	Mapai: 46	Mapam: 19	65	.41
1951	Mapai: 45	Liberal: 20	65	.44
1955	Mapai: 40	Herut: 15	55	.38
1959	Mapai: 47	Herut: 17	64	.36
1961	Mapai: 42	Herut: 17 Liberal: 17	59	.40
1965	Alignment[b]: 45	Gahal[c]: 26	71	.58
1969	Alignment[d]: 56	Gahal[c]: 26	82	.46
1973	Alignment[d]: 51	Likud[e]: 39	90	.76
1977	Likud[e]: 43	Alignment[d]: 32	75	.74
1981	Likud[e]: 48	Alignment[d]: 47	95	.98
1984	Alignment[d]: 44	Likud[e]: 41	85	.93
1988	Likud: 40	Labor: 39	79	.98
1992	Labor: 44	Likud: 32	72	.73
1996	Labor: 34	Likud[f]: 32	66	.94
PM 1996	Netanyahu 50.5%	Peres 49.5%	100%	.98

a. Competitiveness ratio = second-biggest winner/biggest winner.
b. Mapai and Ahdut Haavoda.
c. Herut and Liberals.
d. Labor and Mapam.
e. Herut, Liberals, and others.
f. Likud-Gesher-Tzomet.

other partners in the amalgam, reducing the organizational and personal tensions usually associated with elections. The relative strength of a partner in one of these arrangements was fixed; if the list did well, the absolute number of representatives in the Knesset increased. This arrangement also afforded the politician ideological benefits. Whereas he (or she) could be extreme (or moderate) in the councils of his own party, he could also explain to his party that in order to reap the benefits of the larger amalgamation, his position must be flexible in negotiation.

The appearance of a breakaway third party tempered the trend of two-party vote concentration. In 1965 Rafi won ten seats, and in 1977 the DMC won fifteen. Most of these votes were at the expense of the Alignment; without their appearance, the trend would be even clearer. A related trend was the growth of the Likud. The advent of the Likud in 1977 was aided mightily by the emergence of the DMC because the DMC took many votes away from the Alignment, lowering the Alignment to the second-largest party.

At independence, Mapai (Labor's precursor) was perceived as legitimate, Herut (Likud's precursor) as illegitimate. The weakening dominance of Mapai and Labor and the achievement of legitimacy and an equal political status by Herut and Likud sum up the political history of Israel since statehood. The key questions of Israel's future are likely to involve legitimacy: Will secular and religious Jewish parties develop a shared notion of the legitimacy of Israel's Jewish and democratic nature? Will Israeli Arabs accept the legitimacy of the state? Will Arab parties ever be regarded as legitimate by Israeli Jews? Dealing with these issues will likely introduce new parties. Will a new political alignment emerge in the future? If the country becomes less entangled with issues of the territories and the Palestinians, will it then be free to come to grips with the real questions of Zionism, including the meaning of a Jewish democratic state? If the political issues regarding the Arabs recede, a secular coalition of Labor and the Likud might emerge that might come to grips with postterritorial issues by competing with Jewish religious parties and/or with Arab parties.

Alignment Parties

One key group in understanding Israel's political system is the Alignment. The Alignment was the name of the list set up in the elections between 1969 and 1984, including the Labor Party and Mapam. Mapam decided to run alone in 1988; the term Alignment (*Maarach* in Hebrew) is still used occasionally to refer to Labor and its affiliates. It relates to those parties that formed and ruled Israeli political life for the formative prestate period and the first generation of statehood. After winning eight elections since independence, the Alignment managed to control the prime ministry only during the 1984–86 and 1992–96 periods.

The Alignment is the appropriate group with which to begin because the history of Alignment parties and their leadership is closely tied to the history of the prestate years, the period of independence, and the first three decades of statehood. Its organizations—the Histadrut, Kupat Holim, kibbutz, and moshav—were mainstays of the country until the 1990s.

THE PRESTATE PERIOD

Ahdut Haavoda was established in 1919, bringing together various organizational undertakings begun under Turkish rule. With the defeat of the Turks by the British in World War I, organizational developments gained momentum. In 1920 the Histadrut was set up, forming a structure to further the social, economic, and cultural interests of the workers. The socialist leaders of Ahdut Haavoda were an integrated group of militants imbued with shared goals; aware of traditional Jewish culture, values, and scholarship; and open to the revolutionary movements and ideas sweeping Europe. Their ideological world was a confluence of the urges for social justice, class awareness, and Zionist aspirations. The instinct of their leadership indicated that their goals of national independence and social justice could be achieved only if the requisite political and organizational work was adequately done by them. Their varying brands of Marxist analysis all led to the conclusion that economic foundations had to be laid for the Zionist enterprise and that the Jews in Eretz Israel had to undergo a radical social transformation in order to realize the Zionist goal of a new Jewish nation.[3]

The 1920s saw the expansion of the Histadrut and its activities, although it was increasingly threatened by a largely bourgeois immigration, which failed to join its ranks, and later by the severe economic crises of 1927, during which major enterprises, including the Histadrut's Sollel Boneh, went bankrupt. By 1930, faced with new issues, Ahdut Haavoda merged with a former rival party in the Histadrut and formed Mapai, led by David Ben-Gurion, who was at the time secretary-general of the Histadrut. By 1935 Ben-Gurion was chairman of the WZO Executive and thus the leader of all Jews in Eretz Israel. As Ben-Gurion and the leadership became ever more preoccupied with national concerns, their socialism waned and became more pragmatic in nature.

As the old Ahdut Haavoda moved to the right with the formation of Mapai, an active left-wing opposition emerged both within and outside the party. The left favored a less centralized and less powerful Histadrut and called for the strengthening of local units, especially the kibbutzim. The left-wing opposition was led by Hashomer Hatzair, the ideological center of the Kibbutz Haarzi, although it refrained from declaring itself a party until the mid-1940s. The group endorsed a vision of Jews and Arabs living together in binationalism, pursuing the class struggle for the mutual benefit of all. It was strengthened in the 1930s with the arrival of immigrants trained in its vigorous youth movement abroad.[4]

The left-wing opposition within Mapai took up the cause of the kibbutzim, which resisted the enhancement of the authority of the Histadrut. Kibbutz Hameuhad, a left-wing kibbutz movement, was influential in urban matters as well, its faction winning a majority in the local labor council of Tel Aviv. The leftist opposition was active in 1935, preventing the ratification of an agreement reached between Ben-Gurion and Zeev Jabotinsky regarding cooperation between the Histadrut and the trade union movement set up by the rightist Revisionist Party. Ben-Gurion had negotiated the agreement without consulting the second stratum of leadership, and most of those leaders opposed the agreement. They were not prepared to compromise with a rival organization that stemmed from a party that had aroused extreme negative feelings in the Yishuv.[5]

The left opposition in Mapai fully emerged in the Mapai Conference in 1941, calling itself Siah B. It opposed the change in Zionist policy that called for the creation of a Jewish state. The left opposed plans for the partition of Palestine and opposed statehood. Instead, these leaders called for socialist control of all positions of power in the country and further settlement and development. The Biltmore Program, named after the New York hotel in which the American Zionist Organization endorsed the goal of Jewish statehood in 1942, became offical Zionist policy in November of that year. Siah B, more favorably inclined toward the Soviet Union and Marxism, demanded recognition within Mapai as a separate faction with the right to veto majority decisions.

At the party conference in 1942 all internal factional activity was banned. But when the opposition faction persisted in its opposition, Ben-Gurion staged a showdown at a meeting of the Histadrut Executive in 1944. Siah B left Mapai, renaming itself Ahdut Haavoda to indicate that Mapai had abandoned the ideals of the old party and that they were being carried on by the new one.

In 1948 Hashomer Hatzair and Ahdut Haavoda formed Mapam. Each component group had a kibbutz movement, which dominated it (Haarzi and Hameuhad, respectively), but these movements were not combined or integrated. This enlarged left attempted to remind Mapai of its socialist origins, even if it could not win power on its own. In 1954 Ahdut Haavoda left the merged party to emerge under that name. Hashomer Hatzair had persisted in its pro-Soviet policy, which was unacceptable to many in Ahdut Haavoda. Moreover, the Ahdut Haavoda leadership, especially the high concentration of the group that had served as officers of the Palmach, demanded a more activist foreign and defense policy than was acceptable to the Hashomer Hatzair faction of Mapam.

Socialism was a major conflict theme running through the history of the Alignment parties. Some of them opted for orthodox Marxist-Leninism; others preferred a Marxist-Zionist brand or a humanistic social-democratic orientation with emphasis placed on nationalistic Zionism. Differing international conditions reflected the line-up of parties at any given time. For example, immediately after the Russian Revolution of 1917, some parties urged following the path of class struggle. After the defeat of Nazi Germany in 1945, some followed the Soviet model, while others opted for a brand of western European social democracy. On issues specific to the country, extreme leftist parties often take a binational position, whereas others take a much tougher line regarding the Arabs. Differences developed within the Alignment over the eventual resolution of the status of territories taken in the Six-Day War in 1967; some were prepared to return most or all of them, others none.

THE STATE PERIOD

In the years immediately following independence, Mapai epitomized the dominant party. The largest vote getter, the key ingredient of any government coalition, the standard-bearer of the society's goals, and the articulator of its aspirations, Mapai also had the tremendous political advantages of a united and integrated leadership; a broad-based, well-functioning, and flexible political organization; no serious political opposition; and control over the major economic and human resources flowing into the country. But Mapai failures, especially internal disputes over political leadership and ineffective party organization, were as important in explaining its eventual decline as was the gradual strengthening of the Herut movement and the Likud.

The point to start with in seeking the seeds of decline is the notorious Lavon Affair.[6] When Ben-Gurion decided to retire (temporarily) from political life in 1953, Foreign Minister Moshe Sharett was appointed prime minister, Pinhas Lavon became defense minister, Moshe Dayan chief of staff, and Shimon Peres director general of the defense ministry. The latter two appointments previewed the emergence of the "young Turks" in Mapai; along with Ben-Gurion, they would oppose the old guard.

In autumn 1954 undocumented reports circulated that Israeli intelligence had ordered a cell of Egyptian Jews to engage in bombing and arson against American installations in Cairo in order to harm relations that were at this time improving between Egypt and the United States.[7] The group of thirteen was detained, and two of them were hanged by the Egyptian authorities. An Israeli retaliation raid in Gaza, killing forty Egyptian soldiers, could not wipe out nagging questions about the degree of training and readiness of the spy unit and the political wisdom of the plan. More critically, Minister of Defense Lavon claimed that he had not given the order for these acts and that his signature on the order had been forged. Isolated, he was compelled to resign. The issue was revived in 1960 when Lavon received evidence that, in his opinion, cleared him. Ben-Gurion declined to exonerate him, reasoning that since Lavon had not been convicted, he could not be exonerated. Dissatisfied with this, Lavon infuriated Mapai by bringing the matter before the Knesset Committee for Foreign and Security Affairs, and the story leaked to the press. Since Lavon was also reported to have called into question the integrity of Dayan and Peres, the developing split within the party along generational lines was brought into sharper focus.

The findings of a committee headed by Justice Chaim Cohen were not conclusive. Next, efforts made by Levi Eshkol brought about a statement by Sharett, acceptable to Lavon, that had the evidence placed before the Cohen committee been available in the middle 1950s, it would have brought a different decision concerning Lavon's role in the affair. A ministerial committee was appointed to study the matter, and it concluded that Lavon was free of responsibility. Nevertheless, Ben-Gurion insisted that as Lavon had evidence that imputed guilt to others, only a court of law could undertake the exoneration.

Ben-Gurion resigned as prime minister on 31 January 1961, bringing about the resignation of the government based on the rules that pertained at that time. New elections were held in August 1961 with Ben-Gurion heading Mapai's list for the last time. The party closed ranks for the elections, and only four seats were lost compared with the 1959 vote. But the party would never be the same again. Ben-Gurion was defeated by his former disciples on an issue that he considered one of principle. Moreover, unlike the situation when Ben-Gurion had resigned ten years earlier, his colleagues realized now that they could assert themselves and run things without him.

Conditions were ripe for Ben-Gurion's split from the main corps of second-stratum leaders in Mapai. These developments forecast tensions in the party for years to come. Ben-Gurion and the young guard he had promoted opposed the alignment with Ahdut Haavoda. The old guard favored it, regarding the Ahdut Haavoda leadership as a counterbalance to the appeal of the young guard and an alternative source of future leadership if the young, ambitious pretenders to leadership actually split from Mapai. More important, by neutralizing the young guard, the leaders of the third *aliyah* would be able to continue their rule. At the 1965 party convention the alignment with Ahdut Haavoda was approved by a vote of about 60 to 40 percent. At the same Mapai party convention the delegates rejected Ben-Gurion's demand that the next government headed by the party reverse the government's decision to approve the recommendation of the ministerial committee exonerating Lavon by a vote of about 40 to 60. The emergence of Rafi occurred when Ben-Gurion simply announced the formation of a separate list. Six weeks later, the party expelled those members who had set up the new list; soon after, a reluctant Moshe Dayan joined the Rafi ranks. The Lavon Affair thus split Mapai, fostered the aspirations of the young guard, and gave the leaders of the third *aliyah* their chance to rule.

The decade between 1963 and 1973 was one of third *aliyah* leadership. Eshkol, the genial conciliator and finance minister under Ben-Gurion, served as prime minister from 1963 to 1968. He was also defense minister until 1967 when, before the outset of the Six-Day War, a National Unity Government was formed that included Rafi and Herut, with Moshe Dayan as minister of defense and Menachem Begin as minister without portfolio. Begin, head of the Gahal faction (Herut and Liberals) in the Knesset, was instrumental in having the National Unity Government formed. He even suggested that his old nemesis, Ben-Gurion, be recalled to power to head the new government. As the prolonged crisis that preceded the war simmered, the old-time leaders of Mapai, led by Eshkol, finally acquiesced. Eshkol's government was expanded to include Dayan and Begin.

The three years of the National Unity Government (1967–70), including the period of the Knesset elections of 1969, were most important in changing the perceived illegitimacy of Begin and Herut in the system. Eshkol agreed even before the war to a proposal (that Ben-Gurion had rejected) to have the body of Zeev Jabotinsky, the Revisionist leader and Begin's mentor, reinterred in Israel by formal decision of the government. After the war, even Ben-Gurion relented in his intense animosity toward Begin and Herut, and the two leaders maintained correct, if not warm, relations until Ben-Gurion's death in 1973.

The National Unity Government symbolically presaged future developments. In 1968, Dayan and most of Rafi returned to Labor, and along with Ahdut Haavoda and Mapai, formed the Israel Labor Party. Begin and Herut remained in the unity government until the summer of 1970; they withdrew when the government decided to consider the proposals of U.S. Secretary of State William Rogers for a settlement of the Israel-Arab conflict. Begin's participation in Eshkol's government did more than anything else to legitimize the former leader of the outcast Irgun as a respectable, and ultimately alternative, leader.[8]

Golda Meir was the second member of the third *aliyah* to serve in the role of prime minister (1968–74). Selected by Mapai on Eshkol's death, she served through the Yom Kippur War and the 1973 elections. Soon after, she resigned. She left an Israel weakened by war, in increasing political isolation, with an enormously inflated defense budget, and a Labor Party that would have difficulty overcoming the shocks of the experience.

When the Labor Party was formed in 1968, its constituent parties comprised its institutions on the basis of the following formula: 57.3 percent Mapai, 21.35 percent each for Ahdut Haavoda and Rafi. The remnants of these three parties were partially intact six years later when the issue of succession arose. The candidate who had the support of the old-time leaders was Pinhas Sapir, an effective finance minister and party kingpin. Even in 1974, fifty-four years after the Histadrut was established, it was clear that the older generation could dictate the choice of prime minister to the party institutions if they had an agreed-upon candidate. While formal power had passed to younger hands, the old guard had the influence and the votes to determine the outcome. Yigael Allon and Shimon Peres were unacceptable to the majority Mapai group because they came from Ahdut Haavoda and Rafi, respectively. That they were now all in the same party and that these candidates were admittedly loyal leaders of the new party did not shorten the memories of an old guard trained in the tradition that the first rule of politics in Israel is loyalty to your faction. Yitzhak Rabin, chief of staff during the Six-Day War and ambassador to Washington until a short time before the Yom Kippur War, became the choice of the convention; his political background was less clear than those of the others, and he had no obvious factional affiliation that could be used to veto his candidacy.

Rabin served as prime minister between 1974 and 1977, with Shimon Peres as defense minister. Before the 1977 elections, Peres contested for the top spot with Rabin and was defeated. Shortly before the elections, word was released of an illegal foreign currency account held by Rabin's wife. Rabin left the prime ministry and abandoned his plans to be number one in the Alignment's list for the elections. Peres was named in his place, and it was his misfortune to lead the party into opposition. Although ideological differences between Rabin and Peres were minimal, competition between them continued. After the 1984 election, Peres became prime minister as part of the agreement that set up the National Unity Government.

The agreement that set up the National Unity Government of 1984 called for rotation between Prime Minister Peres and Foreign Minister Shamir after two years. Despite tensions and crises, the agreement held, and Peres exchanged ministries with Shamir in 1986, assuming the office of foreign minister. Although Peres earned high grades as prime minister for curtailing the runaway economy and for withdrawing the Israel Defense Forces from Lebanon, and he was effective in winning control of party institutions, many in the party and in the public preferred Rabin.

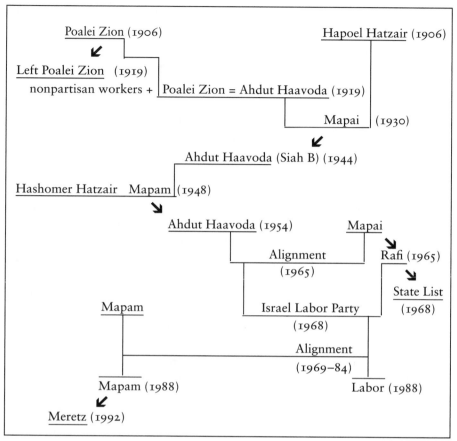

FIGURE 5.3

SPLITS AND MERGERS IN THE ISRAELI LABOR MOVEMENT

SOURCE: Aronoff, *Power and Ritual in the Israeli Labor Party* (Assen: Van Gorcum, 1977).
NOTE: Solid connecting lines indicate mergers; arrows indicate splits.

As a result of the inconclusive 1988 elections, in which Labor won thirty-nine Knesset seats to the Likud's forty, another National Unity Government was established. But this time, rotation was not part of the agreement because Likud support among other potential coalition partners was greater than in 1984. Rabin was made defense minister, Peres finance minister.[9]

Before the 1992 elections, Rabin again challenged Peres in Labor's convention and barely won the 40 percent needed for victory on the first round of voting. Had he fallen short, Peres would most likely have won in the second round because other candidates who ran in the first round had supported Peres in the past against Rabin. Rabin led the party to electoral victory in 1992 and appointed Peres foreign minister, while Rabin served as prime minister and defense minister.

Having had terrible interpersonal relations for decades, they worked more closely than ever in this period. With the collapse of the Soviet Union, the prodding of the United States, the high cost in life, moral rectitude, and property extracted from Israel by the Intifada, Rabin and Peres drastically changed Israel's foreign policy. Israel and the PLO agreed in Oslo in 1993 on mutual recognition and on a cessation of terrorist activities. In ceremonies viewed with favor by much of the world, Rabin and Peres were celebrated as peacemakers. The two of them, along with PLO Chairman Yasir Arafat, won the Nobel Peace Prize.

The relations of conflict and cooperation between the two men ended on 4 November 1995 with the assassination of Rabin in Tel Aviv. The cruel act threw the country into a period of extended mourning, culminating in an unusually quiet election campaign in May 1996. Unfortunately for Labor, Peres again failed to lead the party to victory.

The Labor platform in 1992 included planks that opposed a Palestinian state and called for the continued control and presence of Israel on the Golan Heights. By 1996, these two planks were erased, giving the Labor Party maximum latitude in negotiations after the election, and were especially appropriate for a party with a single dominant leader. In the past, platforms had been used as instruments of constraints for leaders in power or documents reflecting compromise over competing positions. The 1996 platform called for a permanent settlement with the Palestinians based on the Oslo agreements including (1) an undivided Jerusalem as the capital of Israel and under its sovereignty; (2) Israel would not rule the Palestinian people; (3) the Jordan River would be Israel's security border on the east with no other army west of it; (4) separation that would provide an answer to security needs and the national identity of the various nations; (5) Israeli sovereignty in the Jordan Valley, the northwestern section of the Dead Sea, Gush Etzion, and other areas critical to Israel's security; opposition to the right of return for displaced Arabs; (6) retaining most of the settlements already in place; (7) no new settlements; (8) a referendum regarding the permanent settlement.

Regarding Syria, the 1992 plank read: "Israel sees the Golan Heights as vital to its security, its peace, and its ability to insure access to its sources of water, even in times of peace." In 1996, the plank changed drastically: "Negotiations with Syria will continue. The desired agreement will be based on secure borders and specific provision for Israel's security, insured access to the sources of water needed by Israel, and complete normalization between the two nations, with special emphasis on economic cooperation. The permanent agreement will be presented as a referendum."

Mapam was the junior partner of the Alignment between 1969 and 1984. In this period, it lost some of its distinguishing features. While it retained its own party institutions, it appeared subservient to Labor's policies and interests, and some voices within Mapam occasionally called for breaking up the Alignment. Its kibbutz attachment remained very strong, although for the first time in its history, a nonkibbutz member, Victor Shemtov, emerged as the leader of the party. When the Labor Party agreed to form a coalition with the Likud in 1984, Mapam left the Alignment.

Mapam remained in the opposition during the period of the National Unity Government between 1984 and 1988. In the 1988 elections, led by a leader who was not a kibbutz member, Yair Tzaban, the party won three seats. In 1992, Mapam joined with the Citizens Rights Movement, and Shinui, to form Meretz, led by Shulamit Aloni. Meretz did very well, winning twelve seats, and participated in the Rabin government supporting the peace initiative and fostering civil rights and social welfare legislation. By 1996, Tzaban and Aloni had retired and Mapam was close to a complete merger with the other parties in Meretz. In the 1996 elections, the party won nine seats.

The entire political spectrum is sprinkled with former Labor activists. A fascinating feature of the party structure is the shift to the right by people originally in the Labor camp. Rafi split in 1968 over the decision of returning to the Labor camp. Some remained in the State List, headed by Yigael Horowitz and Zalman Shuval. They later were leaders in such parties as La'am and Ometz, but were ultimately incorporated into the Likud. A second group with a similar history was the Greater Israel Movement, led by Mapai leaders such as Zvi Shiloah, Eliezer Livne, Moshe Shamir, and Avraham Yaffe. Some of these former Mapai activists founded Tehiya after rejecting the Camp David agreements with Egypt.

The 1996 version of this phenomenon was the founding of the Third Way, which won four seats, by Labor Knesset members Avigdor Kahalani and Emanuel Zissman, among others. For many of the founders the parting with Labor was painful, since they were leading members of the defense establishment, personal friends, and devoted followers of Prime Minister Yitzhak Rabin who split with him because they were disappointed with his government's course. The platform of the Third Way was almost indistinguishable from the security-oriented Labor Party platform of 1992, especially regarding the Golan Heights, an area populated mostly by Labor followers, which they considered vital for the country's security. Its plan for a territorial compromise in Judea and Samaria was basically a modified version of the Allon plan, essentially Labor's platform for over a quarter of a century, calling for the Jordan River to be Israel's security border.

Likud Parties

Likud parties also had many components. Before the elections of 1996, Gesher and Tzomet formed a single list with the Likud. The Likud itself was an amalgamation of a number of other parties. Like Labor, the Likud found itself attracting a wide variety of like-minded political leaders.

Herut was the most important element in the Likud, in a political and ideological sense. The Herut movement was set up by former Irgun leader Menachem Begin in 1948. The Liberal Party was the political continuation of the General Zionists of the prestate and early state years, and it represented a bourgeois point of view.

A third party of the pre-1988 Likud list was La'am, a remnant of the Rafi faction of Mapai that refused to return to the Labor Party camp in 1948 when the united party was formed. After Ben-Gurion's death, La'am aligned itself with the Likud. In the 1988 elections, its representatives ran on the Likud list but were not part of the newly united party.

As with the Alignment parties, the period of amalgamation began in 1965. Gahal was a bloc of the Herut movement and Liberal Party and competed in 1965 with the Mapai-Ahdut Haavoda Alignment and in 1969 with the Labor-Mapam Alignment. In 1973 the Likud was formed, joining the Free Center and La'am to Gahal.

HERUT

The Herut movement is the direct ideological descendant of the Revisionists, a party founded in 1925 by Vladimir (Zeev) Jabotinsky.[10] The movement's name derived from the party's belief that the policies of the Zionist Organization had to undergo immediate revision if the goals shared by all Zionists were to be achieved. Opposing the paths of conciliation and gradualism advocated by the socialists, the Revisionists demanded militancy in achieving their nationalistic goals. Jabotinsky offered a myth of martial strength to compete with the myths of the conquest of the land offered by the socialists and *tora veavoda* (religious law and toil) offered by religious Zionists. Not by the patient accumulation of another cow and another *dunam*, but by blood and iron, would the country be won. The Revisionist youth movement, Beitar, was named after Joseph Trumpeldor, whose heroism and labor ideology made him a hero in both Revisionist and labor camps.[11]

Jabotinsky, a fiery speaker and original thinker, had been active in Zionist circles for years before resigning from the Zionist Executive in 1923 and conceiving the idea of forming a political party and youth movement. At first, the Revisionists worked within the frameworks of the General Zionists and the WZO, but Jabotinsky's ideas were seen as too militant and were unacceptable to the leadership. In the 1931 elections to the local Electoral Council, the Revisionists won 23 percent of the delegates, the second highest, with only Mapai's 42 percent having a larger share. In the 1931 elections to the Zionist Congress outside of Eretz Israel they did even better, winning 21 percent compared to Mapai's 29 percent. But by 1933, with the advent of Hitler and the murder of Chaim Arlozoroff, Mapai surged to 44 percent and the Revisionists slipped to 14 percent. By 1935 the Revisionsts had given up hope of taking over the WZO and formed their own New Zionist Organization. It was precisely during this period that Ben-Gurion and Mapai consolidated power in the WZO, with Ben-Gurion named chairman of the Zionist Executive. Jabotinsky's refusal to cooperate with the organized Yishuv headed by Mapai would earn him Ben-Gurion's political enmity to the end.

With participation in the organized Yishuv voluntary, there was no possibility of coercing dissident groups. The Revisionists were outside the organized Yishuv and were stigmatized by the establishment, which effectively denied them legitimacy. They were branded as irresponsible opportunists, unworthy of support and likely to pose a danger to the Zionist cause. Three incidents left a larger layer of ill will: Arlozoroff's murder, the "season," and the sinking of the *Altelena*.

In June 1933, Arlozoroff, a prominent leader of Hapoel Hatzair and a gifted thinker and writer, was gunned down at the age of thirty-four at the seashore near Tel Aviv. The leadership of Mapai was convinced that the Revisionists were behind the murder.[12] The young immigrant Revisionist arrested and convicted of the murder was later released for lack of evidence. While Histadrut leaders were certain that Arlozoroff's murder was a Revisionist plot, the Revisionists were equally sure that the trial was the product of a conspiracy between Mapai and the British police. Years later it was revealed that two Arabs had confessed to the murder but had been silenced by British authorities so as not to force the police to admit that they had falsely charged the Revisionist. In 1982 an official commission of inquiry was established to look into the matter, indicating that memories and passions had not faltered that much.

The "season" occurred at the end of 1944 and beginning of 1945. It amounted to cooperation by Jewish authorities with the British mandatory power in rounding up members of the Irgun and Lehi.[13] The Irgun Zva Leumi was the major nucleus of Herut; it was formed in 1937 after Jabotinsky negotiated a return to the Haganah command structure of dissidents who had formed Haganah B in 1931. These dissidents numbered 100 at the time of formation and 3,000 at the 1937 reunification. They were more militant than the Yishuv leadership and feared what they considered the pacifist policies of Histadrut leaders.

In 1940, after World War II had broken out, the Irgun was faced with the issue of cooperation with the British in fighting the war. The Yishuv adopted Ben-Gurion's formulation of fighting the war as if there were no White Paper (severely limiting Jewish immigration) and fighting the White Paper as if there were no war. Jabotinsky called for a truce with Britain, giving priority to waging war against Hitler. Abraham Stern rejected this path, and immediately after Jabotinsky's death in 1940, Stern took the majority of Irgun members with him in establishing Lehi (Lochamei Herut Israel). Stern's plan was to trade Europe's Jews for Lehi's support in defeating Britain and aiding the Germans to capture Palestine.

The Haganah, the military force of the organized Yishuv, had long operated an intelligence unit to follow the activities of other underground organizations, but rounding up and turning in fellow Jews to the hated British was an unusual act. The willingness of the leadership to participate in this activity followed the assassination in Cairo of Lord Moyne, the British minister of state in the Middle East, by two Lehi agents. This high point of the campaign of terror against the British helped Yishuv authorities agree to cooperate with the British security forces in detaining Irgun and Lehi "freedom fighters." This was often done in a clandestine manner in order to ease the troubled conscience of a Jew turning in another Jew—and this at the height of the European nightmare. The "season" successfully dampened the activities of the nonestablishment underground, but it did not extinguish its fire. Its leader, Menachem Begin, successfully avoided capture, and young, new enthusiasts volunteered, filling the ranks thinned by arrest.

Some six weeks after independence, less than a month after the establishment of the Israel Defense Force and a few days into the truce worked out by the United Nations, a third trauma poisoned relations between the nationalist right and the socialist left.[14] The *Altelena* was a ship procured by the Irgun and carried some 800 volunteers, 5,000 rifles, and 250 machine guns and ammunition. Irgunists claimed that the government knew about the shipment and that negotiations were under way for its distribution. Ben-Gurion did not disabuse his cabinet of the impression that the shipment was against the law and was meant to arm the Irgun's men, thus defying the authority of the government. The ship was scuttled by army fire with the loss of the much-needed ammunition. After the public agitation died down, Ben-Gurion appeared to be the victor. He had upheld the rule of law and had crushed possible defiance of the primary rule of the modern state—that it is to have a monopoly on the use of violence. The Irgun disbanded, and many of its members reorganized as the Herut Party. The traditions, leadership, and values of the Irgun and Lehi were transferred to Herut, but the new organization clearly accepted the supremacy of governmental decisions.

The images the leaders had of one another and the groups they led lingered for decades. Fissures were so deep that only time could heal them. This is why Herut's achieving legitimacy and eventual power was so long in coming. Ben-Gurion and Mapai understood that to deny legitimacy to another enhanced their own. The causes of the antagonisms have faded, but the mutual recriminations and passionate expressions of political views have been passed on to the next generation.

Menachem Begin was thirty years old when he became commander of the Irgun in 1943; five years later, he set up the Herut movement in which were to be found many features of the Revisionists, the Irgun, and Lehi. Most obvious was the role of the leader. Begin was still "commander"; his former staff became his aides. He tended to surround himself with his "fighting family" (former members of the Irgun and Lehi) and retained the fiery rhetoric and tough posture that had characterized his underground life. His first years in Herut were as stormy as the Irgun days. Immediately after the sinking of the *Altelena* and a round-up of Irgun and Revisionist Party members, Begin declared that the State of Israel had become a totalitarian state. During the debate over German reparations in 1952, he said that there should be no negotiations with Germany under any conditions. Mobs influenced by Begin's stance attacked the Knesset, and the future of Israel's parliamentary life seemed imperiled. A less intense furor took place seven years later when the issue of the sale of Israeli arms to Germany came up.

Ben-Gurion declined to call Begin by name, referring to him in Knesset debates as the man seated next to Dr. Bader. Ben-Gurion called Begin a fascist, a particularly weighty word in Israel right after World War II. Political passion was never higher, nor was Ben-Gurion's popularity. The combination of the two forced Begin to bide his time. His efforts were mostly parliamentary, attempting to provide the Israeli Knesset with a dynamic opposition; this he effectively achieved, especially on matters dealing with Israeli and Jewish honor and defense.

In the early 1950s Begin removed himself as head of Herut after the party lost almost half its Knesset seats in the 1951 elections, but he soon returned to head the party with added gusto. In 1965, after the newly formed Gahal did more poorly in the elections than anticipated against the newly formed Mapai–Ahdut Haavoda Alignment headed by the lackluster Levi Eshkol, a challenge was mounted against Begin's leadership of Herut by a group led by Shmuel Tamir, an Irgun veteran and a prominent criminal lawyer. After a bitter fight, Tamir lost and was suspended for a year by a party court. Perhaps taking his cue from the "young Turks" in Mapai, Tamir split with Herut to form the Free Center.

Because of the party's relatively poor showing in the 1969 elections,

Ezer Weizman tried to wrest control from Begin. Weizman too was defeated by Begin's superior control of the party's institutions. Weizman went into political limbo to return as architect of the Likud's electoral victory of 1977 and as minister of defense in Begin's cabinet. After Weizman resigned in 1980, arguing that the government was not pursuing the peace treaty with Egypt energetically enough, and even voting against the government on a no-confidence vote sponsored by Labor, he was expelled from Herut.[15] He returned to head a list called Yahad in 1984. This list won three seats; by 1988 Weizman and his group were full members of the Labor Party, and Weizman was seventh on the Labor list and ran its election campaign. He promised to make Peres prime minister, just as he had done for Begin eleven years earlier. But this time he was less successful. He became minister of science and development in the 1988 National Unity Government. He was elected president of the country by the Knesset in 1993.

Begin retired from politics in 1983, soon after the abortive Lebanon war of 1982 and the death of his wife. Some speculated that the post-Begin period would introduce instability to Herut and the Likud, but it turned out that Shamir's "temporary" ascension to leadership was long-lived. Shamir proved to be an accomplished political tactician, and despite tensions with younger leaders such as David Levy and Ariel Sharon, he maintained power. This was especially impressive because it was the first time since 1940 that Herut had been led by anyone but Begin. Moreover, as leader of Herut and as prime minister, Shamir became the caretaker of Begin's Camp David agreement with Egypt and the United States, even though he had abstained on the Knesset vote and the man he appointed as foreign minister in 1988, Moshe Arens, had voted against it.

Shamir outlived the end of the National Unity Government and the "dirty trick" move by Shimon Peres to replace him as prime minister in 1990. Shamir led the country to the Madrid Peace Conference in 1991, but it was never clear how committed he was to his peace policies. He continued the mass expansion of settlements in the territories, and the payments to religious parties for their continued support of his government. He headed the Likud's list in the 1992 elections opposed by Labor's Rabin and saw the Likud fall from forty Knesset seats to thirty-two. He resigned as head of the party but retained his Knesset seat. In 1993, in an unprecedented vote among Likud members, Binyamin Netanyahu was selected head of the Likud.

As Herut's electoral fortunes improved, the visibility of its leadership cadre increased. There were old guard leaders, especially Shamir, and those who rose to prominence when the Likud came to power in 1977, such as Arens. Then there were the sons of former leaders, such as Benny Begin and Dan Meridor; Sharon, the former general; and politicians with special representational qualities, especially Sephardim (David Levy, Moshe Katzav) and the young (Roni Milo, Netanyahu, and Ehud Olmart). In the 1993 municipal elections, Milo was elected mayor of Tel Aviv, and Olmart defeated Teddy Kolleck in the race for mayor of Jerusalem.

A serious rift occurred between Levy, who had opposed him and lost, and Netanyahu over a purported videocassette of Netanyahu's extramarital behavior. Netanyahu accused Levy of being behind the exposure; in fact, no videocassette existed. The rift came to a head over the details of the upcoming Likud primaries. Levy wanted a large proportion of the 1996 Knesset list to be reserved for the party's districts, an arrangement that would enhance his power. Levy left the Likud and formed a new party, Gesher (Bridge), together with one ally, David Magen; however, they continued to be members of the Likud's Knesset faction. This strange development came about because the law regulating political party financing from the public treasury required that at least a third of those Knesset members elected on a list would have to resign from the faction in order to have it recognized as a new faction. Since Levy was far from that number and the money would be lost to both the Likud and to the breakaway faction if they resigned from the Likud, Levy and Magen remained members of the Likud Knesset faction.

Levy announced that he would run for prime minister. Gesher was duly registered, and a list was selected. Finally, Ariel Sharon was successful in convincing Levy to return to the Likud fold in order to avoid a first-round election for prime minister that would feature a united left and a divided right. Should Peres win the needed majority in that contest, a runoff between Peres and Netanyahu would never take place. Levy acceded, succeeding in placing seven of Gesher's candidates among the Likud's top forty places, promising for his new party much better results than they were likely to have achieved by facing the electorate on their own. "Raful" Eitan's Tzomet (Intersection) won the same terms that Gesher had been given, allowing for the emergence of Likud-Gesher-Tzomet in 1996.

The peace treaty with Egypt in 1979 saw the emergence of new political organizations to the right of Herut. The Tehiya (Rebirth) Party emerged when Herut movement leaders Geula Cohen and Moshe Shamir left the party in opposition to the treaty negotiated by Begin, which mandated Israeli withdrawal from the Sinai. Tehiya was led by Yuval Neeman, nuclear physicist and former president of Tel Aviv University. In 1984, Tehiya was joined by Eitan's Tzomet; "Raful" Eitan was a former chief of staff of the Israel Defense Forces. In 1984, Tehiya was the third-largest party, winning five Knesset seats. In 1988, Tehiya and Tzomet ran separately, and won three and two seats, respectively, but by 1992, Tzomet won eight seats as a major benefactor of the Likud's loss of voters, while Tehiya failed to win the minimum number of votes to gain representation. But in 1996 Tzomet folded itself into the Likud.

Another ultranationalist party, Moledet (Homeland), led by former General Rehavam ("Ghandi") Zeevi, won two seats at its first attempt in 1988, three seats in 1992, and two seats in 1996. Moledet called for the transfer of the Arabs from the territories to Arab countries. This idea was first introduced into the political discourse of Israeli politics by Rabbi Meir Kahane, but his list, Kach, was not allowed to run in the 1988 elections. The Central Elections Committee ruled, in a decision later upheld by the Supreme Court of Israel, that Kahane's party disqualified itself from running in the elections because it had an anti-Arab racist platform. Some of the votes that might have gone to Kach were undoubtedly won by Moledet, others by the Likud and religious parties.[16] Rabbi Kahane was assassinated in New York in 1990.

Herut's ideological plank on foreign policy changed over the years depending on conditions. At first it expressed Israel's claim over all of the territory of Palestine held during the period of the British Mandate. It refused to recognize the 1949 borders as legitimate, arguing that this would prevent Israel from taking advantage of circumstances if war was forced on it. When the Herut movement formed Gahal with the Liberals, no changes were needed; each party retained its own platform. Herut supported the idea of *shlamut haaretz,* an undivided Eretz Israel, and after the Six-Day War its platform stressed the importance of continued Jewish settlement in Judea, Samaria, Gaza, Sinai, and the Golan Heights. Immediately after the 1967 war, Begin, along with the rest of the National Unity cabinet, agreed to return Sinai to the Egyptians as part of a peace treaty. The Arabs refused; a decade and a bloody war later, Sadat and Begin agreed to the same thing.

The Likud forcefully opposed the peace accords with the PLO, and its boisterous rallies during this period were part of the verbal violence that foreshadowed the assassination of Prime Minister Yitzhak Rabin in 1995. But when forced to write a plank for its 1996 platform, the party changed its tone. As prime minister, Netanyahu would abide by Israel's treaties, although he would be more careful in ensuring that the other side was carrying them out fully. The PLO would have to be dealt with, but President Arafat would be shunned because of his terrorist past. Most of the Likud leadership went along with this moderation of tone and content; Benny Begin was a notable exception in the Likud, opposing contact with the PLO under any circumstances.

A nationalist party, Herut's social and economic planks favored free enterprise, but not in a dogmatic sense. If government activity or intervention was needed to achieve national goals, this was ideologically permissible. The socialists and Mapai were anathema to Herut for historical, organizational, and ideological reasons. The Histadrut was perceived as a tool of the socialists to exploit the workers, and strikes were seen as a poison in the nation's system. After the General Zionists did so well in 1951, jumping to twenty seats from seven seats in 1949, Herut attempted to appeal to General Zionist voters by adopting a more liberal-bourgeois economic and social platform in 1955. While not a religious party, neither was Herut anticlerical, as the socialists were purported to be. The platform said, as did the original statement of the New Zionist Organization that Jabotinsky set up in 1935, that the movement would "implant the eternal values of Israel's heritage in the life of the nation."

LIBERALS

The Liberal Party was the successor to the General Zionists. The General Zionists represented the core of the World Zionist Organization; their goal was to remain politically united for the common purpose of achieving Zionist programs. In the 1920s the General Zionists split into two factions. Faction A was led by Chaim Weizman, then president of the WZO, and had a prolabor policy supportive of a conciliatory approach to the mandatory powers. Faction B, which was more bourgeois and middle class, supported private enterprise in Eretz Israel and had a more activist policy against the British.

Faction A, bolstered by the German immigration of the 1930s, came to be called the Progressives; Faction B retained the name General Zionists. By 1961 the two factions merged and formed the Liberal Party, but the merger was short lived. They again split in 1965, this time over the issue of electoral cooperation with Herut.

The Progressives retained their gradualist ideology and favored cooperation with Labor, a position they regularly achieved over the years by participating in Labor governments (and even joining the Alignment in 1982). The majority of the Liberal Party opted for the formation of the Gahal list, and the party split. The Liberals (former General Zionists) retained the name Liberal; the Progressives called themselves independent Liberals, which seemed to refer less to their independence of thought or action and more to their independence from the General Zionists and Herut.

Clearly, parties such as these were at a disadvantage compared with the ambitious and well-organized parties of the left and the religious groups whose members were in networks that extended beyond the political dimension of life and encompassed social, cultural, and often economic dimensions as well. As their name proclaimed, the General Zionists were interested in the generalized goals of the movement and less so in the specifics of the project. They supported free enterprise and tended to disdain grassroots organizational work, believing that their enlightened ideas would carry the day.

The General Zionists and the Liberals tended to resemble middle-of-the-road European parties believing in limited government, a constitution, and free enterprise. They believed that if each individual was allowed to pursue his or her own goals, it would be to the advantage of the nation as a whole. Their prominent role in the WZO afforded them close ties and organizational advantages with important organizations such as Hadassah, Maccabee, and WIZO; but the General Zionists never developed patterns of party control over these organizations as did the parties of the left and the religious parties over organizations within which they were dominant. The General Zionists did not identify with the class politics of the left stressed by Mapai; they perceived the importance of the economic and agricultural enterprises undertaken by the socialist parties of the Histadrut in national terms and not in sectoral or political party terms.

The Liberals of the Likud were always relegated to second place. Because no leader of national stature ever emerged from the party, its decision to accept Begin's leadership made political sense. The relations between Herut and the Liberals in the Likud were governed by rules set up over the years to divide power and jobs, by the practices that developed, and by compromise. The Liberal leader Simha Ehrlich was "kicked upstairs" from the job of minister of finance to the deputy premiership when the economic policies he introduced after the 1977 elections not only liberalized the economy but brought about an inflation rate of more than 130 percent a year. As he was the leader of the second major partner in the Likud, firing him outright would have been out of the question. Ehrlich's opposition to the appointment of Ariel Sharon as minister of defense, after Ezer Weizman resigned, prevented the appointment before the 1981 elections. Once the elections were out of the way, Begin could overcome Ehrlich's implicit threat of the Liberals rocking the Likud boat and appointed Sharon. The Likud council had decided that Begin would have the right to appoint ministers to his government, and so Ehrlich's and the Liberal's veto powers were overcome formally. This was one more indication of the weak political role of the Liberal Party. In 1984, Herut leaders tried to reduce drastically Liberal representation in the Likud list. After a tense period of negotiation, a moderate reduction of Liberal strength was agreed to.

Before the 1988 elections, the Liberals and Herut formally merged into a party called the Likud. Their leader, Yitzhak Modai, was third on the Likud list, and Moshe Nissim was in seventh place. Both of them had been ministers of finance in the 1984–88 National Unity Government. While both were also ministers after the 1988 National Unity Government was formed, it was clear that the Liberals had lost their clout. Modai was made minister of economics, a largely planning function with no political punch, and Nissim was appointed minister without portfolio. Modai ran on a separate list in 1992 and failed to win representation. Before the 1996 elections Nissim resigned; two other Liberal leaders, Zalman Shuval and Gideon Pat, failed to win high places in the Likud primaries.

The Independent Liberals were once considered to be at the center of Israeli politics. After achieving a handful of votes for years, their fortunes were cruelly dashed when the Democratic Movement for Change (discussed later in this chapter) reduced their power to one Knesset seat in 1977. By 1981 even that had disappeared. Their economic and settlement organizations, especially Haoved Hatzioni, allowed them at least a formal existence. In 1984, they opted not to run independently and accepted a place on the Alignment's list. They accepted the third place in the centrist Shinui (Change) list for the 1988 elections; unfortunately for the Independent Liberals, Shinui won only two seats. By 1992, they were no longer partners in preelection negotiations.

Religious Parties

On the whole, religious groups came to terms with Zionism late, if at all. Although religious motifs, groups, and leaders were affiliated with Zionism from its inception, the most vociferous opposition to Zionism among Jews came from religious circles. It is therefore not without its irony that these religious parties are growing and certainly are the most stable organizationally of the groups competing in Israeli politics.

All of the competing parties in Israeli politics are Orthodox Jewish parties. The uninitiated should be warned that we are discussing the distinctions among Orthodox, ultra-Orthodox, and ultra-ultra-Orthodox Judaism. Do not be confused into thinking that Reform or Conservative Judaism is being discussed. These last groups are simply not in the picture, although they make efforts, especially through the courts, to win approved status.

Three topics are useful to differentiate the religious parties. First is the willingness of these Orthodox parties to cooperate in the Zionist enterprise.[17] The second has to do with representation of Sephardim in these parties, which were largely formed and run by Ashkenazim, and the third is the degree of militancy displayed regarding the territories.

The original religious parties in Israel were the Mizrachi, Hapoel Hamizrachi, Agudat Israel, and Poalei Agudat Israel. The NRP was made up of two major former parties, the Mizrachi and Hapoel Hamizrachi. The most willing to cooperate in the Zionist enterprise was the NRP, as its name attests. Its cooperation with the secular parties of Zionism in building the Jewish state has been complete, with its sons (and some daughters) serving in the armed forces and the party being a member of the "historical partnership" with Mapai and Labor in the formative years and then a member of the government coalition with the Likud.

At a lower level of cooperation are the *haredi* parties of Aguda, Poalei Aguda, Shas, and Degel Hatorah (the Torah Flag). The word *haredi* connotes awe-inspired, fearful of God's majesty, in the same way that the Christian Quakers and the Shakers use the term. The haredim maintain separate organizational and social structures, although they agree to limited political participation. They do not participate in Zionist institutions, such as the World Zionist Organization. They do not consider themselves Zionists and see their role in influencing the Israeli government as similar to their role of influencing the local government in Boston or Brooklyn, where some of them also have large numbers of adherents. To ensure their support Israeli governments (led by either Labor or Likud) have allowed them unusual privileges such as exempting their sons from army service while studying in yeshivas (daughters are completely exempt) and allowing them to maintain an "independent" school system partly funded by public moneys but not controlled by the Ministry of Education. Although the Aguda has participated in government coalitions, its participation has been restricted since 1952. Until 1977, Aguda leaders often cooperated with Alignment policies but refrained from assuming cabinet positions. This pattern continued after the ascension of the Likud in 1977, with the Aguda formally agreeing to support the Begin government but not accepting a cabinet appointment. Aguda leaders were awarded chairmanships of important Knesset committees. In the 1996 Netanyahu government, as in the 1988 National Unity Government, the Aguda was given responsibility for a ministry (Housing in 1996, Labor in 1988), but since it declined having a minister participate in cabinet meetings, the portfolio was formally held by the prime minister, and an Aguda deputy minister was appointed to handle the day-to-day operations of the ministry. It also held the crucial position of chair of the Knesset Finance Committee.

Religious separatists, including the Eda Haharidit and other extreme elements (some of whom are in the Aguda), pursue a policy of noncontact with Zionists, seeing in them a threat to religious purity. Neturai Karta, a small group of a few hundred families in Jerusalem and Bnei Brak (a religious suburb of Tel Aviv), refuses to recognize the legitimacy of the State of Israel to this day and accuses those who do of blasphemous behavior. There have even been reports that members have conspired with elements of the Arab world to rid themselves and their Jerusalem of the Zionist oppressors.

Three religious lists won representation in 1996: the National Religious Party, Shas, and United Torah Jewry (made up of Agudat Israel and Degel Hatorah). They won 20 percent of the vote and twenty-three Knesset seats—an unprecedented achievement. Before 1996, the highest number of seats won by religious parties had been eighteen seats, which they had won in 1959, 1961, 1969, and 1988. In 1955, 1965, and 1977, they won seventeen seats. In 1981 and 1984, the religious parties won only ten and twelve seats, respectively (see table 8.1). The religious parties have adopted various forms of electoral cooperation in the past. In 1949 they all ran together as the United Religious Front, and in 1955 and 1973 Agudat Israel and Poalei Agudat Israel ran together on a joint list as the Torah Religious Front.

The 1996 display of strength by the religious parties continued the pattern begun in 1988 in which non-Zionist religious parties won more seats than did the Zionist religious parties. Until 1988, the Zionist religious parties bettered the non-Zionist religious parties by a ratio of two to one. In 1988, the NRP—the only Zionist religious party to win representation in that year—won only five of the eighteen seats, and the other three non-Zionist religious parties won thirteen seats. In 1996, the division was nine for the NRP and fourteen for the others (ten for Shas and four for United Torah Jewry).

If there was ever an example of a political group whose power is greater than its strength in the country, the religious parties provide it. The third-largest winners in Knesset elections after Labor and the Likud, religious parties have usually served as coalition partners with the biggest winner. To the big winner this makes good sense. It is better to pay the smaller price demanded by the third-biggest winner than to pay the higher price that the second-biggest winner could demand. With the exception of a number of months in 1958–59, a number of weeks in 1974, and a number of years in the 1990s, the largest of the Zionist religious parties, the National Religious Party (NRP), has always been a coalition partner, whether that coalition was formed by Labor or by the Likud. In the 1984 and 1988 National Unity Governments, and in the 1996 Netanyahu government, most of the religious parties participated.

The splits and divisions with which it has been plagued indicated the issues it faces. One cleavage is ethnic, the other nationalist. In 1981, Tami, lead by Aharon Abu-Hatzeira, scion of an important Moroccan rabbinical family, split from the NRP over the issue of ethnic representation and won three seats in 1981 and one seat in 1984.[18] By 1988, Abu-Hatzeira had been co-opted into the twelfth place on the Likud's list. The nationalist split was related to Gush Emunim, the organization supporting settlement in the territories. In 1981 and 1984, the NRP lost strength to nationalist lists such as

Tehiya and Morasha. Morasha was set up by Rabbi Chaim Druckman, a former NRP Knesset member, and Hanan Porat, a former Tehiya Knesset member, both Gush Emunim leaders. When they failed to set up a joint list with the NRP in 1984, they ran with Poalei Agudat Israel and won two seats. By 1988, Porat had returned to the NRP; in 1996 he was sixth on the NRP list.

The passion for pioneering that characterized the left in the first half of the century shifted to Gush Emunim after the Six-Day War. Gush Emunim sprang from the ranks of the NRP. Its members brought to the project of settlement and redeeming the land of Israel the same kind of youthful excitement, dedication, and self-sacrifice that early generations identified with the kibbutz movements.[19] One clear indication of this is the size of the youth groups in the country. Labor-related youth groups were the largest by far in the preindependence period and in the first decades of statehood. In 1996, the NRP's Bnei Akiva was the largest youth group according to a survey by the Ministry of Education. Bnei Akiva registered 28 percent of youth group members, the Labor-related group had 23 percent of the total, and the nonaffiliated scouts accounted for 16 percent.

The eclipse of the labor movement even in this field is especially ironic, since the kibbutz movements have continued to settle; both Labor-led and Likud-led governments supported settlement in many ways. But the public mind seemed to identify settlement with Gush Emunim. Part of the reason was that Gush Emunim broke with past practice and settled in Arab-populated areas of the territories taken in the 1967 war. Another reason was that the Labor-led governments tended not to publicize its efforts in this field because it could be antagonistic to its peace policies. Likud-led governments were not bashful about their efforts, but they had neither the personnel nor the organization to undertake tasks such as Labor did. Identifying themselves with Gush Emunim pioneers was a reasonable solution for them. The NRP benefited from this development; the Youth Faction and others strongly supported this behavior; still others, such as the religious kibbutz federation, were more cautious. Also, the shift of policy in the NRP in support of an activist settlement and foreign policy coincided with the structure of opinion and changing demography of the country. Gush Emunim, with the implicit and often explicit support of the NRP, could capitalize on the religious claim to the land of Israel, and the national and security importance of the territories, while using forms of settlement developed mostly by others in earlier times.

In addition to the Sephardi and nationalist challenges, another factor that weakened the NRP came from Meimad (Dimension). This group broke off in 1988 and presented a more moderate platform regarding the territories than did the NRP. Meimad won 15,000 votes in 1988, enough to drain off support from the NRP, but not enough to win representation in the Knesset. Meimad still existed in the 1990s, but did not field a list.

In 1996, fourteen of the twenty-three seats of the religious group went to the haredi non-Zionist Shas and United Torah Jewry (Agudat Israel and Degel Hatorah). To understand the politics of these ultra-Orthodox parties, one must know something of the mindset of deeply religious people whose first loyalty is to their theology (not to the laws of any nation-state), who try to live religious lives in a secular country that is strongly nationalist. The ultimate authority for their political decisions (as well as religious decisions, of course) is the Council of Torah Sages. Some political parties have one council that is made up of party leaders, and they make the important ideological and practical decisions for the party. In these ultra-Orthodox parties, however, the senior rabbis decide what is to be done, and a secondary group of politicians (many of whom are also rabbis) carry it out.

Ethnic tensions and personal rivalries are two other dimensions needed to understand the developments in these haredi parties. To understand the complicated story of these three parties, it is important to know that Agudat Israel is the oldest one among them. Traditionally led by Ashkenazi rabbis, the Aguda was surprised in 1984 when a group of Sephardi rabbis (headed by Rabbi Ovadia Yosef, former Sephardi chief rabbi) broke off from the Aguda and set up a list called Shas (Guardians of the Torah). Shas split off after the Aguda rabbis refused to place enough Sephardi candidates on the 1984 Aguda list.

In 1988, additional actors became involved: Chabad (an ultra-Orthodox group led by Rabbi Menachem Schneerson from Brooklyn, the Lubavitcher Rebbe) made its first appearance in Israeli electoral politics. Chabad had long been in religious, educational, and social welfare work but had never before been active politically. Chabad's purpose was to bolster the Aguda's share of the vote by providing the Aguda with Chabad's experienced organizational cadres. The Lubavitcher Rebbe would gain influence in the Israeli political system through the Aguda's Knesset delegation. But rivalry between Chabad and other groups, notably the one headed by Rabbi Eliezer Shach, an old and venerable rabbi from Bnei Brak, and an old-time Aguda leader, split the ranks. The relations between Rabbi Shach and the Lubavitcher Rebbe (and their followers) had been tense for many years on theological as well as other grounds. For example, the followers of the Lubavitcher Rebbe were convinced that their rabbi (who had never set foot in Israel) was the messiah and should be recognized as such; Rabbi Shach and his entourage characterized their position as blasphemy. The competition between them was for political turf and, as this example shows, for otherworldly stakes as well.

Rabbi Shach's relations with the Aguda became more tenuous over the years, and, in parallel fashion, his relations with Rabbi Ovadia Yosef and with the Shas Party improved. Before the 1988 elections, Rabbi Shach and his court set up the Degel Hatorah Party to appeal to his Ashkenazi supporters, but continued as a spiritual leader for the mostly Sephardi Shas. Shas, while predominantly Sephardi, was not exclusively so. For example, Uri Zohar, a very popular comedian in his secular days before he became an ultra-Orthodox rabbi, was an appealing Ashkenazi spokesman for Shas.

The competition between these parties was fierce, involving cajoling, threats, and charges of election fraud. In one of the highlights of the 1988 election campaign on television, for example, Shas presented the proceedings of a rabbinical court that absolved the oaths of potential voters who had promised to vote for the Aguda. The intense competition and the fervent organizational efforts paid off: Shas won six seats, the Aguda five, and Degel Hatorah two. After that election, it became illegal in Israel to try to influence voters by promising to provide a blessing or by threatening to withhold a blessing or to curse someone for voting (or not voting) for a specific party, just as it is a crime in Israel to buy votes with money or favors. In 1996, despite this legislation, the fierce competition for votes continued, and the use of amulets and promises of blessings for "correct" voting were reportedly widespread.

The religious parties in Israel today are the clearest cases of total interpenetration of religious, social, cultural, political, and often economic life. Their members tend to live in religious districts, send their children to religious schools and youth groups, read religious party newspapers and journals, pray together, and vote together.[20] Their organizations provide housing, schools, and even food to the members. In the prestate period this interpenetration existed among socialist groups as well; there are still strong remnants of it, especially in kibbutzim. One of the last sizable communities in which political life is still so intertwined with social life is the religious neighborhoods. The educational activities of the religious parties are much more clearly identified organizationally and in terms of social and political values with their parties than is the case in parallel secular situations; less so in the state-religious school system controlled by the NRP, more so in the "independent" school systems of the haredim, which receive public money without being supervised by the state. Religious youth groups are more successful in recruiting and conveying a clear social, cultural, and political message. The unifying effects of national sovereignty have only partially penetrated their value structure. Whereas statism (see chapter 11) tended to blur differences among parties in the secular camp, especially in schools and youth groups, members of the religious parties retained a central core of religious belief that differentiated them from the general population. This particularistic orientation was reinforced by the social, educational, and political structures that existed in their environment.

The existence of separate communities is reflected in the dress of the adherents. In modern Israel it is likely that a man whose head is covered (unless he is in the sun) is religious and supports a religious party. But the differentiation is likely to be even more fine. A knitted *kipah* (skullcap) has become a symbol of the NRP and especially of its youth movement; a nonknitted *kipah*, by extension, is likely to indicate support for the religious point of view but probably not for the NRP. Black wide-brimmed fedoras and suits generally identify non-Zionist Orthodox supporters—popularly known as "black hats" in Israel. The more traditional garb (common to nobles in Poland in the Middle Ages) of long-flowing robes and fur hats identifies the dress of the Aguda and their supporters and separatists. Different subgroups also have different-colored socks, gowns, and other identifiables. The above is a rough measure only, presented here to point out how complete is the penetration of the community into the lives of the adherents, including the clothes they wear.

As one would expect, the competition within the religious parties is intense. Each group grades the other in terms of categories important to it. The Aguda argues that the NRP is not religious enough, finding fault with the NRP's record of compromise and cooperation with secular governments and policies. The NRP emphasizes its record of contribution to the Zionist cause and education, arguing that a separatist Aguda can have no impact on the larger society and its values. The rabbis of the Council of Torah Sages, the spiritual and ideological guides to the Aguda, Shas, and Degel Hatorah, took to task the chief rabbis of Israel, formerly associated with the NRP, for their interpretations and scholarly exegesis of the Halacha. This competition is made possible because both sides accept the same basic texts, the Bible and the rabbinical teachings, as holy and binding. All ideologies face the issue of interpreting dogma (witness Marxism), and all use the argument of ideological orthodoxy to bolster their interpretations.

Challenge from the Center

The Israeli political party system is firmly rooted in its historical origins; party leaders of the Alignment and Likud parties perceive themselves as representing the left and the right, respectively, even if this is sometimes difficult for voters or observers to understand. Their ideas, vocabulary, organization, and imagery come from the first half of this century and not the second. Their political world is one with a strong and leading socialist party and a beleaguered but persistent right.

And so it came to pass that the two serious challenges to the established parties since independence came from within the left establishment and attempted to fill the void perceived to exist between the dominant Alignment and the revisionist right. The first challenge emerged in 1965 with Rafi, the second in 1977 with the Democratic Movement for Change (DMC).[21] Both lists appeared only once, but in their single appearances they were more successful than many long-established parties had been. Rafi won ten seats and the DMC fifteen. Both parties consciously attempted to fill the political and ideological middle ground between what they saw as a decaying Alignment and an irresponsible and out-of-touch Likud. Both tried to project the image of a centrist party. As the major groups were amalgamations of smaller, more ideologically oriented parties, it was not always easy to perceive the differences between the Alignment and the Likud. The insertion of a center party into the formulation allowed the larger parties to continue thinking of themselves as left or right. Both new parties perceived themselves as parties of the future, rejecting the Alignment and the Likud, which they considered parties of the past. Both took their major leadership and electoral strength from the Alignment camp, returning most of these resources to the Alignment after the aborted experience ended.

But there similarities end. Rafi split from Mapai and, with the exception of Ben-Gurion and the renegade La'am group, returned to it. As time passed, former Rafi leaders played more and more important roles in the Labor Party and in the country. Shimon Peres was to become prime minister; both Moshe Dayan and Peres were to serve as defense ministers, roles previously reserved for the Mapai leadership. Yitzhak Navon and Chaim Herzog were to serve as presidents of the country. Ben-Gurion's bright "young Turks," impatient in their youth with their likely rates of ascent up the ladder of political power in Mapai, achieved positions of importance in Labor despite their disloyalty to Mapai. This was all the more likely because of the lack of alternative leadership in Mapai itself.

If the Rafi challenge came from the heart of the party system, the DMC challenge came from its periphery. The existing parties could ultimately ignore the challengers because the threat could not be sustained over time. Their leadership was ad hoc, without the bonds of mutual respect and understanding necessary for sustained political action. Rafi returned to the fold, the DMC disintegrated. Neither was characterized by effective organization at the grassroots. Neither was especially effective among the lower class, the workers, or the Sephardim (groups that often overlap). The appeal for good government and to "throw the rascals out" worked in certain middle-class and professional groups but could not compete with the organization of Mapai in 1965 or the shift to the Likud in 1977 among many Sephardi voters.

The twelve years between the Rafi and DMC challenges to the prominent parties saw two important wars. In both Israel was victorious militarily, but in the second Israel suffered terrible political and psychological blows, which shook national self-confidence. The Rafi campaign was a direct challenge to the leadership of Mapai and hurried the process of party amalgamation by bringing about the Mapai alignment with Ahdut Haavoda and, in reaction, that of the Herut bloc with the Liberal Party. Rafi featured a young generation of political leaders straining to assume major roles of power and sponsored by a charismatic political patron (Ben-Gurion) who felt wronged by the party he had set up. The generational effect was central to its appeal for efficiency and modernity, and in the face of a ruling power that spawned bureaucracy and was perceived to equate the good of the party with the good of the nation.

The DMC also had a reformist air about it, but the conditions that led to its creation were dramatic and troubling. The 1973 election took place weeks after the Yom Kippur War, and the lists submitted before the war were still in effect. The 1977 elections, then, were the first elections at which the terrible frustrations of the war and its aftermath could be expressed. The protest groups that had grown in strength and volubility after the war had largely disappeared (except for Shinui). The Labor Party had also witnessed cases of corruption by key officials and even the suicide of a minister, Avraham Ofer, who evidently feared that he was being investigated. The unrest within the Labor Party was at its height, and many leaders felt that the organization was too brittle to be able to change in any meaningful way.

The differences notwithstanding, the common plank in the Rafi and DMC platforms was electoral reform. The Israeli penchant to see cultural and political problems in procedural terms was again expressing itself. Change the method and you change the system, this point of view argues. Neither Rafi nor the DMC was successful in bringing about this change, although the electoral achievements of both were impressive.

The DMC leadership disintegrated along with the movement during the tenure of the ninth Knesset between 1977 and 1981. Never an integrated leadership group to begin with, it attempted to set up a party with democratic structures, and this presaged its downfall. The three major components of the DMC were the Democratic Movement, led by Yigael Yadin, former chief of staff of the IDF and a renowned archaeologist; Shinui, headed by Amnon Rubinstein, who had been dean of the law school at Tel Aviv University and was a prominent newspaper and television personality; and part of the Free Center, led out of Herut by Shmuel Tamir. Preparations for the organization of the movement were rushed, partially because Prime Minister Rabin had surprised the country by having elections in May instead of in the fall. The DMC decided on an open primary for determining its Knesset list, and for the first time in Israel political history, some 30,000 citizens participated in setting up a Knesset list. Allegations of noncollegial behavior, heard even before the results were counted, stemmed from practices of recruiting members and arranging deals to vote for (or not vote for) certain candidates.[22] But the enthusiasm of the volunteers and the vocal public support pushed these concerns to the background as the excitement of a new, reformist party prepared for election day. The DMC determined the conditions for its participation in the government, most of them procedural and constitutional, the most important being an immediate revision of the electoral law and a call for new elections.

After the elections, it turned out that Begin could form a coalition without the DMC. He did so, relying on the coalition-wise NRP and Aguda parties. Realizing that they did not hold the balance of power, many DMC leaders pressed for participation in the coalition anyway, feeling that their constituents expected action and not loyal opposition. The call to join the Likud-NRP-Aguda coalition split the party, and Shinui withdrew. Some DMC leaders attempted to curb the excesses of Likud policy, especially regarding further settlement in the territories during the negotiations with the Egyptians and the Americans after Camp David, but on the whole their role was marginal. By the end of the term, Yadin returned to the Hebrew University and his archaeology, Tamir tried unsuccessfully (despite Begin's acceptance but lukewarm support) to return to Herut, and Minister of Welfare Israel Katz joined Dayan's largely unsuccessful (two seats) Telem list in the 1981 elections. Thus ended one of the most promising, yet disappointing, chapters in Israeli politics for those who wanted to see new blood and new ideas reinvigorate the business-as-usual atmosphere of intrigue and personality groupings. Shinui persisted and won two seats in the 1981 and 1988 elections and three in 1984, a quiet echo of the clarion call for change heard in 1977. In 1992 and 1996 Shinui was the smallest partner in Meretz.

With both Rafi and the DMC we can detect a reluctance on the part of the electorate to support the challenging party. We can see this by comparing the results of the party in Knesset and Histadrut elections. The two parties ran in both elections, and in both cases they did relatively better in the first of the two elections. In 1965 the Histadrut elections were held before the Knesset elections; Rafi won 12 percent of the votes of the Histadrut members and 7.9 percent of the votes for the Knesset. This is surprising because a new, young party should have been especially attractive to the emerging professional middle class, many of whose members were likely not to be Histadrut members. Making some liberal estimates, we may conclude that Rafi barely held its own between the Histadrut elections and the Knesset elections. About two-thirds of Israelis were members of the Histadrut, and Rafi's 80,000 votes in the Histadrut elections were almost two-thirds of the 118,500 votes it won in the Knesset elections. In other words, Rafi was unable to pick up a disproportionate share of the non-Histadrut voters or, alternatively, was unable to keep the loyalty of those who voted for it in the Histadrut elections until the time of the Knesset elections. Mapai's political machine worked overtime in 1965 to try to overcome the appeal of Ben-Gurion and his Rafi list. Judging from these figures, the machine was at least partially successful.

The DMC case in 1977 reiterates some of these points. In the Knesset election the DMC won more than 200,000 votes, or 12 percent of the total. In the Histadrut elections six weeks later, it received only 8.1 percent, with about 75,000 votes. That is less than 40 percent of the votes it won at the Knesset election. We can again use the alternative explanations we used with Rafi—that the DMC was unsuccessful in picking up an unusually large share of Histadrut members; or that the Alignment was successful in returning voters to its fold by the second vote. Both explanations are partially true. Parties of the center that have emerged from the Alignment have not been able to attract masses of Histadrut members' votes. There appears to be a homing mechanism that works in favor of the Alignment when faced with this kind of challenge; many Alignment voters return to the fold and leave the new party with a feeling of only a victory and a half instead of two complete victories.

Arab Parties

In the early years of statehood, Arab voters were afforded symbolic representation by having delegates in the Knesset in lists sponsored by Mapai, the dominant party. Arab leaders of a nationalist bent found an outlet for their activities in Maki, the Israel Community Party, dominated by Jews.[23] Rakah, the New Communist List, which split from Maki in 1965, was more clearly anti-Zionist and non-Jewish, calling for recognition of Israeli Arabs as a national minority. In 1977, Rakah merged with the Jewish Black Panthers, headed by Charlie Biton, to form Hadash, the Hebrew acronym for the Democratic Front for Peace and Equality. Biton left the party in 1990. Hadash, headed by Hasham Machmid, is the largest party among Arab voters, winning five seats in the 1996 elections.[24]

By 1984, the Progressive List for Peace emerged, composed of the

Arab Democratic Movement for Peace and the Jewish Alternative. The nationalist Arab group was the dominant one, and most of the votes of the party came from Arabs. The legality of the party was challenged before the 1984 and 1988 elections on the grounds that the party opposed the existence of the State of Israel, but the Supreme Court denied the petitions.

The communist Rakah Party and Progressive List for Peace allowed expression of Arab nationalist goals. A more moderate Arab position was advanced by Abd Daroushe, an Arab who was elected to the Knesset on the Alignment list in 1984. For the first time in 1988, an indigenous Arab party competed. That was the Arab Democratic Party, headed by Daroushe. It had a more moderate platform than Hadash, calling for influence and not only protest. Daroushe had been a member of Knesset on the Labor list, but resigned from Labor soon after the onset of the Intifada (Arab uprising) in 1987. In 1988 the Arab Democratic Party won one seat, in 1992 two seats, and in 1996, in conjunction with the fundamentalist Islamic Movement, it won four seats.

The Arab vote has increasingly gone to these Arab parties, and less to Zionist ones. The year 1996 was a record year in terms of Arab participation in the elections (about 77 percent) and in terms of the percentage of the vote that went to Arab parties (about 70 percent). Arab parties have never been in government coalitions, and no Arab has ever served as a cabinet minister. While Arab parties helped block the formation of a right-wing government after the 1992 elections, thus allowing Labor to pursue the peace accord with the PLO, they were not officially members of the government. Arabs have served as deputy ministers, but these were from Labor or left-wing Zionist parties.

Other Parties

The parties that once made up what are Likud and Labor, plus the religious parties, explain most of the action of Israeli politics. Sometimes the support of small parties became crucial to the system because of the contribution to the stability of the government. It is less likely that these small parties will be as crucial in the future, with the advent of the direct election of the prime minister and the virtual disappearance of one-person parties as a result of raising the minimum percentage for representation from 1 percent to 1.5 percent.

Successful ethnic lists are rare. While all parties want Sephardim and Ashkenazim on their lists for their electoral potential, ethnic groups in Israel have rarely been successful in winning Knesset seats on their own. There was a Sephardi list in 1949 that won Knesset representation *before* the massive influx of Sephardi voters in the early 1950s, and Abu-

Hatzeira's Tami in 1981. The Progressives/Independent Liberal Party had large measures of support in the 1950s from German immigrants and was largely dominated by them, unlike almost all the other parties (even the Arab-based communist Rakah Party), which were dominated by East European Jewish political elites.

In 1996, there were two exceptions to this rule, expressing the group consciousness of Jews of North African and Soviet Union backgrounds in Shas and Israel b'Aliyah, respectively. Shas had been growing in its ultra-Orthodox environment as a Sephardi version; it reached ten seats in 1996, making it the third-largest delegation in the Knesset. There was a Russian immigrant list in 1992, but it did very poorly. But in 1996, Natan Sharansky's Israel b'Aliyah list won seven seats.

Many of the successful small parties were headed by leaders who were once in bigger parties but who broke off and ran in elections on their own. Shulamit Aloni was elected to the Knesset on the Alignment list in 1969 but antagonized the party leadership by her outspoken stands in party and Knesset debates. It was clear that she would be relegated to a low position on the 1973 list, making her reelection very doubtful. Before the 1973 election (and war), she presented a list along with a women's group and a group advocating electoral reform. Her Citizens Rights Movement (CRM) list won three Knesset seats with support from voters who wanted to punish the Alignment for its mishandling of the opening phases of the war but who were not willing to vote for the Likud. In 1974 her three seats became crucial in Rabin's attempt to form a government without the National Religious Party. The CRM was in the government until the NRP joined it, at which time the CRM withdrew. In 1988, the CRM, still headed by Aloni, won five seats, and it became one of the mainstays of Meretz in 1992 and 1996.

Aharon Abu-Hatzeira's Tami Party found itself in a similar position in 1981. The list was set up after the leader withdrew from the NRP a short time before the deadline for submitting lists to the Central Elections Committee. Abu-Hatzeira was annoyed at the lack of support he had received from the NRP leadership during his trial on charges of accepting bribes and because of the lack of representation in the NRP of Sephardi Jews. (In the 1981 trial he was acquitted because of insufficient proof; in a different trial involving misuse of public funds, he was found guilty and sentenced to serve a three-month prison term.) The three votes Tami won were instrumental for Menachem Begin in setting up his sixty-one vote coalition. In 1988, Abu-Hatzeira's Tami ran as part of the Likud list.

Moshe Dayan headed Telem in 1981. In 1984, four such small splinter parties were Ezer Weizman's Yahad; a list headed by a former Likud finance minister, Yigael Horowitz; one headed by a former Labor Party secretary-general, Lyova Eliav; and another headed by a Likud minister and former Dayan running mate, Mordechai Ben-Porat. It is not clear from the 1984 experience if running alone was good electoral strategy: The first two won representation, the second two did not. By 1988, three of the leaders were elected on major lists, Weizman and Eliav with Labor, and Horowitz with the Likud. By 1992, this practice decreased, at least in part because the minimum percentage needed for representation was increased to 1.5 percent.

Barring a role in coalition politics, small parties lend local color (and at times comic relief) to Knesset deliberations, but their political role is insignificant. Individual party members may play an important educational or moral role, and the work of individual Knesset members may be important on Knesset committees, but since we are talking about political arrangements in which votes count, the small party is almost always at a disadvantage. Examples of colorful Knesset members whose presence enhanced the visibility of the Knesset were Uri Avneri, editor of *Haolam Haze* and head of a list by the same name; Meir Pail, who represented the New Left and Shelli; and proclaimed representatives of lower-class Sephardim, such as Charlie Biton of Rakah. Rabbi Meir Kahane's anti-Arab positions added a tense dimension to Israeli parliamentary life until his party was disallowed before the 1988 elections.

While Israel's electoral system no longer encourages very small parties, its political and cultural traditions do not prevent them from having a role in governing. They are given a platform for their ideas in the Knesset, if they know how to use it. There is no constitutional barrier to a small party's using this platform as a springboard to grow into a major party. While this has not happened, it could.

6. Party Organization

The party is the focus of contention for politicians ambitious to run the country or at least on the fringes of power. It is the forum where ideological issues are raised, if not ultimately and formally decided. It is where the rules are drawn under which a candidate may have a good chance of being elected to the Knesset; and Knesset members are generally considered the natural reservoir of those with increased probabilities of attaining significant levels of power. Most crucially, the political party is the prime agent in selecting the person who will be candidate for prime minister.

A political party is a group organized for the purpose of achieving power and holding office within a political system. This distinguishes it from a pressure group, which is intent on influencing policy on a certain issue. Israeli politics can be thought of on three levels: *electoral politics, coalition politics,* and *bureaucratic politics.* All three levels are associated with the political party. The electoral list was historically composed by the party, and lately the major parties have held primaries in which party members vote to form the list. Voters perceive elections as a contest among parties and the leaders of parties. Coalition decisions stem from the strength the parties have won at the polls and the decisions of party leaders. The efforts of the politician to achieve advantage in his or her organization by increasing influence and concentrating resources is a basic characteristic of bureaucratic politics, and a major locus of this behavior is the political party.

Political parties fill many functions. They set the political agenda; they select candidates and choose leaders; and they contribute to the process of political socialization of the electorate by transmitting political values and information to voters. They are also a force for unification in the divisive Israeli political system, for while the campaign is usually intense and the interelection period is marked by stinging attacks, the democratic contest among parties has generally been conducted within the rules, although the system was sorely tested by the assassination of Yitzhak Rabin in 1995. This controlled competition tends to bridle antagonism and stresses shared goals and ideals as much as it highlights differences among the parties.

The Party System

At first glance the Israeli party system seems to fit the multiparty pattern. In 1996, twenty lists ran for election, and ten gained at least the 1.5 percent of the vote needed for election. But simply counting the number of parties in a political system does not reveal enough about the functioning of the system. While Israel has always had many political parties, for much of the prestate era and for the first twenty-nine years of independence, political power was centered in one party. Since the subject of politics is power and not merely formal, legal, or constitutional issues, two additional dimensions must be considered in the analysis: the *competitiveness* of the system, and the *rotation* of power between parties.

On closer reflection, the multiparty model with its implicit assumption of government instability is inadequate. At least until 1977, the Israeli case is an important example of a dominant-party political system. A dominant-party system is characterized by one party's winning a plurality of the votes over a long period of time. But most important:

> A party is dominant when it is identified with an epoch; when its doctrines, ideas, methods, its style, so to speak, coincide with those of the epoch.... Domination is a question of influence rather than of strength: it is also linked with belief. A dominant party is that which public opinion *believes* to be dominant.... Even the enemies of the dominant party, even citizens who refuse to give it their vote, acknowledge its superior status and its influence; they deplore it but admit it.[1]

In Israel we have an example of a democratic system in which competition was allowed and free elections took place, yet the ruling party was not rotated out of power. Italy, India, and Japan in the decades following World War II, and state politics in certain regions of the United States at times, have also been known continually to elect members of one party (e.g., the Democrats in the South and the Republicans in the Midwest), even though competitive politics was allowed.

One attempt to come to grips with the dilemma of competition without rotation in a democratic system was proposed as "an alternative way to democracy,"[2] an analysis relevant to Israeli politics into the 1970s. The argument was essentially that a nonrotative system could be democratic if the internal organization of the ruling party was open to competition among its constituent elements. Moreover, the party could be responsive to shifts in public opinion in the country by revising its formula for coalition formation. Having a plurality, not a majority, of the seats in the Knesset meant that the government was always formed by a coalition of parties. This meant that power was diluted, at least to some extent.

In the years immediately following independence, Mapai was presented with an opportunity shared by few parties in democratic polities —that of presiding over the creation of the constitutional and political order. As a consequence, it was closely identified with the new state, and it was the party of those segments of Israeli society most involved with those heroic years. It was able to translate this identification into an organizational network that complemented and amplified the advantages conveyed by its image. Furthermore, most of this network consisted of channels maintained largely at the expense of the state, with the result that party and government tended to merge in the popular mind. The role of governmental personalities in this image-building process was most important, and until 1977 almost all were from parties that broke away from or were associated with Labor and left parties.

The strategy of the dominant party vis-à-vis other parties in the system thus has two principal goals: (1) to keep the party near the center, where the action is; and (2) to mobilize and demobilize segments of the population selectively in relation to the needs and absorptive capacity of the party. In the development of this strategy the party benefits from its symbiotic relationship with the society in that its dominance ensures it a major role in the definition of where the center is. Moreover, its orientation toward power encourages it to move with long-term shifts in public opinion regardless of its ideology. Party strategists labor under obvious and not so obvious handicaps in moving the party in new directions; there is nothing inevitable about their success, just as nothing is inevitable about the continued dominance of the party. Wrong interpretations of public opinion, inadequate attention to the demands of major groups, misjudgments concerning the importance of marginal groups, poor organizational work —all can lead to disaster.

As long as the dominant party performs intelligently, the opposition can do little that is effective. As Maurice Duverger has written: "The dominant party wears itself out in office, it loses its vigor, its arteries harden. It would thus be possible to show . . . that every domination bears within itself the seeds of its own destruction."[3] Even bad decisions by the dominant party are not disastrous unless the opposition is in a position to take advantage of them, which is seldom the case. And it is not in such a position because the dominant party has systematically excluded it and its leadership from positions of control and from the symbols of legitimacy.

As a result, the dominant-party system is remarkably stable. Disorder and even violence may be recurring features of the system, but they are surface disturbances that lead to little change. The opposition cannot replace the dominant coalition. The frustration of the opposition leads only to superficial instability. Although governments may not last long, the same parties and usually the same politicians continue to dominate the coalition. The faithful are rewarded, the opposition is shut off from power.

As in other dominant-party systems, in Israel the role of centralized hierarchical structures (especially bureaucracies) in the society is very important. The democratic internal processes that often exist in two-party systems are absent here.[4] The apparatus of mobilization typical of single-party systems is likewise negligible as a base of power, though it exists. Society tends to be held together by hierarchies that serve as the principal links between government and citizen. Indeed, these lines of communication, extended and humanized by networks of personal ties, are the true instruments of control in society, and they are either co-opted or controlled by the dominant party.

Mapai and Labor were identified with an epoch and its values, and provided the leadership and ideology of the first thirty years of independence. With the passing of Labor from its position of dominance in 1977, it was clear that the Labor leadership had failed to remain attuned to changes within the society. All the problems are discussed at length elsewhere but listing them here is instructive: A new generation of leadership was not groomed after the old guard passed from the scene; the passing of the old guard coincided with a blow to Israel's military, political, and psychological prowess in the Yom Kippur War of 1973; the party's organization had grown lax, and nasty evidence of corruption had surfaced; the steady change in the demographic structure of the country was not responded to in a convincing way. In sum, not only had the opposition become convinced of the dominance of Labor, but Labor leaders themselves had fallen into the reassuring trap of believing in perpetual dominance. This was the start of their undoing.

What follows a dominant-party era? The question is not easily answered. Some Labor supporters assumed that in 1981 Labor would return to dominance after its temporary setback in 1977. This was not to be. Another possibility was rotation between the two large parties. Labor's partial return to power in 1984 showed that many symbiotic relationships that characterized the first generation of Israeli politics had withered. It took Labor until 1992 to put in place a candidate (Rabin), organizational work, and structural change adequate to regain the support of some of the working-class and Sephardi voters it once claimed to represent. But in 1996, those gains were diminished, and Peres was unable to retain the office.

A third possibility was that the Likud would emerge as Israel's new dominant party, and thus the dominant-party system would continue but with a new dominant party. But just as the loss of dominance is not an abrupt matter, so too the establishment of dominance is a process rather than a moment. If the Likud was to emerge as a dominant political party in

Israel, it had to overcome the lack of organizational contact with the citizenry on an extended basis. Likud parties never had the organizational strength possessed by Labor and left parties, a factor that facilitated Labor's dominance.

The Likud in the late 1970s did not capitalize on three characteristics that it could have used as levers to dominance: (1) a major national turning point, the peace process with Egypt; (2) broad support among growing sections of the population, the young and the Sephardim; and (3) the absence of serious ideological opposition from the Labor-Mapam Alignment. These three necessary conditions were not sufficient for the emergence of a new era of political dominance.

The Likud failed to emerge as a dominant party. Competitiveness between the two big parties, not dominance, marked the party system in the 1977–96 period. By 1996 it appeared that the peace issue had been forfeited to Labor, that the support of the Likud by the young and the Sephardim was to be shared with religious parties, and that while Labor posed no serious organizational challenge, the Likud had failed to develop its own organizational dynamic.

The Likud tried to play the peace card by agreeing to the Madrid Peace Conference in 1991, but only reluctantly. Moreover, the Likud led a recalcitrant, militant policy regarding the territories, the settlements, and the PLO, leaving the peace issue in suspension until it was picked up by the Labor Party in Oslo in 1993. Labor and Peres set the campaign agenda and the Likud and Netanyahu were forced to compete for the political center by accepting the outlines of the peace initiative in their 1996 election platform, including the Oslo agreements and dealing with the PLO. Labor and Rabin succeeded in 1992 in attracting enough young and Sephardi voters from the Likud's power base, and they, along with a majority vote of the Russian immigrants, made the difference for Rabin and Labor.[5] In 1996, these groups also supported religious parties in unprecedented numbers. It appeared that competitiveness would be the major feature of the second republic's party system.

Organization

As power shifts in a society, organization of the political party changes. In a society run by the nobility and clergy, politics is confined to the shifting coalitions in the king's court. When elections determine the division of power, it becomes politically advantageous to organize the electorate better than your opponents do. When the important resources are controlled by the state, it is advantageous to coalesce with opponents to assure a steady flow of money.

Maurice Duverger's *Political Parties*,[6] published in the early 1950s, dealt with parties in general, but his discussion of the cadre party, the mass party, and the devotee party provides important insights into the workings of the Israeli party system. With the two additional concepts of the catch-all party and the cartel party, we shall have the analytical tools needed to make sense of the Israeli political scene.

There is no ideal form of party organization, and forms of organization are not static. Party organization adapts to meet existing conditions. Organization reflects interests, needs, and motivations, but it also generates all of these. And in so doing, party organization itself changes.

Various organizational forms of political parties may coexist at once in the same country. Parties court different audiences; pressured by differing forces, they are susceptible to varying pressures. The forms used by the winners are often mimicked by other parties, but in so doing they invariably change the original forms to meet their own special needs. The organizational structures of new winners are copied in their turn. Many organizational structures may exist, but a smaller number will be dominant.

Different organizational forms correspond to specific historical periods. The *cadre party* flourished in a time of limited suffrage when the leadership was made up of notables and the appeal was to the middle and upper classes. The *mass party* was introduced by the socialists between 1890 and 1900; shortly thereafter, the fascists and communists introduced the *devotee party*. The *catch-all party* was a post–World War II development, and the *cartel party* appeared after 1970.

The mass party was the most successful form in Israeli history, spawning the parties that reigned between the 1930s and the 1970s. Adopted by parties of the left, secular, and religious, mass forms quickly spread out among other parties in an attempt by the latter to imitate the success of the former. The basic organizational unit of the mass party is the branch, and the working class is the major focus of organizational efforts. Organization must be conceived in a broad sense; not only the attainment of office is at stake, but it is also necessary to transform society and the minds and lives of the workers organized in the parties.

The mass party generally has a socialist orientation, one in which centralization and discipline are strong. Properly motivated individuals do not need explicit instructions about how to act in their jobs or their public lives. The good of the party incorporates notions of the good of the state and individual good. Leadership tends to be oligarchical; elites of mass parties are developed by the parties themselves. This is perhaps one of the few instances in history in which political power can be obtained through organizational skill alone, rather than in conjunction with military, commercial, or ecclesiastical skill or office.

Membership in a mass party is very important, for the party not only needs sources of financial support but must also promote class consciousness among the membership. The number of members desired is very large, and the enthusiasm expected of the membership is high. Doctrine is important in a mass party to keep enthusiasm high, to stir class consciousness, and to suggest that the political and social payoffs for the party's strivings are attainable in the near future.

The proliferation of party-related bureaucracies in Israel followed neatly from the concept of the organization of a mass party and from the special conditions that existed in the country. Not only was there a scarcity of social services, but the country lacked the basic economic infrastructure of roads, docks, and energy that are a prerequisite for economic growth and development. In the case of the Yishuv, the situation was basically unique because the political elite preceded the bulk of the population in arriving in the country and making plans for its future. Political organizations, then, provided some services and much ideological instruction, as they did in many European parties; in addition, the socialist parties of the Yishuv were key agents of socialization as new waves of immigrants arrived in the country. The immigrants were dependent on these parties, which absorbed them not only in the sense of party members benefiting by their party's activities but also in the sense of immigrants grateful to the absorbing authorities.

The development of parties of social integration stemmed from ideological and organizational needs. Peter Medding described the reality well when he wrote:

> the activities in the party branch embraced much of the member's social life and were his major source of information and guidance in political and social affairs. His employment, friendships, cultural interests and leisure hours were all deeply influenced by his party membership focused on the local branch. Attempts were also made to encourage the member to live in politically homogeneous Histadrut housing developments. In addition, he read the Histadrut newspaper, *Davar,* which because of Mapai's control of that body, was in reality a Mapai paper, and subscribed also to one of the party journals, such as *Hapoel Hatzair.* A Mapai member could, if he so desired, lead his life in a completely party circumscribed environment, hardly coming into major political contact with outsiders, and barely subject to competing political influences or conflicting sources of information.[7]

It was inevitable that the large scale of membership-oriented activity should lead to drives for more budget, larger membership, and an ever-increasing bureaucracy. Larger bureaucracies also meant more political control because more people were dependent on party activities for a livelihood. These people could easily be mobilized when demonstrations or elections took place. Larger bureaucracies also meant more jobs in the cities for an immigrant population that was, on the whole, of urban origin and was not eager to fulfill the ideological imperative of agricultural settlement. And so the clerks, bureaucrats, and apparatus members involved in the delivery of health services, culture, economic activities, and education grew in number as the parties grew in power and control. As the bureaucracies expanded, more programs were sought, and the role of the bureaucracies and their leaders in the party strengthened.

The devotee party is also evident in certain communist, fascist, and religious party organizations in Israel. There is a basic justification in grouping these forms of party organizations together, for despite ideological differences, there is a basic similarity in the kind of individual to whom these parties appeal. They demand fanatical devotion to the party, to the cause the party supports, and to the dictates of the party. There must be a basic acceptance of the notion that, whatever the behavior, the party is working for the good of the class or the cause; blind adherence to the leadership must be forthcoming. While communists may be considered on the extreme left of the social and economic continua and fascists on the extreme right, and religious fundamentalists on a different continuum altogether, there is a sense in which all of these adherents are very close to one another. In figurative terms, the continuum must be bent and the extremes joined as the continuum becomes circular. Then it is clear that in psychological terms the values and attitudes of communists and fascists (and fundamentalists too) tend to be authoritarian, antiliberal, and closed-minded, unwilling and unable to put up with the frustrations and compromises necessary in a democratic form of government.

Perhaps the greatest similarity is in the extreme authoritarian structure of leadership within these forms of party. Whether it is the Council of Rabbinical Sages, or the politburo, or the supreme leader, decisions are made at the top and obedience is expected from the members. Sanctions may be positive or negative and may include promises of blessings, jobs, or contacts, or threats of curses, expulsion, or worse, depending on the organization and its ideology. What is similar is that leadership is developed by the party, and fundamental obstacles to rotation are built into organizational structures; stable, if not always inspiring, leadership tends to emerge. Stability lasts as long as the leader lasts. After that, the crisis of succession is often severe.

Characteristic elements of the devotee party were in evidence in the Israel Communist Party and Mapam, especially the features of democratic centralism in the former and ideological collectivism in the latter, in which party members were required to accept the rulings of the party's decision-making bodies as ideologically binding. Debates and division of opinion are appropriate only until the party's authoritative bodies have ruled; after that, the membership must acquiesce in the decisions adopted.

Elements of devotee organization were evident in the Revisionist movement and its successors. Jabotinsky was given absolute power by a referendum of the membership in 1933; the leaders Ahimeir and Yevin openly advocated a totalitarian party led by a dictator.[8] The underground military organizations of the Irgun and Lehi continued this tradition, which also answered the needs of a secretive fighting unit. The values of discipline and obedience were exalted, and the use of ceremony and pomp was familiar to those who followed developments on the continent of Europe during the 1930s. In Herut, Begin was called the "commander" by members of the "fighting family" who followed him from the Irgun to Herut. When he arrived flanked by uniformed motorcycle guards at a Tel Aviv outdoor election rally in the early 1950s, the imagery for many was indelibly imprinted.

The major organizational difference between the forms of organization outlined earlier have to do with the basic organizational units used by each party. For the communists it is the cell—a secretive, small group of party members organized at the place of work. The location of organization was an important innovation of Lenin, emphasizing the Marxist analysis of the importance of economic factors in the life of the individual and the state. The cell can fill functions of encouragement, disruption, intelligence, or dissemination of ideas, all according to the needs of the moment. The branch of the mass party is connected with an individual's place of residence, thus making party activity an after-work enterprise. The branch therefore concentrates on providing individual services as well as cultural, educational, and instructional activities because members lack a common place of work. The branches of mass-membership Israeli parties, especially in the heyday of party activity, filled all these functions and were augmented by a complementary organization of the workers at the place of employment by the Histadrut. There, the political and occupational work of the parties could be pursued. The *militia* was the form developed by fascist parties as the unit of organization. Recruiting mainly from middle and lower middle classes (as opposed to the working-class appeal of the socialists and communists), the fascists used the militia with its overtones of army discipline and patriotic symbolism to increase levels of allegiance of members.

The emergence of catch-all parties occurred in the 1960s and 1970s as leaders of various parties began to enjoy a capacity to appeal to the electorate at large. The mass parties weakened as the mass media developed, as the children of the immigrant generation came of age, and as social services were transferred from party-related organizations to the state.[9] Voters were beginning to behave more like consumers than active participants. This new model of party was sometimes incorrectly identified as part of the process of Americanization of Israeli politics. Elections were seen to revolve around the choice of leaders rather than the choice of policies or platforms, especially in the 1980s, while the formation of those policies became the prerogative of the party leadership rather than of the party membership. Popular control and accountability were weakened as the public seemed to judge politicians prospectively rather than retrospectively, in terms of promises rather than record, in terms of what they would do in the future rather than in terms of what they had done in the past.[10] The persistence of national unity governments in the 1980s also contributed to this pattern. Parties were not over, nor were they in decline; they were changing.

The cadre party model presupposes that the elected notables can identify and pursue the national interest, while the model of the mass party was one of competing visions of appropriate social policy. Where the cadre party relied on the quality of supporters, the mass party relied on the quantity of supporters. The mass party became a victim of its own success as the state began to provide on a universal basis the welfare and educational services that had been the responsibility of the party. The improvement of social conditions increased social and electoral mobility. The catch-all party recruited members on the basis of policy agreement rather than social identity. Parties began making universal appeals directly to voters rather than communicating principally to and through their core supporters, further weakening the ties between particular parties and particular segments of society. The party began to act as a broker between the electorate and organized interests, rather than in its traditional role of organizing and then representing interests.

The capacity of a party to perform the brokerage function depends not only on its ability to appeal to the electorate, but also on its ability to manipulate the state.[11] A party that can use the state in the interests of its clients can also use it in its own interests. In their role of law-makers it was "natural" for party leaders to turn to the state to provide and regulate financial support for political parties, and to acquire an easy access to the electronic media, controlled by the state, to pursue their goals. The introduction of party financing in 1969 and the generous amount of free television and radio time provided during election campaigns in the Israeli case, fit this model perfectly. In a sense, the state is invaded by the parties; the state rules are determined by the parties in concert, providing resources to existing parties to ensure their own survival, and aiding them to resist challenges from newly mobilized alternatives. The state becomes an institution-alized structure of support for sustaining insiders while excluding outsiders. The parties now become absorbed by the state rather than acting as brokers between the state and other groups. No longer trustees (cadre party), delegates (mass party), or even entrepreneurs (catch-all party), party leaders become functionaries of semi-state agencies. In this sense a cartel emerges, in which all the existing parties share in resources and in which all survive.

In present-day Israel, Likud and Labor are good examples of cartel parties that rely on government support to persist. They still have branches and place a premium on membership, but these are holdovers from mass party forms; these are occasionally important resources in intraparty fights, but they are no longer vital for the survival of the party organization. This explains how leaders of such parties could even consider "open primaries" in which any citizen, whether a member of the party or not, could participate in choosing the party's candidates for office. The NRP still retains the forms and functions of a mass party, although it too enjoys the legislation for funding parties passed by the other cartel parties. The haredi parties are closest to cadre parties, with their established rabbinical leadership, and the total unimportance of membership and party branches. They flourish by providing their supporters with access to government money and ideological clarity.

The Iron Law of Oligarchy

Michels's iron law of oligarchy is one of the most insightful concepts in the study of political parties and is worthy to be described here at some length.[12] The notion is especially relevant to the reality of Israeli politics; Michels might have been writing about Israeli political parties and not German ones. Although he died twelve years before Israel was declared a state, Michels wrote (not about Israel) almost prophetically that "the social revolution would not effect any real modification of the internal structure of the mass. The socialists might conquer, but not socialism, which would perish in the moment of its adherents' triumph."[13]

The iron law of oligarchy posits that true democracy in any organization is impossible. Autocratic tendencies in an organization are neither accidental nor temporary; they are inherent in the nature of the organization. "He who says organization, says oligarchy" sums it up well. Michels details the reasons that the masses are unable to control their destinies. There are technical reasons, such as the difficulty of assembling in one place or the need to make quick decisions on complex issues that demand great expertise. There are psychological reasons, including the fact that most people are apathetic about public issues, not knowledgeable enough or engaged enough to participate in decision making. More important, argues Michels, most people want to be led.

Which brings us to the crux of the matter. Michels distinguishes between the mass of members in an organization and the leadership. The many financial, political, diplomatic, and informational tasks that must be performed cannot be performed by all. Organization implies a division of labor and a hierarchy of command. Whenever something must get done, someone has to do it; someone must see to it that this thing is done. Leadership necessarily arises in an organization and will act independently of the will of the masses. The leaders will likely speak in the name of the masses and of a democratic ideology, but Michels would counsel that we pay very little attention to what the leaders say and instead look at what they do.

One indicator of the psychological dependence that develops between the leadership and the mass is a phenomenon that might be called the customary right to office. Although formally a leader can be replaced when new elections are held, the fact that he has held office is thought to give him a moral claim on that office or some other leadership post in the organization. Playing to these sentiments may lead politicians to threaten resignation. This is generally very alarming to the masses because it causes uncertainty and denies security, and to other leaders because it may lead to unpleasant confrontations and disclosures—and it tends to be avoided, with the proper concessions generally made to the threatening leader. There is always the chance that the resignation will be accepted, and the prudent politician assesses these probabilities before he undertakes the gamble. On both grounds—the customary right to office and the threat of resignation—Michels would be quite comfortable in Israeli politics. Ben-Gurion, Golda Meir, Yitzhak Ben-Aharon, among many others, successfully used the threat of resignation as a powerful tool to force their will on the group.

As Machiavelli pointed out, when the mass is deprived of its leadership in time of action, "they abandon the field in disordered flight."[14] This happens in politics and organizations as well. This need for leadership on the part of the passive masses makes them dependent on leaders and grateful for their efforts; concomitantly, it makes leaders of mass parties or the state extremely busy people. Soon the leaders as a group are perceived by the masses, and perceive themselves, as indispensable to the organization. The leadership develops power independent of the mass membership and is constituted as an informal subgroup. This is clearly evident in the salaries, expense accounts, and fringe benefits leaders vote for themselves from organizational funds—amounts that are larger than the wages of the workers they represent. This they justify by their enormous efforts and indispensability to the organization; the members, after rightly protesting this autocratic maneuver, approve the increases.

The leaders develop a sense of group superiority vis-à-vis the masses, and soon the leaders themselves change. This drive for power is not only self-seeking but is also based on the belief that their continuance in power would most benefit the organization because of their superiority, sacrifice, and indispensability. The extreme form of the development is that stage at which the leader "identifies himself completely with the organization, confounding his own interests with its interest. All objective criticism of the party or nation is taken by him as a personal affront.... If, on the other hand, the leader is attacked personally, his first care is to make it appear that the attack is directed against the party or nation as a whole."[15]

Peter Medding's book on the role of Mapai during the first twenty years of statehood details many of the situations and manipulations discussed by Michels. For example, Medding notes that Mapai "stood at the apex of a whole interconnected network of organizations and institutions that it controlled and directed from within" and that "the party was thus left as final referee, arbitrator or decision maker."[16] Medding writes that the party displayed a wide latitude in conducting the affairs of institutions it ran on behalf of the party—it was rarely upset by "lack of concern with constitutional formality [which] led to centralization of control in the hands of narrower executive bodies, and the inevitable lessening of the influence of the wider representative bodies." Strangely, after all this and more, Medding concludes that "the internal decision making process as we have analyzed it provides impressive evidence against Michels's theory of political party organization." Since many decisions were made in Mapai in many committees and institutions, and not all were made by the handful of major leaders, Medding concludes that Mapai was an example of "consensual power relations: the views of many groups were put forward or taken into consideration, and bargaining and mutual compromise characterized the discussions." Medding's analysis confronts the iron law of oligarchy with essentially trivial exceptions to the thrust of Michels's argument. Mapai was an excellent example of Michels's iron law of oligarchy, and Medding's thorough research chronicles an oligarchical party at the height of its power.

Adapting to New Conditions

Israel's two biggest parties, Likud and Labor, and some of the others, including Meretz and Tzomet, have increasingly added an element of mass participation in the running of the party. The party primary, in which the membership as a whole plays a role in selecting the leadership, has become more and more widespread. This development accentuates the increasing openness of Israel and its institutions, but it also underscores the extent to which conditions have changed in the political life of the country.[17]

Israeli parties remain oligarchical, top-down parties. To get ahead in Israeli politics, one should still plan a career in a political party. But the skills needed have changed. In the Israel of the 1990s, the public mood and popular demands concern party leaders more than do issues of ideological consistency and organizational necessity. A subtle but crucial switch has taken place: for the prestate and early state parties, elections were necessary inconveniences to be tolerated in order to further ideological and organizational goals. Today, partly because of the competitive nature of the political system and partly because party organization has fewer resources at its disposal, elections become a magnetic source of energy for party leaders and members.

Changes in the electorate also make a difference. If party leaders once controlled resources needed by a population exhausted by war and emigration, today, two generations later, an independent and educated electorate makes demands on government ministers eager to be reelected. This opens politicians to charges of pandering to the public with populistic promises, but the threat of losing a leadership position because of a poor showing in the primaries, or losing the next election, adds a healthy shot of uncertainty to the political process.

Israeli society is more affluent and diverse than ever, and alternatives are available. While communal, ethnic, and religious ties remain central for many, there has also developed an overlay of consumer-oriented, individualistic, atomized cultural elements. Structural developments highlighted the relaxation of the norms of similarity and uniformity. Privatization and competition are the slogans of governments controlled by parties of the right or the left. Increasingly, many aspects of private life are affected by these principles, including health delivery systems and education, with the emergence of private clinics and universities. International travel is more widely available, aided by the lifting of the travel tax; local newspapers and radio stations have provided different messages to different audiences; widespread availability of the VCR, a second television channel, and cable television broke the long domination of the government-related channel. The political genius has yet to emerge who can harness the electronic superhighway to the organizational needs of the political party, but the older ways of organization have clearly become outdated.

The addition of a bottom-up feature in top-down parties reflects changes in the country. The three most obvious causes of the change in the parties in Israel are the contraction of the benefits to be gained from the parties, alternative sources of income for the parties, and the growing role of the mass media (especially television) in the Israeli polity.

First, the roles of the party changed slowly after independence as functions such as defense, education, and employment were gradually transferred to the state. Inevitably the citizen was less dependent on the party than before, and although habits persisted, these new realities were perceived over time. The fact that the party leadership (especially in Mapai) became the national leadership reduced the perceived importance of party membership. Affinities were shifted as services were no longer undertaken by the party leadership. The provision of health services, one of the last bastions of party strength and patronage, was nationalized in 1995 (see chapter 11).

Second, parties have developed alternative sources of income over the years, while gladly accepting the revenues generated by the recent increase in membership. Up to 1969, much of the parties' budgets came from groups and corporations affiliated with them or those anxious to support them, and from their political organizations abroad. The financing of parties and their election campaign expenses by the government treasury was begun in 1969. Party leaders obviously favored this type of funding since, unlike other moneys, there was no uncertainty about receiving government funds, and the decisions regarding the funding were completely in their control.[18] Funds are not provided to individual members; rather, they are given to the Knesset delegation. Leaders obviously have more access to these moneys than do those lower down in the hierarchy. Leaders of small delegations may have even more leverage over these moneys than do Knesset members who are low on the lists of large parties.

The legislation mandated payments to the parties in proportion to their representation in the Knesset. The party receives one "unit" for each Knesset member. In 1996 the "unit" was about $17,500 per Knesset member per month—or a total of more than $25 million per year. In addition, funding for elections in 1996 came to an additional $350,000 per Knesset member, for a total of $42 million. The $67 million of public money for the 3 million votes cast in 1996 comes to more than $22 per vote, making Israel the most expensive democracy per voter in the world. The rationale is democratic because parties are central to a functioning democracy; the outcome is that the biggest winners are also the biggest earners for their organizations' ongoing expenses.

Special funding is made for election periods, and lists are granted a proportion of the funds based on the size of the delegation in the outgoing Knesset. Parties that do better in the new elections are reimbursed; if they lose strength, they may owe the treasury. One outrageous feature of the 1996 legislation was to base the allocation on 126 members of the outgoing

Knesset, and not on the actual 120 number. This allowed financing of six members who had broken with their parties and were running on separate lists, but it simultaneously allowed the original parties to enjoy the public funding that they had expected, as if the renegade Knesset members still belonged to their parties. The large parties in 1996 were big losers of Knesset seats, and in public financing as well; the deficit for both Likud and Labor reached almost $4 million. It would not be out of character for them to coalesce and propose legislation to cover these considerable campaign deficits.

In 1992 the "unit" was set at $300,000 per Knesset member per year, with an additional unit in an election year to defray campaign expenses doubling the total. That was an increase of a third over the amount in effect in May 1991. Litigation prevented the increase from taking effect (the High Court of Justice ruled that it would have to be approved by an absolute majority of the entire Knesset since the Committee's decision to link the quarterly increase in the unit to the cost-of-living index was not included in the original legislation) and it remained at "only" $200,100 per year. Had the "reform" taken effect, the total of public funds going to the parties in an election year would have been $72 million, or about $29 per vote! This was about the level of 1988. Since the change was thwarted, the election year bill for the parties in 1992 was $48 million, coming to "only" $19 per vote for the election year's expenses. Politicians from different parties, who are often split by deep ideological divisions, usually manage to agree on raising the funding unit for the parties. In 1992, they were stymied by the High Court, but not before they went to unusual lengths. The most flagrant of these occurred when members of the Finance Committee who opposed the increase were replaced by their party's leaderships for the meeting of the committee with members who supported it.

The generous payments made by the public treasury to the political parties have been accompanied by the introduction of more public oversight and scrutiny in the affairs of the parties. Most notably, legislation passed in 1994 took the task of setting the amount of the "unit" out of the hands of the Knesset Finance Committee and delegated it to a public commission headed by a retired Supreme Court justice. However, the "unit" is linked to the cost-of-living index and increases regularly. In addition, Knesset members can legislate additional moneys for the parties for purposes outside the scope of existing laws, such as the direct election of the prime minister or strengthening contacts with the voters.

The law limits to $400 direct or indirect contributions from corporations or households, and even these must come from registered voters. The State Controller report has regularly documented the inappropriate use of state-allocated funds for elections, and it is an open secret that the major parties raise many millions of dollars in Israel and from abroad through donations to organizations set up to circumvent the provisions against large and foreign donations. Important parties are well-connected, and it is clear that the State Controller is not apprised of all money transfers undertaken by the parties or for their purposes.

Third, technological innovations revolutionized the manner in which political communication was conducted. Election broadcasting time on television and radio is distributed in proportion to the strength of the party in the outgoing Knesset, giving party leaders a crucial resource because they control who will appear for their parties. Opinion polls proliferated, and talk shows multiplied the sources of information and biases. No more were precinct workers of party bosses immediate and reliable sources of political information and encouragement. No longer were large crowds anxious to hear a party leader speak on the issues of the day. No more were political relations cemented only by a social visit or other informal behavior. For the vast majority of the population, the message of the television signal, every day for the four years up to the elections, and even more so in the weeks before the elections, filled the functions of sizing up the leadership and comparing competing images.

In the prestate and early state years, party members may have been motivated by ideology or material considerations or both. What is certain was that they could more easily involve themselves in ideological discourse or in achieving material benefits if they were party members. Today, people who join parties do not expect to determine the pace of the peace process; they look to the state, not to parties, to achieve better housing, education, or health services for them. They join to participate in the selection of the party's Knesset list or to register support for the ideas of the party or its leadership. They may be indirectly connected with the party hierarchy, or hopeful that party success will favorably affect their activities at the local level. But many fewer career opportunities are to be found in direct party activity or in party-related groups; accordingly, the expectations for direct material benefits are unlikely to be the motivating factor for most of today's members. Change in the political parties was caused by, and affected, change in the society.

Membership

The development of political party organization in Israel is highlighted by a tendency toward mass-membership parties with oligarchical tendencies. The tone was set by the parties of the left, both secular and religious, and the other parties followed. We might have expected that a bourgeois party with centrist ideological inclinations, such as the Liberal Party (General

Zionists), would have organized differently, but at least at the formal level, many characteristics that occurred in the more successful parties of the left were copied by the Liberals. There is obviously a tendency in political life to mimic success, and this may explain why, at least on paper, most parties in Israel seem to resemble one another.

Today the organizational structures of most Israeli parties are similar. There have been historical differences of emphasis depending on the type of party. Take membership, for example. While formally all Israeli parties wanted members, this was more important in parties whose ideologies demanded political and educational work in the electorate, whose program called for party activities that demanded budgets and bureaucratic organizations, and for outlays of funds otherwise unattainable. Obviously, these characteristics better corresponded to socialist parties than to the General Zionists. This was especially true before the state was founded, for then much of the activity was based on party-related organizations, especially the Histadrut (to which the General Zionists did not belong).

In the prestate years, membership was very important for a number of reasons. First, in order to raise money. A steady stream of funds flowing in from the payment of dues was an organizational innovation of extreme importance in the history of the political parties. But it was predicated on the assumption that parties did something, that they provided services. All Zionist parties engaged in fund-raising activities abroad, and none of them relied exclusively on membership in Eretz Israel to fund their activities. But the General Zionists and Revisionists had two advantages: (1) the level of their activity in Eretz Israel was much lower than that of the other parties, and (2) their success at fund raising was greater abroad than it was in the Yishuv. Members' dues in Eretz Israel for the socialist mass-membership parties were relatively more important.

Second, parties provided important services that were available only to members. The polity of the Yishuv was a voluntary structure, and few services were available to all because no central authority existed. The party (often through the Histadrut) could provide housing, employment, and health, cultural, and educational services. Being a member of the "right" party could enhance the probability of receiving these services.

Third, membership was important because it was believed that in the political struggle each additional member raised the likelihood of success. Membership was not conceived of as a passive role entered into only to receive material benefit. Membership was perceived to indicate agreement with the party's ideology and the efforts of the party's leadership. The party played an important role in educating the public through the education of its members.

Fourth, the assumed relationship between voting and membership was always at the back of the minds of party leaders. Growth in membership indicated growth in the potential of votes at the next election. Besides granting the leadership important psychological support, added members seemed to indicate that the party's program was growing in acceptability.

Fifth, the party machine, its bureaucracy, was very interested in members as a sign of its success. Short of elections, no clearer indication of organizational success was available than membership. Another incentive for the bureaucrats was that with each jump in membership, additional programs, and hence additional funds and additional jobs, must be added.

An important distinction to be made is between direct and indirect membership. A direct member applies to the party and is accepted on an individual basis. In most Israeli parties during the period when strong ideological divisions seemed to separate the parties, an applicant had to be recommended by a party member in good standing, in addition to accepting the party's platform and paying periodic dues. A much more practical arrangement in terms of the party organization is indirect membership. In this form one becomes a party member by virtue of membership in another organization, most often a trade union. Not only is the member offered a social support system within the party, but he is represented in party affairs by the same leaders who represent him in union affairs. In reality, as we can imagine, the worker is not overly aware of his party membership because he joins automatically when joining the union.

The conveniences for the organizational bureaucrats are clear. They can count on a steady income from the dues of the union membership deducted from the workers' salaries and forwarded directly to the party by the union. No more uncertainty regarding membership funds; no more fear that party positions will alienate members and bring about large-scale resignations. Another aspect of the same "benefit" from the point of view of the party bureaucrats is that they can now deal with trade union bureaucrats on political matters and no longer have to deal with the members themselves. The two sets of bureaucrats are likely to have similar backgrounds, goals, and life styles; hence they will probably get along quite well with each other.

A key dispute regarding the National Health Insurance Law was the relationship between party membership and other activity. The practice had been that the Histadrut's sick fund was available only to Histadrut members, and since the Histadrut was composed of political parties, a portion of the dues went to those parties. The reformers wanted a clear separation between health insurance provision and political party activity; the Histadrut leaders wanted to retain the connection. After a bitter fight (see chapter 10), the reformers won, and the Histadrut today does not have the regular and automatic income for its constituent political parties from those insured. Provision has been made for a voluntary deduction for political activities, but that is much closer to direct membership than to the indirect membership of yesterday.

A good example of indirect membership comes from the National Religious Party. When the Mizrachi and Hapoel Hamizrachi merged in 1956 to form the NRP, the merging organizations were not disbanded. Hapoel Hamizrachi handled issues of labor, agricultural settlement, the protection of rights of workers, and the development of labor and pioneering values. Members of Hapoel Hamizrachi had access to Histadrut sick-fund facilities on the basis of an agreement drawn up in the 1920s. Hapoel Hamizrachi members (but not all members of NRP) were provided services by the Histadrut, while their organization transferred a percentage of their dues to the Histadrut sick fund. These individuals were not members of the Histadrut, although they paid the same dues as did Histadrut members. They were members of Hapoel Hamizrachi, and by virtue of indirect membership, NRP members as well. This complex arrangement allowed Hapoel Hamizrachi to continue providing these services to its members without renegotiating the agreement, and allowed it to merge with another party to form a new one and yet retain its original organizational identity.

This arrangement was continued even after the advent of the National Health Insurance Law and the reorganization of the Histadrut after its 1994 elections. The decision by the Histadrut to renew its historical alliance with the National Religious Party and Agudat Israel workers' organizations meant that affiliated workers would join the Histadrut and that more than half of the organization tax paid from their salaries would be refunded to the religious parties.

Indirect membership still exists in Israel today, but at a much lower level than in the past. This is a sign of the times, and of the relative weakness of the parties. The introduction of the party primary came about in part because leaders wanted to increase party membership (and the dues generated), and because older alternative forms of membership had withered away. In a party with a weakened bureaucracy, calls for democratization were more likely to be heeded.

Membership rates fell with the lessening ability of the parties to provide material benefits. The percentage of respondents in surveys reporting that they were party members fell from a high 18 percent in 1969, to a low 8 percent in the 1984 and 1988 polls, and then up again to 9 percent in 1996 (see figure 6.1). The downward trend was gradual but consistent; the upward swing was slower than might have been expected.

A new cycle has been added to Israeli party politics. With the introduction of primary elections, membership drives have taken on new importance. Members are now important not only for the dues they generate but

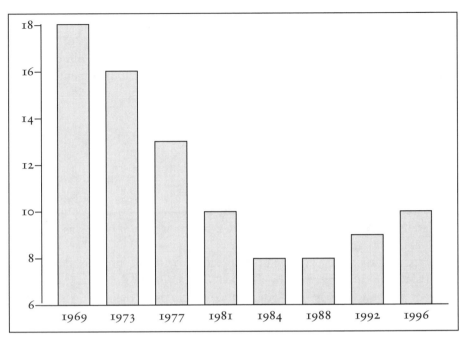

FIGURE 6.1
PARTY MEMBERSHIP, 1969–96 (IN PERCENTAGES)

also for their votes at the primary election. It becomes imperative for a candidate to recruit people on whose votes he thinks he can count. These drives inevitably raise charges of corrupt practices, with reports of activists recruiting members by questionable means.

The character of party membership has changed. No longer simply a matter of ideological motivation or material profit, party membership may be important to further the career of a leader who matters to you. Following the changed electoral rules, the candidate seems to have replaced the party as the prime object of relationship. This change can be inferred from the discrepancy between the rate of party membership as reported by the public in surveys and the observed rate of membership according to the figures of the parties. Based on the parties' membership drives, registered party members totaled at least 500,000 Israelis in 1996. With about 4 million eligible voters, the membership rate should be about 12 percent. But the reported rate in the polls was only 9 percent for Jews, compared with 24 for Israeli Arabs.

Political parties still control the path to power in Israel. But if in the past members were at the bottom of a top-down structure, today they control one key step on that path—the party primary election. Groups and individuals sign up to further their own candidates or issues, or they are courted in the hope that they will support a candidate. Membership in more than one party is illegal, and in 1996, some 30,000 cases of joining two parties were discovered by the office of the Registrar of Political Parties. Individuals were notified that they had to relinquish their membership in all but one party to be eligible to participate in any party's primary election.[19]

Forming the Lists

The way to get on a party's list in the past was to be appointed to it by the party's top leadership. The proposed list, which had been prepared by a nominating committee often peopled by the leaders and their cronies, was generally presented to the party center for approval, which was almost always always automatically given.

A major break in that pattern occurred with the first primary elections in Israel in 1977, held by the DMC. Reacting to the criticism of the role of machine politicians in other parties in choosing their lists, the DMC decided to hold a primary election among its 30,000 members to determine its list for the Knesset. Paradoxically, but not surprisingly, the most well-known candidates received the most votes. If democracy implies free access to decision-making positions, it was not attained by the DMC's primaries. The list of the DMC, chosen most democratically, was most heavily peopled by luminaries; the list of the Labor Party, selected in 1977 in a smoke-filled room by party stalwarts, was much more representative.

Herut had been another pioneer in a more participatory form of list formation. Herut's center had an active role from the 1980s in determining its Knesset list. It selected the candidates for the Knesset list in a ranking procedure within clusters of seven. Herut has traditionally exempted its leader (first Begin, then Shamir) from the rigors of competition, reaffirming the leader's selection by acclamation. In 1988, in fact, the Herut center was identical to the Herut convention, because the latter was bitterly divided among the followers of Yitzhak Shamir, Ariel Sharon, and David Levy, and was unable to select a smaller center. Thus, in 1988, with some 3,000 participating, the election of the clusters of seven proceeded.

In 1988, the Citizens Rights Movement selected its candidates by using a secret ballot in its council. Many competed, including five who were then members of the Knesset. Not surprisingly, the first five on the CRM list were the five Knesset members, and they then were installed as the CRM Knesset delegation after the list won five seats.

The 1988 Labor Party decentralized the system somewhat. There were two ways of getting on the Labor list: through the party's districts and through election by the center. Competition took place for fifty places

—twenty-three positions on the list reserved for the party's districts and twenty-seven to be selected by the center by secret ballot. The district elections were held in the various districts (Tel Aviv, Jerusalem, kibbutzim, moshavim, etc.) by the district councils of the party. Alternatively, a candidate could be nominated for election by the party center. Eighty-six candidates competed for these twenty-seven slots. To assure representation, provision was made that at least one Druze, one Arab, one young person, three women, and one candidate from development towns be selected. After these first rounds of selection, the 1,340 members of the center met. (The center itself had been selected by the 3,201-member Labor Convention. The constitutional size of the convention was 3,001 members, but another 200 members had been co-opted for organizational and political reasons.) The center's task was to determine the positions on the Knesset election list of fifty candidates (twenty-three from the districts and twenty-seven from the central list), using a system of voting for clusters of ten.

The results indicated the difficulties inherent in democratization: the big losers were the districts. Their candidates were ranked in low positions in the runoffs that determined how high on the list a candidate would be. Of the twenty-three district candidates, only nine were finally elected to the Knesset—and seven of them were in the last ten places on the list of those elected. Although the districts may be closer to "the people," they controlled fewer votes in the center. Those who were known by many center members and enjoyed national visibility were more likely to be elected. Still, an unusually large percentage of new and young candidates emerged. Having achieved at least a partial success, Labor followed Herut into an era of greater, if not perfect, democracy in the selection process. In 1992, Labor switched to a primary election in which all dues-paying members could participate. The Likud (dominated by Herut) retained its cluster system in the party center.

The task of the primaries was to select a fixed list to be presented to the voters on election day. A variety of considerations came into play, since the job is different from simply selecting one of a number of candidates to represent the party. Two competing ends, both desirable to those who wrote the rules, were broad participation and representation. The dilemma was that popular elections often select well-known people; how does a list generate a balance between well-known and lesser-known figures, between representatives of majority and minority groups, between representatives from various geographical regions, and so on?

By 1996, both Likud and Labor used primary elections to select their candidates for the Knesset. They both used a mixed national-district system; members had multiple votes, but the party institutions had almost no role to play in them, other than approving the rules and supervising the election. Both parties held membership censuses that ended close to the day for primary elections. Mass enrollments were alleged by vote brokers or by labor organizers. There were charges that people were coerced by their employers in public or Histadrut-owned enterprises to register as Labor members and pay the dues. An internal Labor inquiry regarding the 1992 primary had confirmed many of these charges. Complaints came especially from the Israel Electric Company and the Egged bus cooperative. In the IEC's Jerusalem district, over 90 percent of the employees registered as Labor members. Egged employees also reported pressure from their superiors, who threatened that failure to sign up would result in either firing or loss of tenure, perks, and advancement.

The mixed national-district selection system used by both Labor and Likud solved the problem by assigning positions on the list to various categories of winners in advance. Thus Likud rules had the first place going to Binyamin Netanyahu, since he had been selected as party leader in a separate election, the next sixteen slots to those who placed on the national list, place eighteen to the Jerusalem district, nineteen to Tel Aviv, twenty to Haifa, twenty-one to the Negev, twenty-two to the Galilee, twenty-three to the next national list winner, and so on. In addition, place thirty-one was reserved for a new immigrant, thirty-two for a non-Jew, thirty-three and thirty-six to women, and thirty-seven to a young person. David Levy had withdrawn from Likud and formed Gesher because he felt that the ratio of national to district seats in the composition of the list would weaken his chances to secure slots for his activists. Fifty percent of Likud's registered members actually voted in the primaries.

Labor used the same principle with different details. Peres was unopposed in 1996 for first place, and so no ballot was required. For the rest of the list, Labor allotted twenty-one slots of the first forty-four slots to its national list, the other twenty-three to district candidates. A voter had to select no fewer than eleven and no more than fifteen of the fifty-six candidates. Labor had one-, two-, and three-member districts; a voter could vote for no more than two in the multimember districts. Candidates had to reside in the districts they sought to represent. Two-thirds of Labor's 285,000 members actually voted in the primaries.

The 1996 primaries were flawed because the leaders of the two biggest parties, Likud and Labor, could not avoid the temptation of tampering with the results of the primary vote. The Likud disregard of the primaries as a selection mechanism was the more blatant of the two. The Likud politicians altered the primary results significantly by agreeing to form a joint Likud-Gesher-Tzomet list after the primaries were held, thereby relegating Likud primary winners to lower positions on the new three-party list. One Likud candidate, a Druze Knesset incumbent, applied to the courts—and

was denied—when his thirty-second place was changed to forty-sixth because of the three-party merger. Since the polls showed that the Likud was
likely to win about forty seats, the change would have meant the difference
between victory and defeat (had the polls been correct).

The Labor leadership engineered a change in the results of the primaries in its party as well. Its rules reserved the twenty-ninth place on the list
for a new immigrant. With more than half a million new immigrants from
the former Soviet Union, this was a crucial group, representing some 15
percent of the electorate. But the new immigrant elected in the primary
was an Ethiopian Jew, Adiso Massalla, whose compatriots represented
about 1 percent of the electorate. His election followed the revelation a few
weeks earlier that the government's medical authorities systematically destroyed blood donations from Ethiopian Jews because of a higher incidence
of HIV-positive blood in this donor population. Furious Ethiopians attacked police at a rally, and the public observed them abandoning their
generally passive demeanor in calling for an end to discrimination against
them. This evidently struck a chord as Labor Party members went to vote
in their primaries, for Massalla won the place on the list reserved for a new
immigrant.

Labor leaders, however, still had the problem of the votes of the immigrants from the former Soviet Union. And so they called for a special
election to fill the place vacated by Ora Namir, the minister of social welfare. Namir was the only woman Labor minister in the government, and
she won the twenty-sixth place in the primaries; Dalia Itzik, a young fire-
brand, won ninth place. This raised the delicate problem of which woman
would serve in the cabinet if Shimon Peres were elected. The problem was
solved by convincing Namir to resign her cabinet position and accept an
appointment as ambassador to China, and by calling a special primary to
fill her slot on the list. And this time, to solve the immigrant representation
problem, only Labor Party members who were new immigrants from the
former Soviet Union were entitled to run for the spot. As designed, a
"new" immigrant from the Soviet Union, Sofia Landver, in the country
since the 1970s and not coincidentally Peres's Russian language teacher,
won the race against weak opposition and filled the slot Namir had originally won. Either because of this manipulation or in spite of it, many of
the new immigrants voted for Natan Sharansky's Israel b'Aliyah list.

It is fascinating to consider the organizational implications of different kinds and degrees of connection with a party, and the meaning of a
high and a low ratio involving these categories. The categories are voters,
members, and those actually participating in party affairs. The leadership
of a party must keep in mind these different types of constituents, and the
timing of appeals to each group must be different. Ideally these three

groups should overlap at the highest numerical level possible, but most people do not become members, let alone activists. A party with high numbers of voters, members, and activists would indicate great appeal and a high likelihood of stability for future elections. A party that registered a high number of voters but a low number of members could celebrate for that one election, but would have to suspect that its performance over time might be unsteady. It would not be unusual for a party in this position to begin a campaign for new members immediately after the election. If the number of members was nearly the number of voters, the party would have a firm nucleus of voter support but might have exhausted its potential because it was not successful in recruiting voters who were not members.

Table 6.1 contains the numbers of voters, members, and those who voted in the primaries for selected parties in 1996 and the ratios between the pairs of numbers. The three religious parties, Shas, Agudat Israel, and the NRP exist in different organizational cultures. The highest ratio of voters to members was for the haredi parties Shas and Aguda, mostly because membership in the party alone is meaningless in these ultra-Orthodox, non-Zionist parties, the former Sephardi, the latter Ashkenazi. Their ranks are fed by congregations of faithful worshippers and students of the Torah, which band together with other communities to form the myriad of sects and courtyards allegiant to diverse rabbinical authorities. Matters of policy and appointments to official positions are controlled by the respective Councils of Torah Sages and are not issues of participatory democracy. Political membership, meetings, and primaries are out of place and unnecessary for these parties.

Shas and Aguda are as close to total parties as one can find in mid-1990s Israel, and their organizations nurture their followers in activities along much of the social, economic, and cultural spectrum. Both parties are committed to the well-being of their membership, providing schools outside the national educational system but largely funded from the public treasury, and both are active in procuring government funding to construct housing in communities earmarked for their membership, and in providing other goods and services. Although there are no manifestations of democratic process, the allegiance of the faithful is very impressive. Many Sephardim who had voted Likud in the past voted for Netanyahu and Shas in 1996 out of identification with or nostalgia for the world of tradition that the party represented.

If Shas and Aguda are classic cadre parties, the National Religious Party is perhaps the clearest extant example of the type of mass party organization that characterized the first generation of Israeli politics. Its member-voter ratio is the lowest of the parties presented in table 6.1. The

TABLE 6.1
MEMBERS, PRIMARY VOTERS, AND VOTERS IN SELECTED PARTIES, 1996

	Labor	Likud	NRP	Meretz	Tzomet	Shas	Aguda[a]
Members	261,169	178,582	107,772	34,111[b]	6,414	141	101
Primary voters	194,788	91,907	—	18,968	3,045	—	—
Voters	818,741	767,401[c]	240,271	226,275	[c]	259,796	98,657
Approximate ratios							
Voters/members	3:1	4:1	2:1	7:1	[c]	1842:1	976:1
Members/primaries	1.3:1	2:1	—	2:1	2:1	—	—
Voters/primaries	4:1	8:1	—	15:1	[c]	—	—

a. Part of United Torah Jewry.
b. Members of the three constituent parties, and members of Meretz.
c. Ran on Likud-Gesher-Tzomet list in elections.

NRP has a vibrant membership based in the synagogues affiliated with its movement; it is closely involved in religious state-supported educational institutions ranging from preschool through universities; it is identified with special training-and-Torah-learning units in the army; it prides itself on the organizational and economic commitment by the party's leaders and most of its members to the settlements in the territories; and it has a very active youth group. The NRP preserves a form of total party activity originally developed and perfected by the parties of the secular socialist left, but which has increasingly vanished from Israeli society.

Labor, the mother of mass-membership parties in Israel, in 1996 retained some signs of its organizational past. One such indicator was its voter-member ratio of 3:1, which indicates that many of its 818,741 voters were organizationally involved in the party. The Likud, less than a mass-membership party but more than a cadre one, had a lower voter-member ratio. Its appeal had to be beyond organizational attachments; the Likud evidently overcame its organizational weakness with an attractive candidate in Netanyahu. But presenting a shared list with Tzomet did not seem to bring the electoral success its leaders sought.

A party would want to have many voters and just about as many members. While its ratio may be steady, this might be misleading if the vote for the party diminishes. This is the dilemma faced by both Likud and Labor. The total vote has become more fragmented, with parties with a higher voter-member ratio increasing their strength among voters at a much faster rate than do the mass-membership parties. The result is a fractionalized party system, with a nearly equal division in 1996 between the two candidates for prime minister. For both Likud and Labor in 1996, the primaries were crucial moments in the life of the parties, which in turn would likely have an impact on the choice of ministers in the government formed after the election by the prime minister. The primaries may have been good for the activists, but they failed to generate the popular support needed to win the elections convincingly.

Of the secular parties, Meretz had the highest voters-to-members ratio. Meretz fielded relatively small groups of leaders and militants but was able to attract others at a high rate. For each member of Meretz, seven voters chose the party in the 1996 elections. Meretz was a conglomerate of three parties: Mapam had 15,517 members, the Citizens Rights Movement 5,132 members, and Shinui 1,311. Before the 1996 elections, primaries were held first in each of the constituent parties, followed by a ranking by all Meretz members (including an additional 12,151 members of Meretz not associated with any of the three constituent parties) according to a key reflecting the relative sizes of the three parties. The three constituent parties agreed to merge into one party before the next elections. The ratio alone could not predict Meretz's future, but it is clear that the party would face organizational problems different from those of Labor or Likud.

Party Institutions

The major feature of internal party structure, in addition to the primaries for the parties that hold them, is indirect representation. This is "an admirable means of banishing democracy while pretending to apply it."[20] Its major characteristic is simple: members cast their ballots only once for the broadest-based instititution of the party. This broadest-based institution elects the next-highest-level institution, the members of the third tier are elected by those on the second, and so on. This arrangement facilitates control of the party by a group or groups of activists while professing concern for the demands and wishes of the broader membership. Indirect democracy can be thought of as a many-layered pyramid with each layer reduced or distilled to form the layer above it until the topmost layer is finally reached. Each layer is called on to select only the layer directly above it, but all higher layers can commit the party as a whole, unless specifically prevented from doing so by the constitution.

Anyone with experience with administration will recognize the pattern and will even applaud its logic and appreciate its potential efficiency. If something is to be done, endless debate and mass decision making can be disruptive and time-consuming. On the other hand, this special version of democracy prevents the sustained control of the organization by the rank and file and lends itself to control and manipulation by groups of activists.

The typical structure of an Israeli party is a multitiered one that includes a broad-based convention, a narrower-based central committee that elects an executive committee, which in turn selects a secretariat. While the number of tiers and their respective sizes may change, the general principle applies. As a rule, the more tiers between the mass membership and the leadership, the more unlikely direct democratic control or, in other words, the more indirect the form of representation.

There is a great temptation in this setting to perpetuate the power of supporters and friends and to shut out the opposition—the very essence of oligarchic organization. As Duverger notes: "Party congresses are just like a meeting of employees facing their employers: obviously the former will tend to keep in office the latter, whose creatures they are."[21]

The major parties in Israel were all constructed on the basis of indirect representation. The Likud convention in 1996 had 3,300 members, its secretariat and executive council about 500. The 1996 Labor Party had a 2,847-member convention, which elected a center of 1,240 members, which selected a leadership bureau of 152 members, which elected a smaller executive. Obviously power becomes distilled to a very refined degree in this situation. The selection of the center becomes crucial in controlling the party, and great efforts are made to achieve a list of center members that will be selected by unanimous consensus. Because so many competing groups struggled for representation in the center in 1981, for example, the Labor Party enlarged the number of center members from 880 to 1,150. This allowed many groups to feel politically satisfied, made many activists proud to be center members, and maintained the proportionate power relations within the party.

Mapam's convention in 1996 had more than 1,100 members, its center some 600, and its executive 50. In addition, it had a twenty-five-member committee and a select committee made up of the general secretary, the political secretary, and the center secretary. Mapam used a method of rotating members of the council in order to afford greater participation. The membership of the convention was constructed so that 45 percent of members were from Kibbutz Haarzi, 45 percent from urban branches, and 10 percent from moshavim and Arab sectors.

The NRP convention's delegates, selected by its 125,000 members, numbered 1,000; it convened in 1994 after a long period of disuse. In 1979, a joint convention was held by the Mizrachi and Hapoel Hamizrachi, and each was represented in the formal decision-making bodies, with an executive committee of 264 members. This committee was the joint meeting of two separate executive committees of the NRP and Hapoel Hamizrachi, with each group represented by seventy-six members. When the two groups sat in joint meeting, 110 additional members were added. Democrats might say that this increased representation; political analysts would point out that this increased honorific appointments and lowered the probabilities that key decisions would be made.

Party conventions are the supreme governing bodies of parties, but they provide imperfect examples of democratic practice. The most important point is that most party conventions do not result from secret elections by members of the party. Elections in many parties for the convention turn into an act confirming the existing leadership of the branch. In all the Israeli parties the vote for a convention delegate is for an individual, with the exception of the NRP, in which the election is by list. While it may be possible for an opposition group to organize successfully in a district or two or in a few branches, it is almost inconceivable for an opposition group to pose a serious challenge to the leadership of the party at the convention because of the enormity of the organizational task facing it. If one must canvass hundreds of branch members in order to be elected, let alone elect enough convention delegates around the country with similar views, the advantage obviously lies with established party leaders and local activists. This is why successful opposition to the established leadership is rarely fielded from the grassroots. What is more likely is for dissension among leaders to galvanize the grassroots into action.

Often, local elections are dispensed with altogether. For Herut's party convention in 1975, only 11 out of 100 party branches held elections, the others being appointed by agreements worked out by local activists. This arrangement has characterized the Independent Liberals as well.[22]

Yet another limitation of the democratic nature of the party convention lies in the fact that additional members are often appointed to the convention by the convention without undergoing election anew. For example, it is customary to elect *en bloc,* as delegates to the new convention, notables of the party such as ministers, Knesset members, and members of the outgoing central committee. This serves the dual function of adding more establishment votes and avoiding the embarrassment of having a national leader lose his election to the party's convention. Usually there is an upward limit to the number of additional members permitted in this fashion, and often they serve in an advisory capacity to the convention without the right to vote.

The more supreme a political body, the less authoritative it is. The cynical point of view sums up the general assessment of party conventions in Israeli politics. Party conventions are large, unwieldy affairs needing careful control. This control is almost always provided by the party leadership. Usually conventions are staged for public relations purposes; they attempt to portray a party characterized by harmony, cooperation, and common cause. There have been notable exceptions to this: The 1942 and 1965 Mapai conventions predated the splits in the party, and the 1981 convention was the site of Peres's victory over Rabin for head of the party. It was at the Herut convention that Geula Cohen attacked Begin for the Camp David agreement, left the party, and set up Tehiya. But, on the whole, party conventions are orchestrated demonstrations of organizational control and political compromise.

Party leaders generally promote a "central list." In the case of Mapai, and later Labor, this list usually included leaders of the local labor councils who were members of the party, leading party figures in the municipality or local council, and key members of the secretariat of the local party council. When contests develop, they tend to be over personalities and not over national or party issues. In the 1964 election for Mapai delegates, only six out of eighty-four branches had hard-fought contests, and these were related to personality clashes. And this at a time when the nation was agonizing over the Lavon Affair and Ben-Gurion's call for a judicial investigation.

The convention delegates, elected and appointed, are usually dependent on the party and the leadership. Sometimes this dependency is material, as when large numbers of delegates are employed in party or party-related jobs.[23] Sometimes it is political, as when a delegate's continued political success depends on a good relationship with the party hierarchy and leaders. Often the dependency is psychological, because delegates develop feelings of organizational loyalty and solidarity with the party. However it arises, delegates' dependency makes them instruments in the hands of party leaders, not active representatives of the rank and file.

Party leaders feel they have the power to commit their membership regardless of the loose linkage they have with members. This is clearly seen by the fact that the founding convention of newly merged parties in Israel has never been preceded by an internal election among the membership for convention delegates called on to ratify the merger. This was true of Mapam in 1948, of the NRP in 1956, of the Liberals in 1961, of the Labor Party in 1968, and of the Likud in 1988. The composition of the merged party's convention was arrived at through negotiation with leaders of the merging parties, and delegates were appointed by agreement. Should we be surprised that the conventions meekly ratified the mergers?

The key body in determining the smooth operation of the convention is the standing committee. This committee has had total control over the convention in the Mapai and Labor parties, controlling the agenda and the preparation of the convention. It generally has presented proposals to the convention that were adopted unanimously. The control of the standing committee has been the crucial element in shaping the convention and those bodies that determined its composition. Once the control of the committee was gained, the rest was only a matter of detail, best understood in terms of ritual and ceremony.[24]

The frequency of the convention is also a sore point of Israeli party democratic practice. The NRP's constitution, for example, calls for a convention once every fourth year (although the constitution does allow for the postponement of the convention). In reality, conditions are much worse; NRP conventions were held in 1956, 1963, 1969, and 1973. All conventions except that of 1973 were "agreed" conventions, with the leaders' factions determining the delegates to the convention among themselves without holding elections in the party.[25]

The convention, the supreme body of most Israeli parties, provides an imperfect link with the membership because of the shortcuts used in its elections. The committee then becomes the agent that embodies the principles of indirect representation by selecting the party's center. The center, a smaller group than the convention, meets more often and plays a more central role in the ongoing life of the party. In the past, the center approved the party's platform and list of candidates and debated important policy issues. As we have seen, much effort is made to select for a convention those who will conform to the leadership's wishes. The efforts extended regarding the selection of the center are no less intense. The selection of the center is the focus of great political activity on the part of political activists and party hacks because the best way to determine the outcome of a vote is to control the composition of the electing body. On the surface the procedure is smooth enough, with a nominating committee presenting a suggested list to the convention, a list that is almost always approved. The real action is behind the scenes in the nominating committee where intense political and personal pressure is often applied to increase the membership in the center of this or that group. It is the job of the nominating group (whether that be a special committee, the standing committee, or a small group of party leaders) to accommodate competing demands and end the process of selection of the center with a show of party unity. The factional parties, the NRP and Liberals, saw to it that the factional division in the convention was simply perpetuated in the center.

The center tends to number a few hundred members and meets no more than a dozen times a year, if that. Generally, it has the last word in electing the secretary-general and approving the party platform. In most parties in the past it was this group that rubber-stamped its approval of the list of candidates for the Knesset.[26]

The center is a microcosm of the convention whose importance is as symbolic as it is practical. What the center does is choose the body next up in the hierarchy, whatever its name. This smaller group is more powerful. Except that when the party is in power, the leaders who made the small-party institution powerful by their presence and personal authority are concentrating their efforts on other matters. When most of the leaders are government ministers, their consultations become crucial not only for national policy but for party policy as well.

Another modifier of the rule of the inverse relationship between size and power of party committees is that the top party leaders must be involved. During the years that Herut was in opposition, the practice of the party was for the parliamentary delegation to decide the party's stand on issues and report to other party institutions. The dominance of the parliamentary party assured that its path would be followed by the party. When in power, the parliamentary party was overshadowed by the government and its Herut/Likud leaders. Netanyahu's original period as prime minister displayed a total disregard for the Likud and its institutions. The direct election of the prime minister gave power to the leader and diminished the importance of the party institutions.

Ben-Gurion's interest in party affairs shifted when he became secretary-general of the Histadrut and then leader of the Jewish Agency. As prime minister he had even less time for party affairs, and much of the real decision making regarding party policy shifted to the Mapai ministers in the government. This process became even more acute in 1954 when the executive of the party was increased to nineteen members in order to accommodate pressures from ministers, parliamentarians, Histadrut officials, party branches, women, young members, ethnic groups, kibbutzim, moshavim, and workers in *moshavot* (smaller agricultural towns). Moshe Sharett, then prime minister, instituted meetings that consisted of Mapai ministers together with the secretary-general of the Histadrut and in effect bypassed the executive. Sharett was anxious to have the support of his colleagues and needed this form of collective leadership, especially after having followed the charismatic Ben-Gurion in office. When Ben-Gurion returned to office, he continued the meetings of this informal, extraconstitutional device.[27]

Once decisions were made in this fashion, the participants were expected to follow the line in public and see to it that it was adhered to in decisions made by the party and governmental bodies. Such an informal network is infinitely stronger than formal constitutional provisions, but it relies on a very high degree of group solidarity and common purpose. A leader who finds himself at the head of such a network is blessed; he can utilize the formal arrangements in a much more successful manner.

Developments in Mapai continued in the same direction; after Secretary-General Lavon of the Histadrut stopped participating in the meetings in 1959, Sharett's committee became a committee of cabinet ministers. The executive had grown to thirty members, and since no real power was at stake, more groups could be given representation. And so, as we should have come to expect by now, another, more compact group was selected. This was the leadership bureau, and in establishing it (without any constitutional sanction) the executive abdicated much of its authority.

This is not the place to document the ins and outs of intraparty politics, but the general picture is clear. Groups jockey for power, and the organizational structure is accommodated to the tides of battle. Control over the party is at stake, and resources are not spared in the effort. The mass of members is generally not brought into the fight—probably most of them do not know of it. Temporary truces are reached, usually giving time to marshal forces for the next battle. When a leader emerges whom the party can rally around, his authority can be brought to bear if he is willing to alienate one side in order to find favor in the eyes of the other. The infighting consumes enormous amounts of time and energy. While the politicians' ambitions and future careers are at stake, it is also important because the winners will be the ones to determine policy.

A larger number of tiers generally means that effective control is that much farther from the rank and file. Additional tiers are usually introduced to solve organizational problems, as we saw in the case of Sharett, and not to introduce antidemocratic tendencies into the organization. The proliferation of tiers usually has its origins in a desire to settle problems or distribute representation among the groups, sections, leaders, officeholders, pretenders to power, and bureaucracies that make up the party.

The impression should not be given that the internal life of a party is static, held in control by the ruling oligarchy. Often the contrary is the case, with the oligarchy striving mightily to keep diverse elements of the party satisfied. Turbulence occurs especially when a group thinks that it should be stronger in the party hierarchy than it actually is in terms of positions, representation, or prestige. Sometimes it can be bought off easily by being provided with more jobs for its people or by having its leader appointed to an honorary position. Sometimes it can be co-opted. Co-optation is a process by which dissidents are included as a minority in decision-making bodies, making them privy to deliberations and responsible for decisions without there being a real possibility that their points of view or program will carry the day. Sometimes there is no other choice but to accommodate them by granting them real power; because replacing members of existing bodies would likely upset other fine-tuned relationships, one strategy would be to bypass existing groups by setting up yet another body within the decision-making structure of the party.

Efficient structure or neat textbooklike organizational charts are not goals of political parties; control and political success are. Even if the organizational structures are messy, the questions we should ask ourselves as political scientists must center on political effectiveness, control, collegial relations, and the generation of an image of unified leadership. The latter will likely count for far more in the end than conforming to the abstract, and unproved, rules of rational administrative science. Party structures become more, rather than less, complex because changes tend to be made to existing bodies. It is unusual to start from scratch. Solving a problem by patching an already barely understandable structure tends not to clarify that structure but to make it even harder to understand.

Once the process is entered into, the momentum toward oligarchy increases quickly. Defenders of the form insist that it provides a satisfactory solution to the conflicting demands of democracy and organizational effiency, allowing the membership to vote and yet concentrating power in the hands of the party leadership. Critics of the system identify this structure as one of the prime resources in the hands of the party leadership, which allows it to perpetuate its control over the organization. For if enough members of the broad-based convention can coalesce around a candidate or point of view, they can see to it that their view prevails in the smaller tier above the convention. In that body, the majority point of view of the convention can also be perpetuated but is likely to be distilled and made stronger. As the body becomes smaller, the proportion of those with divergent views is likely to shrink. This, critics say, is the ultimate result of the system and its principal fault.

The primaries involve the membership in parties that conduct them. Regarding the broad-based representative bodies, the system does not ignore them but tends to convert them to rubber stamps. Sometimes decisions or nominations are brought before broad-based party groups and are approved by near-unanimous votes; the authority of the leadership is often brought into play, and the convention is not about to upset the precarious compromises worked out in late-night sessions. The convention feels a sense of responsibility to the party and its leadership and typically abdicates its authority. This very understandable, very human, reaction still causes critics of the system to question whether the party must remain as centralized and hierarchical as it typically is in Israel.

It should be pointed out very clearly that this is not a problem invented by the Zionist movement or even by Israeli politicians. This is a fundamental problem in the life of organizations and is faced by kibbutzim, labor unions, university councils, voluntary organizations—by any organization that considers it a positive value to order its internal life in a democratic manner.

To those who despair of democracy in view of the inevitability of oligarchy, Michels's words are important. He expresses that famous dictum about democracy compared with all other forms: "If we wish to estimate the value of democracy, we must do so in comparison with its converse, pure aristocracy. The defects inherent in democracy are obvious. It is none the less true that as a form of social life we must choose democracy as the least of evils." His view of the role of scientific observation is an important one. Democracy is to be desired, but oligarchy will always remain. The goal must be to put some limit on the absoluteness of oligarchy. For this we need detachment and objective analysis. "Nothing but a serene and frank examination of the oligarchical dangers of a democracy will enable us to minimize these dangers, even though they can never be entirely avoided."[28]

Israeli political life, as exemplified by its parties, its organizations, the Knesset, and the government, is oligarchical and hierarchical. The changes that have occurred, the direct election of the prime minister and the primaries for instance, have provided choice among candidates to the rank and file at the expense of a collective vision and group responsibility. Politics, especially in its democratic form, means hard work, frustrations, and setbacks. Those who cherish democracy must ponder the appropriate balance among competing values. Those who work within the existing parties must learn the rules of representation and the secrets of organization. Those who despair of the existing parties and attempt to set up new structures must take into account that past history and the laws of social science indicate that their new organization will not be immune from the rules of oligarchy described here.

7. The Electoral System

The voting act is conditioned by influences and pressures brought to bear on the citizen and by political arrangements that characterize the system within which the vote takes place. Electoral laws have political consequences, hence many constitutional issues in the realm of elections—reapportionment, extension of suffrage, financing elections, type of ballot, use of voting machines, single-member district as opposed to proportional representation, rules of party and candidate eligibility, and formulas for distributing the leftover vote—are matters that provoke the politician's serious concern and attention. The multiplicity of electoral arrangements is clearly a monument to the ingenuity of political man and a manifestation of his striving for power. Far from being objective rules to regulate the game, electoral laws are never neutral; they favor one political rival at the expense of another.

Legal arrangements are not the only constraints on the system of political competition. Social and historical factors can be just as powerful in limiting the range of potential outcomes the development of a system may produce. These factors may not be causal in determining who shall rule and for how long, but they set parameters on the political struggle and its possible outcome.

Elections for the Prime Minister and the Knesset

Israel conducted direct elections for the prime minister for the first time in 1996. Until then, the Knesset had selected the prime minister, as is customary in parliamentary systems. The new system provides that the tenure of the prime minister and the Knesset shall be four years long and that they shall be elected simultaneously but separately by the voters. This dual system, under which the Knesset and the prime minister are selected separately, is a major departure from usual practice. The capstone of the parliamentary system is that the people elect the parliament and the parliament selects the prime minister. The prime minister serves as long as the confidence of the parliament is maintained. Once that confidence is lost, either a new government is formed or new elections are held, depending on the political circumstances and the laws of the country.[1]

Now the prime minister is elected directly by the voters using a winner-take-all system, and a second round between the two candidates getting the most votes in the first round two weeks later if there is no winner in the first round. The old rules remain in place for electing the Knesset, using a strict system of proportional representation. This dual system combines methods familiar in presidential and parliamentary systems and is unique among electoral systems. However, this major constitutional undertaking lacks a coherent constitutional concept.

The Knesset may remove the prime minister by a special vote of eighty members, on which new elections for the prime minister take place. The prime minister, with the agreement of the president, can dissolve the Knesset; such a step would also end the prime minister's tenure and would force new elections for both. The Knesset can also remove the prime minister by expressing no confidence by a majority vote (sixty-one votes) or by failing to pass the national budget, but then new elections for both prime minister and Knesset are held.

In contrast, Israel's Knesset is elected by a proportional representation list system and very few procedural or technical obstacles face a group that chooses to compete. All registered parties may run in the election. Registration of parties is regulated by law and is quite easy, providing that the party does not oppose the existence of Israel as a Jewish and democratic state, that it does not advocate racism, and that the party is not a cover for illegal activity. In addition, it is not permitted to register a party using an offensive or misleading name, or using a name that is the same or similar to one used by another party. The minimum age for a candidate is twenty-one.

One hundred citizens may apply to the responsible official to be recognized as a political party; the Registrar is to determine that the party is run in a democratic manner and that its platform is consistent with democracy, that it keeps records of its accounts, and that its income is reported to the State Controller. A new party must pay the equivalent of about $10,000 to cover the costs of announcing its registration in the newspaper; a party not represented in the outgoing Knesset that wishes to run in the next elections must also submit the signatures of 1,500 supporters.

The list must be submitted some thirty-five days before the election date. The Central Elections Committee, made up of representatives of the various parties in proportion to their strength in the outgoing Knesset and headed by a Supreme Court justice, is responsible for conducting the election, including the approval of lists. The law that applied in 1988 gave the committee the right to disallow lists that denied the Jewish nature of the State of Israel, opposed its democratic regime, or were racist. The committee prohibited Rabbi Meir Kahane's Kach party from running in the 1988 elections because of its racist and antidemocratic platform.[2] An attempt to disallow an Arab-Jewish mixed list called the Progressive List for Peace, on the grounds that its call for the establishment of a Palestinian state negated

Israel as a Jewish state, failed. Attempts to disallow the two lists were repeated before the 1992 elections, except that Kahane had been assassinated in New York in 1990, and a "Kahane Lives" list was formed and disallowed. The Progressive List for Peace ran in 1992 and failed to win the 1.5 percent needed.

In 1996, the Registrar reported that thirty-one parties were duly registered, but twenty lists actually ran. Some parties chose not to run in the elections for various reasons. Two lists each contained three parties: (1) Likud-Gesher-Tzomet and (2) Meretz (CRM, Mapam, and Shinui). Yahadut Hatorah was formed by the merged list of two parties, Agudat Israel and Degel Hatorah. Two other lists withdrew from competition, although their ballots were nonetheless available to voters. One list, headed by Dr. Ahmed Tibi, concluded that the list would not get the needed 1.5 percent of the vote for representation and would thus deprive other Arab lists from needed votes. Another extreme right-wing party made the same move from the other end of the spectrum.

The voter chooses the entire list as submitted and cannot alter the order of names on the list or delete candidates, as is possible in some other electoral systems. If a party wins a third of the vote, entitling it to forty seats, the first forty names on the list become members of the Knesset. If during the Knesset's tenure a seat is vacated, the next person on the list automatically fills it. Neither by-elections (as in Great Britain) nor appointments (as in the United States) are permitted.

Voting for the Knesset is actually done by choosing the letter symbols of the competing lists. Each party chooses a Hebrew letter or group of letters, which must be approved by the Central Elections Committee, and campaigning and voting are conducted using these letter symbols. An interesting sidelight of the campaign is the symbolism involved in the parties' choices.

The letter combination the Labor-Mapam Alignment requested and was assigned was AMT—*aleph, mem, taf.* A good argument could be made for this combination, since the *aleph* (revealingly, the first letter of the alphabet) was traditionally the letter of Mapai, the *mem* the symbol of Mapam, and the *taf* that of Ahdut Haavoda, all of which were in the Alignment until 1984. But this special combination of letters was more than a throwback to the days when these parties ran as separate entities. For AMT (pronounced *emet*) means "truth" in Hebrew. And who can be against truth? The letter B used by the NRP and the D used by Poalei Agudat Israel, both religious parties, have both been used in campaign rhetoric in highly symbolic and suggestive ways.[3] So was the Z (besides the name of the letter, a signifier for the male sexual organ) used in the 1970s by the Black Panthers, a group of Sephardi Jews who felt they were discriminated against by the authorities, and by the Male Rights in the Family Party in 1996, indicating succinctly that each group felt that it was being "screwed."

If the list submitted by the party (or a group of parties) receives 1.5 percent or more of the vote, it wins representation in the 120-seat Knesset. The citizen, on entering the voting booth, chooses the letter or group of letters assigned to the party he or she wishes to vote for and places the slip of paper with the letter(s) of his choice into a blue election envelope. (A yellow envelope is used for the prime minister vote.) Votes are counted on a nationwide basis, and Knesset seats are allocated in direct proportion to the strength of the list at the polls.

The Date of Elections

Elections in Israel are held every four years unless earlier elections are called. There is a date for the elections set in law, but it can be changed if the Knesset approves a different date. In other words, the date set for elections, like most topics in Israel, can become intensely political. The general instruction in the Basic Law: Knesset sets the tenure of the Knesset at four years unless early elections are called. It provides that the elections shall be held on the third Tuesday of the Hebrew month of Heshvan (which occurs around November) of the year in which the Knesset ends its term, unless the previous year is a leap year according to the Hebrew lunar calendar (which happens seven times in each nineteen-year cycle), in which case the elections shall be held on the first Tuesday of Heshvan.

The tenure of the Knesset has been substantially shortened three times and has been lengthened once. The 1951, 1961, and 1984 elections were each scheduled earlier than the previous elections, held in 1949, 1959, and 1981 respectively, would have mandated. In 1973, when elections were scheduled for the end of October and the Yom Kippur War broke out at the beginning of that month, elections were postponed for two months, until the end of December.

The ruling party would probably attempt to manipulate the election date for political advantage, if it thought it could. But because the campaign period is so long and political developments are so unpredictable, Israeli politicians seem to understand that trying to turn a swing in public opinion into electoral advantage is a risky bet. Shortened Knesset terms in the past have generally resulted from political crises. After the Six-Day War in 1967, at certain stages of the peace negotiations with Egypt in 1978, and after the Rabin assassination in 1995, the Alignment, Likud, and Labor, respectively, probably could have benefited from early elections, but they were not called.

One explanation is that elections must be called well in advance. A Knesset law mandates a 100-day cooling-off period for a civil servant who wishes to run in the elections (although in 1996 it was shortened to 60 days because an early election date was decided on). Since many parties infuse their political ranks with fresh blood from the military, diplomatic, or administrative services, it is customary to set the date for elections well past the 100-day period. A politician knows that in three and a half months his rosy prognostication might well change, and he might regret the move.

The history of the 1996 election date provides a case in point. The Labor Party and Shimon Peres, its leader, enjoyed a cascade of popular support in the months following Rabin's assassination in November 1995. Since the government was in the midst of negotiations with Syria over the future of the Golan Heights and Lebanon, however, it remained committed to the mandated election date of late October 1996. Peres preferred an election campaign based on a draft peace treaty with Syria and thought that face-to-face negotiations between President Assad of Syria and Peres were necessary to reach an agreement in time. Assad finally agreed to face-to-face negotiations but would provide no firm date for the meeting. Peres's assessment then was that Syria would not be forthcoming, and Labor opted for elections at the end of May 1996, and the party leaders set out to reach an agreement regarding the election date with the leaders of other parties.

The crowded Hebrew and Israeli calendars of the spring (Passover, Holocaust Day, Memorial Day, Independence Day, Lag BaOmer, Jerusalem Day, the feast of Shavuot, and memorial commemorations for those killed in the 1967 Six-Day War and the 1982 Lebanese war) combined with very practical political considerations to make the task of setting a date difficult.

Labor favored holding elections in May. This preference was influenced by the wording of the new law regarding the runoff elections for the direct prime minister vote and by patterns of behavior in leisure time by Israelis. The Likud and the religious parties preferred June. At this point, it seemed likely that a runoff election would take place for the prime minister. This was before two of the other announced candidates for prime minister, Rafael ("Raful") Eitan of Tzomet and David Levy of Gesher, swung their support to Netanyahu for prime minister as part of the deal they had worked out to form a joint list with Likud. A runoff, if required, would take place on the Tuesday "two weeks after the announcement of the original vote results." If the first round of elections were held in the beginning of June, the official results announced a few days later, and the runoff two weeks after that, many Peres voters might be out of the country on summer vacation on the day of the runoff.

There were also constraints on calling the elections too early. The official in the Interior Ministry in charge of overseeing the elections warned that holding elections on 20 May would not give his office enough time to update the lists and include in the official roster all those who were eighteen years of age on election day. Labor wanted the voting done by 20 June, the last day of classes in Israel's high schools. After that date (and certainly by 30 June, when the elementary school students finish class), many families make travel plans and the national attention is difficult to focus. Besides, the European Cup Soccer Finals were to be held in that period, and the politicians wanted no distractions from their show. Summer elections in the past had dealt unkind blows to Labor, which reasoned that its relatively more affluent voters were more likely to be away than were those of the Likud and the religious parties. Moreover, the groundswell of grief over the Rabin assassination seemed to be spearheaded by young, first-time voters. The risks of their being shut out for administrative reasons if the elections were held too early, or of their being out of the country if the elections were to be extended to late June or to July, seemed real.

One practical thing that could be done to reduce the risk was to control some of the uncertainty by having a firm date for the second round of voting. Even though this timing was part of one of the Basic Laws (which are supposedly the building blocks of Israel's constitution), the politicians had no qualms about altering it to fit their immediate needs. The revised wording placed the runoff two weeks after the original elections, rather than two weeks after the announcement of the results.

The Likud preferred June, but also favored 21 May, a few days after Jerusalem Day. The Likud felt that the call for keeping Jerusalem united as Israel's capital, and the media attention to Jerusalem on that day, played in their favor and against Peres's more conciliatory positions. But 21 May was only days before Shavuot, the holy day commemorating the receiving of the Torah at Mount Sinai. For haredim and other religious Jews, the days preceding the holyday are for prayer and withdrawal in symbolic preparation for receiving God's word. The thought that some 300,000 haredim might be too withdrawn to turn out and vote made the Likud and Netanyahu reconsider the May date.

In the end, the elections were scheduled for Wednesday, 29 May 1996. In the past, elections had always taken place on Tuesdays. But political expediency led to calendar flexibility. While Israeli politicians are ever cognizant of political advantage (even in such matters as setting the date of elections), it is very doubtful that their willingness to manipulate the situation is matched by their success in affecting the results. At the end of February 1996, when these calculations were taking place, no one knew of the series of suicide bombings awaiting Israel or of the inconclusive result of the

Grapes of Wrath campaign in Lebanon, nor of the impact of these events on the voters.

Constitutional Provisions

The Basic Law: Knesset (section 4) states that "the Knesset shall be elected in general, national, direct, equal, secret and proportional elections," and section 3b of the Basic Law: Government provides that elections of the prime minister shall be "general, national, direct, equal and secret." The six requirements for the election of the Knesset are the legal basis for the relatively pure form of proportional representation embodied in the election of Israel's Knesset.

"General," allowing no discrimination among qualified voters. Every Israeli citizen eighteen years of age and older is entitled to vote. The issue of suffrage was a major scene of political battle in Western democracies. Israel was spared these battles, always opting for universal suffrage. In the Yishuv period, religious groups demanded the exclusion of women from the list of voters because, the argument ran, women have no role to play in public affairs. So furious was the debate that some groups boycotted the elections of Yishuv institutions because of the rules on women's suffrage in the election. Others permitted only males to vote and then had the weight of the male vote doubled in order to compensate for the lack of women's votes.[4]

"National," that votes will be counted on a national basis, although administrative provisions are made for conducting elections and reporting results on regional, city, district, subdistrict, and precinct levels.

"Direct," that each voter must complete the voting act by himself or herself. No delegation of authority, except for the blind or infirm, is permitted. Absentee balloting is not permitted, although special arrangements are made for persons serving with the Israel Defense Forces on election day, for those in official positions abroad and their families (3,638 eligible voters in 1996), for sailors working on Israeli flagships (415 sailors on nineteen ships), and for prisoners. Persons hospitalized on election day were added to those permitted to vote even though they did not come to their polling stations; this added another 30,000 in 1996, enough to select one Knesset member.

"Equal," that each voter has the same amount of influence as every other voter. This ideal is probably unattainable in the real world because in all electoral systems some votes are "wasted," and the electors of "wasted" votes have less influence on the election results than do other voters. The percentage of nonvalid or "wasted" votes in the Knesset vote was 2.2 in 1996. This included those who voted for parties that did not receive the minimum 1.5 percent as well as those who voted improperly, for example by putting two ballot slips in the envelope. In the balloting for the prime minister the rate of invalid votes was 4.8 percent, including those who put in their envelopes the name of neither candidate. Since 1981, the rate of invalid votes had not been higher than 1 percent. In the 1955–73 period it ranged between a high of 4.2 percent (1969) and a low of 2.1 percent (1973).

On the whole, the Israeli electoral system receives high grades for equality of its election of the Knesset, with two reservations to this generalization, discussed below.

"Secret," that it not be possible to identify the vote of the voter.

"Proportional" (pertaining only to the Knesset elections; this provision is not included in the law regarding the direct election of the prime minister, since it is based on a winner-take-all principle), that each list be represented according to its strength in the electorate, providing that it achieves at least 1.5 percent of the vote.

The two reservations regarding the equality principle stem from the fact that, ultimately, the result of the electoral process is to select the Knesset. The 120-member Knesset is selected by determining the "quota" of each seat. If there are 1.2 million valid votes, a list will win a seat in the Knesset for each 10,000 votes that it gets. But reality is not that neat. Parties do not win votes in increments of 10,000; instead, one party wins 9,994 and the other 14,968. What is to be done?

The first reservation regarding the generalization of the equality of the system used to select the Knesset is that the minimum needed for winning a seat is 1.5 percent of the valid voters. That is, for the first seat in our hypothetical example, 10,000 votes would not be enough. One and one-half percent of 1.2 million is 18,000, and that is the number of votes it would take to win the party's first seat. A higher price must be paid for this first seat than for those following it. The second seat is cheapest by far, since 2/120 = 1.67 percent, only 0.17 percent more than the 1.5 percent already paid for the first seat.

This minimum rate was raised before the 1992 elections with the express purpose of limiting the number of single-member parties. And it worked very well. Single-member parties were eliminated in 1992, and the number of parties decreased in 1992 to ten from fifteen in 1988. In 1996, eleven parties won representation, and most received at least four seats, with only one winning two seats.

The second reservation concerns the distribution of the "surplus vote." Between 1961 and 1969 the party with the largest remainder won the vacant seat or seats. In 1949 and since 1973, the d'Hondt system has been used. Widely used in Europe, the method is popularly known in Israel as the Bader-Ofer Amendment, after the Likud and Alignment politicians who sponsored the bill and saw it through the legislative process.

The d'Hondt system provides for a floating quota after the original allocation of seats takes place. Each list has its quota recalculated in order to allocate the surplus votes; the new quota is the number of votes won by a party divided by the number of seats already allocated to that party plus one. Inflating the denominator in this manner obviously works in favor of larger parties to the detriment of smaller ones (see table 7.1).

The method works as its proponents desired. Of the three additional seats allocated in the 1973 elections, the Alignment won two and the Likud won one using the Bader-Ofer calculation. In 1977 the three largest parties (Likud, Alignment, and DMC) won a total of five additional seats compared to the largest remainder formula; the middle-sized NRP did not win or lose, but five small parties lost five Knesset seats among them.[5] In 1996, three of the six additional seats went to the two largest parties (two to Likud and one to Labor), the others going to smaller parties (see table 7.2).

Proponents of this deviation from the principle of equality argue that the relative size of the electorate that supports a list must also be taken into consideration in determining the allocation of seats. A party supported by a million voters must be treated differently from a party supported by 20,000 voters. The d'Hondt formula expresses this preferential treatment. Opponents argue that this is a case of the majority legislating against the minority; indeed, all the small parties in 1973 banded together, regardless of ideology, to oppose the passage of the Bader-Ofer Amendment. In a system in which the multiplicity of opinion and political organization is legitimate and even encouraged, it is unfortunate that the two large parties "ganged up" on the smaller ones, even if the overall damage to the principle of equal representation is relatively slight. In order to safeguard the principle of majority rule, the law states that a party will not win a majority of the seats in the Knesset if it fails to win a majority of the valid votes in the electorate. This contained, slightly, the hue and cry that the amendment generated.

An offsetting feature of the distribution system comes from *apparentement,* the French term for the formal linking of party lists at the stage at which parliamentary seats are allocated. The term roughly translates into English as "cartel" or "association,"[6] and is referred to as a surplus vote agreement in Hebrew. Party lists appear separately on the ballot and the initial allocation is for each party. If there are still seats to be distributed after the count is completed, parties that have entered an *apparentement* participate in the next stage, with the surpluses of the associated parties merged. In 1996, six surplus vote agreements were made (between

TABLE 7.1
LARGEST REMAINDER AND D'HONDT METHODS
OF ALLOCATING SURPLUS VOTES

Party	Votes	Seats	Surplus votes	Largest remainder	d'Hondt calculation	d'Hondt index	d'Hondt allocation
A	667,000	66	7,000	+1	667,000/67	9955	+1
B	415,000	41	5,000	0	415,000/42	9880	+1
C	118,000	11	8,000	+1	118,000/12	9833	0
Total	1,200,000	118					

KEY: Voters = 1,200,000; seats = 120; quota = 10,000.

TABLE 7.2

ISRAEL'S 1996 ELECTION RESULTS: LARGEST REMAINDER AND BADER-OFER METHODS OF ALLOCATING SURPLUS VOTES

Party	Votes	Seats based on quota	Numerical remainder	Largest remainder	Bader-Ofer calculation	Difference	Total
Labor	818,741	33	1,034	0	+1	+1	34
Likud-Gesher-Tzomet	767,401	30	24,031	+1	+2	+1	32
Shas	259,796	10	12,006	0	0	0	10
National Religious	240,271	9	17,260	+1	0	−1	9
Meretz	226,275	9	3,264	0	0	0	9
Israel b'Aliya	174,994	7	1,541	0	0	0	7
Hadash	129,455	5	5,560	0	0	0	5
United Torah Jewry	98,657	3	24,320	+1	+1	0	4
Third Way	96,474	3	22,137	+1	+1	0	4
Democratic Arab	89,514	3	15,177	+1	+1	0	4
Moledet	72,002	2	22,444	+1	0	−1	2
Total	2,973,580	114		6	6		120

NOTE: Minimum needed for representation (1.5%) = 45,782 votes.
KEY: Voters = 2,973,580; seats = 120; quota = 24,779.

Labor-Meretz, Likud-Shas, NRP–Yahadut Hatorah, the Third Way–Israel b'Aliyah, Hadash-Arab Democrats, and Moledet-Telem). The law states that each party of the *apparentement* agreement must win more than the minimum 1.5 percent of the vote; since Telem failed to do so, only five party-couples participated in the calculations.

To illustrate with the 1996 Knesset election results: The quota was 24,779 (2,973,580 votes for parties that achieved the 1.5 percent minimum divided by 120 seats). Division of the votes of each party by 24,779 allocated 114 seats, disregarding remainders, leaving 6 seats to be allocated to reach the full 120-member Knesset. The next step was to add together the votes and seats of those parties that had entered into surplus agreements. For example, Labor received 818,741 votes; when divided by the quota of 24,779, Labor received thirty-three seats, leaving 1,034 surplus votes after the original 33 seats had "used up" 817,707 votes (33 times 24,779). Meretz, which received 226,275 votes, won nine seats on the first allotment, leaving it 3,264 votes in surplus beyond the seats it had won.

Apparentement calls for the calculation of the new quota by dividing the two parties' *total* votes by the *total* of their seats plus one (1,045,016/43). The new quota was 24,302. Even though the two parties only had 4,298 surplus votes among them, that new quota was high enough to win for the two parties together one additional seat. The next step was to determine whether Labor or Meretz would get this seat, for which one reverted to the numbers won by the individual parties to the agreement. Labor's new quota was 24,080 (818,741/34), and the new quota for Meretz was 22,627 (226,275/10). Accordingly, Labor won this seat because its quota was higher.

Of the five surplus agreement party-couples, Likud and Shas won one extra seat each, Labor won one, Yahadut Hatorah won one, and the Third Way won one. Four of the parties that won extra seats were the smaller of the party-couples, confirming that *apparentement* modifies the other features of Israel's proportional representation system that favor the bigger vote-getting parties.

Electoral Reform

Electoral reform is an eternal feature of Israeli politics and discourse. The interest shown by the press and the involved public stems from the belief, strongly rooted in the Israeli political culture, that changes in the law can change behavior, that the formal rules of the game are central in determining the nature of the game and the way it is played. In a sense this is correct because the electoral laws ultimately determine who is elected and how much support they will have. But the debate regarding electoral reform is usually cast in much more general terms. Reform is championed as the way of changing the nature of the political system, making the members of the Knesset responsible and responsive to voters and altering the very moral climate of the country.

Electoral laws are as much a result as they are a cause of the political culture of a country. They project the political values and interests of the times and the ruling groups. Like other laws, they benefit certain interests and groups at the expense of other interests and groups.

The important point is that electoral laws have political consequences. They provide no magic formula for curing the ills of the nation. The laws are incapable of making politicians honest, officeholders responsible, or voters wise. In a simplistic sense, when officeholders perceive that it is in their or their party's interest to be more responsive to the demands of the electorate, they are likely to be so. A change in the electoral laws may also coincide with this perception, but the change in behavior (responsive officeholders) cannot be attributed solely to a change in the rules. The system is much too complex and the interrelations too many to use a simple mechanistic model to expect change in the political system as a result of legislation.

Israel is an example of a representative democracy with authoritative decisions being made only by the duly elected parliament.[7] Other countries have introduced techniques of direct democracy, most notably the referendum. The principle of republican government exemplified in the Israeli system rests on the belief that an elected parliament weighing alternative proposals will best serve the national interest, while forms of direct democracy run the risk of having shifting majorities of varying degrees of intensity making key decisions.

No referendum has ever been held in Israel, although the method has been suggested a number of times. Ben-Gurion suggested using it in 1955 to reform the electoral system. In 1958, Begin proposed legislation that would allow 100,000 citizens to demand a referendum. In a Knesset debate in 1994, Deputy Defense Minister Mordechai ("Mota") Gur, obviously representing Prime Minister Rabin, promised a referendum regarding a possible withdrawal from the Golan Heights as part of a peace treaty with Syria. This effectively defused the political opposition to the continuing negotiations, and since they did not end in an agreement, no referendum was held. In the 1996 election campaign, Prime Minister Peres promised a referendum before signing the permanent status agreement with the Palestinian Authority, but since he was not reelected, he was never put to the test.

Two major democratic systems of elections—the single-member district system and proportional representation—provide us with a framework for considering the pros and cons of various electoral systems, making comparisons among countries, and inspecting criteria for judging electoral systems.[8]

The single-member-district system (SMDS) is associated with government stability, while proportional representation promotes democratic representation. The first is widely used in Anglo-Saxon countries, the second is more prevalent in continental Europe. In SMDS, the candidate who wins a majority of the vote is elected; variations include electing the candidate who receives the most votes even if he fails to receive a majority, or electing the candidate who receives the most votes provided that it is more than a certain amount (say, 40 percent, as in the election of mayors in Israel).

Proportional representation provides for the election of representatives in proportion to the strength of the competing groups in the electorate. Usually individuals do not compete in this system, although in some variations the voter may rearrange or delete names on the list presented by the party or even choose candidates from different lists. Other details also vary from one example to another. For instance, the country may be one electoral unit (as in Israel) or may be divided into districts with competition taking place in each district according to the rules of proportional representation (as was the case in Italy). Another limitation may be the minimum percentage needed in order to win representation. It may be a single arithmetic function of the size of the group to be elected and the number of voters (1.5 percent of the 120-member Knesset, as in Israel), or the number of votes needed for winning a seat may be fixed. Regardless of variation, the principle of representation according to electoral strength is the key. Usually proportional representation generates many competing parties (twenty in Israel in 1996). Small parties generally oppose reform because they would be disadvantaged by a change to a constituency system.

The size of the electoral districts is the critical factor in approximating the ideal of proportional representation: the larger the electoral district in terms of seats, the more proportional the representation will be.[9] This is why the NRP, a party that has traditionally opposed electoral reform to a constituency system, argued in 1977 for dividing the country into five large districts; and why the DMC, whose platform heavily stressed electoral reform, opted for sixteen. The DMC reform would have increased local visibility of the constituency's representative at the expense of proportionality.

Many systems discuss reform, but it is implemented only rarely. Discussions for revamping the American electoral college or the British constituency system have continued for decades. The French are much more active than most, having changed their system for electing the National Assembly from a constituency method to a proportional system and back again since the 1980s. The 1990s have seen a rash of electoral reforms, including the Italian shift from a proportional system to a mixed proportional-constituency system, New Zealand'a move from a constituency method to a proportional one, and the Japanese change from a multi-member single-alternative vote to a more proportional method. The Israeli shift from a pure parliamentary system to a mixed parliamentary–direct election of prime minister system also occurred at that time.

Since there is no perfect system and since electoral reform is not a magic formula to cure the ills of political or social systems, what does electoral reform try to achieve? Put another way, in order to make up your mind regarding electoral change, it is important to know what goals you are trying to reach. What are the important criteria for judging electoral systems? What is the experience of other democratic countries? Which system tends to be associated with which results? Four important criteria are system stability, democratic representation, the link between the elected and the electorate, and the role of the party.

STABILITY

In a parliamentary system in which the executive is elected by the legislature and the parliament is fragmented into many parties, the probability of instability rises. Often no clear majority is achieved by any party, coalitions are necessary for organizing the parliament and for legislation, and no easy agreement can be reached as to who should serve as prime minister.

This condition has prevailed in many countries in Europe—in France before the Second World War and in Italy after it. The British system, by contrast, is more stable because only two or three large parties are in Parliament and the leader is more clearly discernible. In Britain, coalitions are rarely needed and stability is the rule. After some fifty years and fifty-five governments, Italy abandoned its proportional system in 1995–96 and adopted a mixed proportional and single-member-district system.

In presidential systems such as in the United States, France, Russia, and Mexico, the identity of the head of government is determined by vote and is not decided by parliamentary coalitions. This is the meaning of the direct election of the head of government, even though technically an electoral college may be involved in the selection, as in the United States.

The presidential system provides for stability of the executive and the government but does not ensure that the executive's relations with the legislative branch will be trouble-free, especially if the legislature is in the hands of another party. In a parliamentary system the stability of the executive is predicated on control of the legislature because the parliament chooses the prime minister.

The system of the French Fifth Republic has been termed semipresidential,[10] but it features (1) a president elected by the voters and (2) an elected parliament that selects a prime minister in the tradition of parliamentary systems. Israel's system is different because it is the prime minister who is directly elected. Israel also has a president, selected by the Knesset; the president performs roles that are largely symbolic and ceremonial. The fact that the prime minister and the Knesset are separately elected by the public makes Israel's system unique.

In the forty-eight years of proportional representation before Israel moved to its unique system of simultaneously electing its prime minister and parliament in 1996, the country did not suffer from excessive governmental instability. When Binyamin Netanyahu received the Knesset's approval of his cabinet, it was at the head of Israel's twenty-seventh government.

Stability is not only a matter of numbers, it is a matter of political control. The parties of Israel's prime ministers have been in firm control of the political situation for the most part. There has rarely been a feeling of lack of stability, despite the fact that Yitzhak Rabin headed minority governments both in 1974 and in 1994, when religious parties were not part of the government coalition.

But if politics is about ruling, and ruling demands a majority, then coalition politics are at the center of a polity like Israel's. The biggest party has never won a majority in the elections, and hence coalitions are a constant feature of Israeli politics. Winning parties can choose to coalesce with some or all of the religious parties, as they have done most of the time, or they can coalesce with the second-biggest winner (and others), as they have in 1967, 1984, and 1988, calling this exercise the formation of National Unity Governments.

The reformers hoped that, by being directly elected, the prime minister would be relieved of the stress and pressures of intense and costly bargaining with medium-sized and smaller parties to form the coalition. Potential partners would have to cooperate with the directly elected prime minister, the thinking went, because there was no way of changing the candidate for prime minister short of new elections. In addition, some who supported the reform hoped that the number of parties would decrease because to win the prime ministry meant winning an electoral majority, and thus splintering of the vote would no longer be rational in terms of electoral and political success.

These expectations were cruelly dashed by the experience of 1996. The system generated a political party system that was fractionalized. With Labor electing 34 members and Likud 32 members in the 120-seat Knesset, the party system was fragmented as never before. Never in Israeli political history had there been a winning party with such a small Knesset delegation as Labor won in 1996. Moreover, the total seats won by the two biggest parties was also unusually small. One must look to the 1949 elections and those in the early 1950s to find the two major parties commanding so few of the votes of the electorate. The results led to the emergence of sectarian interests, such as the new immigrants, the religious, and the Arabs, and a weakening of the concentration on national issues. This was obviously facilitated by split-ticket voting, by which a voter felt that he could send differentiated messages because he voted twice—once for the prime minister and once for the Knesset. This sophisticated use of the ballot box by the Israeli voter left in its wake a party system in shambles and a Knesset fractionalized and weakened compared to the prime minister and the executive branch.

The extent of bargaining with small and medium-sized sectarian parties to form the coalition was as great in 1996 as it had been in the past, if not greater. The prime minister had to satisfy many different demands, and that put pressure on the public treasury. What emerged was a very costly agreement likely to be renegotiated often during the lifetime of the government as new issues pose threats to the stability of the coalition. The prime minister would also have to pay more in terms of his own time to calm his coalition partners and more in terms of the national budget in order to keep the coalition together.

DEMOCRATIC REPRESENTATION

The premise of proportional representation is that opinions in the legislature accurately reflect opinions in the population. This is unlikely if only because many people do not have firm opinions on many issues of public importance, and even those who do are unlikely to follow the "party line" on each of them. Furthermore, many voters are influenced by matters peripheral to the central issues, such as the candidate's television appeal, the persuasiveness of the campaign, or some emotional attachment with one party or another.

The modern political party should not be understood as the mechanism for reflecting distribution of opinion in the population; it is more accurate to think of the party as the mechanism that transforms votes into public policy and political power. What the voter "really" meant is always a matter of interpretation. Proportional representation must be understood in terms of proportional political party representation and not in terms of proportional representation of public opinion or policy alternatives.

On the whole, proportional representation may not produce an identical image of the electorate in the legislature, but the distortion is not nearly as great as it usually is in the constituency system. Choosing someone to represent a district may pinpoint responsibility, but it denies representation to all those voters who did not support the person elected. The ideal of proportional representation is the faithful representation of all shades of opinion. This is a profoundly democratic notion and is in fact relatively modern. The idea of a single member constituency originated in predemocratic days when legislators were expected to represent corporate bodies such as localities, universities, and economic corporations, rather than individuals. The British idea of constituency representation grew out of its feudal heritage and has remained the dominant political expression of the British system.

The anomalies of the constituency system are well known. For example, in the 1988 Canadian elections, those who opposed the free-trade treaty with the United States were in the majority, but because of the constituency system used in Canada, a majority of the parliament members favored the bill. While public opinion was not accurately reflected in the vote, what was more important was that Canadians saw the results of the elections as a legitimate expression of the nation's will, and the free-trade treaty was ratified.

THE ELECTORATE AND THE ELECTED

A third criterion for the assessment of electoral systems is the proper relationship between the electorate and the elected. Two classic models are the free agent and the delegate. A free agent will vote his conscience regardless of the interest of party or constituency; the delegate will do as he has been instructed to the best of his ability. Modern representative government arose out of the proper relationship between the representative and his constituency. The free-agent model assumes that the representative is only remotely attached to his constituents and that his understanding of the national interest will guide him.

In the Israeli system, an oft-heard criticism of the electoral system is that voters do not know who represents them. The party, especially the large party, is too anonymous for many voters. Technically there is no representative who can protect interests, hear pleas, or present proposals. Israeli parties have been seeking to strengthen the connection with their members.

Five of the largest parties introduced some type of primary election to select their lists before the 1996 elections (see chapter 6). Likud, Labor, Meretz, Tzomet, and the NRP all used primaries among registered party members to select the list of candidates for the respective parties. Israel went through an intense period of primaries, but efforts to limit headline-grabbing sensationalism and to regulate expenditures were only partially successful.

The fundamental question is on what basis groups are represented. Many Knesset members were selected by their party leaders in the past because they were part of an important ethnic, occupational, geographical, or ideological group. Both the Likud and Labor based their primaries on district representation for a part of their list and assured representation for special groups such as women, ethnic groups, or Arabs. Also, many Knesset members are in fact approached by interested parties to promote legislation or solve a personal problem.

SMDS promotes geographical representation. Proportional representation promotes functional representation. In England or the United States a representative is identified by his (or her) association with a given district or state. In Israel he or she is identified by the fact that he is Moroccan (or Polish), lives in a city (or development town), is for an aggressive settlement policy (or against it), and so on, regardless of where the representative lives. Obviously in SMDS it is simpler to identify your representative.

But the facts also indicate that even in constituency systems many individuals do not know who their representative is, let alone come in contact with that person for political purposes. We should not be misled into thinking that if we know who our representatives are, we suddenly become better citizens by participating more in debate over public issues. In Great Britain about half the population knows the party of their district's representative in Parliament. A lower percentage knows the representative's name. In the United States the parallel figures are even lower. The proper relation between the electorate and its elected representatives is an extremely important issue, but it will not be determined simply by legislating a constituency system.

Once the lists are presented, the Israeli voter chooses between them as they are, without the possibility of altering the party's list to the Knesset. He or she must indicate a preference among the lists offered without the ability of adding, subtracting, or changing the order of the names that appear on the list. Contact with the candidate is minimal both before and after the election. While the argument can be made that exposing the candidate to the judgment of the electorate would make him more responsive, the other half of the dilemma is that perhaps responsiveness to the momentary whim of the public is not in the national interest—in short, is not a responsible act. We return to the dilemma of the free agent and the delegate, which, in turn, leads us to the next major topic.

THE ROLE OF THE PARTY

The fourth criterion is the proper role of the party, especially the role of the party machine. Israeli parties in the past tended to be hierarchical, and small elite groups appointed the candidates for the party's list. This began to crumble in 1977, to the point that in 1996, with the introduction of the primaries and the direct election of the prime minister, the role of the political party itself was called into question.

In the past, party leaders not elected by the public acted as king-makers. In 1996, the system itself appeared to have selected the king, a leader who had little obvious reason to consult with his party. While the law required the prime minister to be the head of a Knesset list, that law did not require the prime minister to consult with his party. The Likud's constitution did not require approval of the prime minister's appointments or policies by any party body, although Labor's constitution did.

A very difficult question for Israeli democracy in the past was whether it was appropriate to have unelected leaders select candidates for high office, which, in effect, limited the choice of the public come election day. The answer to that question was that Israel was a free country. Anyone who disliked the way a certain party selected its list could either vote for another party or set up another list. As long as competition was open and unhindered, proponents of this view argued, there was no damage done to the democratic ideal. Alternatively, they argued, individuals who felt this way could involve themselves in the party and change the rules. The general argument was that parties were keepers of an ideology, and as such they were in the best position to determine who was qualified to serve that particular ideology in the Knesset.

The direct election of the prime minister puts enormous power in the hands of the prime minister. It is true that the individual elected was chosen to have that power, but power unchecked is a dangerous commodity in a democracy. The recourse of holding new elections is so extreme that it is unlikely to be used often. The troubling dilemma for Israel's democracy is the emergence of a leader popularly elected but unaccountable to a political party. The institution that has traditionally mediated between the people and the government is the political party. The party must be nurtured to be a vibrant channel of communications if the prime minister is to work well with the Knesset.

To carry the day in the Knesset a party needs party discipline in order to govern. Party discipline demands Knesset members who are willing to be "delegates." On the other hand, it is important to attract to the Knesset individuals with skill, ambition, and talent. Is a talented person likely to want to play the role of party faithful and be disciplined when matters of importance are at stake? Will party interests always, or even often, meet the criteria of personal or national responsibility? Will a dynamic, thinking individual be popular enough to meet the test of popular success in parties with primaries, or acceptable in parties that use nominating committees? Independent thinkers may not be looked upon kindly by the primary voters or by the nominating committees and may be left off the list or placed in low spots the next time around. And yet these are the very people needed by a dynamic, creative party. The dilemma is that discipline enhances stability but also stagnation and a lackluster effect. To recruit first-rate people to the Knesset means allowing them more creativity; this demands a high degree of visibility to win a primary and an ability to overcome the power of the party bosses.

This problem is not unique to Israel. Some countries try to solve it by allowing alterations by the voters of the lists presented by the parties, others by allowing the constituency to select its candidate pending approval of the central office (as in Britain). The primaries were a reasonable way of determining the place on the list of the competing leaders; while it was technically possible that they would not be elected, none doubted that the top leaders would be high on the list—the only question was where.

With these four criteria in mind—stability, representation, link, and role of party—we face the question of electoral reform. Different priorities will generate different systems. If democratic representation is considered more important than a direct link with the representative, perhaps proportional representation will be preferred. If government stability is considered more important than the underrepresentation of minority viewpoints, then perhaps a form of constituency system will be preferred. All criteria cannot be fulfilled equally; some ranking of priorities will inevitably occur.

Debate over electoral reform has become a regular feature of Israeli political life. Prime Minister David Ben-Gurion's problems in the early 1950s with religious party partners in his government coalition led him to suggest that a referendum be held to adopt the British electoral system of single-member constituencies. The central committee of Mapai adopted this position in 1954, and since then electoral reform has been a constant issue of Israeli politics. Rafi in 1965 and the DMC in 1977 both made the issue of electoral reform central to their election platforms. Tinkering with details of the system has been rather frequent, including the shift to the d'Hondt system of allocating surplus votes before the 1973 elections, and the raising of the minimum needed for representation from 1 percent to 1.5 percent before the 1992 elections.

One Reform Plan Not Yet Accepted, One That Was

Many proposals have been made for electoral reform in Israel. Many of them contain a provision similar to what the Knesset approved by a wide margin in a first reading just before the 1988 elections, although it never became the law of the land. The legislation contained two proposals; the common feature was that part of the Knesset would be elected by districts and part on a proportional list basis.

Gad Yaacobi of Labor had spearheaded such proposals for years.[11] An early version of his proposal was that there would be eighteen five-member districts accounting for ninety members, with thirty others to be elected proportionally. This proposal would have added districts to the electoral system, but not direct election of representatives in the British or American sense. His plan would have had all Knesset members elected on a proportional basis, but instead of having one national constituency, there would be eighteen smaller constituencies and one national one. Each party would submit up to nineteen lists, eighteen five-person lists and a single thirty-person list. The person elected would be determined by the number of votes won by the party in the district, not by the candidate. The voter would not be able to identify his or her representative directly nor be able to influence the party's choice of candidates.

Note that the minimal price paid for each seat would increase dramatically. Under the present system the minimum is 1.5 percent; under the reform proposal it would in effect be 20 percent in the districts (one in five) and 3.3 percent for the national list.

An important question with this type of system has to do with the choices that would be required of the voter. Would the voter have two ballots or one? That is, would he (or she) be able to split the ballot by supporting an attractive district list of the Likud, say, and still voting his national preference by casting his ballot for Labor? Or would he be forced to choose only one party? Would the voter be allowed to alter the order of the names submitted by the party? Would he be obliged to vote for five candidates, or could the voter decide for how many candidates (up to five in a five-person constituency) he wanted to vote?

Another problem is that of gerrymandering, or drawing arbitrary districts, in order to benefit the party that controls the apportionment process. An example would be grouping predominantly religious neighborhoods with four or five religious kibbutzim in order to make more likely the election of religious candidates. In fact, while gerrymandering comes to politicians easily, it is not too difficult to prevent. A nonparty body headed by a Supreme Court justice in charge of apportionment would likely be above reproach. In the Yaacobi proposal the districts envisaged are relatively equal in size and contiguous in land area in order to avoid gerrymandering.[12] Alternatively, administrative districts could be made into electoral districts and the number of representatives could be adjusted depending on population shifts.

There have been tremendous groundswells in favor of electoral reform. Rafi stressed electoral reform as one of its chief planks in 1965. Yigael Yadin was active in the electoral reform movement long before he entered national politics in 1977. Amnon Rubinstein's Shinui and Yadin's

DMC spoke enthusiastically of electoral reform, although most politicians preferred to speak in generalities and avoid details. The evidence of public support for electoral reform was striking. In 1972, 30 percent of a sample reported support for a mixed proportional-district system; by 1977 that figure had almost doubled to 59 percent. After the 1988 elections, with the religious parties making enormous demands in order to join in a governing coalition, appeals for electoral reform surged again. Many who called for electoral reform really wanted to change the political outcome of the election. But they concentrated on changing the electoral system.

Politicians, faced with this groundswell, were forced to react, and almost all parties indicated some degree of support for electoral reform in the 1977 elections. But in reality party politicians were very uneasy about electoral reform because it would add yet another element of uncertainty to their already precarious occupation. The foot dragging could be clearly seen in negotiations among the Likud, the NRP, and the DMC to expand the coalition government set up after the 1977 elections to include the DMC. The DMC had an ideological belief in and had made a public commitment to electoral reform. The NRP, as a middle-sized party with most of its voters in a few concentrated geographic areas, had every reason to oppose reform. The Likud, and especially Herut and Prime Minister Begin, were never enthusiastic supporters of reform but had committed themselves to it in the election campaign.

The lines of argument were classic, with the NRP wanting five districts of sixteen members each (we must recall that large districts increase the chances of approximating proportional representation) and the DMC arguing for many districts with few delegates, since its plank had been one of district representation. The problem was solved in a typical Israeli way: a decision was made not to decide. The parties agreed to set up a committee that would bring a proposal within a certain time. That period passed and no recommendation was made. The lack of enthusiasm on the part of most politicians was hard to hide.

The coalition agreement setting up the 1984 and 1988 National Unity Governments called for a special committee that would look into changing the electoral system. With Labor and Likud controlling the government coalition and the Knesset, it would have been an ideal time for the two large parties to legislate reform that would favor their political interests. But the perceived need of having a good working relation with the religious parties—potential future coalition partners—proved overpowering. In 1984, an implicit part of the bargain in with the smaller parties that also joined the National Unity Government was the understanding that reform would be deferred. After all, the coalition agreement called only for setting up a committee. In 1988, the pressure for reform was even greater, but the countervailing forces were also substantial. Electoral reform had not yet come about.

Electoral reform was passed in a first reading by the Knesset before the elections held in 1988, as already stated. The proposal to have part of the Knesset elected by districts and part on a national list sounded loud danger signals in the halls of the small (especially religious) parties. Leaders of the religious parties appealed to Prime Minister Shamir to prevent further Knesset action in the last moments of the legislative session, forcefully reminding him that he was likely to need their support in forming a coalition after the upcoming elections. Shamir acceded to their pleas, and further legislative action was stymied. Although Shamir could have formed a coalition with the religious parties after the elections, he ultimately constructed the 1988 National Unity Government with the Labor Party and other parties.

After the inconclusive elections of 1988, it seemed that the only way to set up a governing coalition was to give in to the demands of the religious parties (who had collectively won 15 percent of the vote) for amending the "Who is a Jew?" definition of the Law of Return and to provide substantial additional funding for their schools. It appeared that the religious parties controlled the future of Israeli politics because they could determine which of the large parties would form a governing coalition in the Knesset. Accordingly, strong appeals rose to prevent in the future the exaggerated power of the minority over the majority.

It was in this period of sharp political division over the future of the territories, and a perceived stalemate between the major parties, that the one major reform of Israeli constitutional transformation—the direct election of the prime minister—was adopted. The ills of the system became more obvious than ever because of the "dirty trick" of 1990, the name given by Yitzhak Rabin to the failed attempt by Shimon Peres to replace the Likud-led National Unity Government with a Labor-led coalition.

The background of the story of the "dirty trick" was a peace initiative put forth by Israel. It gained support in Washington and Cairo, but when U.S. Secretary of State James Baker pressed the Israeli government to be more flexible regarding details, Prime Minister Yitzhak Shamir recoiled. The Knesset expressed no-confidence in its government for the first time in Israeli history, and the Unity Government fell.

Yitzhak Modai, minister of finance, and his group of four other Knesset members (former members of the Liberal faction of the Likud), for a total of five votes, demanded recognition as an independent Knesset faction in return for their support of Shamir's position. The approval of their demand was granted just before the vote of no-confidence. On 15 March 1990, the government fell by a vote of 60 to 55, defeated by the votes of

Labor, the Arabs, the left, and ultra-Orthodox Agudat Israel. The key to the "victory" of Peres and Labor was the fact that five of the six Knesset members of the ultra-Orthodox Shas party absented themselves from the vote.

With the fall of the government, Shimon Peres was appointed by President Chaim Herzog to form a government. Peres had to placate his own party, made up of hawks and doves, and to fashion a government of religious parties and the extreme left. He needed the votes of Arab parties too, but he could not plan on negotiating away territory if their support was seen as pivotal. To succeed, Peres had to find Knesset members of the other camp willing to desert to the Labor side. Israeli constitutional practice at that time did not prohibit the Knesset member from switching allegiance. The three most promising turncoat candidates had all been placed on the Likud list in deals cut to solve previous coalition crises. One was Yigael Horowitz, leader of Ometz (two seats), who had left the Labor Party years before; another was Aharon Abu-Hatzeira, former head of the Tami list; finally, there was the Modai group, with five seats, recently liberated from the Likud and now recognized as an independent Knesset faction.

Things went poorly for Peres. Agudat Israel, the ultra-Orthodox haredi party, agreed not to participate in a Likud government and to support a Labor government without formally joining it. On the other hand, the deciding rabbinical council of the Sephardi, ultra-Orthodox, haredi, non-Zionist Shas, decided to back a government headed by Shamir. Charlie Biton, of the Communist list (Rakah), was wooed to Labor's ranks. Avraham Sharir, one of Modai's group who felt that Prime Minister Shamir had slighted him in the past, seemed to be leaning to Labor, and Modai was also reportedly wavering. It was a seller's market. Peres and Labor agreed to appoint Sharir minister of transportation and to give him a sure place on the Labor list for the next two elections.

Meanwhile, the Likud was busy trying to block Peres's attempt and prenegotiating its own government. Shamir met with Modai; the Likud promised him an important ministry (foreign, defense, or treasury), another for one of his colleagues, five certain places in the next Likud election list, and a $10 million security deposit to guarantee these pledges. After petitions to the judicial system, and a massive demonstration calling for constitutional reform, Modai backed down from his demand for a cash deposit, and agreed to make do with the signatures of all the Likud ministers backing the agreement with him. When four of them refused to go along, Modai reopened negotiations with Labor.

Peres planned to present his government to the Knesset on the last day of his twenty-one-day mandate to form a government. By adding

Sharir to the sixty votes that had brought down the Unity Government, Peres thought he had enough votes. But his plans unraveled when two of the Aguda supporters bolted, despite the discipline that Aguda Knesset members had always demonstrated to the dictates of their party's Council of Torah Sages. Verdiger and Mizrahi chose to disobey party dictates rather than allow the creation of a government headed by Peres. The president gave Peres a fifteen-day extension to form the government. The Aguda lined up Verdiger, one of its two wayward Knesset members, after extracting a promise from Peres that new elections would be held before any territory was returned. Mizrahi was to be tried before a rabbinical tribunal for breaking his promise to follow the dictates of the Council of Torah Sages. Ultimately, he resigned from the Aguda and set up his own one-member faction in the Knesset (to run unsuccessfully in 1992).

The uncertainty grew. After a meeting with David Levy, Sharir seemed ready to shift his support back to the Likud. The deal with Modai's group drew sharp criticism; many Herut members were incensed that much of the next Likud list was being given away. Once Peres failed, it was Shamir's turn, and he had troubles of his own. He won the support of Mizrahi of the Aguda list, and turned a Labor Knesset member, Ephraim Gur. With them, the Likud could count on sixty-two Knesset members. Both were rewarded with appointments as deputy ministers, and Gur was given a promise of a secure place on the Likud list for the next Knesset.

Reform followed. In February 1991 the Knesset reacted to this unseemly chain of events by passing legislation intended to change basic parliamentary norms. The legislation stipulated that a Knesset member who resigned from the party on whose list he or she was elected, or who voted no-confidence against the decision of the party on whose list he had been elected, would be penalized. The offending Knesset member would not be recognized as a member of any other party grouping within the Knesset; would not be allowed to run in the next elections on a list represented in the current Knesset; would not be allowed to serve as a minister or a deputy minister during the term of the Knesset in which the prohibited act occurred; and would not be entitled to party financing from the public treasury.

The other reform to emerge from this messy political period was the direct election of the prime minister. Originally conceived of as one of a series of constitutional reforms by a group of law professors,[13] the proposal took on a life of its own and led to a well-funded public campaign sparked by petition drives and demonstrations.[14]

The reform was presented as governmental reform, more to protect the incumbent parliamentarians (the cynics said) than to increase governmental efficiency. The opposition Labor Party supported the direct election of the prime minister, mainly out of short-term electoral considerations; Likud wavered, with Prime Minister Shamir explicitly and publicly opposing the plan. The vote of a young Likud politician, Binyamin Netanyahu, would prove crucial, ultimately ensuring Knesset approval of the bill for the direct election against the wishes of the Likud leadership.[15]

The legislation, though passed in the twelfth Knesset, before the 1992 election of the thirteenth Knesset, would be applied only from the fourteenth Knesset of 1996. But the politicians were alert to the potential of the new electoral system. Labor conducted its 1992 election campaign as though these were direct elections for the prime minister, placing Rabin firmly at the center of its campaign and exploiting the themes of change and Likud's opposition to reform. In anticipation, the party went so far as officially to call itself "The Labor Party Headed by Rabin." Netanyahu was preparing for the election of a new head of Likud, should that party lose in 1992.

The direct election of the prime minister was Israel's first major electoral reform. While it weakened the Knesset compared to the prime minister, the law did not tamper with the method of electing the Knesset. The politicians could declare that they had passed reform, without changing the manner by which they themselves had learned to be elected. The "dirty trick" set the stage for major changes in Israeli political life: the direct elections of the prime minister, the primaries in the major parties, the ascendancy of Rabin over Peres, the election victory of Labor in 1992; the primaries victory of Netanyahu in the Likud after Shamir stepped down as party head; and the ascendancy of Netanyahu as the first directly elected prime minister.

Before the direct election of the prime minister was actually carried out in 1996, a head count of Knesset members revealed that 77 of the 120 would support repealing or delaying the implementation of the plan if party discipline were lifted so they could vote freely. Shimon Peres, who had consistently opposed the plan, felt an obligation to the assassinated Rabin, who had consistently supported it. And so Peres blocked delay or repeal, and paid for it with his job. Had the old system been in place, he would have been given the first opportunity to form a government, since his party was the largest winner in the 1996 election.

After the 1996 elections there were calls to return to the parliamentary pattern of having the Knesset select the prime minister, or having the prime minister be the head of the largest party in the Knesset, but the Netanyahu camp and the middle-sized parties that did well in 1996 were not anxious to undo the system that had brought them power. Another reform that was proposed was the constructive vote of no-confidence, under which the prime minister and the government could be toppled by the

Knesset only if a majority had already agreed on an alternative candidate for the position of prime minister.

Whether electoral reform should take place is a matter of belief, preference, and evaluation. Whether it takes place is a matter of politics. Public support has generally been stronger for electoral reform than has been the resolve of the political leadership to bring it about. Those who did well under the old system find little reason to explore a new one. Reforming the electoral system generally happens only when politicians back into the project with their eyes closed. And that is precisely what happened with the adoption of the direct election of the prime minister.

8. Electoral Behavior

The distribution of political power in a democracy is determined by the electoral rules employed, by the party system and the actions of parties, by political events, and by the behavior of the voters (see table 8.1, p. 208, for election results).[1]

Voting Participation

Voting turnout in Israel has always been high; about 80 percent of the eligible voters voluntarily cast ballots on voting day. Absentee balloting is not available to the public, although special arrangements are made for persons serving with the Israel Defense Forces on election day, for those in official positions abroad and their families, for persons hospitalized on election day, for sailors working on Israeli flagships, and for prisoners.

The highest rate of participation was in the first Knesset elections in 1949, in which 86.8 percent of the eligible population voted, and the lowest rate was in 1951, with only 75.1 percent participation. The number of eligible voters between the two elections increased by 70 percent as a result of large-scale immigration; the dislocation as a result of this immigration probably explains the lower participation rate. By 1955 the rate was back up to 82.8 percent.

Non-Jews have had high rates of participation in elections. In 1996 their rate of 77.6 percent almost equaled for the first time the rate of Jews (79.3 percent). In 1981 the participation rate for non-Jewish settlements had fallen to 69.7 percent and the rate for Bedouin tribes to 53.3 percent. In 1988 voting participation in Arab communities was 73.8 percent.

The motivation for nonvoting in Jewish and Arab sectors is different. Few Jews abstain for political reasons; their reasons are generally technical in nature. The most important cause of nonvoting among Jews has to do with the way in which the rate of voting is calculated. It is based on the population registry, and those out of the country on election day are counted among those who did not vote. The incidence of leaving the country (sometimes for years) is more common among Jews than non-Jews, and this practice deflates the rate of Jewish voting. Other technical reasons include illness, improper registration, and lack of identification documents.

Among non-Jews, the dominant reason for nonvoting is that they choose not to vote; in 1973, 54.6 percent of the non-Jews who said they would not vote gave purposeful abstention as the reason for not voting, compared to 12.8 percent of the sample of Jewish nonvoters.[2] In the 1996 survey, 8.2 percent of Arabs declared they would not vote, with almost half of them giving the reason that no party was right for them, and the other half expressing their anger at the Israeli Grapes of Wrath campaign in Lebanon. Among the Jews, 2.7 percent said they would abstain from voting, 59 percent of them claiming that no party is right for them, another 28 percent indicating technical problems.

With the possible exception of the Bedouin tribes, voting participation is not associated with levels of modernization. The 1977 Bedouin voting rate was only 64.3 percent, much lower than other groups, but high by the standards of other countries. In 1981, following a very divisive campaign, many Arabs refrained from voting; but in 1988, in the midst of the Intifada, Arab citizens used their votes to express their preferences in the hope of influencing the political process. In 1996, with the extremely close race for the prime minister, non-Jews voted at the highest rate ever.

Explaining the Vote

Besides asking whether people vote, political scientists are concerned with why people vote as they do. The answer to this question is usually complex but can conveniently be thought of in terms of the individual's political socialization, the major issues of the campaign, the candidates offered, and the voter's socioeconomic position.[3]

As a rule, people learn political symbols and values in much the same way they learn other values—through the family, the school, and peer groups. In the case of an individual whose political learning is reinforced by all the socializing agents with which he or she comes in contact, the result is likely to be high levels of belief and behavior consistent with the expectations of the environment. A good example is the voting behavior of kibbutz members. Their vote for the party with which their kibbutz federation is associated is generally very high. The pressures for voting for the party are rarely opposed by significant others. Just as most Israeli Jews accept their Judaism as a matter of course, so too most kibbutz members accept their socialism and identification with a political party as a matter of course.

The situation is more complex when cross-pressures come to bear. Among residents of a city, for example, where levels of political organization are much lower, socialization into political life or into voting for a specific party is likely to be lower and less intense. Voters who were affiliated with party-sponsored youth groups and internalized the values and identity of the party and were reinforced by the home environment in this

TABLE 8.1

KNESSET ELECTION RESULTS (120 SEATS)

	1949	1951	1955	1959	1961	1965	1969	1973	1977	1981	1984	1988	1992	1996
Participation rate (%)	86.9	75.1	82.8	81.6	81.6	83.0	81.7	78.6	79.2	78.5	79.8	79.7	77.4	79.3
Labor and Left														
Mapai[a]	46	45	40	47	42	45	56	51	32	47	44	39	44	34
Ahdut Haavoda[b]			10	7	8									
Rafi[c]						10								
Mapam[d]	19	15	9	9	9	8						3		
DMC/Shinui[e]									15	2	3	2		
CRM/Meretz[f]								3	1	1	3	5	12	9
Arab lists	2	1	4	5	4	4	4	3	1		2	2	2	4
Communist	4	5	6	3	5	4	4	5	5	4	4	4	3	5
Likud and Right														
Independent Liberals[g]	5	4	5	6		5	4	4	1					
Liberals[h]	7	20	13	8	17									
Herut[i]	14	8	15	17	17	26	26	39	43	48	41	40	32	32
Tehiya/Tzomet[j]										3	5	5	8	
Moledet/Kach[k]											1	2	3	2
Religious														
NRP	16	10	11	12	12	11	12	10	12	6	4	5	6	9
Aguda parties[l]		5	6	6	6	6	6	5	5	4	8	7	4	4
Shas											4	6	6	10
Others														
Other parties	7	7	1			1	8[m]	3	5[n]	5[o]	5[p]			11[q]

a. Joined with Ahdut Haavoda in 1965 and the other Labor parties in 1969.

b. See note a.

c. Joined the labor Alignment in 1969 minus the State List.

d. Ahdut Haavoda included in Mapam in 1949 and 1951; Mapam included in Labor-Mapam Alignment between 1969 and 1988; Mapam included in Meretz in 1992 and 1996.

e. DMC in 1977; Shinui between 1981 and 1988.

f. Meretz in 1992 and 1996 made up of CRM, Mapam, and Shinui.

g. Included in Liberal Party in 1961 and independent again since 1965; in 1984, part of Labor-Mapam Alignment.

h. Until 1959 known as General Zionists, joined Herut to form Gahal in 1965, and part of the Likud in 1973.

i. Jointly with the Liberals since 1965 and part of the Likud in 1973.

j. Tehiya in 1961 and 1964; in 1988, 3 seats for Tehiya, 2 for Tzomet; Tzomet in 1992; in 1996 Tzomet part of the Likud.

k. Kach in 1984; since 1988 Moledet.

l. Poalei Agudat Israel, Agudat Israel, and Degel Hatorah.

m. Includes the State List (4 members), the Free Center (2 members), and Haolam Haze (2 members). The first two joined Herut and the Liberals in 1973.

n. Includes Sholmzion (2 members), which joined the Likud after the elections, Shelli (2 members), and Flatto Sharon (1 member).

o. Includes Tami (3 members) and Telem (2 members).

p. Includes Yahad (3 members), Tami (1 member), and Ometz (1 member).

q. Includes Israel Aliya (7 members) and the Third Way (4 members).

learning are obviously more likely to continue voting for that party in later years.

It is almost impossible to know why people *really* vote the way they do. One way of trying to assess the vote is to ask voters what factor was most important in determining their vote. Another way is to ascertain what factors are associated with voting for one party and not another. In both cases we must take into account that factors we have not tapped are also at work.

Israeli voters report that ideological considerations are important in motivating the vote. The Israeli political system is, and is perceived to be ideological in nature; one is tempted to say that this is the ideology of the system. This is so even when strong, popular leaders are running for reelection (Golda Meir in 1969, Menachem Begin in 1981, and Yitzhak Rabin in 1992). In none of the seven surveys (see table 8.2) does the candidate carry as much weight with the voters as the platform of the party. This is even true for the direct election of the prime minister in 1996; the rate of mentioning the candidate in that situation (34 percent) was more than twice as high as the rate of mentioning the candidate regarding the election of the Knesset (16 percent), but still lower than the reported importance of the platform or ideology (42 percent).

These data seem to be challenged by the observation that the candidates for office in Israel are very important in attracting voters or, on the contrary, in repelling voters. Offsetting this in 1996 was the fierce debate on the future of the territories, reinforcing the centrality of the party platform or ideology. On many other issues ideological differences among parties are not great, although their style, emphases, and images may be. In a fascinating twist driven by the direct election of the prime minister, Netanyahu tried to present himself as less militant than his image and his party platform, and Peres tried to present himself as more militant. Both were appealing for the votes of the center, and both feared that they had positioned themselves incorrectly for that task.

The reported importance of identification with the party peaked in the 1980s, although the introduction of the primaries saw membership in parties grow in the 1990s. While the role of the candidate is growing in the television-dominated election campaign, and party differences are made to seem larger than they really are during the campaign, the fascinating point is that Israelis report that their voting decision is dominated by ideological considerations. The Israeli voter has internalized the expectation of democratic theorists that voters make their decision by virtue of rational, cognitive processes. Obviously other factors are also at work, but this is the way Israelis present themselves to others.[4]

TABLE 8.2

DETERMINING FACTOR IN THE VOTE
(IN PERCENTAGES)

"Which factor is the most important in influencing a person to vote for a particular party?"

	1969	1977	1981	1984	1988	1992	1996	1996PM[a]
Identification with the party	17	26	31	32	32	28	27	20
The party's candidate	21	15	18	10	21	12	16	34
The party's platform/ideology	37	46	38	53	41	55	54	42
The party being in government or opposition	7	6	7	4	3	3	2	2
Other reason; no answer	18	7	6	2	3	2	1	2
N =	1,314	1,372	1,237	1,259	873	1,192	1,168	1,168

a. In 1996, the first time the prime minister was directly elected, an identical question was added regarding the choice of the prime minister.

Voting Stability and Change

Patterns of support for the major political groups have been quite constant. Political change came about because the strength of support of various groups has shifted from time to time. The dominant Mapai, now Labor, found support among all groups, but especially among those who identified with the epoch in which the party rose to its peak and to the epoch's dominant values. The highlight of Mapai's (Labor's) achievements was the gaining of independence. All the projects undertaken by the Jews in Eretz Israel—immigration, building the land, security—were highlighted by achieving independence. After the founding of the state, these undertakings were continued, sometimes within different organizational settings and institutional arrangements, but with much of the same symbolism and ideological justification. One who lived through the independence epoch in Israel was more likely to identify with the dominant party. In the process of having party and movement values permeate the society, the distinction between party and state was often blurred. Achievements of state accrued to the benefit of the party. Jews who immigrated to Israel before independence and immediately thereafter continued to support Labor heavily. The rate of support fell off for those who immigrated after 1955, and for Israeli-born voters.

Much of the program and appeal of the dominant Labor Party at the time of independence must be seen in the light of the social and political realities that the Labor leadership knew in eastern Europe in the first decades of the twentieth century. The precarious position of the Jews, the restrictions on economic and political activity, the unbalanced nature of their occupations, the spread of rationalist feeling, the undermining of traditional religious belief and behavior—all these things led to the creation of the socialist-Zionist experiment. The Labor leadership, almost exclusively of East European origin, developed a party and an ideology that answered the needs of the nation as they saw them and experienced them.

The constituent parties of the Likud, and especially the Herut movement, had always seen the problems of the country from a different ideological perspective and consequently found support from different groups. Labor was notably successful among earlier immigrants and among those born in Europe and America. Likud appealed more to the native-born than to any immigrant group, and more to the Asian- or African-born than to the European- or American-born. The symbols Labor used to evoke the epoch of independence and nation building were more effective among the old than the young, more effective among those who came before independence than among those who came after independence or were born in Israel, and more effective among those born in Europe than among those born in Asia or Africa.

The Likud, in opposition until 1977, gave the appearance of being broadly based in its electoral support (as was the Labor-Mapam Alignment) because it blended the appeals of its two major components, the right-wing nationalistic Herut movement and the bourgeois Liberal Party. But much of this spread was an artifact of the difference between the groups that supported Herut and the Liberals. Herut was a party that appealed disproportionately to the lower class and to lower-middle-class workers, and to Israelis born in Asia or Africa, although obviously many Ashkenazim also supported it. The Liberals, in contrast, were a bourgeois party that received most of its support from middle-class and upper-middle-class merchants and businessmen. Since the followers of the Liberal Party had higher levels of education than did supporters of Herut, the spread evident for the Likud was a balancing of two countertendencies; thus it is misleading to read into the data that the Likud before 1977 was beginning to generate the appeal characteristic of a dominant party.

The support of the Likud came heavily from the young, from native Israelis, from Israelis of Asian or African background, and from those with lower education and income levels. Undeniably, many of these cleavages overlapped with strong differences in political opinion and religious observance. To give but one example, the same groups that tended to support the Likud tended to have hawkish opinions on foreign and defense policy. Those who were older, had more education, and came from a European background, and supported Labor, tended to hold more conciliatory views.

The religious parties generally have received about 15 percent of the vote, although in 1996 this shot up to 20 percent, and they were regular coalition partners in the majority of governments, whether headed by Labor or by Likud. Their support came from traditional Jews from Asian or African backgrounds with low income and low education levels; highly educated intellectuals from European origins; and Israeli-born educated youth imbued with religious ideals through formal schooling in the state-supported religious schools. The NRP lost votes in 1988 to the Likud for ideological reasons, and to Shas for ethnic ones. Its rebounding in 1996 was the result of moderating its ideological appeal, retaining its nationalist base, and by successful organizational efforts.

On the whole, the religious parties were relatively more successful among those with lower levels of education. The picture was more complex, however, when support for the religious parties was considered in the light of both education and place of origin. Among the European- or American-born, support for religious parties tended to decrease with educational attainment. The Israeli-born provided the opposite picture, with religious party support increasing with additional education. In the 1980s and 1990s, Shas emerged as the major religious party. A Sephardi ultra-Orthodox party, it won its major support from traditionalists with lower incomes, lower levels of education, and an Asian or African background.

Issue Voting and Demography

Issue voting grew dramatically in Israel in the 1980s and 1990s, especially regarding the divisive issue of the future of the territories, while the grasp of social allegiance on voting patterns remained constant. Social and economic differences have traditionally been considered good predictors of voting behavior, although there has been a general decline in the importance of such cleavages throughout the Western world, and a simultaneous increase in issue voting.[5] As the electoral importance of the territories issue grew, the role of demographic factors either remained stable or receded.[6]

Consider table 8.3, in which the votes of Jews for prime minister and the Knesset in the 1996 elections are broken down by demographic background categories. In 1996 gender played a bigger role than it usually did in Israeli elections, with women tending to support Peres and Labor more than men did; as usual, age was a good predictor of the vote, with the young more likely to vote for Netanyahu and the Likud, the old for Peres and Labor.

Years of education correlated with the vote, especially for those with higher education. Those with more than twelve years of education split two to one in favor of Peres, while respondents with lower levels of education were almost evenly divided between Peres and Netanyahu. The left and Labor also did well with this group of voters, while the Likud did much better among those with twelve years of education or less.

Continent of birth was also related to vote choice. Those born in Europe or America, or whose fathers were born there, were much more likely to support Peres and Labor. Those born in Asia or Africa, or whose fathers were born there, were much more likely to choose Netanyahu and the Likud.

The strongest predictor of the vote reported in table 8.3 was the extent of religious observance. As observance increased, the probability of voting for Netanyahu and the religious parties grew in a linear fashion, and the chances of voting for the Labor Party decreased with the same regularity. Among the very observant the Likud attracted only partial support, evidently since religious parties were available to be voted for; on the whole, however, the Likud did much better among observers than among nonobservers, and certainly much better than Labor did among observers.

The correlations in table 8.4 provide important clues as to the nature of partisanship in Israel. The correlations are between the Labor/Likud vote and various demographic and issue variables for the 1969–96 period,

TABLE 8.3

DEMOGRAPHIC PROFILE OF JEWISH VOTERS,
1996 (IN PERCENTAGES)

	Sample size	Peres	Netan-yahu	Left	Labor	Likud	Reli-gious
Total	100	52	48	6	44	42	9
Gender							
Male	49	49	51	6	41	43	10
Female	51	54	46	5	46	41	8
Age							
18–21	10	42	58	7	32	54	7
22–29	25	56	44	10	43	37	9
30–59	49	48	52	5	42	44	9
60 and above	16	63	37	3	58	32	7
Education							
Up to 8 years	9	43	57	0	39	51	10
9–12 years	56	46	54	4	39	51	7
More than 12 years	36	64	36	10	53	25	12
Continent of birth							
Asia, Africa	14	35	65	2	30	61	7
Europe, America	28	37	63	2	34	56	8
Israel (father Israel)	17	60	40	13	45	32	10
Israel (father Europe, America)	23	65	35	4	61	29	7
Israel (father Asia, Africa)	18	63	37	12	49	27	12
Religious observance							
All	10	10	90	1	7	34	57
Most	17	26	74	1	20	67	12
Some	52	54	46	3	51	45	2
None	22	83	17	19	63	18	0

and the Peres/Netanyahu vote in 1996. Age has had a consistent relationship with vote, with the young somewhat more likely to vote Likud, and the old, Labor. This relationship has been generally regarded as indicating generation rather than life-cycle effects.[7] This correlation peaked in 1973 and 1977 and reached its nadir in 1992. The 1977 reversal was led by the young: youth abandoned Labor for the promises of the Likud or the DMC. The Likud, always strongest among this group compared to other age cohorts, won 36 percent support in 1969 compared to 44 percent in 1973 and 51 percent in 1977 and 1981. The Labor-Mapam Alignment lost half its

TABLE 8.4

CORRELATIONS[a] BETWEEN LIKUD AND LABOR, DEMOGRAPHICS AND ISSUES,[b] 1969–96

| Survey[c] | N | Demography | | | | | | | Issues | | |
		Age	Gender	Density	Education	Income	Religion	Ethnicity	No territories for peace[d]	Capitalism/Socialism[e]	State/Religion[f]
Oct 69	1,017	.17	(.05)	.07	(.00)	(−.04)	.08	.13	.15	.23	.12
May 73	1,062	.27	(.01)	.15	(−.02)	(−.01)	(.04)	.13	.23	.17	g
Mar 77	620	.29	(−.03)	.18	(.01)	(.06)	.18	.32	.28	.22	.17
Mar 81	798	.13	(.06)	.07	.09	(.00)	.19	.23	.27	.16	.20
Jul 84	807	.20	(−.03)	.25	.22	.08	.37	.53	.57	.32	g
Oct 88	532	.16	(.04)	.09	.15	(.01)	.27	.27	.61	.30	.24
Jun 92	657	.10	(.07)	.13	.24	(−.02)	.40	.35	.57	(.05)	.29
May 96	798	.13	(.04)	.18	.21	.12	.36	.30	.66	(.07)	.35
PM96	1,113	.09	(.06)	.20	.18	.12	.44	.28	.63	(.08)	.41

a. Pearson correlations, significant above the .05 level, except for those in parentheses.

b. The coding for these correlations was Likud = 1, Labor = 1, Netanyahu = 2, Peres = 2. Low scores for the other variables indicate young age, female, high density, low education, low income, high religiosity, Sephardi, unwillingness to concede territories for peace, favoring capitalism over socialism, and favoring public life in accordance with Jewish religious law, respectively.

c. Preelection surveys used. In years for which multiple surveys were available, the one which contained the most variables used in the table was chosen.

d. Before 1984, a question concerning the maximum amount of territory Israel should give up in order to achieve a peace settlement. In 1984 and after, constructed from two questions, the first asking preference between return of territories for peace, annexation, or status quo, and a follow-up question forcing a choice on those who had opted for "status quo." In 1996 a 7-point answer was used.

e. The question asked about preference for the socialist or capitalist approach. The 1973 question asked if the Histadrut labor union should see to it that public life in Israel be conducted according to the Jewish religious tradition.

f. The question asked whether the government should see to it that public life in Israel be conducted according to the Jewish religious tradition.

g. Not asked.

support in this youngest age group between 1973 and 1977, the same amount of support that the DMC attracted. The Alignment more clearly than ever became the party of the older, more conservative voter; the Likud, the choice of the young, even though the DMC was a party of young adults. In 1992, the Likud was forsaken by both the young and the old; young voters were more attracted by the parties further to the right, but Labor was more successful than in the past in attracting voters across generations.

It is in the youngest voting group that the significant change comes about. A tantalizing prospect emerged in the 1988 data, with Labor and Likud getting almost the same percentage of support among first-time voters. This hinted at a change in the pattern of the past two decades in which the young chose the Likud, but Labor's optimism was only partially fulfilled, since young voters in 1988 and 1992 tended to support parties of the extreme left and the extreme right as well as Labor and Likud. Labor and Rabin won in 1992 by attracting a substantial part of the young vote, while the Likud lost a sizable portion of it.

In 1996, first-time voters split in favor of Netanyahu at about a three to two rate, despite the impression that the Rabin assassination had galvanized the young generation on Labor's behalf. The assassination did have the effect of mobilizing emotional support for Labor among the young, but especially among those first-time voters who would have supported Labor anyway. Although much was made of the "candles generation" of young people supporting Peres while grieving for the slain Rabin in 1996, there was no evidence that this promise materialized in the elections.

Gender has never been related to vote choice in Israeli surveys to a statistically significant extent.

Class differences have mattered to a degree, although correlations have been neither consistent nor strong. There was usually no relationship between the Likud-Labor vote and income, but the income variable is not the best measure of class in Israel, as it is the kind of topic an Israeli is unlikely to discuss in an open manner with an interviewer-stranger. Two other measures of class, living density (the number of persons per room) and education, tell a different story.

Class differences appeared with the reversal of 1977, with lower-class voters abandoning Labor in favor of the Likud. Education gained in importance after 1981, with the return to Labor of more highly educated voters who had deserted for the DMC in 1977. This process of class stratification continued in the 1980s and was still in evidence in 1992, although over time the education variable was stronger than the living-density indicator. But based on the inconsistent and not too strong correlations of the vote with class indicators, combined with the pattern of correlations between the vote and the socialist versus capitalistic views, the class cleavage does not seem to be the driving force behind electoral choice and change in Israel. Note that in 1992 and 1996 there is virtually no relationship between voters' preferences as to the structure of the economy and their vote, and in 1977 the correlation was of the same magnitude as throughout the 1970s. Moreover, the responses to this question are to be seen as an indicator of whether or not a voter belongs to the camp of socialism-Zionism socially, politically, and culturally, rather than of ideological commitment. And class is not the most potent correlate of the vote in Israel.

Religion and ethnicity were strongly correlated with the vote decision. For both of them, the critical election year was 1977. Before that year, both dimensions barely distinguished Labor voters from Likud voters. Religion (measured by extent of religious observance) gained in importance over time, reaching all-time highs in the 1992 election and in the vote for prime minister in 1996. The relationship between ethnicity and the vote reached its highest point in the 1984 election and has receded since.

The ethnic theme has changed over time as the proportions of the groups in the electorate have changed (see tables 2.2 and 2.3). In 1977, the majority of the electorate was Ashkenazim (53 percent), 43 percent were Sephardim, and 4 percent were Israeli-born with fathers also born in Israel. In the 1988 election, for the first time the Jews of Sephardi background outnumbered the Jews of Ashkenazi background in the electorate. In 1992, with the mass immigration from the former Soviet Union, most of which was of Ashkenazi origin, the proportions were 48 percent Ashkenazim, 44 percent Sephardim, and 8 percent Israeli-born whose fathers were also born in Israel, and by 1996 the Ashkenazim had grown to 50 percent, the Sephardim had gone down to 39 percent, and the Israeli-born with fathers born in Israel had grown to 11 percent.[8]

The relationship between voting and origin is not a new one in Israeli politics. In the 1948–77 period of Labor dominance, it regularly won support from most groups in the society. This was especially true of new immigrants, who were often in awe of the "miracle" that had returned them to the land of their fathers. These immigrants were dependent on the bureaucracies of the establishment for the whole gamut of economic, educational, health, social, and cultural needs. An increasingly large share of the electorate was of Sephardi origin, and Mapai maintained its dominant role as the largest plurality party and the leader of every government coalition. More than that, attempts to appeal to the Sephardi population at election time by lists set up by Sephardim largely failed. It was only before the mass immigration of the early 1950s that representation to the Knesset was achieved by any lists manifestly linking themselves with Sephardim and Yemenites.

The shift away from Labor by the Sephardim was gradual. In the 1970s the tendency became more pronounced, beyond the general trends of the Likud's growth and of Labor's decline. Ethnic voting among the Israeli public continues: ethnicity predicts the vote for both the Likud and the Alignment. In 1984 the preference ratio for the two parties among each ethnic group was about three to one, with the Sephardim preferring the Likud and the Ashkenazim the Alignment. In 1988 and 1992, the preference ratio declined, as smaller parties of the left and right extremes won more of the Ashkenazi and Sephardi votes, respectively. In 1996, both parties performed poorly, but the respective preferences of the ethnic groups persisted.

The ethnic cleavage manifested itself in voting behavior dramatically in the 1977 election when many voters abandoned their long-standing practice of supporting Labor. But they shifted largely along ethnic lines. Sephardim gravitated to the Likud and Ashkenazim to the DMC. These two defections so weakened Labor that the Likud could take over the reins of power, resulting in the beginning of the Likud era of Israeli politics. In 1981 and 1984 many of the Ashkenazim were back with Labor, and the campaigns were especially bitter, focused on the feelings of exploitation toward Labor felt by many Sephardim. The ethnic vote was most pronounced in the 1984 elections, although the 1981 election campaign was most taken up with the ethnic cleavage.

The fortunes of the Likud and Labor were transferred to the second generation as well. The Likud generally retained the loyalties of the Sephardim born in Israel, while Labor did better among Ashkenazim who immigrated and among their Israeli-born children. The Likud in the 1980s gained most among the youngest and fastest-growing groups; the Alignment, losing support within all groups over time, did best in the group that was oldest and was shrinking rapidly.

In the elections of the 1980s the term "ethnic voting" was used often. It was supposed to portray the support of Jews from Asia and Africa and their children for the Likud. The fact was that the Alignment was closer to being an "ethnic party" in this sense than the Likud was. About two-thirds of Labor's voters were Ashkenazim, and a similar percentage of the Likud voters were Sephardim. This had not always been the case. In the past the bulk of both the Likud's and Labor's support had come from Ashkenazim; after all, the Ashkenazim constituted a majority of the electorate. Polls going back to the late 1960s indicate that then, too, about two-thirds of the Alignment vote was from Ashkenazim, even though Sephardim also voted for the Alignment often. In the late 1960s both parties were predominantly Ashkenazi; by 1981 the Alignment had stayed that way, and the Likud had become predominantly Sephardi. The turnabout seems to have occurred in the election of 1977 when a majority of the Likud vote was Sephardi for the first time in history.

Likud in 1992 was more heavily Sephardi than in 1977, with two-thirds of its votes coming from that group in 1992 compared with about half in 1977; Labor was much more balanced, with half its voters Ashkenazim, a third Sephardim, and the rest second-generation Israelis. The Likud came close to being left only with its hard-core supporters, while Labor in 1992 was able to enlarge the circle of its voters. Labor and Peres in 1996 were unable to accelerate this trend, leading to a very close race and ultimately to defeat.

The question may also be turned around by asking how members of the two ethnic groups divided their votes between the two large parties in the 1980s. Again, a mirror image is provided. About 60 percent of the Ashkenazim voted Labor, and about a third, Likud. About 60 percent of the Sephardim voted Likud, and about a third, Labor. By 1984, the Ashkenazi vote was more concentrated in the Alignment than the Sephardi vote was in the Likud—about 70 percent for the former, about 60 percent for the latter. In 1988, with the relative success of Mapam and the Civil Rights Movement among Ashkenazim, Labor's support among that ethnic group fell to about half; Likud's support among Sephardim came close to 60 percent.

As the proportion of Sephardim grew in the electorate, it was clear that Labor would always have an uphill battle regaining power until it could increase its share of the Sephardi vote. That shift occurred in 1992. The trend was not overwhelming, but the movement of Sephardim to Labor was substantial enough to provide the bounce that Labor needed to regain power. This transformation worked only because it occurred in conjunction with two other developments: the movement of other former supporters away from the Likud to parties of the right, and the impetus given Labor by the new Soviet immigrants who supported it. In 1996, Netanyahu won two-thirds of the Sephardi vote, a third of the Ashkenazi vote, and 40 percent of the Israeli-born whose fathers were Israeli-born. Peres's numbers were reversed.

Meretz did more than three times better in 1992 among Ashkenazim and second-generation Israelis than among Sephardim, and the parties of the right were twice as popular among Sephardim as they were among Ashkenazim. Most of Meretz's support came from Ashkenazim, similar to the three out of four rate of the DMC in 1977.

Two-thirds of the voters for the parties of the right in 1992 were Sephardim. The most notable shift was for the religious parties. They successfully adapted to the demographic shifts in Israel after 1977. From a situation in which three-quarters of their vote came from Ashkenazim, in

1992 half their vote was Sephardi, one-third Ashkenazi, and one in seven was a second-generation Israeli. The pattern of their support was almost identical to the distribution in the general population, representing an enormous political achievement. The religious parties drew equally from all ethnic groups in 1992, very different from their 1977 pattern, which showed strong support among Ashkenazim.

In 1996, Netanyahu's vote came primarily from Sephardim, Peres's from Ashkenazim. The surge of religious parties in 1996 was based on broad ethnic support, with different ethnic groups supporting the three religious parties. Yahadut Hatorah was largely Ashkenazi, Shas mostly Sephardi, and the NRP drawing from both ethnic groups. From a situation in which three-quarters of its vote came from Ashkenazim, in 1996 NRP's constituents came from the entire spectrum of Israel's ethnic groups.

If indeed the two major parties in the 1990s may be defined as ethnic parties, it is only in terms of their electorate. One has to keep in mind that about one-third of each ethnic group voted for "the wrong party." Neither party organized to further specific ethnic ends or along ethnic lines. Both Labor and the Likud were run by Ashkenazim, as has been the case with most parties in Israel. Sephardim were high on the lists, but representation was not the issue. The Likud and Labor were ethnic parties only in the sense that the vote for each of them was closely associated with ethnicity.

There were two ethnic lists in the 1996 elections: Shas and Israel b'Aliyah, the party of immigrants from the former Soviet Union. This was the fourth time that Shas ran, and its strength grew from four seats in 1984, to six seats in each of the 1988 and 1992 elections, and ten seats in 1996. Israel b'Aliyah won seven seats in 1996.

Despite the fact that it had held power since 1977 only in the 1984–86 and 1992–96 periods, the Alignment remained identified by many as the party of the establishment. Sephardim, and especially their Israeli-born children, tended to reject Labor because of the persistent inequalities these voters perceived. Ashkenazi voters tended to reject the populism of Likud governments and longed to return to a more familiar and pragmatic past. The hawkish image of the Likud also correlated with attitudes prevalent among Sephardim. Sephardim tend to be more traditional about religion than Ashkenazim. Begin (although not the Likud Party generally) was very successful in utilizing the symbols and language of religion. Many thought of Labor as antireligious, especially since it supported Meretz positions during the 1992–96 period, and because of Labor's attacks on the religious parties for what Labor termed disproportionate gains through coalition bargaining. During the 1996 race, Peres pleaded with the rabbis for the support of the religious vote, but to no avail.

The twin issues of God (religion) and nationalism (the territories) were powerful predictors of the vote. On the state-religion issue, the trend of increasing correlations persists over time. The identification of Labor as an anticlerical party has strengthened, while the Likud has played to the traditional sympathies of much of its voting base, even though the origins and ideology of the Likud are very secular.[9]

Since 1984, the elections in which Shamir replaced Begin as the head of the Likud, the correlations of the territories issue with the vote were high. Over time, Labor has more unambiguously identified itself as the territories-for-peace party, and the platform of Labor has become less vague on this issue. The public perception of the difference between these two parties on the territories issue did not change much; almost two-thirds of the respondents in the 1981, 1984, and 1992 surveys thought these differences were big or very big. By 1996 the figure jumped to 80 percent, although Netanyahu strained toward the middle in the election campaign.

The years 1992 and 1996 were different from previous elections in that many more voters said that the territories would be an important consideration in their voting decision. In the 1996 sample, 71 percent said that the issue of the territories would very greatly influence their vote, compared with 52 percent in 1992 and less than a third in previous elections. Adding the next category of response, 90 percent in 1996 and 81 percent in 1992 said that it would influence them greatly or very greatly, compared with 63 percent in previous elections.

We have seen that respondents report that ideology drives their vote and that issue voting has risen. Although the territories issue may drive the vote, it does not necessarily dominate the campaign. One way of assessing the mood of the times is to consider the recurring question asking respondents to identify the major issue with which the government should deal. Breaking the answers down into foreign and security issues on the one hand (security, terror, peace, etc.) and domestic issues on the other (housing, health, education, immigrant absorption, etc.) shows how much the public agenda varied over the years (see figure 8.1). In 1969, 1988, and 1996, foreign and security issues were mentioned by more than 70 percent of respondents. But in 1981 and 1984 no more than 30 percent mentioned those issues and concentrated instead on domestic matters. Equally fascinating is the fact that supporters of both big parties shift their attention in the same direction, with small differences.

It is easy enough to "predict the past" and to provide "explanations" for these differences. It is much more difficult to predict them. The years for which the security response was high came on the heels of important security developments: the Six-Day War of 1967, the beginning of the Intifada in 1987, and the Oslo agreements with the PLO of 1993 and 1995. The years 1981 and 1984 were years of the emergence of Sephardi voting

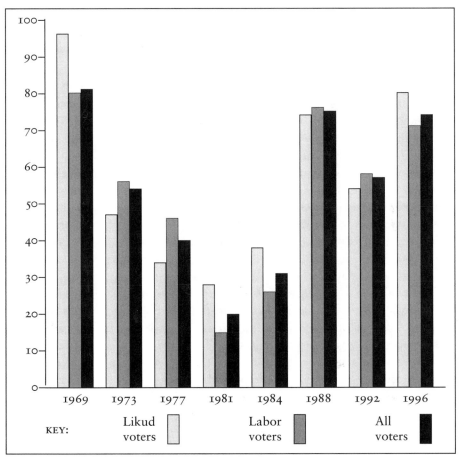

FIGURE 8.1
SECURITY AND/OR PEACE AS MAJOR VOTE ISSUES,
1969–96 (IN PERCENTAGES)

SOURCE: *Statistical Abstracts.*

power and its finding a powerful voice in its support for the Likud. To this issue of the ethnic vote we now turn our attention.

The chances for the continued success of a democratic regime rest in part in having social groups overlap. In Israel today we witness a lack of overlapping social cleavages, so much so as to point to a possible danger to Israeli democracy. When the political system is polarized, with one group concentrating within it the religious, Sephardim, and less educated and lower-status workers voting for the Likud and religious parties, and the other group having a disproportionate share of secular, upper-class Ashkenazim voting for Labor and Meretz, the chances of intolerance, lack of communication and understanding, and violence grow. These patterns are not immutable, and it may be that with changes in the leadership of the two major parties the system will become very fluid, and new affiliations will emerge within the polity.[10]

In many countries the amount of the vote variance explained by social structure and attitudinal variables has been reduced from the 1960s through the 1980s. This has not been the case in Israel. The difference lies in the nature of the issues that have captured the agenda. In most Western countries issues involving postbourgeois versus materialist values, gender issues, public versus private consumption, and state employment have gained ascendancy. In Israel these issues have energized only limited publics and have not become as central, critical, and engulfing as the major issue dimension in Israeli politics: the territories and the Israeli-Arab conflict. Voting in Israel became more structured, and security issues became a more important determinant of it over time.

The changing bases of electoral behavior have been attributed to greater individual- and aggregate-level volatility in the vote. And this liberation, where it occurs, means that the fortunes of political parties and leaders have become much less certain and are dependent more on leadership skills than on organizational factors.[11] The 1992 elections, for instance, seemed to empower the electorate, and the Labor Party was called on to lead for the next term, with the implicit threat that it too could be replaced in future elections. As it was in 1996.

Split-Ticket Voting

Split-ticket voting was the dominant feature of the 1996 election. Almost half the voters selected parties different from those of the two candidates for the office of prime minister, as is clearly seen in table 8.5. Netanyahu received about 55 percent of the votes of Jews, Peres more than 90 percent of the votes of non-Jews, most notably in Nazareth, the largest Arab city in the country. Communities with strong concentrations of observant Jews, such as Bnei Brak (largely haredi) and Jerusalem (both haredi and Orthodox-Zionist), as well as Jews living the territories (such as in the city of Ariel) went heavily for Netanyahu. Peres did very well in kibbutzim (collective settlements), and slightly better than Netanyahu in secular Jewish cities such as Tel Aviv. The settlers of the Golan Heights, the former Syrian area seen by many as crucial to Israeli security, were largely Labor supporters; they split almost evenly in the prime minister's race because they were concerned that Labor was planning to return the Golan.

The rate of invalid votes in the prime minister's race was 4.8 percent, more than double the rate (2.2 percent) for the Knesset. The difference be-

TABLE 8.5

VOTING SUPPORT FOR NETANYAHU AND PERES,
LIKUD AND LABOR IN SELECTED COMMUNITIES,
1996 (IN PERCENTAGES)

	Eligible voters	*Invalid votes*	*Netanyahu*	*Peres*	*Likud-Gesher-Tzomet*	*Labor*
Total	100	4.8	50.5	49.5	24.8	26.6
Jerusalem	7.4	4.3	69.9	30.1	25.7	16.4
Tel Aviv	7.9	5.1	44.9	55.1	26.7	34.0
Bnei Brak (haredi)	2.0	4.3	89.0	11.0	11.3	6.7
Nazareth (Arab)	1.3	8.6	1.4	98.6	8.6	3.4
Ariel (in territories)	.3	1.8	89.3	10.7	50.5	1.8
Katzrin (in Golan Heights)	.1	4.2	43.2	56.8	25.3	24.3
Yagur (kibbutz)	.04	3.7	2.4	97.6	1.6	80.6

tween the rates indicates that it was not a lack of understanding of the election rules that caused the high rate of invalid voters for prime minister; instead, it points to an unwillingness to choose either of the two candidates on the part of a sizable number of voters. This reluctance was generalized throughout the system, not concentrated in one area or voter category. In Arab Nazareth, 8.6 percent of those who voted in the prime ministerial election cast blank or invalid ballots, while in Jewish Tel Aviv the percentage was 5.1, and in observant Jerusalem and haredi Bnei Brak it was 4.3 percent in each. Considering that the difference between the two candidates was less than 30,000 votes, these abstentions were crucial.

The Israeli voter used the ballot box in 1996 in a sophisticated manner and left in the wake of the vote a weakened party system and a Knesset that was fractionalized and unnerved compared to the prime minister and the executive branch. Splitting their tickets, many voters sent differentiated messages by using differently the two votes available—one for the prime minister and one for the Knesset—and thereby blurring the clarity of the Knesset election results regarding national issues. In the 1996 survey conducted in the weeks before the election, respondents were asked how they would vote if the old system were in place and they had only one vote each. Almost all Likud and Labor voters reported they would vote as they did, a third of the left-wing Meretz voters said they would vote Labor, and

12 percent of the voters for religious parties reported that they would vote for the Likud.

The Floating Vote

Despite social and economic change, the political system of Israel seemed on the surface to be remarkably stable until 1977, with one party (Mapai, later Labor) consistently receiving a plurality of the votes. But the Israeli political system was hardly static. Appearances notwithstanding, it would be misleading to depict the election results as robotlike behavior on the part of the public, election after election. To sustain this kind of analysis, we would have to make herculean assumptions about the unimportance of population change due to the exit of some from the voting public (death, emigration) and the entrance of others (coming of age, immigration). The anomaly of the Israeli case stemmed from the very large change in voting publics (primarily due to immigration) from election to election, and the apparent stability of the voting results. Part of the effect was illusory: votes changed, but the government did not.

The proportional representation system and the emergence of a dominant party system in Israel prevented the translation of voting change into government change until 1977. Changes in the vote, however, were accurately reflected in the size of the delegations that represented parties in the Knesset. Between 1965 and 1969, 25 percent of the respondents reported that they had voted for different parties in the two elections. A stability rate of 74 percent is very similar to the results obtained in Britain in a study that concluded that "electoral change is due not to a limited group of 'floating' voters but to a very broad segment of British electors."[12]

Prior to 1973, a good deal of the change of vote in Israel was among factional groupings. For example, the parties of the left lost voters to one another. We have seen that the individual party may be exposed to a substantial swing in its votes from election to election. But when examined in terms of factional groupings, a much more stable picture emerges. Parties of the left (including the communists) never won fewer than sixty-four nor more than sixty-nine seats in the 120-seat Knesset in the seven elections through 1969. In 1973, they won fifty-nine seats. The center parties ranged between twenty-seven and thirty-four seats (forty-three in 1973), and the religious parties between fifteen and eighteen (fifteen in 1973). Hanoch Smith divided the parties into six such groupings and calculated the average deviation for each grouping between 1949 through 1969.[13] The average deviation from the 1949–69 average vote for the parties in the Labor grouping (excluding the communists) was only 1 percent. The average deviation for the center and religious groupings was even lower: .8 and .6

percent, respectively. The overall strength of factional groupings was relatively stable. Changes were occasioned by mergers and splits, alignments and divisions that characterized the relationships among the parties within factional groupings. But these swings should not obfuscate the basic fact that the parties of the Labor grouping, especially Mapai, dominated the voting results and politics of the entire period.

The period following the Yom Kippur War of 1973 is best thought of in terms of a realigning electoral era. In a realigning election (or a critical election, in V.O. Key's phrase), a new party balance is created. Key characterized an election as critical when "more or less profound readjustments occur in the relations of power within the community, and in which new and durable election groupings are formed."[14] Many thought that the 1973 war could be seen as a turning point in Israeli politics because it shattered so many myths and previously held conceptions. The publication of the 1973 election results soon after the war provided a rare opportunity to compare the voting behavior of large segments of the population. Since much of the population was serving in the army on election day, the results were especially informative, for the army is rather homogeneous in its composition—predominantly young and male (although women and the not-so-young are also represented).

If the experience of the 1973 war was to have far-reaching effects in the future, it would have been best to search for signs of these effects in groups directly involved in the war and among those whose political beliefs and partisan attachments were still relatively flexible. If the army went Likud by a large majority, we might interpret the war as a shared experience of the generation then reaching maturity that would have an impact on the politics of the future. The new tendency would be different from the dominant one in the previous generation; the younger generation, which constituted a larger share of the electorate and was raising its children in a new climate of opinion, would eventually prevail.

The election results did not indicate that the voters behaved very differently on election day from the way they had behaved before. The army results gave the Likud 41.3 percent of the vote, as opposed to 39.5 percent for the Alignment. In the general population the division was 30.2 percent and 39.6 percent, respectively. (In 1977 the results were even more dramatic in the army: 46 percent Likud, 22 percent Alignment, 16 percent DMC.) It is true that the Likud outpaced the Alignment in the army returns. But even before the war it was well known that the Likud was strong among younger voters. The Alignment won from the army voters the same share as it did from the general population. Using this indicator, it was inappropriate to conclude that the 1973 elections were critical; at most, tendencies already in process were accelerated as a result of the war.

There was no clear, large-scale shift of group allegiances from one party to another. Previous patterns were accelerated; no new patterns were obvious.

In a dominant-party system it may be more useful to discuss a "realigning electoral era"[15] rather than a critical election. During such an era the dominant party's electoral support slips from its grasp. As time passes, as "dominant doctrines" shift, the power base of the dominant party may well be eroded. No one act or failure is enough to explain this decline. The Labor Party, the pivot of all government coalitions until 1977, became entrenched in office. Socialist values notwithstanding, it became conservative. It was anxious to preserve the gains it had won for the state, for the citizenry, and for its functionaries as well. Many of the revolutionary socialist ideals that were part of Labor's legacy became only verbal goals. The fact that Labor had difficulty in attracting the votes of the young—the generation that had grown up since independence—indicated a partial short-circuiting of the party's claim to dominance. This decline was evident in the voting results.

The 1977 elections ended the realigning era by deposing the dominant party. As we would expect in a dominant-party system, the opposition itself did little to depose the ruling party. The Likud's strength increased steadily; demographic and ideological forces were harnessed behind it. The Alignment's greatest loss was to the Democratic Movement for Change. Alignment votes that went to the DMC determined the fall of the Alignment and the rise of the Likud. Later victories by Labor in 1984 and 1992 could not restore its position of dominance. Dominance is a set of power relations, and a state of mind. Dominance is difficult to deny to the party that has it and extremely hard to rewin for the party that has lost it. The results of the 1981 elections strengthened the impression that a basic change in Israeli politics had come about as a result of the critical election era. Despite its relative success compared with the 1977 election, the Alignment was unable to stymie the continued growth of the Likud. In 1984, although the Alignment won more votes than any other party, it was far from a position of dominance and had to share power with the Likud in a National Unity Government. In 1988, Labor lost additional votes and was smaller than the Likud. Labor finally agreed to continue the National Unity Government with the Likud, but Labor could not demand that the prime ministry rotate out of the hands of the Likud's Prime Minister Shamir. The 1992 elections brought Labor back to power, but that advantage was lost again in 1996.

In 1973, after the postponement of elections as a result of the Yom Kippur War, the rate of vote stability remained remarkably high. To be sure, the Alignment was weakened and the Likud strengthened. The Likud won 8 percent of the 1969 Alignment vote, while it lost only 1 percent of its own 1969 vote to the Alignment. But when the overall rate of stability is calculated by dividing the number of stable votes in the two elections by the number of voters who reported a 1969 vote, the stability rate was 68 percent. The religious parties voters were most loyal, with 79 percent reporting identical votes in 1969 and 1973. Only two-thirds of the 1969 Alignment voters reported that they voted for the Alignment in 1973, with 17 percent reporting a vote for the Likud and 4 percent for the Citizens Rights Movement list.

If the rates of stability and floating vote were not all that different in 1973 from what had occurred earlier, what was different was the unbalanced nature of the tradeoff. Usually the floating vote is a multisided affair with the losses of one party made up by the gains it wins from another. Many of the losses sustained by the Alignment this time were net gains for the Likud. Perhaps this is the uniqueness of the 1973 results—not in the scope of this shift but in the relatively uniform movement of its direction.

In 1977 the rate of voting change was very high (see table 8.6). If between 1965 and 1969 it was about a quarter, and between 1969 and 1973 about a third, between 1973 and 1977 it was half of the sample; between 1977 and 1981 it fell back to about 40 percent (see table 8.7); and in the elections of 1981, 1984, and 1988, it retreated to a quarter. Most of the change was among those who had supported the Alignment in 1973. Of those (44.5 percent of the sample), less than half voted for the Alignment again in 1977, with 20 percent going to the Likud and 18 percent to the DMC.

TABLE 8.6

STABLE AND FLOATING VOTE, 1973 AND 1977
(IN PERCENTAGES)

| 1973 | 1977 | | | | | | |
	Likud	Align-Align	DMC	Religious	Other	No answer, no vote	Total
Likud	**19**	.5	2	0	.5	2	24.0
Alignment	9	**20.0**	8	.5	1.0	6	44.5
Religious	2	0	0	**5.0**	0	0	7.0
Other	1	0	2	0	**1.0**	2	6.0
No vote	5	.5	2	0.5	.5	4	12.5
No answer	0	0	0	0	0	**6**	6.0
Total	36	21.0	14	6.0	3.0	20	100.0
							(N = 465)

SOURCE: Based on June 1977 survey data.

NOTE: Stable vote in **boldface** type.

TABLE 8.7

STABLE AND FLOATING VOTE, 1977 AND 1981

(IN PERCENTAGES)

			1981			
1977	Likud	Align-ment	Religious	Other	No answer, no vote	Total
Likud	27	3	1	3.0	5.0	39
Alignment	2	18	0	1.0	3.0	24
DMC	1	4	0	2.0	2.0	9
Religious	1	0	3	.5	.5	5
Other	1	1	0	1.0	0.0	3
No vote	4	2	1	2.0	1.0	10
No answer	3	2	0	1.0	4.0	10
Total	39	30	5	10.5	15.5	100

(N = 1,203)

SOURCE: Based on May 1981 survey.

NOTE: Stable vote in **boldface** type.

The 1973 Likud voters remained loyal on the whole, with some 8 percent supporting the DMC in 1977. Those who did not vote in 1973 gave the Likud 40 percent of their vote, the DMC 16 percent, and the Alignment a scant 4 percent. The DMC received two-thirds of its voters who had participated in the 1973 elections from the Alignment, and the Likud almost 30 percent of its 1977 vote from the same source.

In 1981, a very tense and polarized campaign led to low levels of tradeoff among the Likud and Alignment voters of 1977 (see table 8.7). Most of them stayed with their previous choices, with the Alignment picking up 3 percent of the sample from those who had voted Likud in 1977, compared with 2 percent of the sample who had voted Alignment in 1977 and shifted to the Likud in 1981. The major movement was the DMC vote, which was overwhelmingly won by the Alignment at a ratio of four to one compared with the Likud. Some 1977 Likud voters voted for other parties, especially Tehiya. But the most crucial datum regarding the future was the attraction of the Likud among those who had not voted in 1977 (mostly young voters): the Likud outdrew the Alignment among this group by a ratio of two to one.

In 1984 (not shown here), 23 percent of the total sample repeated their 1981 votes for either the Alignment or the Likud. Four percent of the 1984 sample who had voted Likud in 1981 switched to the Alignment; 5.5 percent switched to other parties. The Alignment lost .5 percent to the Likud, 2 percent to others. Among the army voters, the Likud and Tehiya won about 50 percent, the Alignment, Shinui, and the Citizens Rights Movement about 40 percent.

In the 1988 elections, the two big parties retained their 1984 voters at about the same rate (not shown here). Some Alignment voters drifted to the left, but others moved to the Likud and the right. A similar pattern for the Likud voters was evident but in the opposite direction. The pattern among new voters (no vote in 1984) indicates just how fractured the political system was, with 5 percent of the total sample selecting the right and the Likud and 5 percent selecting Labor and the left.

Rates of retention were very different for Labor and Likud between 1988 and 1992 (see table 8.8). The Likud lost more than a third of its 1988 vote, while Labor retained most of its 1988 vote. Those defecting Likud voters went to Labor and to parties of the right. The result was a much-weakened Likud, allowing Labor and Rabin to take office in 1992. New voters split evenly among the right and the Likud, on the one hand, and the left and Labor, on the other, with a substantial number of them choosing religious parties.

The 1996 elections were different because of the addition of the direct election of the prime minister. Focusing only on the Knesset vote reveals the difficulty both big parties had retaining their 1992 voters (see table 8.9). New voters did not provide an answer to the Knesset vote question in the survey at a very high rate; those who did choose split evenly between Labor and Likud.

TABLE 8.8

STABLE AND FLOATING VOTE, 1988 AND 1992

(IN PERCENTAGES)

			1992				
1988	Right	Likud	Labor	Left	Religious	No answer, no vote	Total
Right	**2.5**	.5	.5	0	0	0	3.5
Likud	3.5	**20.5**	4.0	.5	1.0	4.5	34.0
Labor	.5	.5	**20.5**	1.5	0	1.5	24.5
Left	2.0	.5	1.5	**6.5**	0	.5	11.0
Religious	.5	1.0	.5	0	**4.5**	.5	7.0
No vote	3.0	3.0	4.0	2.0	1.5	1.0	14.5
No answer	1.0	.5	1.0	.5	0	2.5	5.5
Total	13.0	26.5	32.0	11.0	7.0	10.5	100.0
							(N = 1,107)

SOURCE: Based on June 1992 survey.

NOTE: Stable vote in **boldface** type.

TABLE 8.9

STABLE AND FLOATING VOTE, 1992 AND 1996

(IN PERCENTAGES)

1992	1996					
	Likud	Labor	Religious	Other	No answer, no vote	Total
Right	4	1	4	0	0	9
Likud	**19**	1	0	0	2.0	22
Labor	2	**24**	0	1.0	3.0	30
Left	0	3	0	3.0	1.0	7
Religious	1	0	**4**	.5	.5	6
Other	1	1	0	**1.0**	0	3
No vote	2	2	0	0	**5.0**	9
No answer	5	4	1	1.5	2.5	14
Total	34	36	9	7.0	14.0	100
						(N = 1,122)

SOURCE: Based on May 1996 survey.

NOTE: Stable vote in **boldface** type.

The factors associated with consistent voting are the same factors associated with a "conservative" vote. Age, for example, has always been very powerful; the older one is, the more likely one is to retain old patterns of behavior, including the vote. Education is also related to voting stability: the lower the education, the higher the stability of the vote. Voters with higher education levels change their votes more often and vote less often for the larger parties and more often for smaller ones.

Party Images

There are many reasons for the change in fortunes of the two parties; the passing of leadership, the weakening of dependency relations, and demographic changes have already been discussed. All these changes are connected with the images the electorate holds of the parties. Just as a social myth is a convenient way of ordering reality, the party's or leader's image is no less important than the actual opinion or personality. While reality is usually complex, myths and images have a simplifying quality about them. They are easily grasped, widely accepted, able to convert masses of detail into an understandable whole. If Peres is thought of as soft and Netanyahu as tough, conflicting evidence can easily be put aside in favor of the widely held image, which allows one to grasp the essence of the person more easily. And when conflicting images are widely held by polarized groups, beliefs tend to be held and expressed all the more strongly. A key aspect of voting behavior involves prospective evaluations of the competing parties —the answer to the question "Who can deliver?"[16]

Prospective evaluations have been found to be very important in explaining Israeli elections.[17] In 1988, short-term issues such as dealing with the Arab uprising were less important than aspects dealing with the long-term future of the territories. The analysis of the 1992 elections showed the security aspect to be crucial in the voting decision compared to the economic one. In the 1996 elections, the risks involved in peacemaking were contrasted with the threats evident in everyday life. Taking all these analyses together, it is clear that the images of the parties in terms of their ability to achieve goals that are generally favored by the electorate are significant factors in voting behavior.

Regarding security matters, the desirable party would be one able to put an end to uprisings and terror, on the one hand, and to achieve peace, on the other. Respondents have been asked over the years to evaluate which political party (Labor or Likud) would best be able to achieve different goals. Labor presented itself as the party of peace and the better one to lead the country in negotiations with the Arabs. The Likud tried to project a firm image regarding security. In 1992, Labor evidently achieved that image with Rabin at the head of the list; in both 1988 and 1996, with Peres, Labor gambled and lost. In 1996 Labor was seen as better able to bring true peace and more likely to preserve democracy in the country; the Likud was perceived as more likely to know how to fight terror and to handle the tradeoff between returning land for peace (see figure 8.2, p. 234).

Evaluations relating to the securing of true peace and the preservation of democracy were the elements that have changed the most (see figures 8.3 and 8.4, pp. 235 and 236), to the detriment of the Likud. This gives us a measure of a changing mood in the country and attests to the issues that swayed many of the switchers during this period. The bold prominence of the bars in figure 8.3 provide a symbolic referent of the Likud image in those years. By contrast, the bars for Labor on the same scale seemed shrinking and meek (see figure 8.4). Only toward the end of the period was there an upward slope in the pattern. But the overall impression was that the resurgence of Labor was tenuous and could quickly be reversed. As it was in 1996.

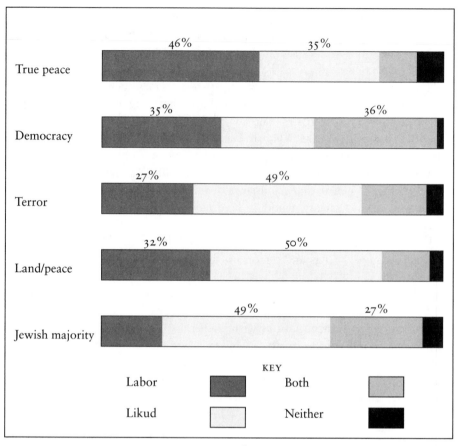

FIGURE 8.2
PARTY IMAGES, 1996

"Which party will better secure _____?"

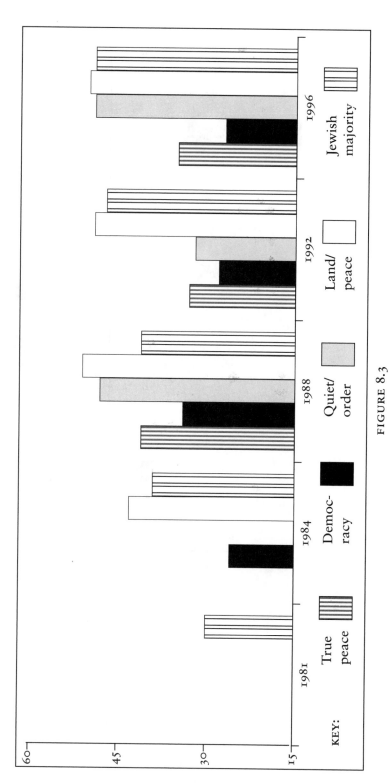

FIGURE 8.3

LIKUD IMAGE, 1981–96

"Which party will better secure _____?"

KEY:

True peace

Democ- racy

Quiet/ order

Land/ peace

Jewish majority

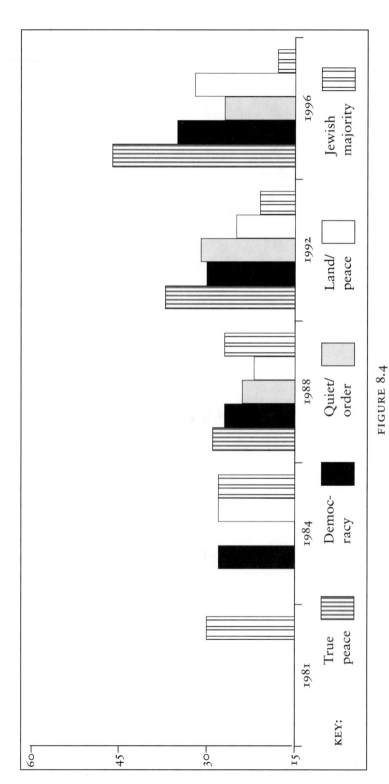

FIGURE 8.4
LABOR IMAGE, 1981–96

"Which party will better secure _____ ?"

KEY:

True peace | Democracy | Quiet/order | Land/peace | Jewish majority

9. The Knesset, the Government, and the Judiciary

The Knesset, Israel's parliament, is the supreme legislative body of the state. It has tremendous symbolic importance as the seat of the people's sovereignty and the most important deliberative council of the nation. Its Speaker stands in for the president of the country should the latter be out of the country or indisposed. He receives the reports of the State Controller. But symbolism should not be confused with power. With the adoption of the law mandating the direct election of the prime minister, the Knesset suffers from self-inflicted inferiority.

The Knesset is born of politics. The composition of the Knesset is determined by the one true expression of mass democracy: the elections. It is organized along party lines, committee appointments are made by party, and even seating arrangements are determined by party. But when the Knesset passed the law of the direct election of the prime minister, it abdicated much of its power.

Some aspects of the Knesset can be traced back to the Parliament of Great Britain, other aspects to continental usage and procedure. The Jewish state, deprived of autonomous independence and institutional development for some 2,000 years, took up parliamentary forms of the late nineteenth century. The long evolutionary process of the emergence of the supreme parliament was bypassed, and the acceptance of the Knesset as the omnipotent legislative body was natural. In fact, the struggle for parliamentary dominance in the world's democracies was protracted and crowned with success in England only in the eighteenth century. The lack of this historical perspective makes it more difficult, and more necessary, to evaluate the functions, strengths, and weaknesses of the Knesset.

The nineteenth century can rightly be considered the golden age of parliamentary supremacy. Legislative supremacy was the prevailing tendency in America and Europe, and representative institutions could successfully cope with the relatively simple conflicts of democratic societies. Governmental expenditures were small, and the state tended not to interfere with the economy so that the legislature could delve into the details of budget making.[1] At this point of legislative evolution the Zionist revolution adopted parliamentary procedures. The Zionist Congresses reflected parliamentary life in turn-of-the-century Europe, and this is the legacy of the Knesset. The link between the Congresses and the Knesset was the Electors' Council (Asefat Nivharim) of the Yishuv, which served as the assembly for the Jewish community under the Mandate.

Two interesting structural features of the Knesset indicate the Israeli parliament's affinity to the continental style rather than the English. First, speakers in the Knesset, as in continental parliaments, speak from the rostrum. This encourages prepared speeches and lengthy oratory and decreases the likelihood of sharp interchanges between the speaker and his listeners. In the English Parliament one speaks from one's seat. At one time Israeli practice introduced microphones at the seating place of each member to assure that interlocutions be heard, but this was discontinued. As a rule, the speaker who has the floor now comes to the rostrum and addresses the Knesset from there.

The second feature is the matter of permanent seating and the capacity of the house to hold all the members. The British case is unique in this sense; members do not have fixed seats, and the hall is too small to fit all the members comfortably. In contrast, Knesset proceedings take place in a spacious hall, and each member is assigned a seat. Members of the government sit at an oblong table in the center of the chamber with members of the Knesset around them in a semicircle. They all face the chairman of the meeting and the rostrum.[2] The party that controls the ruling coalition sits to the left of the Speaker, not for ideological reasons, but because that provides the most advantageous angles for the television cameras that broadcast the proceedings.

The Absence of Checks and Balances

An important school of thought argues that the institutions of constitutional and representative government are central to democracy. One of the central issues determining the viability of a democratic political system concerns the relative merits and demerits of the parliamentary and presidential systems in terms of the relations between the legislative and executive branches of the government, the accountability of one to the other, and the overriding question of separation of powers and checks and balances.

Almost all governments have executive, legislative, and judicial functions differentiated in different branches. There is mixing in the functioning of the branches in all systems, as when judges fill administrative functions regarding implementation of judicial decisions, the division of land, and bequests. Deviations from the principle of division of power are especially blatant. The administration deals with secondary legislation in amounts that surpass the output of the Knesset in primary legislation and administrative justice becomes more important as the degree of intervention of the central government grows.[3] The deviations of the courts and the legislature may be considered marginal, as when the Knesset takes on judiciary powers in deciding to revoke the immunity of a Knesset member.

Even before the adoption of the new system of simultaneous election of the prime minister and the parliament, it was clear that the legislature was not the equal of the executive, although formally the legislature generated and controlled the government. The legislature in Israel simply did not have the status or the power of the executive. The strong party system on which both rested made it a political inevitability that the dependent Knesset members would support their party leaders, who were also government ministers. The new system underscores the strength of the prime minister and the weakness of the Knesset even more forcefully.

One of the important myths of Israeli political life is that checks and balances exist within the system. This is simply not so. Even in the past, the legislature was important, and in some hypothetical situations even crucial, but in the political sense it was merely a staging ground for the government and the executive branch. There were cases when a move by a Knesset member from party to party could threaten the stability of the government coalition. But that type of calculated behavior on the part of a representative is hardly an appropriate base for a constitutional separation of powers. In the new system, partly by design, partly by accident, the prime minister is much more autonomous than before.

Prime Ministerial Government

The executive branch in Israel always had disproportionate importance compared to the legislative branch. The introduction of the direct election of the prime minister in 1996 has enhanced that power. As of 1996, Israel embarked on the uncharted waters of "presidential parliamentarism."[4] The prime minister is elected directly by the voters using a winner-take-all system, with a second-round runoff between the two highest vote getters two weeks later if no candidate receives a majority in the first round. The Knesset is still elected as in the past, using a strict system of proportional representation.

The new system raises serious questions of political control, accountability, and legitimacy. If the prime minister comes from a party with a different set of political values from the majority of the members elected to the Knesset, deadlock and paralysis are possible. Who would be responsible for the continued running of the state? And whose will would prevail? The kinds of dilemmas that may await the system in the future would be more appropriate in a country in which inaction is championed, or one in which gratifications could be denied while deliberations took place. The

Israeli system has neither of these qualities, and hence the crisis, should it happen, is likely to be very severe.

The system of separately electing the prime minister and the legislature is unique among the nations of the world, since it fuses the two dominant forms of democratic government, consensus rule and majoritarianism. The answers to two questions highlight the differences between the two systems of governing: Does the legislature select the chief executive? Is the chief executive dependent on the legislature's confidence? Two "yes" answers identify the system as parliamentary, two "no" answers as presidential (see figure 9.1).

| | | Is the chief executive dependent on legislative confidence? | |
		Yes	No
Is the chief executive selected by the legislature?	Yes	*Parliamentary government*	**Switzerland**
	No	**Israel 1996 (Second Republic)**	*Presidential government*

FIGURE 9.1

FORMS OF GOVERNMENT

SOURCE: Adapted from Arend Lijphart, *Democracies* (New Haven: Yale University Press, 1984), 70.

This major constitutional undertaking lacks a coherent constitutional conception. Some of its provisions seem whimsical; the legislation was the result of tough negotiations and compromises and is a good example of Bismarck's admonition to beware of examining too carefully the process by which two things are made—sausage and laws.[5] The law introduces a balance of political terror, making the prime minister and the Knesset hostages of each other. While there are many negative sanctions, the positive ones are few and far between.

The Knesset may remove the prime minister by a special vote of eighty members, on which removal new elections for the prime minister take place. In contrast, the prime minister, with the agreement of the president, can dissolve the Knesset; such a step would also end the prime minister's tenure and would force new elections for both. The Knesset can also remove the prime minister by expressing no-confidence by a majority vote (sixty-one votes), or by failing to pass the national budget, but then new elections for both prime minister and Knesset would be held.

The prime minister, although elected directly by the people, must win approval from the Knesset for his cabinet ministers. The law limits the size of the cabinet to a minimum of eight members and a maximum of eighteen, including the prime minister, and at least half must be Knesset members. A minister may be removed either by the prime minister, or by the Knesset, with a special majority of 70 of its 120 members. If approval of the cabinet is denied by the Knesset, both the prime minister and the Knesset must stand for elections again within sixty days. If the prime minister fails a second time in winning the Knesset's approval of the cabinet, that person may not stand again for prime minister in the next elections.

Eligibility rules also indicate the ambivalent nature of the new law in terms of a parliamentary format and a presidential system. The people elect, yet the Knesset's role is crucial. The candidate must be at least thirty years old and meet the qualifications for Knesset membership. If the elections for prime minister are held in conjunction with Knesset elections, he must be the head of a party list. If special elections for prime minister are called, he must be a Knesset member. The candidate may be nominated by a party faction in the outgoing Knesset with at least ten members, provided that faction is running in the next Knesset elections, or he may be nominated by a combination of Knesset factions whose total representation is more than ten, provided that they are competing in the upcoming elections. Fifty thousand eligible voters may also nominate a candidate who heads a list running in the Knesset elections. A term limit is also in place: a prime minister who has served for seven consecutive years cannot run for reelection in the next election.

Israel was a good example of the parliamentary system before the adoption of the dual system of elections. The Knesset was elected by the people, and it in turn selected the executive branch based on its membership. The leader of the plurality party was usually called to form the government and stand at its head. Since no party ever won a majority of the votes, a coalition government was always formed.

Confidence in the government was assured as long as the coalition remained intact. Lack of confidence was often moved; there were 99 votes of no-confidence in the 1992–96 period, and 150 in the 1988–92 period. None of the motions was successful. Only one government failed a vote of confidence in Israel's political history; that was in 1990, when Shimon Peres orchestrated the fall of the National Unity Government headed by Yitzhak Shamir with his "dirty trick" maneuver. In the end Peres was unable to win a majority of the Knesset, and Shamir formed another government without Labor.

While the coalition held, it was almost inconceivable that the government would fail to pass its legislative program in the Knesset. The government ceased its term in office if the Knesset expressed no-confidence in it, if it decided to resign, if the prime minister no longer could or wished to serve in that capacity, or if a new Knesset were elected. In all four situations the outgoing government continued as a caretaker government until a new one was appointed. A caretaker government had all the powers of a regular government and none of the political liabilities. It was hermetically closed (Joshua 6:1); ministers could not be appointed or replaced. A no-confidence vote could not be expressed in a caretaker government.

The result of a vote of no-confidence, or the resignation of the government or the prime minister, was that the government fell. New elections were *not* a result of any of these developments. The only way in which new elections could be called in Israel was through a law of the Knesset. No one could dissolve the Knesset. Israel was a very pure example of the parliamentary form of government.

The previous system had a certain degree of flexibility. The president of the country could empower the leader of a minority party to form the government. This happened in 1983 when Shamir was asked by the president to form a government after Prime Minister Begin's resignation, even though the Likud's Knesset delegation was smaller than the Alignment's. The person who was to form the government had to win a majority of the Knesset's votes, and if the choice of the president was inappropriate, his candidate would be unsuccessful in his task.

The Knesset had the ability to call for new elections, but since the Knesset is made up of politicians and political parties, and the decision to disband the Knesset and call new elections demanded a majority of the house, the governing coalition could almost always determine whether this move would happen or not. New elections were called against the wishes of the ruling majority only once. This occurred before the 1984 elections when Tami, although a party in the governing coalition, used its three votes to support an opposition motion to hold early elections.

The dual system of separately electing the prime minister and the Knesset will test many of these patterns. No clear relationship exists between the legislative and executive branches. The prime minister is in place (a feature of a presidential system), but he can be replaced only by new elections should he find it difficult to win the legislative majority needed to govern, and not by the emergence of an alternative coalition in the Knesset (a feature of a parliamentary system). In the new system, a majority of at least sixty-one Knesset members is needed to remove the prime minister; in the past, losing a vote of confidence by any majority was sufficient. This is another sense in which the Knesset has strengthened the prime minister at its expense.

There are no checks and balances in place to regulate their interactions: the prime minister cannot veto legislation, nor can the Knesset overturn prime ministerial actions. The sole recourse to political crisis is new elections. Calling a time-out for two months to conduct new elections in the face of a crisis situation seems a flawed method even before it is tested by reality.

The elementary fact of Israeli political life remains that the government, now headed by a directly elected prime minister, and not the Knesset, is the focus of political power in the country. In the past, ministers of the cabinet were leaders of the political parties in the coalition. As ministers, they had not only political power and prestige but generally also the patronage and budget to enhance their political positions and that of their parties. As leaders of political parties that tended to operate oligarchically, they knew that the other Knesset members of their party realized that it was in the interest of the party—and often in their personal interests—to toe the line. The new system gives rise to the distinction between ministers and secretaries in the sense of American government: advisers or experts serving at the pleasure of the leader (the prime minister in Israel, the president in the United States). It is too early to tell if this model will develop, but the constitutional provisions are in place for its emergence.

Under the former system, the strength of the government was achieved by a process of condensation in which, at each successive stage, the potency of the remaining actors increased. Within a voting population of 3 million, the power of an individual voter was not great. The relative influence of each of the 120 members of the Knesset was obviously greater. If members of the government coalition parties numbered, say, sixty-five, and members of the government eighteen, power was concentrated even more. Now, if you were one of the seven who happened to be ministers who were members of the major party and, say, among the ministers of the major party you also happened to be in the dominant faction, of which there were only three members, your power grew greatly.

In contrast, the person directly elected prime minister takes on the role of producer and director of the entire show. The process of condensation, once the major feature of the Israeli political scene and enhanced by the governmental institutions developed, dissipates. The smallness of the country, the electoral system, the parliamentary system with coalition government, the supremacy of the executive, and the direct election of the prime minister—all these things enhance the centralization of the system even more.

The law regulating the direct election of the prime minister is likely to lead to a different role for the cabinet. First, by law it is a smaller body, eighteen members at most, compared to governments that reached the mid-twenties in the past. Second, up to half of its members can be detached experts, or at least not members of the Knesset. Yet it retains the connection to the Knesset and its parties by the other half, who have to be Knesset members, generally meaning party leaders. Ministers are responsible to the prime minister, but they are obligated to report on their activities to the Knesset. Third, the prime minister can hire and fire ministers and can define the scope of activities and responsibilities of the various ministries. All these moves would have been very difficult under the old system; under the new one, they may still be moves of import, but, depending on the personality and style of the prime minister, they may be much more possible. In effect, the ministers will be hostage to the political will of the prime minister. Fourth, the prime minister becomes the clear leader, not merely the first among equals. The prime minister still has to be concerned with the stability of the coalition, but in general that stability will be shaken only if Knesset party leaders are willing to run the risk of standing for new elections, an activity that is universally unpopular among politicians. The major fault of the law in this context is that the major relationship that exists between the legislative and executive branches is the fear that one of them will bring both to judgment day (new elections) sixty days from now.

Coalition Politics

The two words *coalition politics* are almost synonymous. In order to construct winning majorities in committees, organizations, or legislatures, coalitions must often be formed. Forming coalitions comes naturally to politicians, and in the parliamentary systems of Europe it has become accepted as a basic characteristic of politics.

As a general rule we would expect coalitions to be formed with the smallest surplus over the resources necessary to maintain a majority in the Knesset. There are costs involved in having another party support your party's platform. Obviously, one would try to keep costs down by entering coalitions with as few other parties as possible. The "minimum size" principle applied to the Knesset would lead us to expect that a coalition of 61 in the 120-member Knesset would be formed. In fact, the Israeli experience has rarely adhered to the minimum-size principle.[6] Most governments formed in Israel between 1949 and 1996 have rested on solid majorities in the Knesset, well above the minimum size needed to rule. These comfortable majorities have given the governments more leeway in actions and have intimidated smaller parties from causing coalition crises because by simple arithmetic it is clear to smaller parties that they are dispensable. Of the twenty-seven governments since 1949, only two have had support from fewer than sixty-five members at the outset. In 1955 the cabinet formed by

Prime Minister Sharett was made up of a coalition of only sixty-four votes, but it lasted only two months. The 1995 government formed by Peres after the Rabin assassination began with the formal support of only fifty-six Knesset members, but it had the informal support of five Arab Knesset members and was in a state of consultation with the six-member Shas delegation about joining the coalition. The special conditions that existed after the assassination allowed the government to continue through the elections a half year later.

During its term of office, a coalition's size may be reduced to the point that it is in danger of losing its parliamentary majority. Thus the Ben-Gurion cabinet of 1951 had the support of only sixty Knesset members after Agudat Israel and Poalei Agudat Israel left the cabinet over the issue of compulsory army service for women. As a result of defections from the Likud and the splitting up of the DMC, Begin's Knesset support fell drastically in 1979. After the 1981 elections, Begin set up a government based on the support of only sixty-one members of the Knesset.

Until 1977, the consistent leader of the coalition was the Mapai-Labor Alignment. Being the pivot of all arithmetical calculations regarding the coalitions, the dominant party consolidated its position by controlling the key ministries of defense, foreign affairs, finance, education, and the prime ministry. Budget allocations, key appointments, and important matters of policy were all in the hands of the Labor Party. With the ascension of the Likud in 1977, the government coalition was constructed for the first time by another party. But its political behavior in terms of forming the coalition was not much different from that displayed by the Alignment over the years.

The basic ingredient of the Likud coalition of 1977 was the same as that used by the various Labor governments—the National Religious Party. With twelve Knesset votes, the NRP was attractive to the Likud without being threatening. Moreover, the NRP was experienced in the politics of compromise, which is the essence of coalition politics. The alternative DMC, with fifteen seats, had a reformist bent to it and insisted on items in the coalition negotiations, such as electoral reform, to which the Likud preferred to pay only lip service. Once the government was set up, it was harder for the DMC to stand by its principles; ultimately it acquiesced in entering the government coalition without receiving the assurances it had sought.

A good working relationship developed between Mapai and the religious parties, although the major crises in the history of coalitions in Israel are associated with problems of religion. In a country so hard-pressed with security and economic problems, it is enlightening to note that cabinet crises usually center on matters peripheral to immediate concerns of government and pertaining more to matters of philosophy and theology. Perhaps this indicates special cultural attainments of Jews and the Jewish state, but it also means that ruling coalitions are relatively successful in governing; government policy is generally assured of support before it reaches the Knesset, and only on matters on which cleavage cannot be overcome do partners sometimes quarrel in public.

Three examples will suffice. The first crisis in Israeli cabinet history occurred in early 1950 over the religious education of children in immigrant camps. A compromise solution was worked out whereby religious schools would be set up in predominantly religious camps and two systems, secular and religious, would operate in others. By the end of 1950 the issue emerged again; the cabinet recommendations were rejected by a Knesset vote of 49–42 with many opposition parties using the opportunity to strike a blow against Mapai as much as to support the claims of the religious parties. Ben-Gurion immediately announced the resignation of the government, and new elections were called for July 1951. This crisis gave impetus to Ben-Gurion's assessment that a national system of education must be established, thereby abandoning party-related tracks that had characterized education in the prestate period. At the government level, he was convinced that effective ways must be found to assure collective responsibility in order to prevent cabinets failing as a result of the defection of coalition members. It also convinced him that electoral reform was needed in order to free the political system from the stranglehold that strong parties had over it.

A second crisis occurred in July 1958 when the two NRP ministers resigned from the cabinet over a directive issued by Minister of the Interior Israel Bar-Yehuda of Ahdut Haavoda. Bar-Yehuda's instructions to registration officials stated that "any person declaring in good faith that he is a Jew shall be registered as a Jew and no additional proof shall be required." This infuriated the religious authorities, for the question of "Who is a Jew?" has historically and traditionally been their province. Indeed, it can be argued that the issue is of prime concern to them because matters of group exclusivity are meaningful only in terms of some preconceived notion of the history and destiny of the group. Ultimately, the NRP resigned from the cabinet and experienced the taste of opposition for the first time. The real issue was not "Who is a Jew?" but *who decides* who is a Jew? The most significant political outcome of the crisis was that between 1959 and the late 1980s, the minister of the interior, who is responsible for registration of citizens, was from the National Religious Party. This pro-NRP conclusion was reached while the party was not a member of the coalition, indicating that even in opposition it had considerable leverage.

The story of the third example of a coalition quarrel began in January 1970 when the Supreme Court ruled that a person's statement that he was a Jew was sufficient to define him as a Jew. The government headed by Golda Meir subsequently amended the Law of Return by defining a Jew as "one who is born to a Jewess or is converted." This is in accord with rabbinical practice and was considered by many a major victory for the religious forces. But the issue soon arose—converted by whom? Conversions undertaken by non-Orthodox rabbis were not regarded as valid by the establishment of Israeli religious leaders. The demand was made that the Law of Return be further amended to have conversion valid only if performed in accord with Jewish rabbinical law (halacha).

Golda Meir's efforts to form a new government after the 1973 elections were held up until March 1974 by this issue. After much effort, a formula was developed. The prime minister issued a statement that since the amendment of the Law of Return, "no non-Jew had been registered as a Jew, and the government intended to continue in like fashion." The NRP gave in for all intents and purposes and joined the Meir government in the light of "compelling security considerations" occasioned by reports of the deteriorating situation on the Syrian border. When Golda Meir resigned as prime minister soon after having established the government, however, the process had to begin again. In this second round, the opponents of the coalition, especially the NRP Youth Faction led by Zevulun Hammer and Yehuda Ben Meir, hardened their line and were successful in preventing the NRP from participating in the new Rabin government. By November 1974 the NRP replaced the Citizens Rights Movement members in supporting the government without achieving any change in the "Who is a Jew?" issue. The NRP was concerned about losing its powerful base in the Ministry of Religious Affairs, which allowed it to control religious councils and chief and local rabbinates. This had happened in the 1958–59 crisis, and the leadership was afraid that it would happen again.

Coalition involves a large number of issues, such as ideology, government ministries, programs, and money. Many of these are tied together. Sometimes behavior explained at the public level in one way is really motivated by something altogether different. One way to examine the nature of the payoffs in coalition politics is to examine the ministries assigned to the various parties. This is harder to analyze than it appears because not all ministries are of equal importance and even the size of the budget is not always an indicator of a ministry's importance. Using government ministries as an index of the payoffs of coalition behavior, we can distinguish between the qualitative and quantitative dimensions. Qualitatively, the important ministries have historically been in the hands of the major party of the coalition. During parts of their terms of office, David Ben-Gurion, Levi Eshkol, Menachem Begin, Shimon Peres, and Yitzhak Rabin were also their own defense ministers. The appointment of Moshe Dayan to the post of defense minister on the eve of the Six-Day War of 1967 was important not only because Prime Minister Eshkol relinquished the post but also because it was given to a member of Rafi, a party outside the government coalition before the establishment of the National Unity Government. Moshe Dayan represents another important exception when, after the 1977 Likud victory, Menachem Begin offered him the post of foreign affairs minister, even though Dayan had been elected on the Alignment list.

The second National Unity Government was set up in 1984. It resulted from the stalemate that the election produced. In an unprecedented manner, the Alignment and the Likud agreed that Peres would be prime minister for the first twenty-five months. Also, most of the other lists elected supported the government, making its promised strength in the Knesset 97 of 120 members. A careful balance was struck between the two large parties over ministries, timetables, and commitments to smaller parties associated with each of the bigger ones.

The National Unity Government that followed the 1988 elections highlighted many of these considerations. Likud (forty members) and Labor (thirty-nine members) were almost equal in size; the religious parties with eighteen members seemed to be likely candidates for coalition. But the religious parties demanded, among other things, ironclad guarantees that the Law of Return would be amended so that only those converted according to halacha would be considered Jews. Halacha is strictly observed by Orthodox Jews, but in lesser degrees by others. Accordingly, Jewish communities around the world (overwhelmingly non-Orthodox) and many Israelis opposed this demand vehemently. The other option was a Likud-Labor coalition.

President Herzog was unusually active as the 1988 government was formed; abandoning the normal passivity of the president, Herzog publicly urged the formation of a National Unity Government. Finally, the unity government emerged, but without the features of rotation in power that had existed in 1984. Most of the religious parties joined the ruling coalition in the end, but as junior partners. Likud was given the prime ministry (Shamir) and the foreign ministry (Arens), and Labor got defense (Rabin) and finance (Peres).

Besides ministries, many other things are bargained over in coalition negotiations. Policy is a crucial one. The government sets up guidelines that are, in effect, the government's platform. These are presented to the Knesset when the cabinet is approved, but the guidelines do not have binding status. They reflect promises made by partners of the coalition to each other. Usually, however, no timetable is set on promises for enacting policy, and often such promises can be overlooked. If the coalition is fragile, however, or if the other party must acquiesce in supporting a policy, the payoff may be that the large coalition leadership fulfills its promise by enacting legislation or pursuing certain policy goals. The coalition has the resources to do this because the Knesset members can be pressured to follow the party line.

Other chips in the bargaining process include deputy ministers, chairmanships of Knesset committees, and budgets. The number of deputy ministers permitted under the law regulating the direct election of the prime minister is six. A deputy minister must be a Knesset member; he enjoys the status of minister and many fringe benefits. Budgets may be promised to kibbutzim or yeshivas or any other favored organization of the party being wooed to join the coalition. The public treasury often pays a high price for the continued existence of the government coalition.

The Cabinet

Formal and informal power rests with the government and its ministers. Obviously there are gradations of power, with the prime minister and those close to him near the top of the scale. Israeli government can rightly be called prime ministerial government. Ben-Gurion could conceive of and plan the Sinai operation without prior knowledge by his cabinet. Golda Meir's decisions regarding Egyptian overtures in the early 1970s and Begin's decision regarding the feasibility of a peace treaty with Egypt at the end of that decade magnify the contention that the predispositions and conclusions of the prime minister can have far-reaching influence in the system. Both leaders were surrounded by colleagues who had differing opinions, but it was ultimately their line that prevailed. The government cabinet declares war and ratifies treaties.

The prime minister has a superior position, in both law and politics, and is the undisputed focus of power. The prime minister's political acumen, personality, or coalition imperatives might lead to the sharing of power, and even to responsiveness to party or public opinion, but the prime minister's near monopoly on power resources must never be underestimated. The incumbent in any political situation has an advantage; when the incumbent is head of government by virtue of separate elections and also head of party, that advantage is increased dramatically. Used judiciously, the combination is almost irrepressible.

Cabinet ministers are not advisers of the prime minister, nor have they been appointed traditionally because of expertise in fields controlled by their ministries. Members of the cabinet are generally there because of their political role as politicians whose parties have decided to join the ruling coalition. There have rarely been more than one or two ministers at a time who were not Knesset members. Under the direct election law, up to half of the ministers in the cabinet may not be members of the Knesset; in Netanyahu's 1996 government two of the ministers were not Knesset members.

The 1988 National Unity Government had twenty-six ministers; five of them were ministers without portfolio. The fact that almost a quarter of the Knesset were government ministers meant that the work of legislation fell on the remaining members. During National Unity Governments (and a third of the period between 1967 and 1988 had such governments), there have been fewer Knesset members in the opposition than there were in the government cabinet. This meant that the coalition parties in the Knesset were usually led by second-level leaders because the first-rank leaders were busy in the cabinet. And this, of course, weakened the Knesset politically.

This has driven support for the so-called Norwegian law, which would have ministers automatically resign from the Knesset on being appointed to the government in order to make room in the Knesset for the next person on the party list, and, not surprisingly, the law would allow a minister who resigns from the government cabinet automatically to resume his place in the Knesset, at the expense of the newcomer. This plan would strengthen the ranks of the government coalition supporters in the Knesset and reward more of the party activists. The reform would be expensive because so many new officeholders would be involved; the real reason that the plan will be accepted or rejected, however, will be political and not economic.

The minister is appointed by his party and is responsible for the voting behavior of his delegation in the Knesset. The prime minister generally does not interfere with the selection of ministers by coalescing parties, although Golda Meir refused to allow Yitzhak Rafael to serve in her cabinet. Until 1981, the prime minister was powerless to fire a minister. To do so would mean a political confrontation with the minister's Knesset delegation, something a prime minister would usually choose to avoid. After 1981, a law made it possible for the prime minister to remove a minister by announcing his intention to the Knesset; forty-eight hours later, unless the prime minister changed his mind, the minister's appointment was terminated. As of 1996, the prime minister can remove a minister, his action becoming effective forty-eight hours later, giving the prime minister time to reconsider.

The government sets up its own rules of procedure, and most of its official decisions have to do with legislation that the government approves before forwarding it to the Knesset. What really is done in cabinet meetings is a function of the personality of the prime minister and the issues on the public agenda. Unfortunately, little is known in a systematic way about the dynamics and interactions within the cabinet. We know the procedures for asking the various ministries involved for their comments on pending legislation. We are sometimes aware of acrimonious debate that takes place in a cabinet meeting, especially if there is a leak or if the debate continues on the evening's television news or in the newspapers. We also know the quantity of legislation and decisions taken (and we may debate about their quality). But the cabinet and its meeting must be thought of as a rather formalized setting for the continuation of the political game. The supremacy of the prime minister and matters of coalition politics, electoral politics, and bureaucratic politics can never be far removed from the minds and actions of the ministers and the government. It is important to be sagacious and concerned with the public welfare, and we all hope that ministers are those things. Being politicians first and foremost, however, it is clear that their motivations are complex and do not always flow directly from trying to achieve the greater good. When there is a conflict within the cabinet, things become more focused and then it is easier to determine the lineup of the players and assess why they act as they do and what they hope to achieve. The personalities of the major actors, especially that of the prime minister, determine much of the governing style of the cabinet.

The government sometimes delegates matters to one of its committees of ministers, and government committees can make decisions in place of the cabinet. A 1991 law required that a ministerial defense committee be established, headed by the prime minister, deputy prime minister, and the ministers of defense, foreign affairs, and finance, and others up to half the members of the cabinet.[7] Since the maximum size of the cabinet under the direct election law is eighteen, the defense committee may have no more than nine members.

The prime minister may participate in any meeting of a government committee, and if he so desires, he may serve as chairman of that meeting. Deliberations of the government and the ministerial committees are secret. The ministers are responsible for the actions of their ministries, and the minister is also responsible for the decisions of the government as a whole. This means that once a decision is taken in the government, all the ministers must support it, in the Knesset and publicly, even if they opposed it in the cabinet meeting. Ministers must also see to it that Knesset members of their delegation vote for the governments' position unless given permission to do otherwise.

In Israeli political history, the resignation of most ministers from the government can be explained in political terms. While there may have been matters of principle or policy at the heart of the issue, the resignation itself must be thought of in terms of its effect on the political structure of the coalition. Parties (and hence ministers) have resigned from the government over religious issues and matters of foreign policy. The examples used earlier in this chapter can be cited as cases of leaving the government on political grounds connected with party principle. Another example would be the exit in 1970 of Gahal from the National Unity Government because it could not agree to the government's position on U.S. Secretary of State William Rogers's plan with its acceptance of UN Resolution 242. Rarely does an individual minister resign on issues of principle, as Yitzhak Berman did in 1982 after the government refused (only to reverse itself a week later) to set up an official commission of inquiry regarding the events in the Palestinian refugee camps of Sabra and Shatilla in Beirut. Government ministers almost never resign out of ministerial responsibility. For example, Prime Minister Meir and Defense Minister Dayan did not resign as a result of the Yom Kippur War, in part because of the support given their view by the Agranat Commission that decisions regarding the war involved the collective responsibility of the entire government.

Knesset Members in Action

Knesset members play more complex roles than simply that of legislator. The Knesset member must be concerned with his (or her) own career, and especially with the upcoming primaries in the party (if they exist). He must maintain ties with those groups within the party or in the public at large from which support was received, with the fortunes of his party and its adherence to his ideals, and with the interests that he represents. As legislator, he also is concerned with the public welfare. His hardest task is synthesizing these sometimes competing roles.

The need to grant special legal status to legislators is recognized by all democratic countries. Representatives must be free to go about their business without harassment by the authorities, the exceptions being treason and apprehension in the act of committing a crime. There are good reasons to protect the independence of the legislator, but it must be done in a sensible manner.

The Knesset member is granted immunity by law. By comparative standards the immunity of Knesset members is extensive. The basic concept is to allow the legislator freedom of speech and freedom of action while pursuing his duties. Parliamentary immunity refers to his actions in the legislature. This immunity is irrevocable. A second form of immunity extends to matters not directly connected to legislative work. The Knesset member is protected from criminal proceedings against him for the entire period of his membership in the Knesset, and even for acts committed before he became a member of the Knesset, although this immunity can be removed by the Knesset on recommendation of the House Committee. Immunity once extended to traffic violations, but this has been reformed.

Some of the crassest affronts to civic sensibilities have been rectified, but a well-known Knesset member still enjoys a considerable social advantage because the Israeli public is very aware of celebrities in their midst.

The removal of immunity is now decided by a public vote in the Knesset. In the past, a secret ballot was used, allowing the impression that at times extraneous issues were at play. Take the case of Rafael Pinhasi of Shas, accused of misuse of funds given to his party from the public treasury under the party financing laws, based on an inquiry conducted by the State Controller. In 1993, upon the request of the attorney general and after the recommendation of the House committee, the Knesset approved the removal of his immunity, but he was granted a second vote by the High Court of Justice on technical grounds. The final vote was fifty in favor, fifty-four against, and eight abstaining. In the 1996 coalition negotiations, Pinhasi was given the chair of the Knesset House committee, the very committee that makes recommendations to the Knesset on such matters. Yet the attorney general renewed his petition to remove Pinhasi's immunity so that he could stand trial; he had to make that case before the committee that Pinhasi headed.

During the ninth Knesset there were three sensational cases of immunity removal: NRP minister Aharon Abu-Hatzeira was accused of improperly using public funds and was found not guilty; Shmuel Rechtman of the Likud was sentenced to prison on bribery charges; and Shmuel Flatto-Sharon was accused of illegal campaign practices and was later found guilty. More than twenty members have had their immunity removed to face criminal charges while serving in the Knesset. Was it any wonder that some thought of the Knesset—and even the government of Israel—as a house of refuge protecting members from the shortened arm of the law?

The Knesset may remove a member from its ranks by a vote of two-thirds of the members if he is convicted of a criminal act and sentenced to at least one year in jail. If a sentence is not yet final, a Knesset member may be suspended until the legal proceedings are completed.

The Knesset member is entitled to serve out his term regardless of his political behavior. This was an important exception to the central rule of Israeli politics in previous years that the political party dominates the Knesset. Even if the Knesset member leaves the party on whose list he was elected and joins another party, he remains a member of the Knesset. The resignation of a Knesset member from his list is always an agonizing affair. The list claims that he must resign from the Knesset, because the voters voted for the party and its ideology, not for the individual Knesset member. The Knesset member invariably answers that if he had not been on the list, his former party would not have done nearly as well.

The Knesset is a fairly reliable prism through which the Israeli political system can be viewed, but it is not to be confused with the heart of the system. The composition of the Knesset is determined by elections, and the relative strength of the parties determines the government coalition and national policy. Even the organization of the house is influenced by the party composition of the Knesset. The delegation of a party or list to the Knesset is the major building block of the house's organization. Political calculations in forming the government are based on the size of the delegation. The assignment of committee membership and chairs is done by the delegation, and for important debates, speaking time is allocated to delegations who in turn divide it among their members; motions of no-confidence must be made by a delegation; and even office space in the Knesset building is provided to the delegation rather than an individual Knesset member.

The parliamentary delegation is obviously an important political force within its own party. Generally there is overlap between the leadership of the party and the leadership of the parliamentary delegation. Party policies are guides for the parliamentary delegation. If the party is represented in the government coalition, government policy in effect dictates the stand of the parliamentary delegation. Often, then, the parliamentary delegation of the party must accept this state of affairs or be open to the accusation that its party platform has been flaunted by the government. The overlapping membership of an individual in government, parliamentary delegation, and party can be used to pressure the government in a direction more amenable to the party platform. This may happen when, behind the scenes, a minister encourages a stand against a proposed government policy and even has the party issue an ultimatum that its continued support in the government will be conditioned on the altering of government policy. Small and medium-sized coalition partners, such as the NRP, Mapam, and the Liberal Party, have used this ploy often. In major coalition parties the party leadership is also leading the government, and thus the usual pattern is for the parliamentary delegation and the party institutions to pass declaratory resolutions supporting the government policy and wishing it continued success.

In ideological parties (Hadash, Agudat Israel, Shas) the primacy of party institutions over the Knesset delegation appears in the party constitution and in its operative procedures. This situation can be manipulated by the political leader when an outside group superior to him, such as the Council of Torah Sages in the case of Agudat Israel and Shas, "demands" that he conform to the group's dictates. The party establishes the identity of the ideological authority, and the Knesset member, as powerful as he may seem, is only a messenger of the ideological party. In the end he may compromise, as all politicians do; till then, he can explain his seeming intransigence by citing the superior authority of his party's decision.

An example of a Knesset delegation being given voting instructions by the party council on a specific issue occurred in 1975 over the Knesset vote regarding the interim agreement with Egypt worked out by U.S. Secretary of State Henry Kissinger. Yaad was a four-member Knesset delegation that thought it would be best to abstain or reject the agreement because it did not go far enough. The party council, after strenuous debate, requested that the Knesset delegation support the agreement. All four members, against their better judgment, did so.

The example of party control of the Knesset delegation is rare in Israeli politics because usually the party councils and the parliamentary delegations are dominated by the same people. The triangle of relationships —party/Knesset delegation/Knesset member—is the source of many conflicts.[8] Party rules find it necessary to state specifically that the Knesset member is subject to the decisions of the party, generally leaving it that vague. It is clear that in the logic of the Israeli political system hierarchical relations exist among the three, with the party usually taking precedence, followed by the desires of the Knesset delegation, and lastly the Knesset member. The member is elected on the party list representing a program or ideology, and he must decide, especially in a party with primaries, whether his personal career will be better off in the long run if he is a loyal party member. Most Knesset members do not have the financial, organizational, or personal qualities necessary for risking a political career on a given issue. For most members, the Knesset is the culmination of a political career, not the beginning of one.

Party discipline is the only way many coalition programs can be passed, argue the advocates. Party discipline promotes mediocrity among Knesset members, who no longer think for themselves, and cynicism in the public at large when parties change long-held views for political advantage and force their Knesset delegation members to toe the line, argue the dissenters. Party discipline even has its expression in the Knesset law that makes the minister responsible for the behavior of Knesset delegation members and can bring about the forfeiting of office because the minister fails to have the delegation's members vote in conformity to the government's decisions on certain issues.

The government coalition has at times permitted abstention on crucial issues by members of coalition parties and has even allowed verbal opposition to its proposals along with abstention on the vote. As a rule, however, members of delegations that participate in the coalition are expected to support government proposals. The major exception applies to issues that the coalition decides are matters of conscience, such as certain religious matters, at which time party discipline is removed. Party discipline may also be rescinded when the government is willing to gamble on its success, as when the Begin government brought the peace treaty with Egypt before the Knesset. Some Likud members opposed or abstained in the vote, but the prime minister correctly calculated that the votes of remaining Likud members and the votes of many more moderate opposition parties would assure the passage of the treaty and support the evacuation of the Sinai. This example notwithstanding, party discipline allows the Knesset to legislate and the government to rule in a stable manner. Party discipline makes meaningful the contention that the Knesset must be understood in political, not ideological, terms.

Two areas in which Knesset members can supposedly influence the Knesset and the government are question time and motions for the agenda. Unlike the British system, in which question time is an opportunity for a sharp exchange between government minister and parliament member, in Israel question time is usually dull. The attention goes to the question submitted and not to the answers, which can take six weeks or longer in coming. Although the answer can be followed by a short oral question to the minister by the Knesset member who asked the question (if he happens to be present), the whole procedure is usually lackluster. Motions for the agenda allow matters of public importance to be aired even if no specific legislation is to be debated and even if the government has not requested the debate. At the end of a ten-minute introductory speech, the minister concerned replies. The issue may then be deferred for a general Knesset debate on the matter, rejected, or referred to a committee for examination and report to the Knesset. So as not to clog the house with motions for the agenda and private members' bills, a quota system has been instituted, based on a party ratio, with a slight advantage to the opposition parties. Urgent motions are outside these quotas. The urgency must, however, be recognized by the chairman of the Knesset.

The organization of the Knesset follows party lines. The chairman is almost always from a major faction of the largest party, and his deputies are generally chosen from the large parties in the house. Aside from his symbolic and ceremonial importance, the chairman has considerable authority in the routine affairs of the Knesset because he largely determines the agenda and is responsible for the day-to-day operation of the legislature.

No quorum is necessary for Knesset deliberations and action. Criticism is sometimes expressed by those who believe that a legislator should sit in the house when business is being conducted. Attendance is very low at most times. The contention made by some Knesset members that they do not attend the plenum because they are busy with the Knesset's really important work in its committees is on the whole unfounded. Many Knesset members absent themselves from committee meetings as well, and the importance of the Knesset committees has been overstated. A more plausible explanation is that as politicians their activities are varied and time-consuming; it makes little sense for them to listen to speeches on matters they or their parties have already settled. Because of the centrality of the party, the dominance of government ministries on legislation, and the nature of the profession of politicians, it is difficult to argue that the absence of Knesset members from the debates in the plenum is a major problem of Israeli democracy. It is a symptom, but not the disease.

Knesset membership imparts important advantages to the individual seeking election. Knesset members have many more resources and relative advantages compared with others. Especially in the age of primaries and television, a shrewd Knesset member can develop clout and visibility. The franking privilege is a major resource of the Knesset member, although this is no longer unlimited after a public outrage when one Knesset member sent 450,000 letters (this was before the 1992 elections in which 2.66 million voted) concerning pending legislation regarding the rights of veterans. Knesset members (and their spouses after their demise) are entitled to 25,000 free telephone message units per year. While it depends where and when the conversation takes place, that allows for a good deal of talking.

Besides political and administrative clout, Knesset members are well off by Israeli standards. It is important to note that many Knesset members are established (if not wealthy) before entering parliament. Many are lawyers, professors, rabbis, kibbutz or moshav members, retired generals, or *apparatchiki* in the labor unions or other organizations related to party life. They earn a handsome salary in Israeli terms from the Knesset, but many of them would do even better if they were not Knesset members.

The present rules prohibit the earning of additional income or the holding of another public position. This matter is especially important for mayors and union leaders, and for professionals such as lawyers and accountants, since in the past some have used their position in the Knesset to advance their careers. Also prohibited is receiving expenses or other material goods such as a car, a driver, or office space from any source. A Knesset member may receive such benefits from his political party. He may also retain ownership of property or stocks, and may receive royalties from literary or artistic efforts. A yearly financial report must be filed.

For the first forty years of statehood, being a Knesset member was not an exclusive undertaking. Knesset members could continue their private concerns while serving in the Knesset. The reason a political party would want a public officeholder to be a Knesset member was political: for the party organization, it afforded control over centers of power; for the individual, it established a power base for additional exposure and influence, and at the same time it allowed the legislator to espouse the interests of his constituency. An interesting exception was the rule passed by the Labor Party that prohibited representatives from holding more than one elected post. The reason for this ruling was that in opposition, the party had to provide positions for its activists and had therefore to limit the number of positions held by each individual. The official reason given was the principle of rotation. From the perspective of the Knesset, however, it obviously weakened the house as a legislative institution. Relegating a day or two a week to matters of the Knesset may be enough for very talented and very busy people, but it also indicates the relatively low stature and importance of the Knesset in the political system.

In 1988 the Knesset expanded the prohibition on outside employment to include Knesset members who had professional practices as lawyers, accountants, and so on. New Knesset members were given a nine-month grace period to withdraw from previous commitments. The law permitted activities in a political party, and in educational and charitable institutions, but not for pay. An attempt was also made in the legislation to regulate the fringe benefits that organizations could provide a Knesset member. Offenders could be brought before the Ethics Committee of the Knesset. The law set up a special committee that could permit exceptions in special cases. The decisions of the committee, set up just months after the law came into effect, made clear how political considerations could outweigh ethical principles of good government. In the light of the upcoming municipal elections, wide-ranging exceptions were made.

There were once extraordinary health benefits and pension rights for Knesset members; while these have been reduced or abolished, some benefits and rights still exist, and they are hard to dislodge. Since Knesset members are sensitive to the charge that they regularly raise their own salaries, they set up a committee to make recommendations regarding their remuneration, proposals that must then be reviewed by the Knesset's House Committee. Two revealing incidents occurred in 1996: the commission recommended increasing the members' salaries by a third (to a hefty $80,000 a year in 1996, about five times the national average, in partial compensation for the new anti-moonlighting law) and lowering the pension rate to 2 percent per year, the general pension rate among salaried workers in Israel. Knesset members had enjoyed a 4 percent rate. The committee approved the first recommendation and turned down the second.

The regulations for cabinet ministers have been more stringent for some time. A minister is expected to devote all his time to his job. Rules against professional and commercial conflicts of interest have been established, and while these expressed expectations have proven largely unenforceable, they make clear the norms of behavior expected of ministers.

In the Knesset, especially for those more active in the day-to-day operations of the house, a clublike atmosphere develops. Common interests and shared experience bring people closer together regardless of party background. As in other social situations and in legislatures around the world, this esprit de corps is an important social feature of the informal life of the Knesset and Knesset members. It undoubtedly gives many of them an enhanced feeling of purposive behavior in legislating for the nation and its needs. The atmosphere cushions the uncertainties surrounding the decisions to be made and the unpredictable nature of the life of the politician. Being accepted by colleagues is sometimes erroneously translated by Knesset members into feelings of success and satisfaction and invincibility at the polls the next time around. Needless to say, while the clublike atmosphere is functional for legislation and for reducing tensions between ideological opponents, some Knesset members are rudely shocked when they are removed from the club by party leaders or the voters.

Legislation

The formal stages of legislation will be familiar to students of European parliaments. There are three readings of a bill. Most bills are initiated by a proposal introduced by the government. It must be placed on the table of the Knesset forty-eight hours before the Knesset takes it up for a first reading. The minister responsible for the legislation generally presents the explanation of the bill in the first reading, and a member of the opposition opens debate on the bill. After the debate, the bill is voted on. If returned to the government, it is in effect a defeat for the government because the Knesset chooses not to consider legislation proposed by it. Almost always, however, the first reading ends with a decision to send the bill to committee, which is tantamount to approval.

The committee by which the bill is considered is generally suggested by the minister. His suggestion is almost always accepted. If there is dissent, the matter is decided by the Knesset House Committee. Important matters are certain to end up on the table of a "friendly" committee. No time limit is set on the committee's deliberations, and no mechanism can be used to force a committee to report on a bill, short of the efforts of committee members themselves to have the bill read out of committee.

In the committee the bill is discussed in detail, and amendments to the bill are suggested. Changes may be introduced by the committee, which then reports back to the Knesset with its version of the bill. The second reading of the bill is concerned with the amendments proposed by the committee. If no changes are made in the committee's version, the second and third readings of the bill can proceed immediately. If additional changes were introduced during the second reading of the bill, the third reading is postponed in order to study the ramifications of the changes adopted in the second reading and give the government the opportunity to withdraw the proposed law in view of the changes made.

The bill becomes law after being signed by the prime minister, the president, the Speaker of the Knesset, and the minister responsible for the bill; it is then published in the official gazette. The right of veto does not exist; the signatures on the bill are mandatory, not discretionary.

In the thirteenth Knesset (1992–96), 395 bills were passed (compared with 354 for the previous Knesset), with some 46 percent of the Knesset legislation initiated by the government. That meant that 54 percent of bills passed originated as private members' bills (compared with about 20 percent for the 1984–88 Knesset). A bill proposed by a private member follows the same procedure except there is a preliminary reading of the bill before it goes to committee to be reported back for the first reading. This tremendous volume in private members' bills, much higher than in other Western democracies, increased dramatically in the 1990–96 period.

Most private members' bills were submitted by members of the opposition in the past. One private member's bill passed in 1960 was known as the Kanovitz law, which intended to regulate the pollution caused by motor vehicles. Shimon Kanovitz was a member of the Progressive Party. While the intentions of the Knesset were good, it took two and a half years for the ministries responsible (Health, Transportation, and Interior) to publish the necessary regulations, and to this day the law is a classic example of one not enforced. The fact that execution of a law is no less important than its legislation reinforces the tendency to rely heavily on government ministries for bill initiation. Government-proposed legislation is initiated only after it has been cleared with the various ministries involved, especially the ministries of Finance and Justice. Since most legislation involves financial costs for additional manpower to enforce the legislation or impinges on other legislation, these ministries are especially active in determining which legislation, and in what form, will reach the Knesset for deliberation. The Knesset, as an institution, is virtually powerless in the face of this development.

With the close of the era of National Unity Governments in 1990, many Knesset members put forward bills that would have failed at this preliminary stage in the past because the proposal was not consistent with government policy and because there was an automatic majority in the Knesset to support the government position. The motivation to propose legislation was certainly there: The visibility afforded by the private members' bills in a television age and a party system dominated by primaries explain much of the increase. These private members' bills were sometimes very expensive to implement (such as a bill that passed providing for cash payments to veterans), but they were too popular to oppose. There have been suggestions that proposals that involve new expenditures must indicate which funds will be cut from other activities to provide for the implementation of the law. But these suggestions have never been adopted. The increase in private members' bills becoming law is an example of the government and the political parties being weakened without the Knesset being strengthened.

The committees of the Knesset are formed along party lines. Soon after the elections, an arranging committee headed by a member of the largest party is established to determine the composition of the committees. Opposition members regularly chair some of the less important committees. The work of the arranging committee is quintessentially political since it must balance the size of the delegations with the attractiveness of the committees.

There are twelve standing committees of the Knesset: the House Committee; the Law, Constitution, and Justice Committee; the Finance Committee; the Foreign Affairs and Security Committee; the Immigration and Absorption Committee; the Economics Committee; the Education and Culture Committee; the Interior Affairs and Environment Committee; the Labor and Welfare Committee; the State Control Committee; the War on Drugs Committee; and the Committee for the Advancement of the Status of Women. There are no more than fifteen members on each committee, except for the Foreign Affairs and Security Committee and the Finance Committee, whose upper limit is seventeen members. Joint, special, and ad hoc committees are also established from time to time.

Assignment to committees is done by the arranging committee, and representatives of the various delegations determine for their own parties where they want their stronger delegates placed. Most members sit on one or two committees, but some have served on three or more. These assignments can enhance a Knesset member's career by placing him on an important committee or weaken him by not doing so. Small delegations are faced with a difficult dilemma because they do not have members on all the committees; they must convince their Knesset colleagues to grant them representation on the committees they deem important. Committee appointments are for the duration of the Knesset's tenure. If a member resigns from his party, the place on the committee reverts to the party, even though he remains a member of the Knesset.

The temporary replacement of committee members who disagree with the government's position is an excellent example of a mechanism of control by the ruling coalition and the passivity of the individual Knesset member. Two important instances of this were the appeal before the Foreign Affairs and Security Committee of the government decision regarding the settlement of Jews in Hebron in 1980, and the decision in the Finance Committee in 1982 to close El Al on the Sabbath and Jewish holidays. In the first case the Likud had agreed to permit the DMC the right of appeal before the Foreign Affairs and Security Committee on settlement issues. In the second case the courts had ruled that a decision by the government to change the charter of a government corporation was not sufficient unless approved by the Finance Committee of the Knesset. Since the defeat of the first issue and the passage of the second were important to the Likud, and since party discipline did not hold in Knesset committees, the leadership "temporarily" replaced unreliable coalition members on the committee until the votes were taken. Subsequently, the rules were changed so that the members of the Foreign Affairs and Security Committee could not be replaced during the three-month period of the Knesset's term.[9]

Committee chairmen are formally elected at the first meeting of the committee, on the nomination of the House Committee. The chairmanship of committees has been used in coalition negotiations conducted after the elections for setting up the government. Rather than agree to give a bargaining party another ministry or deputy minister, an important Knesset committee chairmanship may suffice. Coalition parties always have a majority in the committees of the Knesset, although some chairs may be from opposition parties, depending on the size of the opposition and the importance of the committee.

As a rule the chairmanships of important committees are reserved for members of the ruling coalition. Three important committees are the House Committee, the Foreign Affairs and Security Committee, and the Finance Committee. The House Committee is important because it has virtual control over the Knesset and its day-to-day operations. Since the Knesset is often in the public eye and is the formal decision-making organ of the state, the ruling majority must be able to control procedural decisions. In this kind of situation, where majorities are automatic, rules of order can determine how effectively the coalition or the opposition will be able to use parliamentary procedure to its advantage.

A second committee usually headed by a member of the ruling party is the Foreign Affairs and Security Committee. Although its membership is select and the matters brought before it are often very grave, its impact on policy is relatively small. The committee has been used as a sounding board or as a mechanism for consulting with members of the opposition on important international matters. This committee provides the government with an opportunity to discuss sensitive security issues without involving the entire house. Various chairs have made valiant efforts to increase the committee's role in policymaking, especially since the membership of the committee has often included former prime ministers, defense ministers, and chiefs of staff, but these efforts have largely been in vain, and the impact of the committee on policy remains relatively small. In addition, sensitive matters regarding topics such as intelligence and the security budget are discussed in subcommittees, thus weakening the committee even more.

The Finance Committee has an active role in policy and has usually been headed by a member of a coalition party. In both the ninth and tenth Knessets, between 1977 and 1984, the committee was headed by Agudat Israel Knesset members. The Aguda was willing to forego government ministries and agreed to support the coalition on condition that a string of legislation be adopted (including tighter control on abortion, tighter observance of the Sabbath and holidays, and more financial support for yeshivas) and that it be assigned the chairmanship of the Finance Committee. Not being ministers in the government gave its members a certain amount of distance from ongoing government policy; they could support the ruling coalition without being responsible for its policies. At the same time they could bargain for budget, legislation, and power because these were commodities more easily available to coalition members than were ministries. In 1988, Labor demanded and received the chairmanship of the Finance Committee. Shimon Peres agreed to be finance minister and knew very well that his economic policies would have a better chance of success if a member of his own party were chairman of this vital committee. The chairman of the Finance Committee after the 1996 elections again came from the Agudat Israel of the Torah Judaism list.

The annual budget is discussed at length in the Finance Committee, and its recommendations to the Knesset on the subject generally are passed. The Finance Committee is also given statutory authority to approve changes in the budget during the fiscal year. The Knesset has allocated decisions regarding the salaries of judges, Knesset members, and ministers to its Finance Committee, as well as the responsibility for setting the amount of money to be allocated for financing political parties. In turn, public commissions have been set up to deal with these two topics and to bring recommendations to the Finance Committee.

The committees meet on a regular basis, and there are Knesset members who are ready to explain that the major task of a Knesset member is work in committee. This statement must be seen in perspective. The power of the Knesset committees does not come close to approximating the power of committees of the U.S. Congress. There, committees play a key role in the legislative process. In fairness it must be pointed out that the American case is unusual. In Europe as a whole, and even in Great Britain, committees of the parliament do not reach the level of importance reached by committees in the American system.

There are two important reasons for this state of affairs. First, the American Congress is conceived of as the legislative branch of government, *independent* of the executive. The parliamentary notion is different, and the Israeli version of the directly elected prime minister and the parliament is unclear. The parliament *cooperates* with the government it chose, while the Congress may *compete* with the president. The Knesset has historically not perceived itself as operating independently or at cross-purposes to the government of the day, although that may develop over time.

The cooperative stance explains the relative weakness of Knesset committees. They could not subpoena witnesses or have them testify under oath. They could not order documents to be brought before them. In the past, they could invite, persuade, and cajole, but, for the most part, they had no legal means of sanctioning those who refuse to cooperate. An in-road was achieved when a 1991 law permitted the Government Control Committee to establish a state investigating committee with the agreement of the State Controller. The Government Control Committee can also demand the testimony of an officeholder discussed in the report of the State Controller, except for the president of the state, the Speaker of the Knesset, and judicial authorities. The 1992 law stipulating the direct election of the prime minister includes a provision permitting forty Knesset members to deliberate, no more than once a month, with the participation of the prime minister. The law also allows committees to require ministers and civil servants to testify before them. This is progress, but it still leaves Knesset committees far from having a forceful role in the legislative process independent of the government and its ministries.

The second reason for the relatively minor role played by Knesset committees in the legislative process is budgetary. To function properly as an independent agency in legislation, a Knesset committee should have a large staff of professionals to gather information, assess it, and put it at the disposal of members of the committee, and, of course, to provide oversight for the activities of the administration. Take, for example, the field of education. Almost a third of Israel's population is in school. Overseeing the ministry and collecting, processing, and analyzing data are just too much even for a conscientious and hard-working member. For in addition to his membership on the Education Committee, he is likely to be a member of a second Knesset committee, he is also a member of a party, and he has a constituency to attend to—in short, he (or she) is a politician whose tasks are numerous and whose time is limited. To provide the Knesset Education Committee with the kind of staff needed to fill this function would be expensive. Besides, there is an easy alternative: the information requested can be provided by the minister and his ministry's staff. They have gathered the information and supposedly have made their policy proposals based on these data. But this is exactly where the independence of the legislature breaks down. The members of the Knesset committees become dependent on the data, experts, and points of view of the ministry and do not exercise their governmental function of overseeing and legislating independently.

Knesset committees do have staff, but not nearly enough. The committees may be granted legal assistance since the concept is that drafting legislation is the job of a lawyer. As a moment's reflection will indicate, this is only partially the case. On occasion the Finance Committee has had economists in a consulting capacity, as have other committees. But a part-time consultant or testimony before the committee by a university professor simply cannot replace staff work done over a long time in a consistent manner. The reason given for the failure to set up independent staffs for the Knesset committees has been the cost of such a proposal. But at the same time Knesset members will agree that being dependent on experts from the ministries weakens the effectiveness of the committees. The point that these Knesset members gloss over is that the matter is fundamentally in their hands. The practice in Israeli government has always been that the government does not discuss or approve the budget of the Knesset. (This is one of the only areas of real independence on the part of the legislature in Israel.) Since this is the case, and since many Knesset members feel that the committees must be strengthened, they could appropriate moneys for this purpose and establish a staff system for the Knesset committees.

It may be that this is a utopian suggestion, for participating in the legislative process in a significant manner means that the responsibility of legislation will also shift (at least partially) from the government ministries to the Knesset. As members of hierarchical political parties, Knesset members in actuality may decline to take a more active role in the legislative process because they are content in knowing (and keeping) their place in a system that does not encourage confrontation between the executive and legislative branches.

The Judiciary

The judicial system provides one of the greatest paradoxes in Israeli civil life. In a culture that is very highly politicized, the judicial system is professional and impartial despite its occasional wavering and despite charges that it is being politicized. Although there is no written constitution, the political system as a whole and particularly the judicial system respect the principle of limited government and have exercised self-restraint in many areas. The country has been declared to be under emergency conditions since independence, yet in many areas of civil liberties (at least in Israel's pre-1967 boundaries) Israel's record is good. The rule of law is much respected as an ideal, although in fact access to justice is stratified by one's wealth, determination, and patience to utilize the judicial system. In a system where most appointees in public life must meet some political requirement, the appointment of judges is widely perceived as based on professional attainment and potential. Increasingly, as the Court has become more activist in matters of civil rights, it is perceived by some as part of the political battle. On the whole, however, the Israeli judicial system is professional and unpolitical and, in that sense, very unIsraeli. This is what makes it such an important bastion of Israeli democracy in a sea of forces that would hasten the erosion of its foundations.

Like most other activities of Israeli government, the judicial system is controlled by the executive branch. For example, the budget of the judicial system is not determined by the Knesset, but by the executive branch, meaning the Finance Ministry. This is an unhealthy arrangement, especially for an activist Court that adjudicates government actions and regulations on a regular basis.

A basic notion of a liberal democracy is the limiting of the powers of government through the existence of a constitution. This document sets the outer limits of the permissible and implies a form of redress through the courts if that limit is breached. Democracy consists of both the formal procedures of electing governments and the freedoms from government interference that protect minorities and individuals from having their liberties infringed by government action. The Israeli experience has always taken a formalistic approach to its understanding of democracy. This is nowhere better seen than in the fact that the issue of electoral reform is studied in schools and debated at length in the press, while the lack of a basic law that covers human and civil rights is taken for granted as a political necessity. The beginnings of a bill of rights have emerged with the passage of basic laws regarding the freedom of occupation and human dignity and liberty, but much work is still to be done before the bill of rights is completed. Great Britain has no written constitution, but Great Britain has a tradition of hundreds of years of guarding civil liberties and developing their meaning. Israel's experience is too fragile to leave the guarding of civil rights to the goodwill of the authorities. The glaring shortfall in the Israeli system is the absence of a written constitution.

The Israeli solution to the lack of a constitution is the stage-by-stage approach.[10] In 1950, when debates over the writing of a constitution were at their peak, it was clear that the two major bodies of opinion created a standoff. Secularists insisted that Israel must have a constitution like other modern, Western, liberal states. Religious spokesmen claimed that the Torah and its rabbinical commentaries made up the written constitution of Israel and that this was superior to any secular legislation, since it was of

Divine origin. As consensus is usually an important goal in Israeli politics, especially regarding matters of principle and public concern, it was decided not to attempt to reach a compromise but to put together, stage by stage, legislation that would, at a later date, form Israel's constitution.[11] This solution has been known as the "Harari decision," named after the Knesset member who introduced it. It is also likely that the leaders of the fledgling state did not want the provisions of a constitution to limit their freedom of action and thereby delayed completing the work of writing the constitution. The Harari decision called for the Law, Constitution, and Justice Committee of the Knesset to prepare the appropriate legislation. The first Knesset, which passed the resolution, was perceived to be a constitutional convention and was in fact called a constituent assembly. Before the three basic laws passed in 1992, all the basic laws except for those regarding the Knesset and Jerusalem were prepared and approved by the government and not by the Knesset Law, Constitution, and Justice Committee. Many of the basic laws do not have limiting clauses, a condition necessary if the legislation is to serve as a constitutional provision.[12]

The basic laws are (1) The Knesset, 1958; (2) Israel Lands, 1960; (3) State President, 1964; (4) the State Economy, 1975; (5) the Israel Defense Forces, 1976; (6) Jerusalem, Capital of Israel, 1980; (7) the Judiciary, 1984; (8) State Comptroller, 1988; (9) Freedom of Occupation, 1992; (10) Human Dignity and Liberty, 1992[13]; and (11) the Government, 1992.

The status of the basic laws was intended to be higher than that of regular legislation. This is obvious, among other reasons, because in passing a basic law the Knesset is continuing the work of the first Knesset, the constituent assembly. This is even more clear when entrenched provisions in basic laws require that changes be made only by special majorities. In general, legislation in the Knesset is passed by a simple majority of those present—abstentions not counting. The Basic Law: Knesset has two entrenched provisions. Article 4, which deals with the electoral system, can be changed only by an absolute majority during each stage of legislation. Articles 44 and 45 of the same basic law exempt the law from being changed by emergency regulations unless two-thirds of the members (at least eighty) concur. In addition, clause 9a states that a law to expand the term of office of the Knesset must be passed by 80 members at least. The Basic Law: Freedom of Occupation and the Basic Law: Government can be amended only by a majority of 61 members. Article 53 of the Basic Law: Government makes the basic law immune to emergency regulations.

The entrenchment clause in the Basic Law: Knesset was the background for the first case that hinted at judicial review in the Israeli system. Judicial review is the power of a court to invalidate on constitutional grounds a governmental action whether it be committed by the executive (administrative) or legislative branch. The *Bergman* case involved the Israeli Supreme Court in a case in which the Court declared an act of the Knesset void for violating a basic law.

Aharon A. Bergman had brought an action before the Supreme Court, sitting as the High Court of Justice, to block the implementation of the (Campaign) Financing Law of 1969. Bergman's complaint was that the law unfairly discriminated against new political parties because it provided governmental funds only for those parties already represented in the outgoing Knesset. He argued that the financing law violated the equality required by section 4 of the Basic Law: Knesset, which had been entrenched and could be changed only by a majority of Knesset members. The financing law had passed its first reading in the Knesset by a vote of 24–2.

Writing for all five justices who participated in the case, Justice Moshe Landau agreed that the financing law was in conflict with the equality required by section 4 of the Basic Law: Knesset. The absolute denial of funds to a new list constituted a major denial of equal opportunity in the democratic electoral process. Justice Landau acknowledged the absence of any provision in Israel's written law that expressly authorized the Court to construe statutes in terms of the natural justice principle of equality of all before the law. "Nevertheless this principle that is nowhere inscribed breathes the breath of life into our whole constitutional system." It was therefore right and just, Justice Landau argued, for the Court to use it in interpreting the law. This story of judicial innovation has a political ending. The Knesset enacted the financing law again—this time by an absolute majority—incorporating changes in the light of the Court's remarks. The issue of judicial review was skirted and the supremacy of the Knesset was upheld.[14]

The power of judicial review of legislation was expanded significantly with the passing of three basic laws in 1992.[15] The Basic Law: Human Dignity and Liberty and the Basic Law: Freedom of Occupation were intended as the first pieces of a bill of rights, while the Basic Law: The Government regulated the direct election of the prime minister. Although the laws appeared limited in scope, they granted the Supreme Court powers to overturn legislation that violates the rights they list.

The Basic Law: Human Dignity and Liberty contains in clause 8 the constitutional basis for reviewing, and possibly declaring unconstitutional, future legislation that does not conform with the law:

> The rights according to the Basic Law shall not be infringed upon except by a statute that befits the values of the State of Israel and is directed towards a worthy purpose, and then only to an extent that does not exceed what is necessary, or by regulation enacted by virtue of express authorization in such law.

The Court quickly made it clear that it would declare unconstitutional ordinary laws that did not comply with the new basic laws. This had a noticeable impact on legislators and administrators who must consider whether their laws or their actions would survive the scrutiny of the Court.

The Court also made it clear that it was prepared to give new liberal interpretation to previous legislation that restricted basic human rights. Thus, for example, the courts compelled the air force to allow a woman to enter a combat pilot course on the grounds that previous administrative regulations violated the principles of the Basic Law: Human Dignity and Liberty.

The basic laws have yet to yield a constitution, nor have they been used by the legislature as a means of training itself and the public to think in terms of a body of law that limits later legislation and governmental action. Despite the need to complete the work of drafting a constitution and despite the fact that the Knesset has the constitution-writing function in addition to that of the regular legislative function, the basic laws have yet to develop a constitutional aura about them. They can and have been changed and amended with ease, and thus lose their strength as limitations on the governing authorities. When in 1979 the coalition parties wanted to appoint a second deputy prime minister in order to solve problems of prestige and coalition formation, or in 1996, when the issue of the election date was being debated (see chapter 7), the Basic Law: Government was amended accordingly.

A severe impasse developed over the Basic Law: Freedom of Occupation in 1993 when a court panel overruled a government ban on importing non-kosher meat as a violation of the importers' right to earn a living. The government had decided to relinquish its monopoly over the import of meat as part of its privatization policy; but the Ministry of Commerce denied a company permission to import non-kosher meat. The High Court of Justice declared the ministry's refusal unconstitutional. A revised basic law was worked out under pressure of the religious parties that would allow ordinary laws to be modified by an absolute Knesset majority in order to be considered an exception to the provisions of the basic law. Such a law, forbidding the import of non-kosher meat, was enacted. But in amending the Basic Law: Freedom of Occupation in 1994, a reference to Israel's declaration of independence was added. This may come back to haunt the orthodox proponents of the amendment, since the declaration refers to the principle of religious equality, which in the future may be the basis for judicial review of special preferential treatment to Jewish Orthodox institutions.

The tension between the limitations on government implied by a constitutional system and the security problems of Israel is best evidenced by the constant state of emergency that has existed since 19 May 1948, five days after the achievement of independence. The legal arrangement is an announcement by the Knesset, or by the government if the Knesset cannot be convened, or by the prime minister if the government cannot be convened, of the existence of a state of emergency. The existence of a state of emergency allows the government to change or suspend any law (except the right of access to the courts, post facto punishment, or infringing human dignity), to increase taxes, and to issue other emergency regulations intended to provide for "the defense of the state, the security of the public and upholding necessary distribution and service."[16] These regulations are generally for a three-month period and can be extended only by Knesset legislation. In effect, emergency regulations have afforded the government an alternative method of legislation. Legislation that might be time-consuming and controversial can be achieved quickly with the emergency regulations. Emergency regulations are often used in defense matters and in economic matters involving labor disputes or taxation.

ELEMENTS OF THE LAW

Israeli law is influenced by four major traditions: (1) Ottoman law, (2) British common law, (3) religious law, and (4) Israeli law. Each element represents a different historical period or cultural influence in the developing Israeli laws.[17]

Ottoman law reflects the impact of the rule of the Turks in Palestine before World War I. It was a composite of Koranic precepts and Islamic customs along with a heavy influence, especially since the beginning of the twentieth century, of French legal models and sources. Ottoman law was not influential regarding personal laws for the Jews, for at that time non-Moslem communities were under the jurisdiction of their own community. But Ottoman law was very influential regarding property law, especially land. The French influence was introduced by the Turks in the nineteenth and early twentieth centuries regarding civil and criminal procedures, and commercial and maritime law. During the Mandate, the British enforced Ottoman law and practice unless specific British mandatory regulations were issued in their stead. The scope of influence of Ottoman law is constantly decreasing as Israeli legislation replaces aspects of the Ottoman law.

The British Mandate lasted from 1922 to 1948. In this period legislative power was vested in the high commissioner. The high commissioner was bound by provisions of the Mandate but had full power and authority to pass ordinances needed to maintain peace, order, and good government while according complete freedom of conscience and exercise of freedom of worship. He was prohibited from discriminating in any way between inhabitants on the ground of race, religion, or language.

By the time of the establishment of the state the substance of British common law and the doctrines of equity and *stare decisis*—the binding force of judicial precedent—had been firmly established in the judicial system. These principles in particular and the British influence on the Israeli judicial system in general are probably the most significant heritage of the British Mandate.

Personal law is largely under the jurisdiction of the courts of the recognized religious communities: Jewish, Moslem, and Christian. In the Jewish communities this means the Orthodox rabbis (see chapter 10), for neither Conservative nor Reform rabbis are recognized in Israel for performing religious ceremonies. This issue has the potential for creating ill will between the various organizations of Jewry because outside Israel the two latter groups are powerful and growing.

The jurisdiction of Jewish religious courts extends to all Jews in Israel, whether Israeli citizens or not. The religious courts' decision is subject to appeal both within the appellate system of the religious courts and through the High Court of Justice. With few exceptions, such as bigamy and abortion, the Knesset has not undertaken to legislate in the field of personal law. In other matters, Jewish law is often taken into account, but wide-ranging precedents from the Western world are usually dominant in legislative and judicial matters.

Israeli law has developed from the special nature of the country's problems. There are still laws from the Mandate on the books and occasionally one hears a call to update them. But, as would be expected, the proportion of Knesset-made law is growing over time.

THE COURTS

If the judicial system is based on a complicated legal order influenced by many sources, the court system is much more straightforward. The courts have a hierarchical structure with little overlap among them. The two major systems are the civil and the religious courts; in addition there are special courts for military, labor, traffic, municipal, and juvenile matters, to name but a few. The civil court system has three levels: magistrates', district, and supreme courts. Magistrates' courts deal with offenses that carry relatively light sentences (a maximum of three years' imprisonment except in the case of drug offenses) and relatively small money claims. District courts may accept appeals from magistrates' courts; jurisdiction of the former covers civil and criminal matters exceeding the limits of the lower courts. There are five district courts in Israel: in Jerusalem, Tel Aviv, Haifa, Beer Sheva, and Nazareth.

The Supreme Court was composed of fourteen justices in 1996 and is the country's highest appellate court. In addition, the Supreme Court has original jurisdiction over petitions seeking the grant of relief against administrative decisions that are not within the jurisdiction of any court. In this role the Supreme Court sits as the High Court of Justice and may restrain or direct government agencies or other public institutions by such writs as habeas corpus and mandamus, as is customary under English common law.

The Supreme Court generally hears cases with a panel of at least three justices, although sometimes larger odd numbers are used. In the appeal of John ("Ivan the Terrible") Demyaniuk, five justices were impaneled; in the 1968 case regarding the registration as Jews of the children of Binyamin Shalit, a panel of nine justices decided the case. In a case involving the future of frozen sperm of a dissolved marriage, a court of eleven justices was impaneled. Trials in district courts generally have a single judge. No jury trials are held in Israel.

An important explanation for the independence and stature of Israel's judiciary is the special method of selecting judges. This is done on the recommendation of a nine-member appointments committee that consists of the president of the Supreme Court and two other justices of that court, the minister of justice and one other cabinet minister chosen by the cabinet, two members of the Knesset elected by secret ballot by majority vote, and two practicing lawyers who are members of the Israel Bar Association and approved by the minister of justice. The justice minister serves as chairman of the appointments committee; the nominees of the committee are formally appointed judges by the president of the state.

Judges serve for life during good behavior until mandatory retirement at the age of seventy (seventy-five for judges of religious courts). Salaries are fixed by the Finance Committee of the Knesset and are graduated according to the level of the court and tenure on the bench. The salary of the president of the Supreme Court is usually equivalent to that of the prime minister, and the salary of Supreme Court justices is equivalent to that of ministers. The court system is technically under the jurisdiction of the Ministry of Justice, too close to the government administration to ensure a large measure of independence by the judiciary.

While the Israeli experience has shown that justices can be chosen in a manner that neutralizes the highly political nature of the national culture, other considerations are still active. For example, it is customary to have at least one religious justice on the High Court, with representation also considered important for Sephardim and women. In 1996, there were two Sephardim and three women on the High Court. No Arab has ever been appointed. Previous judicial experience is not required in the appointment of judges. Two-thirds of the thirty-six Supreme Court justices who served between 1948 and 1978 had prior judicial experience; of the first five appointed, only one did; of the next twenty, fourteen did; of the next eleven, nine did. Of the judges promoted from the district court to the Supreme Court, none had obvious political affiliations. Others were more visible in the public spotlight; their previous posts included general consul in a diplomatic mission, legal adviser to the government, legal counsel of the Histadrut, and university professor.

The judicial elite of Israel is similar to the political elite discussed in chapter 4 in terms of its demographic characteristics. Of the thirty-six judges who served on the Court during the country's first forty-five years, all were Jews, thirty were Ashkenazim. Ten were born in Poland; nine in Germany, eight in Israel, six in Russia and Lithuania, and one each in Iraq, England, and the United States.[18]

The judicial system in Israel is the foremost guardian of civil liberties in Israel.[19] There is no written constitution and no bill of rights. Most legislation is designed to permit the authorities to limit freedoms by, for example, giving the Interior Ministry the task of licensing printing houses or giving the police the task of granting permits for demonstrations. The record of the Interior Ministry and the police has been generally good in protecting the rights of the individual to freedom of the press, speech, and assembly, but these rights are *granted* to the individual by the authorities, rather than *assured* the individual. It is true that in moments of crisis laws cannot thwart a determined antidemocratic force, yet the existence of a constitutionally endowed right tends to have a limiting influence on enemies of freedom and sets up norms that may be difficult to overcome. To make the point perfectly clear, limiting rights is a matter of interpretation as to whether the public safety is jeopardized; the burden of proof is on those whose rights are being limited. If rights were constitutionally protected, they could of course still be abused, but then the burden of proof would fall on the government that agreed to limit freedom.

In the Israeli judicial system the role of the Supreme Court stems from the ability of the Court, when it sits as the High Court of Justice, to act before an action is taken by the authorities. The common-law principle is that damages can be recovered after the act has been perpetrated. Imagine a wall shared by you and your neighbor. The neighbor decides to tear down the wall without any concern for your rights or your house. After your house fell in because your wall was destroyed, you could collect damages. Equity demands the ability to pursue justice even before the act is committed. You are entitled to petition the Court to have the neighbor prevented from tearing down your joint wall without your permission. The same principle applies to actions of the authorities. The High Court of Justice can prevent government actions instituted illegally, and that will be harmful to your rights or property. A private citizen may petition to challenge the actions of a government agency, a ministry, the army, a minister, and even the prime minister.

Six examples of the functioning of the High Court of Justice:

1. In 1953, the Court overturned the interior minister's decision to suspend publication of the Communist newspaper, *Kol Ha'am*, and its sister paper in Arabic. The Court held that it had to be shown that it was "probable" that an article's publication would endanger the public peace; a "mere tendency" in that direction was not sufficient.

2. The Registrar of Companies had refused, in 1962, to register a printing firm set up by Al-Ard, an Arab nationalist organization, on the grounds that it would use the company to spread views that endanger state security. The High Court upheld Al-Ard's petition to be registered, saying that control of freedom of expression was not one of the purposes of the Companies Ordinance.

3. Regarding land requisitioning in the territories (the cases were based on international law and not Israeli law, since the territories are under military rule), the Court determined that requisitioning land from its owners could be done only if the proposed settlement was necessary for military reasons. Since the Court was convinced that this condition was met regarding Beit El but not Elon Moreh, it vacated the order for the confiscation of land in the second case and upheld it in the first.[20]

4. The High Court of Justice decided in 1984 to overturn the decision made by the Central Election Committee to disallow Kach and the Progressive List for Peace from running in that year's election. The High Court of Justice ruled that the law did not empower the committee to take that decision. The law was subsequently changed and the two parties were again banned by the Election Committee in 1988. The High Court of Justice was again brought into the picture, and this time ruled that the committee was correct in banning Kach, but not the Progressive List.

5. In 1986, the Court upheld president Chaim Herzog's pardon of several Shin Bet security agency operatives involved in covering up the murder of two captured terrorists involved in the bus 300 incident. The Court rejected arguments that Herzog's pardon power could not be exercised before legal proceedings had begun.

6. In 1990, an appeal was made to the Court of the decision by the government's attorney general not to prosecute the heads of Israel's banks in the 1983 stock-fixing crisis, which brought about enormous expense for the government after it decided to cover much of

the loss. The Court ruled that the decision by the attorney general was "substantively unreasonable" and ordered the attorney general to proceed with the prosecution. The trial ended years later with guilty verdicts for most of those involved.

Israel's Supreme Court has acquired, by traditional role and by the abdication of other institutions, the task of major guardian of justice and civil rights in Israel. The Court was reticent in interfering in political issues, and its asserting itself in the *Bergman* case (its first foray into the field of judicial review) was tentative and unsustained. Since the mid-1980s the Court has developed into a very dynamic one. It has not shied away from questions brought to it, but has extended itself in broadening the meaning of justice throughout the system and ensuring for itself the role of fearless guardian of inherent rights.[21]

Israel's courts are highly aware of civil rights and respect the tradition of the Enlightenment that sees the individual and his rights at the heart of the society. The role of the Court is to protect rights and to limit the authorities in their unwarranted use of power. With no constitution and few laws on which to base this protection, however, it falls to the Court to set the tone of self-control for the authorities in respecting rights. The Court has moral weight, and the power to hold in contempt those who do not obey its rulings, but it has no police or army with which to enforce its decisions, and so it must be aware of the norms prevailing in the society.

Considering that civil liberties are not firmly entrenched in law and that the system rests on the discretion of the authorities, Israel's record in this field is quite good. The blemishes on the system are the religious requirements that, when applied, restrict certain liberties taken for granted in other liberal systems and the emergency regulations that transfer to the executive functions that would otherwise demand the public deliberation of the legislature.

From the early 1980s, the judicial activism of the Court became clear. In the political sphere, the Court overturned the ban by the Central Elections Committee of two parties before the 1984 elections (see chapter 5) and, citing the public's right to know, required political parties to make public the details of coalition agreements (a provision that would emerge as part of the Basic Law: Government that instituted the direct election of the prime minister). Apprehension about its decision caused Labor and Shas to remove a clause in a draft coalition agreement stipulating that the government would introduce legislation circumventing any Supreme Court decision that impinged on the religious status quo.

In censorship cases, the Court virtually eliminated the practice regarding theater productions, reduced it for movies, and decided that the army censor could not block publication of an article that included criticism of the head of the Mossad unless there was a "near certainty" that the content of the article posed a danger to national security. It also backed the right of newspaper reporters not to reveal their sources.[22]

In the religious sphere (see chapter 10), the Court ordered the registration as a Jew and the granting of new immigrant status to an American woman who had undergone a Reform conversion, forced a political leader who also served as a judge in the high rabbinical court to relinquish his judicial position, ordered the inclusion of women in religious councils and in the electoral groups that selected candidates for religious councils, and ordered El Al, the national airline, to provide a homosexual employee's partner the same benefits it provided to the spouses of other married workers.

One dominant personality driving all these changes was Aharon Barak, a justice since 1978, and president of the Supreme Court since 1995. He was appointed attorney general in 1975, and Begin drafted him to head the legal team at the Camp David peace talks with Egypt. Soon after, at forty-two, Barak went to the Supreme Court.

As attorney general, he decided to press charges against Asher Yadlin, who was about to become governor of the Bank of Israel on charges of financial misconduct while heading Kupat Holim; Yadlin was eventually imprisoned. Barak was also involved in probing the case of Avraham Ofer, a Labor housing minister charged with financial malfeasance. As the probe dragged on, Ofer shot and killed himself. Barak also decided to press criminal charges against Leah Rabin in 1977, rather than allow her to pay an administrative fine quietly. She had a bank account in the United States, a violation of Finance Ministry regulations that barred Israelis from holding bank accounts abroad. As a result, her husband, Prime Minister Yitzhak Rabin, decided not to run at the head of the Labor list in the 1977 elections, opening the decades-long competition between Shimon Peres and Rabin.

Barak has been directly involved in the constitutional revolution taking place in the country.[23] In addition to his role in judicial review, he was instrumental in expanding the right of citizens to petition the Court. In the past a citizen could petition the Court only if he had been directly affected, but now the Court will hear any petition it deems to be in the public interest.

Barak has led in applying the test of "reasonableness" under which the Court can annul a cabinet or Knesset decision if it is unreasonable in the extreme.[24] This doctrine signifies the Court's changed perception of its role in the political system, going beyond adjudication to the application of substantive criteria in its review of laws and policies.[25] The use of the doctrine of reasonableness to invalidate legislation or administrative action, known as substantive due process in the United States, was accelerated in the 1980s. In one important case, the Court overturned the government's appointment of ex-Shin Bet agent Yossi Ginossar as Housing Ministry director-general, determining that he was not fit for public office because he had perjured himself in two security service scandals. Although he had never been convicted, the High Court struck down the nomination on the ground that such a decision was so unreasonable that it could be regarded as illegal and therefore null and void. In other cases, the Court forced the resignations of Shas Minister of the Interior Deri and Shas Deputy Minister Pinhasi, who were being investigated on criminal charges, although Deri had promised in writing to resign if charges were pressed in court. The High Court also forced the attorney general to reconsider decisions not to file charges against bank managers involved in the 1983 bank-shares debacle and against the chief of police.

Activist courts raise active opposition, and the Barak Court is no exception. Political opponents, especially in religious circles, accuse the Court of forwarding its own liberal political agenda. Calls have been made to have the Knesset alter the Basic Law: Judiciary to limit the scope of Court jurisdiction. The Court's reputation for liberal decisions is complemented by its restraint regarding matters involving security.[26] Thus, the court upheld the expulsion of 418 Hamas activists without a prior hearing, it approved house demolitions, and it did not overturn the practice of using "moderate physical force" in interrogations of Islamic fundamentalists. Similarly, after declaring null and void the criteria used by the Interior Ministry for recognizing conversion to Judaism (and thus being eligible for citizenship under the Law of Return), the Court referred the matter to the legislature rather than order the ministry to register the petitioner as a Jew.

If the issue of civil rights in Israel is complex, it is more so regarding Arabs.[27] Israeli Arabs are full-fledged citizens, granted all formal rights. They vote and are represented in the Knesset and in municipalities. But since they do not serve in the army (and probably do not want to), they are deprived of access to the whole of the system, including welfare benefits provided for veterans, political access to the highest levels of decision making, and the psychological satisfaction that goes along with the identification of country, religion, and nation. Psychological satisfaction may not be a civil right, but it would be shortsighted to assess the position of Israeli Arabs using only formal legalisms; besides, reforms in the 1992–96 period were intended to remove some of the existing bureaucratic inequalities. There may be no easy solution for their dilemma, but denying its existence, as many Israelis do, is no solution either.

West Bank and Gaza Arabs present a much more difficult problem.[28] Before the establishment of the Palestinian Authority, they could petition the High Court of Justice, although they were not citizens of Israel. If conceived of as evolving in a battle zone, then the Israeli record of dealing with them was reasonable in the history of warfare. But if the judgment were based on the norms of a regular country, the Israeli record was much weaker. Military occupation is difficult under any circumstances, and its chances to be perceived as humane over time are very low.

The court system is crowded and sluggish.[29] While the quality of judging is generally regarded as high, and the system is adding staff and acquiring equipment, access to justice is painful, costly, and slow. Recent legislation has introduced a public defender system to provide legal representation for all. Lawyers proliferate; the system seems so built that only they can manage to navigate in the murky waters of bureaucrats and special regulations. The Israel Bar Association is a statutory body whose tasks include licensing and controlling practitioners.

In general, Israel is a nonpunitive society. Penalties prescribed by law for many crimes are low compared with other countries. The death penalty appears on the books, but it is never applied. The one exception was in the case of the Nazi Adolf Eichmann. The crime rate is increasing and is a topic of public concern, but it has never become a political issue as it has in other Western countries.

10. Interest Groups and Public Policy

It is appropriate for political scientists to concentrate on groups that try to influence public policy. We do well to remind ourselves that policy decisions benefit some groups at the expense of others, that political decisions are made by a small portion of the population, and that groups try to influence decisions.

The right to assemble and organize has long been regarded as a fundamental political right, and that is precisely why it is one of the first rights denied by authorities in periods of tension or upheaval. That like-minded citizens can organize to have their interests expressed in policy is a keystone of the democratic process. Unlike a political party, whose primary function is to aggregate various interests in order to compete in elections with a view to gaining control of the government, the interest group articulates the demands and attitudes (the "interests") of group members in order to bring about policies in line with their views. Whereas the party is primarily concerned with elections and ruling, the interest group is geared to the policy outputs of the system. Political theorists have often taken the existence of a large number of active interest groups as evidence of the vitality of democratic institutions in the country.

The theory of political pluralism posits the struggle among myriad interest groups as a highlight of the democratic process. For a writer like David Truman, the extensive organization of competing groups is evidence that power is widely shared and that no group ever loses completely, although none always wins either. While the pluralist school points to some groups as stronger than others, it also recognizes that new groups ("potential groups" in its parlance) can organize and take part in the political process to their advantage.[1]

The terms *interest* and *interest group,* although pervasive in political science, are very difficult to employ as analytical tools. What is an interest? The empirical referents of the term are many at best and ambivalent at worst. In the final analysis it appears that most commentators have employed the term interest as synonymous with group activity to achieve desired results. But are we not all characterized by the interests we support? And if we only support interests but do nothing to achieve them, can we be thought of as participating in the political process?

We all have interests. At the most basic level there are the interests of survival and sustenance, but even these "interests" involve policy issues. Are subsidies to be enlarged, reduced, or maintained? Does security demand lengthening or shortening the extent of army service? Are settlements to be expanded or not?

Quickly it becomes clear that interest is often synonymous with politics. What we want is, almost by definition, opposed by others and hence part of the political game. And if there were no groups or individuals fighting over it, if there were no interests, we would not be concerned with it. Years ago, before there was widespread awareness of the limits of our planet's natural resources, clean air was not a political issue. And precisely because there was widespread belief that there were sufficient amounts of clean air for all of us, no interests felt jeopardized and no groups felt vulnerable. But with the development of greater awareness of the finiteness of the earth's resources and the growing awareness of the role that these matters play in maintaining our quality of life, the issue entered politics. Interests were perceived in maintaining low levels of ozone in the atmosphere and low degrees of chemical concentration in lakes and rivers. Economic "interests" brought on an era of concern about nuclear plants for the production of electricity and the safety of automobiles on the roads, about material fire-resistant enough for the making of children's pajamas, about where to locate electricity generating plants, and about the carcinogenic character of the foods we eat.

"Interest" is so pervasive a phenomenon, and so closely related to the group organization designed to further it, that it must be used very carefully. It is important to keep in mind that in order to understand the phenomenon better we must characterize two things: the interest and the group. The term may refer to personal interests or social or general ones. Support for increasing the minimum wage may stem from personal motivation for a low-paid unskilled worker, or it *may* be an altruistic goal for greater social equality on the part of a group or political party. One's orientation is likely to be affected according to whether a personal interest is involved. Another helpful distinction may be between sectoral interest, such as business or labor, and promotional groups that have more altruistic goals in mind.

The organization of the group is also a key to understanding the role of interest groups. A loosely coordinated group with part-time leadership and a low budget behaves very differently and most likely has a different impact on the system than a well-organized, bureaucratic group with a large budget. The outcome is not a foregone conclusion. The former group and its membership may be sufficiently motivated for a large effort on a relatively short-term basis (stop the war, or lower taxes), while the latter organization is better able to handle long-range protracted contacts with government authorities. A bureaucratized interest group inevitably faces organizational problems of the growing conservative nature of its bureaucracy and a tendency to oligarchy; the other kind of organization may be able to be more dynamic, at least in the early phases.

A popular notion of interest-group activity is that it must be public and loud. This notion must be reconsidered. The most effective pressure groups are those we hear of least. Confrontational politics and long petitions are not necessarily a sign of strength in a system such as Israel's. The popular notion of interest-group behavior in pluralistic political cultures has the lobbyist wage a brave fight in the name of the interests of the masses. But the truly effective lobbyist is the one known only by those he needs to maintain the policies desired by patrons. The basic fact is that most policy matters are indeed decided behind closed doors on issues most of us would not understand or become agitated about. It is the rare issue that excites public passion, and on such issues unusual tactics might be employed. But for most policy matters, interests are expressed, promoted, and transformed into policy in much more subtle and mundane ways.

Some groups have won reputations as effective lobbyists for positions they favor. Politicians are likely to fear the clout of such groups long before they have organized petitions, mass mailings, or demonstrations. In the United States the National Rifle Association (which opposes limiting the right of Americans to bear arms) and the so-called Israel lobby are two examples of groups whose potential is enhanced by their previous behavior and successes. Israeli counterparts to such groups are difficult to find because Israeli interest groups are more likely to be ideologically, if not organizationally, linked to a political party or point of view. The appeal by Gush Emunim, Peace Now, or the Histadrut would tend to reinforce existing political divisions rather than add a new dimension to the forces at work on a given policy area.

Other groups, such as the Council for the Prevention of Traffic Accidents or various ecological groups, are largely financed by public moneys and promote causes rarely embroiled in partisan politics. One clear success was achieved in 1991 by the Constitution for Israel movement in leading the call for electoral reform and the direct election of the prime minister. Fueled by the anger of the electorate with the politicians, and with a budget of millions of dollars in contributions, the movement managed to translate the verbal support historically given to the notion of electoral reform by most of the parties and politicians into votes for the new law in the Knesset.

Rather than think of competing interest groups, it is best to think of political parties attempting to colonize bureaucracies or public policy issues or both. The ruling party has dominated defense, the Alignment has run the Histadrut and has colonized the agriculture bureaucracies, and the NRP has nationalized the religious issue and has made it its own. Pluralism is not in evidence; competing political parties are.[2]

The Israeli Case

An analysis of interest-group activity must begin with a careful consideration of the system to be influenced. The trait that makes the pluralistic model described above not completely relevant to Israel is the relative lack of points of access in the Israeli political system. In a large, decentralized system such as the American one, points of access are many, and the role of the media in launching nationwide campaigns is crucial. With a Congress composed of 435 congressmen and 100 senators and a president whose political antennae are always up, the potential for interest-group activity is great. But in a centralized, bureaucratized system such as Israel's, the same rules do not apply. In Israel the major focus of policy-oriented pressure must be the few senior civil servants responsible for the area under discussion or the leaders of the two or three important parties in the government coalition. This handful of people is likely to have the political and administrative power needed to satisfy the demands of the group making application. The new system of direct election of the prime minister focuses power even more than in the past; the fact that Knesset members from the larger parties must win in a broad-based primary election changes the nature of the appeals and promises they make, but not the power and influence that the individual Knesset member has.

Israel, a small country whose politics and politicians are thoroughly acquainted by those active in the field, is a case of a democratic system whose interest groups work in a very compacted environment. Groups organize and jockey for power and influence, but because the space is so small and the system so intense and so dense, the interplay that might exist in other countries is not evident.[3] This is so for at least three reasons. First, Israel's system is so centralized and party dominated that there are only two or three effective access points into the system. The direct election of the prime minister has made this situation even more acute. The Knesset, as we have seen, is run by a coalition of parties that also controls the government. Most legislation is initiated by the government and is generally assured of passage by coalition parties in the Knesset. Why, then, lobby individual Knesset members? The effective interest group would concentrate on the two or three major parties that make up the government coalition. Within each party there is likely to be a handful of individuals whose support would be critical in bringing the issue on the agenda and having it passed. But since the Israeli system is so centralized, so party dominated

and bureaucratic, lobbying can be much more concentrated and even secret. How different from the 535 congressmen and the president who can
be lobbied in the American system! Their techniques of sophisticated communication networks and computerized mailing lists become irrelevant in
Israel. Having access to the party leadership or the hierarchy of the government ministry dealing with the issue is infinitely more important than
fancy organizational techniques developed in and for a different culture.

Second, there is a lack of free-floating issues in the system. Few issues
in Israeli public life are not already being processed. It is very hard to find
an issue that might raise public attention that is not already being discussed, debated, studied, or researched by a government, public, or semi-
public agency. The absence of free-floating issues decreases the potency of
interest groups and gives a tremendous advantage to the ruling party if it
can regulate the introduction of issues being processed by the system. The
timing of the infusion of issues into the system, as much as anything else,
allows powerholders to nip in the bud movements that might otherwise
gain public momentum and divert attention to the areas they favor.

The success or failure of the ruling party in managing demands has
depended very little on the party's ideology. Issues of labor relations,
wages, and economic policy have been troublesome for any finance minister who has tried to deny the workers what they wanted. Labor governments may have had a slightly easier time because the Histadrut was under
their control, but the parties have differed more in style than in substance.
Likud governments, having had no control over the Histadrut, could be
sniped at by this Labor-dominated institution from time to time. Religious
issues have generally been called up by the religious parties on a political
timetable that they have controlled. At times, religious issues were raised
close to the period in which the coalition they participated in appeared to
need their votes in order to avert its fall. Sometimes the religious issue was
propelled into the public sphere by competition among various religious
parties and factions.

Insertion of issues by groups outside the party system has traditionally been more easily contained. The number of demonstrations and petitions in Israeli politics is high,[4] but this does not mean that they are effective on the whole. What it seems to mean is that an extraparty level is
sought for asserting pressure because party channels are either clogged or
overloaded. The Wadi Salib riots in 1954 and the Black Panthers in the
early 1970s, both examples of the introduction of the ethnic issue into Israeli politics, were handled by setting up a committee, by co-opting a number of the leaders, and/or by initiating some policy changes. These groups
tended to be small, their efforts episodic, and their achievements in concrete terms marginal.

It is instructive that the largest returns for the least effort are always won in the Israeli system by groups affiliated with one of the major parties. Numbers can certainly make a difference, but numbers in themselves are not enough. The fact that hundreds of thousands signed a petition supporting the annexation of the Golan certainly was noted when the annexation was finally legislated. But in and of itself it was insufficient. After all, the petition had been circulating for years; poll after poll and election after election indicated that popular support for the idea existed. Numerical strength, coupled with the appropriate political and diplomatic conditions and the political will of the leadership, preceded the legislation.

The third reason that Israeli interest groups must be understood as existing in a compressed environment is that interest-group leaders are often in a hierarchical relation with the party politicians they are trying to influence. They are not likely to be anonymous callers lobbying for some obscure issue but members of the party's institutions whose votes were or will be needed on one issue or another, or for some candidate. More crucially, it is likely that the party leadership approved, or at least did not veto, the appointment of these individuals. We are talking of a process of severe selection in which those who come to make the case of the kibbutzim are not anonymous farmers from the back country but leaders of the kibbutz or moshav movements whose interests often define the actions and policies of the Labor parties. What is more, these movement leaders may one day become important party influentials.

This process occurs even in the army. At the highest levels of the army, meetings may be between politicians serving as government ministers and officers who are potential and even aspiring politicians. The military has always been an important recruiting ground for party politicians, and it is likely that the politicians at the meeting will on some occasion be consulted about the promotion or appointment of these senior military leaders to their next military or political positions. As in all other social situations, people tend to like those who agree with them and agree with those they like. A community of interest builds up based on a commonality of positions and lifestyles. Interest-group activists are often the product of the process of selection that will determine the cast for years to come. The point is that the cast is limited in number, in background, and in social class. Once, the member of the cast was born in Europe and was an immigrant of the second or third *aliyot;* today he is likely to be Israeli-born and university educated. Efforts are increasingly being made to increase the number of Sephardim in this group, but overwhelmingly it is still Ashkenazi. Women and Arabs are almost totally absent from this group.

It is useful to think of Israeli politics as being of the closet and not of the caucus. Then it will be easier to understand that surface motion is not motion, that basic policies are set far from the displays in the Knesset or the headlines of the papers. Important policies are set and important groups operate without fanfare, without headlines, without the public demanding similar concessions. For most groups with economic interests, publication of their victories is counterproductive. If the pilots win concessions that are likely to upset the delicate balance of wage differentials in the country, neither the pilots nor the government want to broadcast this fact—the pilots because they want to retain their relative advantage, the government because it wants to prevent others from demanding similar concessions. If the kibbutzim win favorable water allocations, they are not likely to gloat in public over their achievement. Most interest-group activity is covert; an interest group's frequent appearance in the news is likely to be an indicator of setbacks to its interests (perhaps temporarily) and not a sign of strength.

Notice how different this description is from the pluralistic theory of interest-group representation alluded to earlier. Absent is the assumption that these groups provide a key linkage between the people and their government or that groups compete with one another. There is no safeguard against one group's interest becoming dominant, and it is not at all clear that resources are substitutable, with, for example, numbers taking the place of budget in the case of a poor group with a popular cause. Most important, the definition of the "public interest" that emerges from pluralistic interest-group theory must be changed in a basic sense: if the competition among groups competing fairly for policy goals is the best assurance that the public interest will be served, in the Israeli system the game is clearly stacked in favor of the ruling parties, allowing them to define the public interest if they have the will to do so. Add to this the corporatist arrangements wherein the government, the Histadrut, labor unions, and manufacturers meet to work out wage guidelines, and the understanding of the limitations of spontaneous groups is more complete.[5]

Based on this analysis of the role of interest groups in setting public policy in Israel, it is clear that questions that might be important to scholars in other settings are less important here. For example, whether Israelis join voluntary groups to a great or a limited extent becomes a moot point. Voluntary organizations, when not party affiliated, tend not to be crucial in setting public policy. The numbers themselves do not provide an indication of political power. An estimated 600 public organizations exist in Israel, and 30 percent of Israeli adults belong to a voluntary organization other than the Histadrut.[6] Before 1995, about two-thirds of the adult population belonged to the Histadrut, and about three-quarters received medical treatment from its sick fund. After 1995 and the initiation of the National Health Insurance scheme, the respective figures were about one-third

Histadrut members and two-thirds enrolled in its sick fund. But these figures tell us little about the contours of policymaking in Israel.

In Israel, as in any other country, nonformal, nongovernmental processes play a role in decision making, and in this field the role of the interest group looms large. A useful typology has been put forward by Gabriel Almond and James Coleman.[7] They identified interest articulation as one of four input functions into the political system (along with interest aggregation, communication, and recruitment and socialization), arguing that in many political systems this function of formulating and expressing political demands would be performed by organized interest groups. They identified four major kinds of groups:

1. The *institutional interest group*, which is a formal organization or a long-lasting informal group within a social institution whose manifest function is something other than interest articulation. A group of military or bureaucratic leaders who are formally authorized to undertake some task but who include in their activities influencing policy outputs would be an example of this.

2. The *associational interest group* is constituted in order to express the interests of the group it represents. To do this it usually develops a staff and orderly procedures for achieving the goal for which the group was established.

3. The *nonassociational group* include kinships and ethnic, regional, or status groups that lack formal organization and through which interests are articulated on an intermittent basis by individuals, family heads, and other spokesmen.

4. The *anomic interest group* is of shortest duration and is not characterized by formal organization or long-range planning. Examples of it would be riots, demonstrations, assassinations, and other more or less spontaneous penetrations into the political system from the society.

Various means of access, styles of operation, and environmental factors affect articulation patterns,[8] and these differences have been used to characterize level of political modernization based on interest articulation. The emergence of differentiated infrastructures, such as associational interest groups, indicates higher degrees of political development. As the polity becomes complex and issues increase in number and severity, articulation of interest becomes more institutionalized.

It is instructive to think of Israeli politics in terms of these four types of interest groups. While we can certainly think of instances of all four types, most interest articulation—and certainly most influence—is institutional and associational. For example, the Israel Electric Company achieves its power from its monopoly status granted by law, rather than by recruitment of public opinion and support. Its employees's union is among the most successful organizations because of the threat that its members will disrupt the flow of electricity to the country. No ruling party has been willing to confront them or fundamentally to change the monopoly status of the company or the fringe benefit of free electricity enjoyed by the company's workers.

Associational interest groups such as the Histadrut are also very important. It seems reasonable to speculate, although no empirical work on the subject has been done, that two kinds of groups (institutional and associational) are the most active and the most successful in the Israeli decision-making process. Nonassociational and anomic interest groups are observed only rarely, although their occurrence is more likely to be noted in the newspapers than is the mundane, day-to-day operation of the first two groups. A demand for ethnic representation or a sit-in in apartments by young couples or a demonstration in support of some foreign policy is more unusual—and therefore more likely to appear in the news—than a report by a committee of experts or a secret political twist of the arm by a Histadrut official to a senior civil servant. But the latter are likely to have the political weight necessary to influence policy; the others probably do not.

There is a close link between political parties and interest groups in all political systems. The Israeli case presents a fascinating laboratory to consider the contention that a weak party system facilitates a strong pressure-group system.[9] The primacy of party in Israel was once evident, but it is now in question. Will the relative weakness of the autonomous system of interest groups change as well? The answer to this question will be offset by the generalization that a fragmented decisional system tends to encourage associational groups, while a centralized hierarchical one tends to discourage them. Israeli political parties seem to be in decline, but the decision-making structure appears to be ever more centralized. Add to this the preference of the system's rhetoric for absolute value orientations. Pragmatic bargaining was always permitted and even desirable behind closed doors; at the public level the pragmatic style that values bargaining is denied, and hence much of the legitimacy of interest groups that espouse that style is also denied.

In the compact conditions of the Israeli political and bureaucratic cultures, those groups do best in terms of policy outcome that are closest to decision-making bodies or decision makers themselves. Lobbying, the effort to secure specific policy decisions or the appointment of favorably disposed government personnel, is undertaken in discreet, covert ways as opposed to the more overt methods that characterize a more open system. One example of "painless lobbying" was the existence in Israel of multiple officeholding, in which it was acceptable for a legislator simultaneously to hold an executive position in a major decision-making organization such as the Histadrut or the Jewish Agency. Mayors were sometimes elected to the Knesset in the past (now forbidden), thus affording the municipal interests an ideal carrier and object for lobbying efforts. Levi Eshkol, while serving as prime minister and defense minister, retained for a time the post of chairman of the settlement division of the Jewish Agency, a politically sensitive post, but hardly one demanding the attention of the prime minister. But it is reasonable to assume that the head of the division had a good deal of access to the very highest decision makers in the land.

Elite interaction is usually a little less intense than the previous example, but it exists nonetheless. Keeping in mind the pyramidal structure of Israeli political life and the relatively small numbers of people at the apex of the pyramid reminds us that the probability of elite members meeting often—formally and informally, in official capacities and socially—is very high. And if these individuals also belong to the same party, the interaction is likely to be frequent and cooperative. The informality and ambiguity attendant on an "off the cuff" conversation between a mayor and a minister introduce severe analytic difficulties for the student of interest groups, but they are likely to be more frequent and significant in terms of policy outcomes than many more overt kinds of pressure.

Activities such as formal lobbying and mobilization of the public are not infrequent occurrences, but it is reasonable to conclude that their impact is slight. Lobbying as a recognized institution does not exist in Israel; there are no requirements to register, nor are there legal limitations on activities such as there are in the United States. Demonstrations, hunger strikes, and petitions are regular occurrences in Israeli politics, but they are generally conducted by groups at the fringes of the power network and not by significant ones. If a group such as the Histadrut or Gush Emunim calls for a mass rally or march, it is likely to be for purposes of group arousal as much as for direct influence on a specific policy area. Demonstrations for these broad, politically well-connected groups have more of a symbolic role to play than a policy role.

In the British House of Commons a substantial proportion of the members have explicit and acknowledged ties to organized groups, and the groups perceive the election of their members as advantageous to their general policy interests.[10] This condition sometimes exists in Israel as well; the election of an "interested member" is yet another indication of the group's connection with the party involved. A kibbutz member, a leader of the

Histadrut or some cooperative, a rabbi, or a leader of a trade organization indeed represents the interests of his constituency, but the connections between his organization and his party are pervasive and continuous. Groups are often active at the party level campaigning for the election of their leader to the party list. The efforts of the group for the leader and the efforts of the leader for the group are often either side of the same coin because sometimes the leader speaks for its group on his own behalf in seeking election.

Perhaps the most important mechanism used by groups in attaining access and influence is influencing the appointment of officials on bureaucratic and statutory boards, including key civil service or political appointments. Groups utilize their proximity to party leaders to try to influence these appointments. During the three decades of Labor dominance it was well understood in Israeli politics that the way ahead led in some fashion through the parties of the Alignment or the parties in coalition with them. Such membership was an important, necessary, although not sufficient, condition for appointment and power. Individuals could be sponsored by groups close to the parties; if an endorsement could not be had, the absence of a veto was also occasionally sufficient. In the first period of Likud rule a good deal of carryover of Labor appointments was in evidence. This was attributed to a desire on the part of the Likud to adopt a merit civil service philosophy or, less kindly, to a paucity of candidates who could pass the Likud loyalty test after its long period in opposition. With their later victories in the 1980s and 1990s it was evident that Likud appointments were influenced by endorsements of groups close to Likud parties.

Independent groups that organize to influence policy are generally short-lived and unsuccessful unless co-opted by some party-affiliated group. More important, in the Israeli system the number of groups proves nothing because of their extreme inequality in terms of power. Power in the system is in the hands of leaders of the party or parties in the government coalition. This power is fortified by an extensive system of interlocking directorates with these leaders or their chosen proxies, in this way concentrating power in the key organizations.

Keeping in mind the difficulties attached with the interest-group concept, we next consider some major areas of interest-group activity. While there are hundreds of groups in Israel, four areas are discussed, although no one area is easily identified with a single group. Analyzing these areas allows us a clearer picture of the issues that excite the political system and the ways these issues are handled and influenced by interest groups operating in each area. The four areas to be discussed are defense, the Histadrut, agriculture, and religion.

Defense

Defense policy provides the best example of an institutional interest in the Israeli political system. Defense is the policy area that commands the most attention, the largest concentration of budget, and years of active service of most Israelis. This policy area has overshadowed all others in Israel's existence, often recruiting top-level individuals to serve its demands and rewarding many who have reached the top of its hierarchies with prominent second careers in politics, business, and administration.[11] Placing a priority on defense has become part of the Israeli way of life, with an overwhelming proportion of the population seeing it as the central issue facing Israel. The defense issue penetrates the value system of the country; symbols of military strength, self-sacrifice, and heroism are given positive recognition in the culture. Complex political issues of international relations are often simplified, and military aspects of problems are often stressed at the expense of the political. Borders and settlements are often the focus of the debate regarding Israel's future, with issues such as the interest of other nations given lesser roles.

In the first forty-eight years of independence (1948–96) 18,211 persons died in the service of the country. Yet, for all its importance and its constant present in Israel, defense is dominated by leaders of the major government party and is rarely permeated by outside groups. Groups outside the defense establishment—even the Knesset Committee for Foreign Affairs and Security, not to mention Peace Now or Gush Emunim—play only a minor role in determining Israel's defense policy, although the latter two may influence political parties. The defense challenges facing Israel are of course enormous, and Israel's success in this field has become legendary. The prolonged state of conflict and the risks taken on the road to peace shaped its perception of reality and influenced its societal and economic arrangements. It is precisely because the topic is so salient and the issue boundaries tend to be so impermeable that it is so central to understanding the political system.

The impact of the defense issue is clearly seen in the arrangements that have been worked out regarding national service. For many, it is a major form of identification with the country; for others, it signifies their isolation from the mainstream of Israeli life. The defense issue segregates the Jewish from the Arab population by requiring army service from the former while denying it (except for the Druze and Bedouin) to the latter. Having served in the army is an important requisite to most positions of power and importance in Israeli life, and non-Jews are effectively shut out from them. Veteran status is also a necessity for certain welfare benefits. Arabs are excluded for security reasons; given their choice, it is likely that many would not be willing to risk their lives for the Jewish state.

Two Jewish groups are exempted from army service for political reasons. The conscription of some yeshiva students is formally deferred (in effect they are exempted) while they are studying. This arrangement began in the early days of statehood when Ben-Gurion agreed to the demands of the ultra-Orthodox that yeshiva students (there were about 500 of them then) be exempted. Today, their number has increased a hundred-fold to 50,000. Religiously observant women may also avoid active service. Both groups are regularly attacked for shirking their duty, and alternative forms of national service are often suggested for religious women and Arabs, but these have never been implemented.

Service has become less inclusive, and it is likely that in the future the society will be divided among those who served and those who did not as the army becomes more professional. If peace develops and the army demands less manpower, this process will be accelerated. This has special relevance regarding the large immigrant group from the former Soviet Union. The army historically played an important role in the integration of successive waves of immigrants. But since the army in recent years has more recruits from which to choose, it can be more selective, thus denying many immigrants the rite of passage that in the past was most important to get ahead in Israeli social life.

An example of the divide between those who served and those who did not is provided by the army records of those elected to the Knesset in 1996. About a third of the 120 Knesset members (mostly Arabs and ultra-Orthodox Jews) had not served in the Israel Defense Force. Many Jews do, and for many years. Men often serve in reserve units into their fifties; women are exempted after having borne a child. Interestingly, one's political positions are not altered by service in the territories or exposure to combat training, although after these experiences one tends to be more critical of the army as an institution and less optimistic about its future than people who have not served or who have served under less demanding conditions.[12] In the past, the pervasive structure of the military enterprise assured that most families had a connection—some more direct than others—with the army. This universality assured a high level of salience for military matters and tended to lend implicit public support to the policies followed. The military, certainly until the Yom Kippur War, enjoyed a very high level of prestige in the society, partially because of the sacrifice inherent in the job and partially because of the successes of the military since independence, especially in 1967. This combination of high participation, high prestige, and the admitted importance of the issue made the defense establishment one of the most important areas of interest-group activity in the country.

No area of Israeli public life is immune from its impact. Major economic decisions in such varied fields as industrial infrastructure, natural resource development, privatization, and urban planning take defense considerations into account. The number of buses available in the country, the future of an airport close to the heart of a city, the routing of roads and their capacity, and the kinds of industries to develop are specific examples of this range of concern. The defense issue also has an impact on cultural matters ranging from religious law to the development of an army slang that makes the army one of the most fertile areas of the development of the Hebrew language. The structure of the education system is influenced by the demands of defense, ranging from the curricula of vocational high schools to the fact that Israeli university students tend to begin their studies after a number of years of army service and are likely to be called up for reserve service, along with many of their teachers, during their years of study. The impact of this reality on Israel's youth is a topic of justified concern among parents, educators, psychologists, and philosophers. Can moral, humanistic values be glorified in an environment of training to kill and destroy? Can the value of life be upheld in a structure calculated to bring death? The answers are not simple, and no single type has emerged as the Israeli soldier; but the dilemma provides the backdrop for the attempt to merge the rich morality of Judaism with the historical developments of Zionism.

The successes of the Israeli army must be seen against the backdrop of the Holocaust and the image of the defenseless Jew being led meekly to death. The trauma of that image undoubtedly goes a long way to explain the primacy of the military in Israeli thought and life. The objective challenges the country faced from a hostile environment before the peace treaties and accords reinforced these traumas. One of the difficulties in the pursuit of peace was the difficulty in conceiving of the neighborhood and former enemies in a new way. The process of differentiating between good Arabs and bad Arabs is far from complete for many Israelis. It is difficult to shift from being a nation in arms, a nation besieged, especially when suicide bombers explode on urban buses. For the decades of strife, Israel was called on to do what few had done successfully: to maintain democratic and liberal traditions under conditions continuously working against those traditions.

Considering the enormous economic, psychological, and cultural burden of defense, Israel's record in maintaining democratic forms and civil rights (at least within the pre-1967 borders) is admirable. Part of the explanation for this success is the small size of the country. Israel's army depends on a vast reserve of manpower that is continually called up and trained. The aphorism that Israelis are soldiers on eleven months' leave catches the spirit of the situation.[13] The dominant values of the country are reflected in the army, and vice versa. No isolated class has developed, no feeling of being aloof or different from the rest of the population. While the image of the army as more efficient or successful is lower than it was, feelings of pride in it are dissipated throughout the society and are not concentrated in a narrow class of officers.

The dilemma posed by the military forces of any nation is clear. Since the state is supposed to monopolize the use of violence and since military might rests with the army, it is essential that the army be under the control of the civilian authorities of the state. Both democratic and communist regimes desire the subjugation of the military to civilian control, for fear of being replaced by those officers to whom the means of violence have been entrusted. Imbuing a "professional" commitment in the army to obey the duly elected leadership is not a matter of empty ideological posturing but is a matter of neutralizing a dangerous potential threat to the continuation of the regime.

In Israel the army was seen as a partner with the political forces in bringing about the national revolution of independence of statehood and not as a competing power. A pattern of dual control developed during the Yishuv period in which the Haganah was responsible to the dominant party, Mapai, and to the voluntary national institutions that were the functional equivalent of civilian authorities of the state. On achieving statehood this dual pattern of loyalty to party and state persisted and prevented the emergence of an instrumentalist army solely controlled by the civilian branch of the state—the ideal model of liberal democracies.[14]

The existence of separate armies with competing political loyalties was a major problem resolved by Ben-Gurion in 1948 when separate commands of the Haganah, Palmach, Irgun, and Lehi were abolished and the Israel Defense Force (IDF) established. But because Ben-Gurion feared that the new army would be open to the same kind of coalition pressures as were other aspects of Israel's public life, the army was never domesticated in the sense of being controlled by the civilian ministry of defense. Ben-Gurion wanted to keep control in his own hands, and while he served as both prime minister and defense minister (1948–53 and 1955–63) this arrangement was possible. But when Ben-Gurion's personal stature was removed from the equation, it became clear that the subordination of the military to the civilian government had not been properly institutionalized.

It was fashionable to talk of the depoliticization of the army, and there was much evidence of this new instrumental pattern emerging. But the basic flaw in the process was the attempt to devise a nonparty solution to a political problem in Israel's political culture, which rests squarely on political parties. Who can keep the army under civilian control and yet away from the politicians and their party interests? Ben-Gurion's answer was to extol the virtues of civilian control while keeping personal control over the major decisions of the IDF. All three times that Ben-Gurion retired (1953, 1954, and 1963) from the dual roles of prime minister and defense minister, he suggested that the roles be filled by two separate individuals. During his tenure he tried to make the defense sphere independent of the civilian sphere and in so doing ultimately made their interpenetration inevitable. "The end result was, therefore, that the dual control failed to achieve either of Ben-Gurion's aims. Though deprivatized, the IDF did not develop into an apolitical, instrumentalist army under the absolute supervision of the state institutions. Instead it ultimately became an army working as a partner in the political process, integrated with the civil power even beyond the national-security field."[15]

The nominal civil control instigated by Ben-Gurion largely succeeded in keeping other parties' influence out of the IDF but made the interpenetration of the highest echelons of Mapai and the highest echelons of the army very intimate. No strong autonomous civilian ministry was set up to oversee the functioning of the military. Since Ben-Gurion the civilian was in charge of the IDF, his oversight was deemed sufficient. The Defense Ministry became a civilian aide for the army, with all major functions of budgeting, procurement, and military strategy situated in the army itself or duplicated in the Defense Ministry. At certain levels, internal party developments influenced the army. Senior ministers would court army leaders for support in conflicts with other ministers regarding policy. The support of the officers was important not just in the sense of professional advisers but as the opinion of the major interest group involved in the area. In periods of generally accepted leaders such as Ben-Gurion and Begin, the role of the military was similar to that of the professional adviser, but when the role of leader was less secure, as with Eshkol and Rabin (both in the 1970s and in the 1990s), the position of the military leadership was an important part of the political calculus.

After Ben-Gurion, the fact that civilian control had not been institutionalized became obvious. One writer categorized relations between the defense minister and the political system as follows: Ben-Gurion had almost complete authority over the IDF and the Defense Ministry. Lavon, his successor as defense minister, had almost none, and not surprisingly from this perspective, the Lavon Affair (discussed in chapter 5) occurred during this period. Levi Eshkol is called a "representative" defense minister. Between 1963 and 1967 he held both positions of prime minister and defense minister, and represented the demands and programs of the military to the political leadership. This is hardly control. The time between 1969 and 1974 had Golda Meir as prime minister, Moshe Dayan as defense minister, and Pinhas Sapir as finance minister. Dayan and Sapir differed over economic and defense matters; also, Dayan had split from Mapai with Rafi while Sapir was leader of the Mapai political machine. This left Golda Meir in the role of arbiter, balancing between the two prominent ministers in her government. The period between 1974 and 1977, in which Yitzhak Rabin was prime minister and Shimon Peres defense minister, was characterized by cabinet rivalry between the two and by professional control by Peres of the military.[16]

Begin's experiences were more varied. With Ezer Weizman as defense minister, Begin tended to support a harder foreign policy line than Weizman, especially regarding Egypt, leading to a tacit coalition between Begin and Chief of Staff Rafael ("Raful") Eitan and ultimately bringing about Weizman's resignation in 1980. Until Ariel Sharon was appointed defense minister in 1981, Begin also served as defense minister. In that period he was slightly more actively involved in defense matters than when he had a defense minister, Eitan playing a dominant role. Sharon's appointment after the 1981 elections removed the political conflict within the triad because all three (Begin, Sharon, and Eitan) were hard-liners. Sharon tended to dominate army as well as government policy until he was forced to resign from the Defense Ministry as a result of the Kahan Commission report concerning his role in the events in the Palestinian refugee camps of Sabra and Shatilla.

Rabin was defense minister from 1984 to 1990, the years of the National Unity Government, and had to work closely with the security cabinet, a group that was made up equally of Likud and Labor politicians. He resumed the dual role of defense minister and prime minister after being elected in 1992 and until his assassination.

The pattern that has emerged is that top government leaders (by definition politicians) are very active in army policy, especially relating to procurement and personnel appointments. The boundaries between the civilian and the military in Israel are not clear; there is no civilian counterpart to the military in the Israeli defense establishment. Top military leaders have been called on to be very active in matters of policy that, according to a purist model, should be the exclusive area of the politicians. A good example was the very active participation of senior officers in the negotiations with the Palestinians and the Syrians in the 1990s, in which the (supposedly professional) judgment of the military leadership carried great weight for the political leadership, especially for Shimon Peres. Since Rabin had been chief of staff, he was more willing to express opinions regarding military matters.

In an effort to change this balance, proposals had been made to set up a National Security Council in the prime minister's office that would be able to counter the preponderance of influence by the defense establishment. Netanyahu finally did not adopt these proposals, which would have transferred responsibility for the arms industry from the defense minister, thus weakening the office considerably. As defense minister, he appointed Yitzhak Mordechai, a general who had recently resigned from the army after being denied the post of deputy chief of staff.

Retired army officers have been very involved in the political debate, especially since the beginning of the Intifada (Arab uprising) in December 1987. Before the elections, groups of senior reserve officers organized to express authoritative opinions about the need to retain the territories in order to defend the country militarily. Contrarily, the Peace and Security Council announced that the security of the country would be furthered by exchanging territories for peace. The reaction came promptly. The Security and Peace Council, also made up of senior reserve officers, stated that holding the territories was necessary for the security of the country.

The problematic nature of civil-military relations is seen more clearly during periods of crisis and war. During the War of Independence, Ben-Gurion had to contend with a revolt among his generals, who were opposed to his proposed appointments, intended to purge the high command of officers who were not Mapai members. Ultimately Ben-Gurion won the battle by compromising with the generals while demanding total political support from his cabinet in such matters. In the Sinai Campaign of 1956, the war was well under way before Ben-Gurion apprised his government of the plan of war. Civilian control, yes, but not governmental control. In the days before the 1967 Six-Day War, intense political negotiations were conducted that ultimately led to Dayan's appointment as defense minister after Eshkol removed himself from the position. Not only were other political parties active in this negotiation, but the leadership of the army also took part in it.

In the 1973 crisis of the Yom Kippur War the porous relations between the civilian and military were most obvious. Ministers were given military appointments, and generals publicly criticized political decisions. The Agranat Commission ultimately focused blame on the military, largely ignoring the acts of omission and commission by the political leadership.[17] In the 1982 Lebanon war the military was divided on the goals and the tactics of the war, as was the civilian community. The lack of a national consensus split the army and crises of morale and resignations, demonstrations, and petitions swept the army. The lines of demarcation between the civil and military are not clear partially because the army is such an integral part of Israeli society and partially because basic institutions of civilian control have never been established.[18] With the army being so esteemed, so prominent, and so important, it is not surprising that it is also so powerful.

Even in a constitutional sense civilian control over the military is blurred. We know who the chief of staff is, but it is more difficult to determine who the commander in chief is. Collective responsibility lies with the government, and often many ministers speak out on military matters to the discomfort of the minister of defense and the prime minister. The Basic Law: Israel Defense Force, passed in 1976 after the evidence of a lack of clear lines of authority in the 1973 Yom Kippur War, formalized the constitutional responsibility. The army is under the authority of the cabinet, and the chief of staff is the commander. The minister of defense acts through authority of the cabinet in defense matters. The chief of staff is appointed by the cabinet on the recommendation of the minister of defense. While this better defines the relations, the roles of the prime minister and the other ministers are still left vague. The defense minister's role is defined neither as delegate of the cabinet nor as leader of the army. It could be both or neither depending on the circumstances.

The appointment of the chief of staff must incorporate both professional and political considerations. At that highest of levels, not even the strongest proponent of civilian-military separation would pretend that a complete divorce of the two is possible. But which quality should be prominent: professional competence or political loyalty? Leaders such as Ezer Weizman, Ariel Sharon, and Yitzhak Mordechai have been candid in expressing their opinions that they were best qualified, but they were passed over because Labor leaders did not trust them politically. They each became defense minister without being chief of staff. Chiefs of staff have done very well politically. The list includes Yigael Yadin, Moshe Dayan, Yitzhak Rabin, and Chaim Bar-Lev, but only Yitzhak Rabin ever became prime minister. The fact that the chief of staff is so important in the political system both during and after his tenure indicates how close the apexes of the political and military pyramids are.

The civilian Ministry of Defense is eclipsed by the IDF. Yitzhak Rabin, former chief of staff and former prime minister, called the Ministry of Defense a ministry of supply for the army. The ministry exists in the heavy shadow of the IDF, and even in those spheres in which its formal authority is recognized, it does not succeed in exerting it.[19] It was Ben-Gurion who made the double decision that the Ministry of Defense would be separate from the army but that it would not supervise the army. The ministry tends to be an appendage of the general staff because later defense ministers have followed Ben-Gurion's practice of utilizing these uniformed officers extensively in the decision-making process and in his practice of choosing not only the chief of staff but other senior officers. Ben-Gurion's practice of keeping research, manufacturing, procurement, finance, and conscription under civilian management was maintained, but in many of these spheres the dictates of the IDF carried the day, and the civilian Defense Ministry was swept along.[20]

The defense minister is an extremely important actor in Israeli politics because of the centrality of the defense issue, but the Defense Ministry as an implement of civilian control is relatively unimportant. The topic was so sensitive that the statement of a senior civil servant to the effect that "the army dominates the defense establishment" was banned by the censor.[21] The rationale of the concentration of power in the hands of the military is that the army, as the body responsible for implementation, must also be responsible for planning, procurement, and deployment of the arms and forces. This may be based on a naive belief that Israel is immune from social forces that have led to military takeover in other countries, or it may be an expression of the high esteem that many Israelis have for their army. While there exists the formality of separation, and while the minister of defense and the cabinet have dominated military planning and moves, Israel lacks the patterns of civilian control in a more institutionalized sense that exist in other countries.

A good example of this is the defense budget. As we saw in chapter 3, the defense budget in effect defines Israel's budget in terms both of domestic spending and of its reliance on funds from foreign sources to offset the purchase of weapon systems abroad. The military, in turn, defines Israel's defense needs. The head of the budget division of the Ministry of Defense (who also holds the title of financial adviser to the chief of staff) prepares a proposal after extensive consultation. His task is made easier in the sense that the army works on a five-year plan, which in effect means that the plan must be updated from year to year. In the case of major change— redeployment of forces as a result of political negotiations or military readjustments—a new plan might be needed. Canceling plans for the advanced jet fighter Lavi because the United States refused to continue to underwrite its development and production, the unanticipated expenses of combating the extended Arab uprising, or the redeployment of IDF forces from the territories are examples of how budget plans may change in midterm, even in the absence of war. But the budget process takes last year's budget as a given and tends to grow from that point. No zero-based-budgeting methods are used to attempt to determine what is really needed to achieve the desired results.

If a single budget proposal emerges from the whole process, it is forwarded through the defense minister to the Finance Ministry and the cabinet. If there are disagreements among general staff members or between the army and the ministry, the matter is brought to the minister. In such a case, however, his role is that of judge rather than leader. When brought to other civilian leaders, the tendency has been to give as much as possible.

Eshkol tended to press the officers to ascertain that their budget was sufficient, and Sapir perceived his role as cashier for the defense establishment. Rabin and his chief of staff, Ehud Barak, redesigned the budget in the 1990s in terms of a leaner and smarter army, thus allowing for the budget to take a smaller part of the country's economic resources, a commodity always in short supply. The cabinet was actively involved in the process usually only when the defense and finance ministers disagreed. While budget decisions need cabinet approval, these tend to be formal decisions ratifying decisions made elsewhere.

The Knesset has developed a special procedure for working on the defense budget. Since it is a secret subject, the entire Knesset is not involved. Instead, a special subcommittee composed of members of the Finance Committee and the Committee for Foreign Affairs and Security scrutinizes the budget in closed session and approves it item by item, while the whole Knesset approves the total sum as part of the national budget. The structure of its preparation and the political process it undergoes assure that the defense budget approved will be quite close to the proposals approved by the general staff and the defense minister. Only those groups at the heart of the preparation stage have a realistic chance of affecting it. Matters as important and far-reaching as the production of a new tank or a new jet aircraft are for all intents and purposes decided in the defense establishment. The Finance Ministry, the cabinet, and the Knesset, in decreasing order of effectiveness, may slow the decision-making process, but it is unlikely that they can turn it around. Arguments made about the tremendous expenses involved and the alternatives that might be economically more sound can be made, but they usually do not, at so late a date, abort the decision. If indeed the Israeli system is a partnership between civilian and military spheres, there is at least some evidence that the military partner is more senior than the civilian one.

The pattern of civilian-military relations in Israel is complex. In a formal sense the civil branch dominates. In a deeper sense the military is not segregated in its barracks but is active in the political life of the country at its highest reaches. What is more, some military leaders enter active political life after retiring from the army. The boundaries are porous and shifting, and this very feature may allow Israel to retain formal civilian control over the military.

The Histadrut

If politics played an important role in an institutional interest group in the defense field, party politics was even more prevalent in an associational interest group such as the Histadrut. The Histadrut was conceived as the organization of the workers' movement run by the labor parties, which would compete among themselves in elections. The Labor Party was clearly dominant in the Histadrut until 1994, so the organization became an important staging ground for political fights within the Labor Party, an important aid to power when Labor ran the government, and an important source of opposition when it did not. Power within the Histadrut was a possible resource to be used in national politics by ambitious groups and individuals within the Labor Party because the budget controlled by the Histadrut was considerable, and the jobs that could be allocated were numerous.

The Histadrut is a voluntary organization of workers that functions as a trade union, but was also much more than that, having played a key role in the prestate period in building the infrastructure of the country's economy, in absorbing immigrants, and in preparing for the political and military challenges that Israel would face (see chapter 3). It claimed more than 1.8 million members before the 1994 reorganization, after which it plunged to some 650,000 members, representing a major fraction of the Israeli workforce. Obviously, such an organization must be taken into account when policies important to it are being considered.

Since its inception in 1920, and until 1994, the Labor Party controlled the Histadrut. The ideology of the Histadrut was it that represented the interests of the workers; in reality, the Histadrut represented the interests of the Labor Party, which controlled the Histadrut. Even the 1994 elections may ultimately be viewed as a fight within Labor for control of the Histadrut. Chaim Ramon, minister of health in the Labor Party government of the day, headed a list which ran against his own party (Labor) and won 46 percent of the vote to Labor's 32 percent.[22]

Since 1994, the economic activity of the Histadrut and its role in social service delivery have changed dramatically. Kupat Holim, the sick fund, is still a Histadrut activity, but the National Health Insurance Law provides that most of its operations will be funded, and regulated, by the government. The Histadrut redesigned itself so that trade union activity was its major function.

Socialist parties are often associated with labor unions. The support may be more direct, as in Germany and Great Britain where the unions actively support a labor party, or less direct, as in the United States where organized labor generally supports the Democratic Party. Often in continental countries each political party has its own trade union and recruits labor's support in that way. Israel's pattern is unique; the Histadrut fits none of these descriptions. The Histadrut is made up of workers who elect their governing officers from competing parties. Until the 1960s the parties that competed were workers' parties or parties that accepted socialist ideals. But since the 1965 Histadrut elections and the participation of a Herut-Liberal list (Gahal), the full spectrum of parties that competes for the Knesset elections also competes for the Histadrut elections, making them an important stage in Knesset elections.

The New Histadrut (the new leaders even changed the name) downsized the organizational structure; the member still has many opportunities to vote. The Histadrut convention still involves more than 1,000 delegates; the post-1994 regime disbanded the Histadrut Assembly, a middle-level body of no great organizational importance. The important executive committee with 137 members, down from 374 members and alternates, emerged from the convention. The seventy workers' councils are also elected, and they were reorganized into twenty to thirty regional units, costing many activists their jobs. Members also vote for the trade union council in their craft or profession, and then there is the election for the workers' committee at the individual workplace. Women also vote for *Naamat,* a women's workers' council.

The elections for the convention and workers' councils use a proportional representation fixed-list system similar to that used in Knesset elections. The minimum percentage needed to win representation in the Knesset is 1.5 percent, but for the Histadrut national convention, the minimum has been 2 percent since the 1981 elections. In 1977 it was 1 percent, and before that time, there was no minimum percentage required. Some of the national trade union leaders and most of the workers' committee members are elected on a plurality basis. This latter system promotes the election of visible and popular leaders; the former system retained the processes of selection and promotion in the hands of the labor establishment. Chaim Ramon won in the 1994 election for the national convention by presenting it as a popularity contest race between him and the Labor bureaucrats, even though technically it was a contest conducted under the list rules of proportional representation. After the election, although it lost control of the convention, the Labor Party continued to control the workers' councils. The appeal of younger leaders, evident in past council elections, had made itself felt at the national level against the old-time establishment.

In the elections to the national convention before 1994, Labor had always won an absolute majority of the votes. Ramon did not win a majority, but he came very close. Control of the Histadrut passed from Labor to Ramon's list. This central feature that had provided Labor control over the economy, patronage, and power, was lost. The same hierarchical structure of the Histadrut that afforded Labor leaders such power in the political economy of the country was also responsible for the conservative image of the Histadrut establishment elite in the public mind.[23]

In addition to streamlining the decision-making structure, Ramon cut the number of workers in the Histadrut administration (executive committee, workers' councils, and tax collection agency) from 3,924 workers in July 1994 to 2,217 a year later. The plan was to cut that workforce to 1,100 to help cover the 1.2 billion shekel deficit faced by the Histadrut.

Losing control of the Histadrut was a serious blow to the Labor Party. No longer could it count on cooperation with the leadership of the Ministry of Finance in the process of wage negotiations when Labor was in power. Without cooperation, the negotiations could be long and stormy. Historically, much depended on the relations between the government and the Histadrut. After the establishment of the state, the Histadrut lost much of its power and leading personnel to the newly formed government. By and large the Histadrut was relegated to second-rank status in terms of setting social and economic policy, although its ideas and leaders were often heard and sometimes promoted to more prominent positions. In the Likud era the Histadrut became a major focus of opposition to the government for the Labor Party. There were two major reasons for this. First, the long years in government had weakened the party as an effective organization, and the Histadrut was more able to fill the gap. Second, the important base of power and patronage for Labor after 1977 was the Histadrut and its related enterprises. Paradoxically, the Histadrut and its leadership were strengthened as a result of the 1977 and 1996 Likud victories over Labor.

The appropriate way to conceptualize labor relations in Israel in general is by seeing the Histadrut trying to further the interests of the workers and its own interests as well. In the pre-1994 period, it was most likely for the Histadrut and government to resolve labor friction through compromise. When arguments developed, they were due to differences over implementation, not over policy. Or, and this happened not infrequently, a group of worker leaders would strive for concessions above and beyond what the Histadrut agreed to. Then, without the support of the Histadrut, wildcat strikes or work actions would wreak havoc on an economic sector. What is fascinating to observe is how much more effective Histadrut leaders were in communicating with the government and/or the employers than they were in dealing with the workers. Under the Likud, the government and Histadrut seemed to perpetuate the kind of relations that existed under Labor in the field of labor relations, but on more general topics—such as social-economic policy or proposals for legislation regarding compulsory arbitration, national health insurance, or state pensions—the differences between Histadrut and Likud government leaders were great.[24] In the post–1994 period, the Histadrut tried to generate an image of militant trade unionism, free from the economic interests that had conflicted it in the past.

Within the Labor Party the Histadrut was an important resource in another sense. The local leadership often used the office of secretary of the local council as political patronage. If it wanted to reward an active member, the party might provide him with that job. If, on the other hand, a member achieved prominence within the council and became its secretary, he almost automatically acquired an important position in the local party branch and possibly beyond it as well. It is the nature of the extended scope of the Histadrut in Israeli labor relations that the secretary of the workers' council has the potential to help solve individual as well as collective grievances and to dispense patronage jobs within the Histadrut network. The economic and service institutions of the Histadrut, weighted down by enormous deficits, became a tremendous economic burden rather than an ideological imperative or a political boon and crumbled in the end. Ram may rejuvenate Labor's power base within the working class, or it may strike out on its own.

With the decline of Labor's electoral fortunes in 1988, it was faced with a twofold problem: (1) to secure government funds, credits, and guarantees for Hevrat Ovdim's overextended industries, cooperatives, and service providers; and (2) then to use the Histadrut as a vehicle to regain political power. The wheel had turned: for forty years, Labor wielded political power by controlling the economy. When Shimon Peres became finance minister in 1988, he hoped to be able to restructure the economy in a way that would save the economic future of the Histadrut and the political future of the Labor Party. Grabbing the reins of the weakened Histadrut in 1994, Chaim Ramon was able to gain status and power for himself while depriving the Labor Party of its former bastion of strength. He also changed its structure beyond recognition by downsizing its economic activity and bringing about the nationalization of the health services.

Paradoxically, as the Histadrut became more important for Labor's future, the role of Histadrut leaders diminished. This pattern was a reversal of what had occurred with independence. In the prestate era, the Histadrut was the focus of action; as the Jewish Agency and later the state became centers of activity, the major party leaders reduced their activity in the Histadrut. As we have seen in chapter 4, that was the pattern followed by Ben-Gurion himself. Ramon did not have serious electoral competition in his quest to win the Histadrut.

In the 1996 elections, Labor suffered from the lack of the organizational effort that the Histadrut had provided it in previous elections. Determined to be singleminded trade unionists, Histadrut leaders were very careful not to involve their organization, now led by Ramon's Ram, in Labor's election campaign. The huge reservoir of personnel and vehicles that the Histadrut institutions controlled was not employed during the campaign. Peres's loss by only 30,000 out of 3 million votes indicates how crucial added organizational effort might have been. It is even more ironic than that because Peres appointed Ramon, the man who had run Rabin's successful campaign in 1992, to be his campaign organizer in 1996.

Agriculture

Agriculture is an excellent example of an important policy area in which interest-group activity is more covert than overt, relying on party, parliamentary, and government contacts available because of the strategic location of the pro-agriculture persons in the system. Agriculture was a penultimate value in the period before the establishment of the state. Through agriculture the Zionist movement could realize two of its major goals: returning to the land of Israel in the most literal sense, and making the Jewish people productive instead of centering their economic activities on trade, craftsmanship, and scholarship. Over time, especially since the 1930s, agriculture was also identified with defense imperatives because it allowed for spreading the population and establishing a physical presence and a kind of military early-warning system.

The earliest traces of modern Jewish agriculture go back to the first *aliyah* and the plantations set up by Baron de Rothschild. These efforts permitted Arab labor and discouraged Jewish labor because the former was cheaper and more experienced. The second and third *aliyot* pioneered new forms of agricultural settlement including the kibbutz and the moshav, and based their program on using Jewish labor while avoiding the exploitation of others by employing only members in their enterprises. These pioneering ventures became the ideological and organizational strongholds of the labor movement, and even though most of the rest of Eretz Israel were always urban dwellers, agriculture became associated with the highest ideals of the system of values that existed before independence. Agriculture was perceived as a mission of the movement and the nation. It was fruitless to search for the boundary of agriculture's lofty influence because the leadership, ideology, and organization of the entire labor movement presented themselves as stemming from the agricultural sector.

The bourgeois farmers and plantation owners associated with nonsocialist ideas were extraordinarily negative in opposing the socialist organization of agriculture. They were divided among themselves, and after the 1930s became more and more marginal in the politics of the country. One of their leaders, Yosef Sapir, even argued that only with decentralized organization could they be true to the ideals of the "free" farmer.[25] The right accepted the socialist ideology, seeing in agriculture a way of life that would lead to national rejuvenation. For the parties associated with Labor, these settlements and their leadership became heads of the entire movement and ultimately of the nation, while the agriculturists of the Likud parties were soon eclipsed and could do little more than make feeble attempts at interest-group activity.

Independence and the establishment of the Agriculture Ministry decreased the autonomy of the Histadrut and the Agriculture Center in agricultural matters and ultimately led to substantive changes. But at least in the first decade of independence the dominance of the Agriculture Center remained intact. Most of the ministers came from agricultural backgrounds in the settlement movements and usually from the kibbutz movement affiliated with Mapai. The organizational and ideological strength of the settlement movement prevented Mapai from actively interfering in agricultural policy; the opposite was true—leaders of the agricultural movements achieved prominent roles in the party and dominated in party affairs out of all proportion to their numerical size. Looking just at kibbutz members, we find that in 1965, six of Ahdut Haavoda's eight-member delegation, six of nine from Mapam, and eight of forty-two from Mapai were from kibbutzim.[26] One can sense the political decline of the kibbutz movement and of the agriculture "lobby" by comparing the 1996 figures: only the Knesset delegations of Labor and the Citizens Rights Movement had kibbutz members, and they had only one each.

The supremacy of Labor and Mapam was obvious when the matter of land allotment was considered. Israel did not have a history of large landowners, and so there was no need for agrarian reform. Land was purchased by the World Zionist Organization through the Keren Kayemet and distributed or leased by it primarily to settlements organized in the Agricultural Center. The Agricultural Center incorporated settlements (kibbutzim and moshavim) affiliated with the Histadrut. This arrangement gave the Histadrut enormous power, and in the early years it was the kibbutzim that won the battle, receiving preferential treatment at the hands of the Agricultural Center over resources provided to it by the Keren Kayemet.[27] The kibbutzim were preferred over the moshavim (the private farmers of the right were almost totally ignored) because the kibbutzim were more closely associated with the dominant party, while the moshavim had their closest contacts with a rival party. The kibbutzim were dominant in the Agricultural Center, and that made all the difference.

The interpenetration was so complete that various kibbutz movements, affiliated with different socialist parties, competed with one another within the Agricultural Center. The settlement division of the Jewish Agency handled training, research, and budget but left the allocation of land to the settlement movements, which set up a committee composed of leading activists. When Mapai won control over the WZO and the Jewish Agency, it quickly took advantage of the resources placed at its disposal to further national, party, and sectoral goals. Since decision-making positions had been "colonized" by the kibbutz, there was no need to exert great pressure to secure favorable policies.

After independence, the dominance of agriculture continued. Huge sums were poured into settlement movements, resulting in impressive achievements in agriculture; in addition, the settlement movements provided organizational strength and a supply of party activists and leaders to Mapai and other parties. This was especially sensible for the kibbutz movement, whose lifestyle provided for the member's and his family's needs and could allow him to absent himself from work on the kibbutz to further the interests of the nation, the party, and the kibbutz. National federations could recruit members—from 5 to 7 percent—from the federated kibbutzim for work within the movement or in national capacities.[28]

In 1959, Moshe Dayan was appointed minister of agriculture. His appointment shocked the political establishment because Dayan was young and many faithful politicians were itching to be appointed, and because Dayan had only recently completed his turn as IDF chief of staff, but mostly because Dayan was seen to represent the moshavim and not the kibbutzim. Dayan changed the sectoral outlook of Israel's agriculture ministers and adopted a statist approach (see chapter 11). This was upsetting to the old order, whose interests were secured by having their people appointed to key positions. Dayan rejected the arrangement of having the Agriculture Ministry deal with the old-time settlements established before the state was founded and the Jewish Agency deal with new ones founded after statehood. The new settlements were predominantly populated by new immigrants from Asia and Africa, who were untrained in agricultural ways and largely without the accompanying ideology with which the early European settlers had begun their settlements. The new settlements were generally set up on poorer land and were very dependent on the bureaucracies, which issued credit, training, and marketing. These bureaucracies tended to be run by veteran Europeans. When Dayan took over the Agriculture Ministry, he found the average kibbutz landholding unit was 105 dunams compared with the average 36.7 dunams for moshavim. The average water quota for the kibbutz unit was 24,300 cubic meters compared with 10,600 for the moshavim. Dayan undertook major changes in this balance. He allocated 100,000 dunams to the new kibbutzim, lowered the kibbutz water quota to 17,100 cubic meters and raised that of the moshavim to 13,500 cubic meters.[29]

Moshe Dayan was the first minister of agriculture who did not perceive himself as a representative of the settlement movements, although he was born in the first established kibbutz and raised in one of the pioneer moshavim. During his term the bulk of the country's land was formally nationalized with the passing of the Basic Law: Lands of Israel in 1960. The law regulated the allocation of land and made the Lands Administration (and not Keren Kayemet) responsible for the national lands, which constituted about 90 percent of the country's land. The minister of agriculture became chairman of the Lands Administration.

Under the Labor-Mapam Alignment the settlement movements could greatly influence government policy because they could count on majority representation on the commissions that interested them. (The commissions for tobacco and olives had a majority of Arabs since much of the production of these items is in Arab hands.) Most of the settlement representatives came through the Agricultural Center, and the government representatives were also favorable to the sectoral demands of agriculturists. Even in the Likud years the federations affiliated with the Labor-Mapam Alignment were well represented on the commissions because most of the agriculture of the country is organized by them. Although the government representatives tend to be less cooperative in following the sector's demands, the influence of the settlements on agricultural policy is substantial; agriculture as an issue area, however, has lost its centrality.

Competition in agriculture between the kibbutzim and the moshavim has a long history. Historically the kibbutzim had dominated the party and hence policy. The other source of conflict that would fester over the years and become more and more evident as the ethnic polarization of the country grew was between the kibbutzim and veteran moshavim, which were mainly Ashkenazi, and the moshavim peopled by Sephardi immigrants. The older settlements did not lead the community in absorbing immigrants who came soon after the state was founded. Whereas they had pioneered in statesmanship, diplomacy, agriculture, and security, they absented themselves from the effort of absorbing the new immigration. This may be understood as fatigue, overload, or dismissal. The labor settlement movements abandoned the task of absorbing new waves of immigrants to the bureaucracies they had helped set up. By thus depersonalizing the process, they accelerated feelings of alienation on the part of the new immigrants toward the more established farmers. The veteran kibbutzim and moshavim have been perceived as a landed gentry in affluent Israel. They were characterized by others as arrogant, as thinking that the leadership of the country was its natural and indispensable role. These people were easily singled out in the antiestablishment, anti-Labor campaigns of the 1980s. Their previous image of folk hero became tarnished and their political power dissipated.

Even the appointment of a kibbutz member as minister of agriculture in 1988 could not help much, because by then the agricultural sector was in deep economic and political trouble. As the country industrialized, and as the service sector became more important, agriculture would not again play the central role it had in the politics of the past. The government arranged to take over some of the debt of the kibbutzim in the mid-1990s (see chapter 3), but even those improved conditions could not restore their previous wealth, power, and status.

In the dominant party, Mapai, agricultural interests were assured because of the ideological tone of the era and the leadership positions that members of the settlement movement attained. This also meant that the party refrained from interfering in the affairs of the agricultural movements. Party interference was greatest in the agricultural organizations of the smaller parties, set up to try to compete with the successful organizations of the labor movement. This included the minuscule movements of Herut, the Liberals, and the Independent Liberals, and the slightly larger movements of the NRP and Poalei Agudat Israel. These agricultural movements often achieved representation within party institutions but never achieved the importance of labor movement organizations.

Four of those who served as agricultural ministers—Pinhas Lavon, Levi Eshkol, Moshe Dayan, and Ariel Sharon—eventually became ministers of defense. Especially in the case of Sharon, agriculture was defined by his activities and concern for settlement of the territories, thus continuing the tradition of the prestate era, which equated agriculture with settlement and defense needs. The ministry was dominated in its early years by ministers favorable to the kibbutz, a dominance that could be seen in both policy and appointments.

The control of water allocations is so important an economic political resource that it caused a furor when Netanyahu attempted to set up the Ministry for National Infrastructure in 1996, to be headed by Ariel Sharon. Water was a key to building a powerful base for Sharon. But water was the province of Raful Eitan, the minister of agriculture, and another important power broker in Netanyahu's climb to the prime minister's office. Eitan was not willing to have control over the water commissioner taken from him. The compromise was that Eitan would continue to have control over water for agriculture, including the amounts used and the rates charged, and that Sharon would control other aspects of water.

In the past, settlement and agriculture were associated with the shared value of building the homeland; in the 1990s building the homeland raised contentious issues of territories and relations with the Palestinian Authority. With the exception of the Golan Heights, the established kibbutz movement refrained from settling in disputed areas; the symbol of agriculture could no longer sustain a national ideology.

A production commission for the control and marketing of citrus fruit was formed in the 1940s and existed until the 1990s.[30] Later commissions were introduced for all branches of agriculture; they were empowered to oversee production, to assure a regular supply of the product, to facilitate its marketing, and to deal with surpluses. Today the commissions are statutory authorities that can enter into contracts and enterprises (six other commissions relating to agriculture have been incorporated). These commissions are composed of those active in the branch; the government has no more than 25 percent of the membership (with representatives of Agriculture, Finance, Industry, and Commerce ministries and sometimes the Ministry of Health); the producers (represented by settlement groups) 50 percent, the marketers 15 percent, and the rest are retailers and consumers. The commissions have a great deal of authority and can set quotas, minimum prices, surplus policy, subsidies and incentive bonuses, funds to encourage export and industrial usages; they even deal with packaging and categorization.

Voting patterns in 1996 (see table 10.1) reflect the weakened links between the political party and the organizational affiliation of both kibbutzim and moshavim. Kibbutz members supported Peres at a 90 percent rate, moshav members at a rate slightly below 50 percent. In the kibbutzim, the Likud won almost no support, while in the moshavim it received the votes of more than a quarter of the voters. Labor secured more than half of the kibbutz vote, but only a third of the vote in moshavim.

Members tended to vote for the party with which their kibbutz movement was affiliated. Voters of the United Kibbutz movement (Takam), affiliated with Labor, were very supportive of that party; members affiliated with the Kibbutz Haartzi, led by Mapam, voted for the Citizens Rights Movement, the list that included Mapam.

Members of moshavim founded after independence were largely Sephardim, and they have been less successful on the whole than the veteran moshavim. The farmers of the younger moshavim are the least loyal to Labor and have shifted to other parties, especially the Likud, just as their urban cousins have. Kibbutzim did not absorb many postindependence immigrants, and so they have been immune from this pattern, maintaining a record of support for their party. But that record is weaker than it was in the past. As recently as 1981, the kibbutz federations associated with the Labor-Mapam Alignment supported their party at rates above 90 percent regardless of when the kibbutz was established.

The NRP's kibbutz federation was loyal to its mother party in 1996. In one religious kibbutz, Kvutzat Yavne, Netanyahu received two-thirds of the vote, Peres only a third. But the NRP won 71.6 percent of the vote, compared to only 58.2 percent in 1992. In the past, some of the leadership of the religious kibbutz federation were active in the more conciliatory religious party, Meimad, which had competed with the NRP. Members of

TABLE 10.1

VOTING FOR PRIME MINISTER, 1996, AND SELECTED PARTIES, 1996 AND 1992, IN SELECTED SETTLEMENTS (IN PERCENTAGES)

	Netanyahu	Peres	Likud-Gesher-Tzomet		Labor		Meretz		NRP	
			1996	1992	1996	1992	1996	1992	1996	1992
National total	50.5	49.5	29.4	31.3[a]	26.6	34.6	7.3	9.3	7.8	5.0
Jewish settlements	55.5	44.4	27.4	33.0	27.7	36.3	7.0	9.2	8.6	5.0
Non-Jewish settlements	5.2	94.7	2.2	8.8	16.6	20.3	10.0	10.0	1.7	4.7
Jewish agricultural settlements	36.3	63.6	18.3	20.1	41.4	44.4	15.3	19.4	9.4	6.5
Kibbutzim	10.0	89.9	3.1	4.2	55.0	53.3	31.0	36.9	4.8	3.0
Moshavim	51.7	48.2	26.8	28.7	34.6	39.5	6.4	7.6	12.9	9.5
Jews beyond Green Line	83.7	16.2	32.2	37.6	10.1	14.7	2.5	3.5	27.0	18.1
Golan Heights	49.7	50.2	16.3	30.6	31.2	41.7	5.1	9.7	15.7	10.4
Bnei Brak	88.9	11.0	11.1	14.9	6.6	11.4	.9	1.6	11.5	9.3
Jerusalem	69.9	30.0	25.6	31.0	16.3	20.8	7.4	10.2	11.6	6.6
Tel Aviv	44.8	55.1	26.6	32.1	33.9	38.5	12.2	13.6	5.5	2.9

SOURCE: Official election results of the Central Elections Committee, as reported in *Hayom* supplement of *Ma'ariv*, 2 June 1996, 8–17.

a. In 1992, Gesher had not yet split, and Likud received 24.9 percent of the vote, Tzomet 6.4 percent.

Amana settlements, the movement affiliated with Gush Emunim, supported parties of the more militant right. In 1996, Meimad did not run, and the right was folded back into the Likud, making the NRP a more attractive alternative.

Religion

The clearest case of political parties reflecting and promoting a set of interests is that of the religious parties regarding the role of religion in the state. For the NRP, Shas, and Agudat Israel, the first a Zionist and the other two non-Zionist parties, the major plank of political ideology is to have the State of Israel organize its public life in accordance with Jewish religious law, halacha. This is the overriding concern of both parties; after that, issues of economic policy, the future of the territories, and all other matters with which a political party concerns itself are addressed. In these parties the religious lobby and the party are synonymous. They have been at least partially successful in creating in Israel a Jewish state that adheres to Orthodox rabbinical law. This has been achieved not through an articulate lobby impressing legislators with its vision but by succeeding in the games of electoral and coalition politics.

Religion is a central issue in Israeli political life. It is crucial because of the broad consensus within the Jewish population that Israel should be a Jewish state. The conflict is over the degree to which legislation and civil life in Israel should reflect the norms and decisions of established (Orthodox) religious authorities.[31] The Knesset has passed legislation regarding some of these matters. For example, (1) the 1950 Law of Return assuring the right of every Jew to immigrate to Israel; (2) the 1952 Law of Citizenship granting citizenship to every Jew, his or her spouse, children, and grandchildren; (3) the 1953 law establishing sole jurisdiction to the Orthodox rabbinical courts regarding marriage and divorce among Jews; (4) a 1951 law making the Jewish Sabbath an official rest day for Jews and requiring a permit to employ a Jew on the rest day; (5) the 1962 law prohibiting the raising of pigs in Israel except in areas in which there is a concentrated Christian population; (6) the 1986 law prohibiting Jews from displaying leavened food for sale during the days of Passover; and (7) the 1990 law allowing local authorities to regulate whether enterprises involved in entertainment (movies and theaters) will be allowed to operate on the Sabbath and holy days.

The issue is made more complex because of the various meanings of Jewishness. Judaism may be thought of as a religion, a nationality, a culture, or all of these, and more. For Orthodox Jews, religion and nationality are one and the same. Religious observance and belief, while desirable, are not essential criteria for membership in the community.[32]

Israelis are split over these matters, as is demonstrated in figure 10.1. It is fascinating to note the different patterns over time in the distribution of answers to questions regarding personal religious behavior on the one hand and the role of religion in public life on the other. Despite enormous change along most dimensions of Israel's existence, the rate of those responding that they observe "all" or "most" of Jewish religious law is amazingly stable at 25 to 30 percent; the other responses provided were "some" and "none." These numbers are consistent with the estimate that about a quarter of Israeli Jews are observant in an Orthodox sense or even beyond that, including 6 to 10 percent haredi, or ultra-Orthodox; that about 40 percent are determinedly secular; and that the rest are somewhere between those poles.

Regarding desired public behavior, the responses vary widely from one period to another. About half of them agree to having public life con-

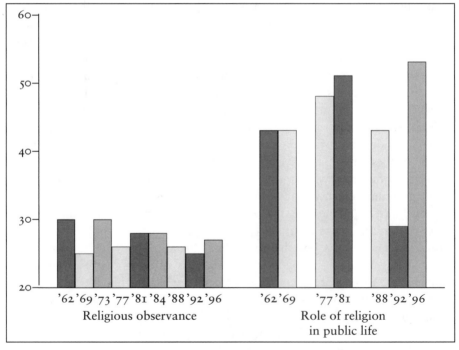

FIGURE 10.1

RELIGIOUS OBSERVANCE AND THE ROLE OF RELIGION
IN PUBLIC LIFE, 1962–96

NOTE: No data for the role of religion in public life for 1973 or 1984.

ducted in accordance with tradition; about half disagree. The question seems to act as a barometer for government policy. When religious parties are in the coalition and the pendulum seems to have gone in their direction, as in the 1960s and 1980s, less than half the respondents answer that they want public life to be conducted according to halacha. The 1992 response seems to indicate a sense that the power of the religious has increased too much and should be curtailed. The 1996 rate indicates that the majority now feels that the secular point has become too dominant in public policy.[33]

The cause of Jewish religious law in public life is promoted by all the religious parties; most other parties are secular or noncommittal, but an antireligious party has yet to emerge. The issue of promoting religion is legitimate in the Israeli polity in a way that promoting antireligion is not. Many would support a pluralistic approach that would allow both freedom of religion and freedom from religion. The problems begin when one group perceives that the behavior of the other is impinging on its rights. The norm of the Israeli political system has been to legitimize both the role of religion and the ethic of a single Jewish people; these are important political issues because it is so difficult to achieve these goals.

The call for the separation of religion and the state has never had wide appeal for at least four reasons. First is the political reason. Religious parties have been active in the ruling Zionist and Israeli coalitions since the 1930s. This cooperation gave rise to the concept of the status quo when the state was founded; this meant that arrangements in effect during the prestate period regarding religion and religious practice would be extended into the state period. And so it has been.

Second is a symbolic-ideological reason. With the exception of a few groups, most Israelis support the notion of Israel as a Jewish state and while there are furious debates about what this could possibly mean in an age of liberal democracy, most identify with this value (see chapter 12). To be sure, there are other than religious options open to the question of how to express the Jewishness of Israel, but once the premise is accepted, the status quo version becomes at least appropriate, if not exciting. Even when the socialists ruled and preferred a different form of expression of the Jewishness of Israel, their coalition calculations and obligations led them to accept the status quo arrangements.

The third reason is simply habit. For many Israelis, the arrangements in effect appear natural because they are the only ones they have known. Besides, for most people in Israel, the arrangements present no serious burden or inconvenience. Most marriages pose no problem, most children born are legitimate, most people do not drive on the Sabbath in areas that the ultra-Orthodox want blocked from traffic, and most rituals can be ignored if one so chooses. Only a small minority is affected negatively by rabbinical rulings, and its anguish has never catalyzed a mass movement for alleviating the situation.

Fourth, the call for the separation of religion and the state is foreign to much of the experience of Jewish history and the people of the Middle East. The focus of religion on the individual is a modern, Western notion, especially evident in Christian contexts. Religion in the traditional sense was a community undertaking, and the individual was identified by his membership in the community. The Yom Kippur service recites that "we have sinned" not that "I have sinned." Jews were dealt with as members of a community throughout their history of dispersion, sometimes achieving large measures of communal autonomy. The Ottoman Empire recognized communities, and this millet system became the basis of practice during the British Mandate and ultimately within the State of Israel.

From this heritage it is a natural development to have marriage and divorce and other matters of personal law regulated by the religious community to which one belongs. Religion, then, connotes social belonging and jurisdiction, not only theological belief. Accordingly, notions of individual choice have never taken hold in Israel. While one might not believe in God, one's personal status would still have to be settled by the religious court. Political authorities and religious authorities have worked hand in hand to strengthen the power of each other. Rules of inclusion and exclusion in the community—that is, Who is a Jew?—became questions given religious answers with the authoritative backing of the secular state.

Israel is not a theocracy; it is a modern parliamentary regime that has opted to allocate decisions on certain aspects of public and private life to religious authorities. For the Jewish population it is the Orthodox rabbinate whose interpretations are binding; for members of other religions, it is the recognized religious authority of the other recognized communities whose rules are binding: Muslim, Druze, and almost a dozen Christian sects.

In regulating religious affairs in Israel the Knesset did not give the Jewish religious courts superior status to the courts of other religions, but it did give the Orthodox religious courts a monopoly within the Jewish community regarding marriage and divorce.[34] The 1953 law gives the rabbinical courts complete jurisdiction over marriage and divorce of the Jews in the country, whether citizens of Israel or not. Up until then, membership in Knesset Israel was voluntary, but from that point on, jurisdiction over all Jews was in the hands of the rabbinical courts. The various solutions to which Jews denied the right to marriage by the religious courts have turned—marrying in Cyprus or marrying through the mail to Mexico or other places—are permitted not by halacha but by the secular state and its rules of registering the marriage of citizens.

The registration of one's personal status is in the hands of the Ministry of the Interior. Control over this ministry has become extremely important for religious circles, and indeed two NRP leaders, Chaim Moshe Shapira and Yosef Burg, held the post for most of the governments and most of the years of the country's existence. The ministry registers both "religion" and "nationality." According to halacha, the two categories are interchangeable, "Jew" being a connotation of both religion and nationality. This interpretation is not the only one possible with, for example, atheists claiming that they are Israeli nationals with no religion, or extreme antinationalists claiming that they are Jews with no special connection to the secular State of Israel. The result has been a standoff with an inclination to little or no modification of past practice. It is only when hard cases are introduced that the authorities must grapple again with these difficult questions.

Such a case was that of Brother Daniel. Brother Daniel was born, reared, and educated as a Jew in pre–World War II Poland. He even spent a number of years in training to immigrate to Eretz Israel. He converted and became a Catholic Carmelite monk, but claimed the right under the Law of Return to come to Israel. The Law of Return, passed in 1950, grants Israeli citizenship to any Jew coming to Israel. Rufheisen, Brother Daniel's name before conversion, claimed that he was a Jew who had converted to Catholicism and was entitled to the same status and privileges granted other Jewish immigrants. In 1962 the Supreme Court ultimately backed the position of the religious parties, namely, that Brother Daniel was no longer a Jew because he had converted.[35] But the Court distinguished between halacha, which regards him still as a Jew by virtue of the fact that he was born of a Jewish mother, and the secular usage, which recognized a convert to another religion as no longer a Jew. The Court's support of the religious position denying Brother Daniel's request was based on secular grounds.

Another hard decision was made in the two cases brought by Binyamin Shalit in 1968 and 1972.[36] Shalit, an Israeli-born Jew and naval officer, married a non-Jewish woman abroad. When they tried to register their two children as Jews under the nationality category, the request was denied. The NRP-run Interior Ministry wanted to leave both the religion and nationality category blank; Shalit, an atheist, was willing to leave the religion category blank but wanted his children registered as being of the Jewish nation. The Supreme Court, by a 5–4 majority, agreed to his request. This was an important decision and different from the Brother Daniel case. In the Daniel case the status of the plaintiff was cloudy, according to halacha; in the Shalit case the children were not Jews according to halacha, but the Court ruled that they must be registered as of Jewish nationality. The Knesset, under NRP pressure, amended the law to read that a Jew is one born of a Jewish mother or converted. When the second Shalit case arose regarding the couple's third child, the Court denied the request, and the child was not registered as a Jew.

The "Who is a Jew?" issue continues to plague Israeli politics. In 1983, for example, the High Court of Justice instructed the Interior Ministry to register as a Jew a woman named Suzie Miller. She was an American immigrant to Israel whose conversion in the United States by a Reform rabbi had been declared "suspicious" by the Orthodox rabbinical authorities in Israel. The Shas party minister of the interior, Yitzhak Peretz, resigned from the cabinet over this decision. Peretz resisted attempts to return him to the government unless the law was changed. It was impossible to placate him, and he remained outside the government until after the 1988 elections. The Miller decision, and others related to the legal status of individuals converted in other places and with varying observance of halacha, led to the firm demand of the religious parties to change the law. Because of the fact that many conversions to Judaism (especially in the United States) are performed by Conservative or Reform rabbis, the religious parties have labored to have the law changed again, recognizing only conversion according to halacha. This would mean limiting legal conversion to Orthodox rabbis. Although most secular politicians oppose these changes, whether they will be accepted depends on coalition calculations and not on philosophical or theological considerations. After the 1988 elections, with the religious parties in a strong bargaining position regarding the future coalition, both Likud and Labor toyed with the idea of agreeing to amend the "Who is a Jew?" definition of the Law of Return so that only conversion according to halacha would be acceptable. Vociferous appeals by Jewish communities abroad, demonstrations within Israel, and intercession by the president of the country finally led to a National Unity Government, obviating the need to agree to this demand by the religious parties.

Had the law been amended at that time, it would have pertained to only a handful of individuals each year. But the symbolic importance of the amendment was enormous. Many Jews abroad have family members who are not Jews according to halacha—either through intermarriage or after conversion by non-Orthodox rabbis. To have their children (or grandchildren) labeled as anything but Jewish was considered an affront by many of these Jews. Besides, the argument went, why should this theological issue be decided by the Knesset, a political body whose members include non-Jews? The 1988 skirmish ended without changing the amendment, but it was clear that the war was not over. It will be fought another day because it is important to both sides.

The 1988 fight over amending the definition of conversion led many to the conclusion that religious parties had power disproportionate to their electoral strength. Many were convinced that changing the electoral system to the direct election of the prime minister, thus insulating him from coalition pressures, would solve the problem. The reason used to raise money from Reform and Conservative Jews abroad by those promoting the direct election of the prime minister was that it would lessen the hold of Orthodoxy. How ironic that in the first election held using the new system, the Orthodox religious parties were strengthened more than ever in the past. The guidelines agreed by the parties that set up the Netanyahu government called for legislation recognizing only conversions approved by the Israeli Chief Rabbinate.

For the Orthodox parties, the Reform and Conservative movements of Judaism are much more threatening than is secularism, or even atheism. The more liberal movements are seen as usurpers, perverting the titles, prayers, and ceremonies of the religion. The common roots are not overlooked; the Orthodox see the other groups as manipulating holy symbols in a subversive manner. As the role of Orthodoxy in Israel grows, and the portion of Diaspora Jews who are not Orthodox expands, nothing less than the unity of the Jewish people may be called into question in the future.

A different but related problem stems from the mass immigration from the former Soviet Union; it has introduced hundreds of thousands of people who are directly affected by the "Who is a Jew?" issue. Under halacha, Jews are either children of a Jewish mother or converts, but under the Law of Return that regulates immigration, one Jewish grandparent is deemed sufficient. Estimates are that almost a third of the immigrants who have come to Israel from the former Soviet Union since 1989 would not be considered Jewish under halacha.

Most of these people are not Jews because their mothers were not Jews, and because they have not undergone the lengthy conversion process. About 10,000 of these immigrants insist their mothers were Jewish, but have been unable to prove it to the satisfaction of the Orthodox state rabbinate. These people, full Israeli citizens under the Law of Return, are sometimes the subject of heart-breaking circumstances, as in the cases of a soldier killed in action or a two-year-old killed in a traffic accident, both denied burial rights in the local cemetery because their mothers were not Jewish. In addition, the number of cases is growing of individuals whose social existence is rooted in the Jewish community of Israel, yet they are not allowed to marry the partner of choice because one of them is not Jewish according to halacha. Or in death, they may not be buried in cemeteries near their Jewish loved ones.

The high cost of conversion hinders many of the non-Jewish new immigrants. The Ministry of Religious Affairs has refused to cover the $1,000 needed to finance circumcision, as it does for uncircumcised immigrant males who have been able to prove their Jewishness to the rabbis' satisfaction. In 1992, only 740 conversions were performed, and in 1993 the number dropped to 600, despite a sharp increase in applications. Sephardi Chief Rabbi Eliyahu Bakshi-Doron, elected in 1993, ordered a limit on the number of converts, reflecting the ultra-Orthodox view that only those committed to living a fully Orthodox life should be converted, a lifestyle very few immigrants from the former Soviet Union would commit themselves to. One who comes to Israel married to a Jew finds it difficult to divorce that spouse in Israel or to adopt a child in Israel. All these matters of personal status, under Israel law, are the province of the religious authorities. Whether or not these difficulties lead to renewed calls for the separation of state and synagogue, the rules in place have led to the emergence of a permanent underclass of people who cannot get married in the generally accepted manner and who are isolated from the mainstream in other matters of lifestyle and personal status.

The actors who determine developments in this issue area are the religious political parties, the factions within them, and the rabbis affiliated with them. These groups compete with one another, often attempting to win public support (within the religious community) by being more exacting in their interpretations of current events in terms of the halacha. This is especially convenient for the more dogmatic, who find themselves in the desirable position of calling into question groups that are more lenient, and this is exactly the tactic used by the opposition factions within each party, by the more ultra-Orthodox parties against the Orthodox (usually the Aguda and Shas against the NRP), and by rabbis affiliated with one party against rabbis of another. The other political parties are absorbed in these dilemmas because of their desire to have the coalition support of the religious parties or to prevent religious parties from supporting the rival secular political party. Thus the government budget becomes a political football, with religious parties pressing for added funds for their pet projects.

When the election of the president of Israel can be determined by religious party votes in the Knesset, political deals are rumored. Or when religious legislation might be defeated because antireligious members of the coalition threaten to vote against the bill or abstain, the leaders of the secular party heading the coalition have been known to put tremendous pressure on the upstarts, including threatening the downfall of the government if the bill fails. The point is that much of the activity in this issue area is motivated by purely political considerations. Israel is divided on the religious issue, but it would be inappropriate to measure that division by the legislation passed on the subject.

The clear political success that the religious parties have had rests on their pivotal role in coalition formation. The results of this success are obvious in law: a series of laws and administrative rulings that have, on the whole, gone in the direction desired by the religious parties on questions relating to such issues as abortion, marriage and divorce, public transportation on Sabbath and holy days, enforcement of the Jewish dietary laws, and the definition of who is a Jew. From the point of view of the religious parties, there are many matters yet to be settled as they would wish, but no one can deny the achievements they have made.

The background to their success is cultural and has to do with the symbol system and the basic premises on which the society rests. But would things change drastically if the religious parties were no longer needed in the government coalition? To what extent is the Jewish character of Israel one of political expediency and to what extent is it part of the civic culture? There is no certain answer to this hypothetical question, but my own guess is that the forms regarding religion and religious usage that have evolved in Israel are more permanent than many secularists would like to think.

The arrangements perpetuated as a result of the status quo are more flexible than is commonly thought. Local authorities have leeway in how strenuously they apply laws concerning commerce or entertainment on the Sabbath and holy days. The local strength of the religious parties plays an important role in the matter. On national issues, a great deal more visibility and uniformity are maintained. All institutions that receive moneys from the government must observe Jewish dietary laws. This includes the army, schools, hospitals, and government missions abroad. The issue whether El Al, the national airline, would operate on the Sabbath and holy days occupied the country's attention in 1982 until the government decided, in accordance with the demands of the religious parties, to stop these operations. The list is a long one, not long enough for some, too long for others, and always changing.

One fascinating dilemma concerned television on the Sabbath. The secularists saw television as an extension of radio, which existed before the establishment of the state and hence was continued into the state period as part of the status quo. (Indeed, early Israeli television was not much more than radio with pictures.) The religionists saw television as especially insidious on the Sabbath and interfering with family solidarity, to say nothing of enticing weaker souls from endeavors of prayer and study. In 1969, the Broadcast Authority Executive Committee approved television broadcasting seven days a week (except on Yom Kippur). The minority appealed the decision to the prime minister, who decided to bring it before the government. In the meantime, the Supreme Court ruled that there was no reason to suspend the decision until the government met, and Sabbath television began on 7 November. Other legal arguments regarding the legality of work permits issued to those who were to transmit the broadcast also failed in Court. In this case the Court spared the politicians from facing the decision of how to interpret the status quo.

The religious parties, especially the NRP, have been constant partners in the ongoing story of Israeli politics. While the parties straddle the fence that divides principle from pragmatism, depending on whether they are in the government coalition or not, the NRP in particular has had to guard its flank from the political sniping of the Agudat Israel and Shas; the NRP is a firmly Zionist party, the Aguda and Shas are non-Zionist. For both ideological and practical reasons, the NRP became the champion of the movement that summarizes developments since the founding of the state—the nationalization of religion.[37] The goal of the NRP is to have religious institutions that might have been temporary or voluntary in the past become permanent fixtures of the religious community by having them established, and funded, by law. The NRP has invested great efforts to influence this legislation and to dominate these institutions, which include the Ministry of Religious Affairs, the Chief Rabbinate, the rabbinical courts, and the religious councils. Through these efforts, the NRP has hoped to establish itself as the major representative of the Jewish religious community.

The institutional instincts of the NRP have been excellent. The web of relations between the party and these religious institutions has provided budget and patronage for the party's leaders. But when its electoral fortunes came on hard times, going from twelve to four seats between 1977 and 1984, the party had a hard time retaining control of these institutions. The haredi parties, and especially Shas, penetrated the systems that the NRP had built, and transformed them in the process. One of the most spirited fights regarding the 1996 coalition was over the Ministry of Religious Affairs. Both Shas and the NRP wanted it, but after they agreed on rotating the minister's position, they found it impossible to agree on who would begin the rotation. As that fight was going on, the Aguda demanded its share of the Ministry of Religious Affairs as well.

The Ministry of Religious Affairs has important administrative, legal, and political functions. It supervises and provides technical services for all the various religious sects in Israel. The ministry, along with the Chief Rabbinate, is very active in the Jewish community. It supervises Jewish dietary laws for public institutions not under the supervision of a local rabbinate and oversees the ritual purity of imported food, especially meat. It provides grants for the building of synagogues and ritual baths, supervises the activities of burial societies, administers holy sites such as the Western Wall, and encourages the development of yeshivas. On the legal level, the ministry initiates legislation on religious affairs and implements legislation after it is passed. In 1994, when Shas left the Rabin government, the ministry was given to Shimon Shitrit of Labor. His activities regarding matters such as burial rights and lists of those ineligible for marriage heartened many secularists and infuriated many of the Orthodox leaders. Being out of power was so upsetting to them, both in terms of office and of policy, that the leaders of the religious parties all but declared that they would participate in the coalition after the 1996 elections no matter who headed it.

The Ministry of Religious Affairs is also important because of the patronage it controls. The selection of personnel of almost every religious institution in the state, Jewish and non-Jewish, involves the ministry. This includes the Chief Rabbinate and the local rabbinates, the rabbinical courts and the religious councils, as well as the state religious school system.

There are two chief rabbis in Israel, an Ashkenazi and a Sephardi. Both of these developments—the fact that there is a Chief Rabbinate at all and the fact that there are two of them—stem from historical considerations; neither is mandated by Jewish tradition. Judaism does not require a rabbinical hierarchy; the Chief Rabbinate emerged more for purposes of managing contacts with the authorities outside the Jewish community. Because of the separation clause in the U.S. Constitution, no chief rabbi was needed in the United States, and none emerged. But in 1921, under the British Mandate and following the practices of the Ottoman Empire's millet system, a rabbinical council was convened in 1921 to manage the affairs of the Jews in Palestine. This council was ultimately recognized by the mandatory power, and the Chief Rabbinate was institutionalized. Only in 1972, however, were its existence and the rules for its election mandated in law by the Knesset. The Chief Rabbinate was recognized as the supreme authority regarding halacha, although with the establishment of a hierarchy of religious courts it ceased to double as the Supreme Rabbinical Court of Appeals. The electoral college to select the chief rabbis was to be composed of eighty rabbis and seventy laymen, equally divided between Ashkenazim and Sephardim, with the mayors of the country and the heads of local religious councils playing a role in the election. There have been appeals to abandon the practice of having chief rabbis, but the practice persists, more for political and personal reasons than for philosophical or theological ones.

The manner in which the electoral college is constructed was meant to ensure the joint influence of the NRP (through the rabbis appointed) and Labor by virtue of their influence in local government when the law was passed. This joint influence has persisted despite the emergence of Shas as a major religious party and the Likud as a major political force at both the national and local levels. The election of the chief rabbis is always accompanied by intense bargaining among political parties; although the ballot was secret, the results showed that the parties had high levels of influence on the rabbis. The Aguda, which rejects the religious authority of the chief rabbis, occasionally calls for the abandonment of the institution and at other times backs candidates of its own.

The local religious councils were established to provide services funded by the public treasury. After much party bickering, a Religious Council Law was passed in 1967 and calls for the religious councils to be recomposed every four years. The law provides that 45 percent of the members be appointed by the minister of religious affairs, another 45 percent by the local authority, and 10 percent by the local rabbi. The members are to be personally religious, but the appointment system was meant to reflect the ethnic and political composition of the community. When the political fortunes of the Likud, Shas, and Aguda improve, they naturally strive to reap for themselves the benefits that flow from the arrangements instituted under Labor and the NRP.

In 1987, a new type of crisis emerged in the ever-engaging sphere of religion and the state. A woman, Lea Shakdiel, an observant Jew and a member of the town council of Yeruham, was selected as a member of the town's religious council. The minister of religious affairs, Zevulun Hammer of the NRP, refused to confirm the election of Shakdiel because she was a woman. In 1988, the High Court of Justice decided, in a decision written by a justice who himself was an observant Jew, that the selection of Shakdiel was perfectly legal and binding, and that denying her this position violated the requirement of equality of the sexes as required by law. Moreover, he argued, halacha did not deny women the possibility of having a role in the selection of public officeholders. Needless to say, the furor was intense. Three years passed before she was seated.

In other cases in Tel Aviv, Haifa, and Netanya, the municipal councils also appointed unacceptable persons either to the electoral college for the religious councils, or to the religious councils, and again passions soared. In some of the cases women had been appointed; in others, observant men but observing according to Conservative or Reform ritual. The Orthodox would have none of it. The inauguration of the Ashkenazi chief rabbi for Tel Aviv was postponed for a year and a half until the legal and political battles subsided. The battles do not end, but there is delay, failure to convene relevant committees, or sometimes the withdrawal of the offending nomination.

The rabbinical court is another institution that the NRP has successfully brought under the jurisdiction of the law of the state, thus perpetuating it. In principle, the rabbinical courts have exclusive jurisdiction over all Jewish citizens in the area of personal-status law. While formally separate from the Chief Rabbinate, the chief rabbis serve as presidents of the Supreme Rabbinical Court of Appeals. The chief rabbis must approve all religious judges before their appointment. The Religious Judges Law of 1955 is similar to the Judges Law of 1953 with the exception that the latter sets out the qualifications for judges; qualifications for religious judges are set by the Chief Rabbinate. A further difference is that judges swear allegiance to the state and its laws, whereas religious judges must swear allegiance to the state only. There are twenty district courts and the Supreme Rabbinical Court of Appeals in Jerusalem. The Israeli Supreme Court, in its capacity as the High Court of Justice, retains the right to determine whether the religious courts have jurisdiction in a given matter, and by precedent it has also intervened when it finds that principles of "natural law" have been violated by the rabbinical courts. For example, the court held in a 1994 case that in divorce, religious court rulings had to be based on the principle of equal rights to joint property requiring them to follow civil law rather than religious law on this matter.

Religion is a potent issue area in Israeli politics. Nevertheless, the density of action within the area makes it unlikely that groups from outside will successfully penetrate and win influence within it. The political parties have large stakes invested and are committed to compromises developed over the years. Many of these compromises have been enacted in law by the Knesset, a fact that makes it even more difficult to alter past practice. The NRP has had to pay a political price for the nationalizing legislation by sharing power with other religious parties and with secular parties. But this "price" has worked both ways: the secular parties also committed themselves to structures that enhanced the worldview of the religious groups, not to mention their political power and patronage.

11. Public Administration and Local Government

In a highly centralized state, issues of public policy and administration are closely entwined. Both are seen as political resources as well as political opportunity. The balance between group and personal benefit, on the one hand, and the public good, on the other, is never firmly settled. The gradual but steady transfer of the delivery of social services from political parties with their particularistic approach to the universal criteria of a national service conflicted with the desire by some of the parties to enlarge their budgets by adding more members. The civil service was also embroiled in tensions between principles of good government and the tendency by many politicians to see the bureaucracy as an extension of their own political will. The roles of the State Controller and national commissions of inquiry have improved the image of impartiality of some state authorities since the mid-1980s. Local government is the public body most closely in touch with citizens and provides many services to them.

Statism

Many of the services in the prestate era were provided by voluntary organizations; the largest and most resourceful of these groups was the Histadrut. The services proved important in establishing the Histadrut and its ruling party in a dominant position throughout the prestate period and the first generation of the independent state. With independence came a wave of nationalization of these services. The ideology was called *statism* and Ben-Gurion was its major champion. The call was taken up by sections of his Mapai Party before he left it in 1965, and it was a major plank in the Rafi platform, the party he founded after leaving Mapai.

After most of the members of that party returned to the Labor fold in 1968, Ben-Gurion persisted in rejecting the Labor Party and in maintaining his call for statism. His State List of 1969 even included the idea in its name, and when that party became part of the Likud, it brought Ben-Gurion's call more forcefully to that part of the political spectrum. There were two elements to the idea: that "services required by all citizens must be provided by the state"[1] and that the Labor Party was unable to separate party interests from national interests and that the latter must prevail.

The process of nationalization of services in Israel is a long and involved story. Since the transfer has been in stages and is still incomplete, the administration of public services has had to face unique challenges. But as the transfer includes more areas, as when health services or pensions are nationalized, the power of the government center increases. Power is transferred from the service providers controlled in the past by the political parties to the civil servants who run the ministries, and to the ministers who head them.

The partial transfer was the product of a political system characterized by coalition politics and was not hurried by those whose political power was increased because they knew how to manipulate the structural complexities that characterized the system. This closed circle was not easily penetrated; interests, symbols, and careers were all involved. The tension between those who attempted to achieve a more complete transfer and those who supported a partial transfer (or no transfer at all) was a major theme in the country's story. Four areas indicate the complexities: defense, education, employment, and health services.

DEFENSE

After independence in 1948, there was no question about Israel's need for a single national defense force. Immediately after the state was established, the Haganah (the largest military organization in the Yishuv, controlled by Mapai) became Israel's army; the future of the other military organizations—Irgun, Lehi, and the Palmach—was in doubt.

The Irgun (also known as Etzel) and Lehi were underground organizations that sprang from the Revisionist movement. The Irgun, headed by Menachem Begin, was the larger and had the support of most Revisionists. When the state was established, the Irgun was dominated by the Herut movement. Lehi was smaller but more extremist in its methods of activity against the British; Yitzhak Shamir was active in its ranks. It had split off from the Irgun in 1940 and was less strongly identified with the Revisionists. The Palmach was identified with the Kibbutz Hameuhad (the kibbutz branch of Ahdut Haavoda) and, to a lesser extent, with Hashomer Hatzair.

Disbanding the Irgun and Lehi can be seen as part of the struggle to ensure the legitimacy of the regime. Neither organization was represented in the provisional government, and thus Mapai had no need to compromise with them. Disbanding the Palmach was more problematic because Mapam, to which the Palmach owed its allegiance, was an integral part of the labor movement and was Mapai's partner in the government when the Palmach command was disbanded. At that time, however, the composition of the coalition was such that Mapam did not have the power of veto because it could not leave the government and abandon Mapai in a minority position. Nevertheless, disbanding the Palmach formations was postponed until Mapam was in opposition. Disbanding the Palmach did not threaten the organizational infrastructure of either the labor movement or the Histadrut. Mapai thus had the support of the party machinery on this issue. The Histadrut, firmly in Mapai's control, also supported its dissolution. The dissolution of the Palmach also had economic benefits for the Histadrut, which had funded it, as moneys were released for other activities. Disbanding the Palmach is best considered as the means by which the dominant party prevented other political bodies from retaining their own militias within the newly formed sovereign state.

EDUCATION

The nationalization of the education system in 1953 did not create a unified school network. The state system was broken down into a general and a religious (Jewish Orthodox) subsystem. Today most Jewish children in Israel attend government schools; however, exceptions are permitted. The kibbutz movements each retained autonomy over the educational systems of their members' children, but as the pressure grew to prepare students for universities, they tended to accept standards used in the general educational system. The "independent" religious track was established for haredi students. These are connected with Agudat Israel, Degel Hatorah, or Shas.

Religious education, sponsored by either the state-religious track, or one of the haredi tracks, envelopes more than a third of the students in the country and more than a third of the teachers in training colleges.[2] Both receive funds from the state; the former is also under state supervision, while the latter are truly independent, enjoying both state money and freedom from supervision. When Labor controlled the Ministry of Education from 1948 to 1977, it generally had an NRP deputy minister to deal with matters of religious education. In 1977 the National Religious Party won control of the Education Ministry, and the institutions of religious education received a serious boost. During the 1992–96 government, Shulamit Aloni and Amnon Rubenstein of Meretz served as education minister, and obviously the focus shifted. After the 1996 elections, the NRP's Zevulun Hammer returned to the ministry he had headed in the past.

The labor movement entered the field of education at a relatively late stage in the development of the educational system of the prestate period. It developed a socialist track that existed in competition with the "general" track (identified with the General Zionists) and the religious track. After the establishment of the state and with the advent of massive waves of immigrants from Europe, Asia, and Africa, education became a prime political issue. The socialist track experienced pronounced growth compared with the general track. In 1948–49 only 29.3 percent of pupils were registered in socialist schools; 43.8 percent were enrolled in general schools. Three years later, the general schools accounted for only 27.4 percent of all pupils, while the share of the socialist schools had increased to 42.6 percent.[3] The labor schools movement achieved outstanding success in the settlements of the new immigrants, but this was the cause of a bitter struggle with the religious parties, which at one stage even boycotted government meetings because of the dispute.

The transfer of the education system to the hands of the government in 1953 did not generate a coalition crisis because Mapam was then in the opposition and was thus effectively isolated and prevented from allying with possible sympathizers in Mapai. The leaders of Mapai knew that Mapam would be satisfied with a guarantee of educational autonomy for its kibbutzim, and when the support of the religious factions was obtained in return for strengthening the influence of the religious faction (Hapoel Hamizrachi) in the religious state schools, no real opposition remained. Thus, in 1953 the particularist school movements were abolished. The socialist and general tracks were, in effect, merged into the national secular subsystem controlled by the Ministry of Education, which in turn was controlled by the labor movement. The NRP retained effective control over the national religious subsystem and after 1977 often controlled the Ministry of Education. Of the parties that had been active in education during the prestate period, only the General Zionists did poorly. This is especially ironic since they had strongly supported the idea of statism and the State Education Law.

Remaining outside the national school system are the autonomous schools in some kibbutzim and those of the "independent" haredi track. The former, which are decreasing in size, choose to meet the standards set by the country's universities, as kibbutzim seek to train a labor force to deal with modern technological advances. The latter are very strong and growing, creating an ever more insular community (and voting group). The "independent" haredi track grew from 5.7 percent of the Jewish students in 1979 to 10.2 in 1995. In the same period the public schools share fell from 74.7 to 68.4 percent, and the share of the public religious track grew from 20.1 to 21.4 percent.[4]

EMPLOYMENT

Labor exchanges run by the Labor Ministry were set up by law in 1959 after a long history of party competition over the provision of employment.[5] Labor exchanges were politically important in the prestate period and the first years of nationhood, during which unemployment was widespread; their importance decreased once the service ceased to be required by the majority of the population. In the poststate era, the Labor Exchange Centers are more important in times of mass immigration and economic slow-down.[6]

Cooperation of sorts developed among the parties in the prestate era. Ben-Gurion reached an agreement with Jabotinsky and the Revisionists with regard to job allocations in 1935 (due to the scarcity of jobs at this time), but Ben-Gurion's premature statism was defeated in a referendum of Histadrut members. Still, other joint ventures were pursued in the labor field, and by statehood cooperation was widespread. A Labor Exchange Center was established and gradually concentrated on employment, despite frequent squabbling among the groups involved. Mapai gave silent consent to the nationalization of the employment service because it was already dominant in the Labor Exchange Center and felt that other parties had achieved overrepresentation there.

HEALTH SERVICES

The total expenditure on health in Israel is large and growing; in 1993 it accounted for 8.2 percent of the GNP, compared with 6.1 percent in 1975.[7] (The parallel U.S. figure in 1993 was 14 percent). Life expectancy is among the highest in the world, while infant mortality is among the lowest. The ratio of physicians to population, the number of specialists, and the level and quality of resources invested in health services compare favorably with those prevalent in the Western world.

The National Health Insurance Law, in effect since 1995, sets forth the state's responsibility to provide health services for all residents of the country.[8] The law stipulates that a standardized basket of medical services (including hospitalization) be supplied by one of the four comprehensive health care organizations that insured most of the population before nationalization. Every resident registers as a member with one of the organizations, each having equal status. The sick fund may not bar applicants on any ground, including age or state of health, and after a year, a person can transfer to a different sick fund. The sick funds are required to supply the services enumerated in the standardized basket, within reasonable time and distance from the insured person's home.

The sources for funding include health insurance premiums paid by each resident, parallel-tax payments by employers and self-employed persons, National Insurance Institute funds, funds from the Ministry of Health budget, and consumer participation payments. Payment of health insurance premiums is compulsory. The National Insurance Institute collects health insurance premiums in the same way it collects national insurance premiums: employees have the premium deducted by their employer; self-employed persons remit them directly to the institute.

The collection of health insurance premiums is progressive; low-income earners pay less and high-income earners pay more. When both spouses are employed, they pay separate insurance premiums: employers and self-employed persons pay 3.1 percent of the portion of the salary that is equal to half of the average wage, and 4.8 percent of the rest of the salary, up to a maximum of four times the average wage. Workers who receive retirement pensions or benefits from the National Insurance Institute, or from the ministries of defense or finance, pay health insurance premiums only on their income from work; pensions and benefits are exempt from payment. Persons receiving old-age pensions pay a premium of 2 percent of the average wage.

The Histadrut's Kupat Holim sick fund (there are three other sick funds in the country) in 1996 provided services for 63 percent of the citizenry, the Maccabi fund for 19 percent. Before the new law took force, the Histadrut's fund had about 75 percent of the insured. Some 16 percent of the country's hospital beds were in Histadrut hospitals.[9]

The National Health Insurance Law was promoted by Chaim Ramon as minister of health, based on the recommendations of public commissions and previous health ministers. The draft law sponsored by Ramon was approved by the Rabin government in March 1993 and passed its first reading in the Knesset in July of that year. But Rabin backed down later under pressure from a handful of Histadrut activists who controlled half the delegates to the Labor Party's convention.

A motion put forth by Chaim Haberfeld, head of the Histadrut, and Nissim Zvili, secretary-general of Labor, and adopted by the Labor Party convention in January 1994, would have changed the basic features of the proposal sponsored by Ramon and under consideration by the Knesset. According to the motion, the draft law would be changed so that Kupat Holim membership would remain conditional on union membership, and the Histadrut would continue to collect the dues and would turn part of them over to the National Insurance Institute to fund health insurance, and keep .8 percent of members' salaries for Histadrut activities.[10]

After losing this vote in the convention, Ramon announced that he would run in the Histadrut elections on a separate list. Ramon's Ram list resoundingly defeated Haberfeld's Labor list 46 percent to 32 percent in the elections held in May 1994. In June 1994 the Knesset passed the National Health Insurance Law (the version supported by Ramon and opposed by the Histadrut) by a vote of 68–0. The Labor Party supported the bill in the Knesset vote; when it lost the control of the Histadrut, it lost its reason to oppose the law. For Ramon it turned out to be a brilliant gamble; he got the law he wanted and positioned himself for a future run for leader of Labor.

Before the law was passed, the Histadrut's Kupat Holim played a primary role in the delivery of services, but increasingly it had to rely on state funds to meet its deficits.[11] Half of the Ministry of Health budget in the past was earmarked for transfer to the sick funds, and other moneys were added indirectly. During Labor governments, ministers of finance were known to provide direct support to the Histadrut's sick fund above the 10 percent of budget received from the Ministry of Health. The Health Ministry opposed these added funds because it wished to maintain control over the health field, even though it had a small budget. In the 1983 and 1987 doctors' strikes similar interdepartmental tensions were evident.[12]

Kupat Holim also competed with other Histadrut functions for budget. By the late 1960s the proportion of Histadrut dues allocated to the sick fund increased to almost 60 percent. Another source of income was an employers' contribution to the sick fund for their workers. Since 1973, this contribution was paid to the National Insurance Institute, which apportioned it among the different sick funds. Because the payment to the Histadrut fund incorporated a contribution to the Histadrut, this arrangement in effect obliged employers to contribute to a trade union.

In the mid-1980s, support from the government treasury to Kupat Holim decreased substantially. Commissions, committees, and experts made suggestions intended to make more rational a system that had an important social mission and a very heavy political and bureaucratic overlay. The non-Histadrut planners, including experts from the Finance Ministry, attempted to reduce the subsidy by having the Histadrut and its members pay more nearly the real cost of medical care; the politicians and the bureaucrats tried to avoid that. The public was not anxious to pay more, but it was also restive about the delivery of health care.

Before the National Health Insurance Law of 1994, Kupat Holim insured 75 percent of the population and had some 30,000 employees. The prime motivation of many members in remaining in the Histadrut was to benefit from the health services it provided; however, the Histadrut benefited because a fraction of members' dues was used for political and cultural purposes. Proposals to transfer the delivery of health care to the state were opposed, since leaders of the Histadrut did not want to lose control over the many jobs that a complex bureaucracy such as Kupat Holim controlled. The supplying of medicines, linen, food, forms, and other goods needed to run such an operation was also a consideration. Not least, it was also assumed that belonging to the Histadrut's Kupat Holim would ultimately accrue to the ideological and organizational advantage of the Labor Party. The transfer of health services was a major blow to the Histadrut and to the Labor Party; both lost their most important source of funds and patronage.[13]

In the past, the fund had provided services not only for its members but also for members of the religious parties. In 1979 those affiliated with the NRP accounted for 6.7 percent of the insured and those of Agudat Israel 1.2 percent. These religious party members received services by virtue of their membership in organizations affiliated with the sick fund, although they themselves are not individual members of the Histadrut. These special relations came with an understanding that these religious parties would not compete in Histadrut elections and formed one of the bases of the long-term political cooperation between the religious parties and the labor movement. One of the important reasons why the religious parties opposed the nationalization of the health services for years was the historic connection these parties had with Kupat Holim. This arrangement was continued even after the advent of the National Health Insurance Law and the reorganization of the Histadrut after its 1994 elections, adding some 37,000 affiliated workers and their families from the National Religious Party and Agudat Israel workers' organizations to the Histadrut. In the end, the sides agreed that the organization tax of .9 percent of their salaries would be paid to the labor federation and that the Histadrut would refund to the religious parties more than half of this organization tax.

The Histadrut's Kupat Holim was by far the most important actor in laying the foundation of the health system during the prestate period. Before the British Mandate at the end of World War I, diseases such as dysentery, malaria, typhus, and trachoma were rampant, and health facilities were practically nonexistent in the land, then a backward and neglected part of the Ottoman Empire. By 1948 when the State of Israel was established, the country's medical infrastructure was already well developed, immunization was standard procedure, and frameworks for improving environmental conditions were operative. In the early years of the state, the health services had to readdress some of the problems previously overcome in order to cope with the needs of hundreds of thousands of refugees from postwar Europe and various Arab countries.

The Labor Party and the Histadrut had always opposed national health insurance; in the past they had supported proposals for making health insurance compulsory but leaving the provision of services to the existing sick funds. Sick fund, Histadrut, and Labor Party leaders appreciated the enormous financial power and patronage opportunities they would lose if sick fund activities were nationalized. In addition, ideological reasons extolling the virtues of mutual aid, self-help, and worker solidarity were voiced. It was clear that the sick fund was the labor movements' main source of strength and that its abolition would mean the collapse of the movements' organizational and financial bases. In the past, only parties that did not have their own health schemes—the General Zionists, the Progressives, and Agudat Israel—had supported the introduction of a national health insurance law, a movement that started in the 1950s and culminated in success in 1994.

Attempts at complete nationalization were thwarted regularly. The terms of reference for a governmental commission set up in 1957 called for general health insurance preserving the multiplicity of sick funds and the autonomous management of the insurees' organizations. The majority report complied; the minority report claimed that the terms of reference were inconsistent with the principles of good management and financial efficiency and proposed a unitary structure. The debate heated up, and suggestions were even made by party leaders keen on statism (including Ben-Gurion) that the sick fund and the Histadrut should be separated and the sick fund left on its own.

Much of this debate coincided with the split in Mapai in 1965. After the elections, in which Rafi took 8 percent of the vote (disappointing for it, but heartening for Mapai, headed by Eshkol), another committee was set up to plan for general health insurance "provided by the insurees' sick funds," in the words of the letter of appointment. The committee again split between those who were loyal to the needs of the government and those who felt that the goals of supervision, avoidance of duplication, planning, and compulsory insurance were not attainable by the proposed method. It was a standoff between the professionals and the politicians.

Within the Labor Party the argument centered on the way in which the sick fund's organizational and budgetary independence could be ensured after the enactment of such a law. All factions of the labor movement were interested in weakening the smaller sick funds by demanding that funds not operating in the more remote settlements would have to subsidize the provision of health services in those areas. Since the Histadrut sick fund was the only organization to do so, this would mean a significant weakening of the smaller sick funds. If such a national health scheme were introduced, the labor movement intended to exploit it for its own ends, namely, to ensure its fund's dominance in the field of health care while ensuring a substantial budget from the national treasury that would both reduce the pressure on the Histadrut and ensure the sick fund's organizational independence. In the ministerial committee that discussed the issue in 1969, the Labor ministers were united in their opposition to the demand made by the NRP and the Independent Liberals to channel the collection of sick fund dues through the National Insurance Institute.

Minister of Labor Yosef Almogi suggested the compromise mentioned above, whereby members' contributions would be paid directly to the sick funds, while employers' contributions would be collected by the National Insurance Institute, which would make the allocation to the different funds. The labor movement wanted to be sure that Histadrut members knew their contributions were going to the Histadrut and that it could continue to use the collection offices for patronage; with regard to the employers' contribution, the fund's only concern was to guarantee its income. The sick funds and the Histadrut were prepared to accept a certain degree of state supervision in return for an expansion in the scope of their activities and an increase in their power. In this case the banner of statism was used as a camouflage for trade union and party interests.

In 1973 the Medical Insurance Law was proposed to the Knesset by the government. It had been developed during the previous two years largely to meet the needs of the Histadrut sick fund and without excessive consultation with the other funds or the Ministry of Health. The proposal was presented a few months before the elections with the hope of impressing the electorate with the legislative activity of the Alignment, although it was uncertain that there was enough time to enact the proposal into law. Items on which the Histadrut sick fund was not prepared to compromise included service provision by the many sick funds, collective membership, and dues collection. No single fund was to be established, although principles for supervision and standardization were proposed. Membership was compulsory, but the Histadrut refused to agree to freedom of choice of sick fund by employees who belonged to organizations (mainly the Histadrut) that had collective affiliation contracts with a sick fund. The proposal to have fees collected by the National Insurance Institute was resoundingly rejected by the Histadrut and its sick fund for fear of losing control of the funds and the patronage of the jobs involved.

The proposed bill included a division of responsibility between the ministries of Health and Labor in providing different elements of the health service. This was crucial, for while the Labor Party never deemed it important to control the Health Ministry, it almost always controlled the Labor Ministry, for both practical and ideological reasons. At subsequent stages the bill was stalled by opposition from those who feared reduction in their influence following the passage of the bill in its proposed form —the smaller sick funds, the Ministry of Health (which basically objected to the role proposed for the Ministry of Labor), and the Histadrut, which feared that the proposed law would lead to an increase in the sick fund's membership and increase its autonomy within the Histadrut.

The ascension to power of a non-Labor government in 1977 raised expectations that legislation would be quickly forthcoming in the health field. But the government soon became deeply involved in negotiating a peace treaty with Egypt and controlling runaway inflation. The Health Ministry went ahead with preparations for national health insurance legislation based on two concepts: organizational unification and administrative regionalization.[14] The plan was to divide the country into regions and "provide health services based on the facilities available in the region—sick funds, public hospitals, institutes, laboratories, etc." No nationalization of health facilities was foreseen; agreements would be arrived at between the health authority and the providers of health services. But most significant, "there [would] be no more membership and no more membership fees, rather residents [would] be eligible to receive all health services by virtue of their being insured by National Insurance." It was not at all surprising that even without seeing the detailed proposal, the Histadrut, its sick fund, and the Labor Party immediately and emphatically rejected the proposal. The legislation was abandoned.

There were many in Labor who were certain that nationalizing the health services would injure the Histadrut in the long run, just as other transfers of services had done in the past. To this day one can hear heated debates in Israel about the disbanding of the Palmach or the nationalization of the education system. Ideologues as well as pragmatists argue that the movement toward statism was one factor that brought about the downfall of the Labor Party in the 1977 elections, and there are indications that a lack of organizational vigor in 1996, after the downsizing of the Histadrut, was instrumental in Netanyahu's victory over Peres. Bases of spiritual and political dominance had been relinquished over the years to anonymous forces opposed to the continued rule of the left.

Another social service of considerable importance is the Histadrut's pension plans. In addition to providing for pensioners, the funds amassed great sums of money that could be used to finance other Histadrut projects. This ability was severely limited in the mid-1990s when the government agreed to ensure the solvency of these pension funds on condition that the financial activities of the funds be controlled and monitored by the Finance Ministry. The clout of the Histadrut was further limited. In sum, the Histadrut, once a world unto itself in many ways in which were concentrated economic, social, and political powers, has been in steady decline. Its many functions, considerable patronage, and economic prowess have been severely curtailed by overextension and nationalization of services.

Public Administration

Israel's public administration reflects many elements of the country's political culture. There is a plethora of rules, bureaucrats, and committees, but the political element is never far from the surface, especially if the issue is considered an important one. Lip service is paid to professionalism and nonpartisanship, but these values are likely to weaken as one climbs higher up the civil service ladder. There is a pretense of modern rational structure, and increasingly computerized techniques have been introduced; still, a solid core remains of a more personal and traditional form of dealing with the citizenry by the administration. Outright corruption is relatively rare or small in scale, but *protekzia*—the use of "pull" or personal acquaintance to speed up processes or obtain favorable treatment—is rampant.[15]

Israel's administrative culture is composed of four strands. The first is the Middle Eastern style in which there is "deference to authority and status, bargaining skills and displays of bureaucratic officiousness." At the same time there is the British legacy, which "is a no-nonsense, orderly, condescending, bureaucratic approach, with little room for bargaining, local initiative or disruption." Third is the strand of traditions brought by Jewish immigrants: "paranoic ghetto attitudes mingle with dynamic, cosmopolitan, liberal entrepreneurship." The fourth strand, the Israeli, uses the experiences with which the people grew up. The older ones, "skilled in political infighting and insurgency tactics, affirm their inherent visionary powers, their pragmatic 'feel' of things, and their confidential, in-group decision-making." Their children, more middle class and likely to be native born, turn more to models experienced in military service or learned in the university, although improvisation is always a possibility.[16]

The public administration is a direct extension of the pervasiveness of bureaucracy. Bureaucracy is a feature of the modern state everywhere, but in Israel it seems even more prevalent. Part of this impression stems from the fact that such a large portion of the population is employed in jobs related to one bureaucracy or another. This is enhanced by the extremely large role of government and its related agencies in the economy and society. This employment pattern fortifies the inclinations of the Jews who come to Israel to continue living in urban areas and make their livings in commercial or service sectors.

Bureaucracy is important in a modern society because it provides for a division of labor and is immune from reliance on a single individual. As transactions are based on written rules and records, it allows for neutrality and constraint. These positive features also provide the background for bureaucracy's limitations and perversions: too much paperwork, too many authorizations needed, too many organizations involved, too little coordination. The proper functioning of the bureaucracy is as much an art form as any human endeavor; ultimately it depends on the people involved, their motivations, and their attitudes. Faults are rarely to be found in the instrument but in the way the instrument is employed.

Bureaucracy is seen as a neutral form that facilitates executing policies. In this theoretical world politicians *set* policy; the public administration and its civil servants merely *execute* policies. In the real world, relations are not nearly that simple. Politicians usually lack expertise in highly complex and technical areas such as welfare delivery, water distribution, or defense allocations, so they turn to senior civil servants for advice and opinion. Civil servants often present to the decision maker a choice between various alternatives, but the structuring of the problem and the implications of the policy are in their hands. Politicians have been known to prefer one policy over another for political reasons; bureaucrats have been known to promote one policy over another because they think that the policy better meets the political goals of the politician. Not least important in this list that confounds the line between administration and politics is the fact that administrators tend to remain, but politicians rotate out of office if their party loses or they move on to other positions.

These considerations point to two major questions regarding the civil service. The first has to do with the degree to which it is motivated by professional as opposed to political considerations. Looked at from another angle, to what extent do appointments and promotions result from merit considerations as opposed to a spoils system in which the victors divide jobs and privileges among their camp followers? The second question has to do with the degree to which the civil service is responsive to public demands and responsible in its actions to the executive, legislature, and ultimately, the voters.

The answers to these questions in Israel are not straightforward.[17] Certainly much lip service is paid to creating a professional, nonpolitical, responsive, and responsible service. And there is evidence that progress has been made. But the evidence is mixed. For example, merit considerations are often spoken of, especially at the lower ranks of hierarchies. But as we move up the ladder of power and prestige, the prevalence of extraprofessional considerations grows.

Israel is a small country, and among the few candidates for a senior position, the front-runners are likely to be known. Past performance and the groups to which a candidate is affiliated cannot easily be separated in the minds of an appointment committee. Charges of politicization have frequently been heard from various sides of the political fence.

The dilemma is not an easy one to solve. It is important that years of service in the public administration be rewarded with promotion; on the other hand, politicians in decision making positions must be able to work with and trust the judgment of senior civil servants. Obviously, this trust will be facilitated by appointing people who are known to the politicians and who have demonstrated their loyalty. For most of the bureaucrats, professionals, and clerks in public administration (some 75,000 without the army and teachers), these considerations are not relevant, but they may be very relevant in determining who will lead their ministry, department, or regional office. The specter of politicization has grown more acute as each political party accuses the others of indulging in political appointments. For our purposes there is no better indicator of the problems of the public administration than its failure to develop as a neutral, professional arm of government.

It is a rule of thumb that when a civil service is strong, it is a meritocracy; when it is weak, it is not. In Israel the civil service is neither very strong nor exclusively meritocratic because the political element is never far from the surface in matters of policy, appointment, and execution. So much of foreign and defense policies is traceable to the prime minister and defense minister, and so much of economic and social policy to the finance minister, that seeking an independent and autonomous civil service is futile. The control of the Finance Ministry is evident from the structure of the arrangements: the Civil Service Commission is a department of the Finance Ministry and thus control tends to be centered in the ministry and not at the cabinet level. One of the first acts of the new Netanyahu government in 1996 was to fire the civil service commissioner, although the act was withdrawn after pressure from the High Court of Justice. Within weeks, however, the civil service commissioner was changed. Many career bureaucrats made the transition in 1977 from Labor to Likud without difficulty, but since this was Israel's first transition, it was more of a personal feat than a characteristic of the system. Since then, two other transitions have occurred, and it is clear that the rules of a smooth and responsible transition are yet to be written.

The relative weakness of the Israeli civil service is obvious from the career compartmentalization that characterizes the system. There is very little real mobility in the Israeli civil service, although almost everyone is rewarded with occasional promotions within the department, division, or ministry. In the United Kingdom it is relatively easy to move horizontally within a department; in the United States it is easy to move vertically from department to department. Both systems provide training for senior civil servants in a variety of tasks and fields. In Israel neither movement is widespread. Everyone in the system crawls forward together, everyone receiving gradual promotions but rarely breaking the pattern of employment into which he or she began work. The lack of lateral transfer promotes inbreeding, which ultimately works to the detriment of the organizations.

One group spared the dilemma of having secure tenured positions without much chance of getting beyond one's original department or ministry includes those few individuals who are in direct contact with the minister: the director general of the ministry, the minister's secretary and driver, and various aides. In all, there are some 45 positions to which the relevant leader can appoint the person of his choice without further examination or competition, in addition to some 200 aides and personal advisers. These are really political appointments.[18] The future of these people depends on their ability and perseverance, and on the political fortunes of their ministers. Young aides have been known to use the protégé relations that develop to enhance their career mobility. Successful director generals have been known to use their experience and connections to good political advantage in promoting their careers. Two examples are Levi Eshkol and Shimon Peres, both of whom served as director general of the Defense Ministry.

It would be too narrow an understanding to think of the public administration as obediently administering policies made elsewhere. The ministries are the major repositories of knowledge and the major collectors of data regarding the topics under their control. As we have seen, most legislation originates in the ministries. Recommendations may or may not be adopted, but that is likely to be a political or budget issue as much as an administrative one.

The role of the minister in the political system is the key to determining how strong the ministry will be. It works the other way as well: top political leaders head the important ministries. A small ministry such as Welfare might become important if the minister holds the balance of power in coalition calculations in the government and Knesset. The major point is that the public administration is an extension of the political system. The organization of the government is primarily affected by political considerations and not by abstract models of rational public administration.

There usually has been an inverse relationship between the number of ministers and the size of Knesset support for the government coalition. Yitzhak Rabin's government between 1974 and 1977 was one of the largest in the country's history and yet was supported by a bare majority of the Knesset. In 1983 there were twenty-one ministers in Begin's government, and it faced constant threats of removal of support from coalition partners. The National Unity Government of 1988 had twenty-six ministers. These situations reflect problems within the ruling party and other parties making up the coalition. After the Likud assumed power in 1977, the leaders declared they would streamline the ministries and reduce the number of ministers. There was some reshuffling (the Police Ministry was merged with the Interior Ministry) and some new names were attached to old functions (energy and infrastructure, building and housing, transportation and communication). What should be clear is that these rearrangements were temporary—and could be revised if political demands required, in this way providing other politicians with ministries.

The 1996 government was the first to be regulated by the law that limited the number of ministers to eighteen and set the minimum number at eight. Still, in order to entice Ariel Sharon into service in the cabinet,

Netanyahu rearranged various functions from other ministries and established the Ministry of National Infrastructures.

The activity and number of ministries are not the only things determined by politics. That is true of deputy ministers and ministers without portfolio as well. The former may fill roles in the administration. When the Education Ministry was in the hands of the Labor Party, for instance, it was usual to have a religious party deputy minister to handle religious schools' affairs. Other deputy ministers may be appointed as part of the delicate political balance within coalition parties. Because the Aguda refused to share in cabinet responsibility, it preferred to control its share of the pie from a deputy minister's post, with the minister as the prime minister or another minister who understood that the Aguda deputy minister would be making the decisions. The new law limits the number of deputy ministers to six.

Ministers without portfolio have also been known to be appointed to solve political problems. They participate in government meetings but have no direct responsibility for the administration of a ministry. This was the role Menachem Begin filled in the National Unity Government between 1967 and 1970. The National Unity Government of 1988 had four ministers without portfolio.

The fact that the minister's political clout is often a key to the ministry's success gives him (or her) the potential for prestige within his ministry. But since the minister is often an outsider to the subject matter of the ministry and dependent on professionals in the ministry to aid him, and since his success as minister is partially connected with the cooperation he receives from his ministry, the minister may become a captive of his ministry. He quickly finds himself representing not only the ministry's policies but also its interests. He becomes the major force in the government committed to retaining or even enlarging his ministry's budget and areas of activity. Universal rules is the goal, but it can be reached only if it is given political backing. There have been cases of a strong minister or mayor or director who achieves benefits for his employees that are a function of his political strength and against stated policy. The center then appears weak because it cannot, or has chosen not to, confront the issue of irregular salaries and benefits.

Decision making in Israel tends to take one of two forms. One is the crisp, often unexpected, decision made by a handful of people that effectively bypasses the public administration. Such decisions reflect the centralized nature of the system and the enormous political power in the hands of a few. The second form is one of organized randomness, with myriad sections and departments within ministries often expressing conflicting points of view, and fights between ministers and ministries regarding policies. In

these latter situations the system is the opposite of hierarchical; it is cha-
otic. Either no clear policy is articulated because of the conflicting demands
or a series of contradictory rules emerge that tend to defeat the policy purpose of any one group.

If leaders think the matter is acute, the first form of decision making
is used; if not, the second. This is the difference between issuing clear-cut
edicts or allowing a situation to develop haphazardly. Michael Brecher has
studied foreign policy decisions in times of crisis, and his figures illustrate
the situation in Israel. Of the crucial decisions regarding the Six-Day War
in 1967 and the Yom Kippur War in 1973, Brecher documents the concentration of decision-making power in the hands of the prime minister and a
small number of hand-picked politicians and senior officials. By way of il-
lustration we may consider the following figures: In the 1967 crisis,
Brecher identifies 97 consultative meetings. Of these, 31 had two participants, 23 had three or four, and 24 had five to ten participants. Of these
meetings, 65 were of an ad hoc nature, with only 13 being institutional. In
1973 Brecher counts 111 meetings, 42 attended by two participants, 8 by
three or four, and 25 by five to ten. Of these, 25 were of an ad hoc nature,
and 50 were institutional.[19]

There tends to be an inverse relationship between the importance in
terms of national security of the issue being discussed and the number of
people involved in the decision-making process. The Sinai Campaign of
1956 and the destruction of Yamit before withdrawing from Sinai in 1982
are examples of decisions taken by Ben-Gurion and Begin respectively,
with minimal if any consultation preceding the decisions. In many other areas, however, the effort that would have to be made to coordinate policy
or the political capital that would have to be expended to sort out conflicting interests and goals would be greater than it seems to be worth. Israeli
public administration has learned to live with this duality of sometimes being ignored in influencing policy and sometimes being frustrated in achieving clear-cut policy.

Planning exists in the system, but it is often irrelevant to the political
exigencies in force when projects are actually implemented. Planning demands an assumption of stability regarding the future environment, and
that is precisely the characteristic that is lacking in Israel. Parties in power
shift, influence within the coalition changes, a new administrator is more
important than his predecessor, new interests must be placated—all these
things and others are insidious to the planner. Besides political surprises,
there are other uncertainties that interfere with planning. Large-scale immigration, a war, a peace treaty, or an economic crisis can have devastating
effects on plans.[20]

Another problem is bureaucratic conservatism. In-place structures generate interests and jobs and a built-in inertia. Conditions often change more quickly than structures do. For example, national bureaucratic structures planned and implemented the creation of water supplies. When that challenge was successfully faced with the establishment of a national water carrier, water distribution became the pressing bureaucratic problem, and the old structures persisted, even though they were clearly unequipped to handle the new challenge.[21]

Oversight

THE STATE CONTROLLER

Overseeing the activities of the public administration is quite developed. The State Controller regularly probes into the practices and policies of ministries and other organizations that receive state funds. Reports tend to be professional and unbiased, and in recent years their impact—or at least their visibility—has increased since the appointment of Miriam Ben Porat, a retired Supreme Court justice, as State Controller. Still, serious failures are discovered year after year. There must be a formal, ministerial response to the report, but many of the problems remain. The very act of revealing is important, but it is a giant step from controlling.

Another institution that has achieved public acceptance is the commission for citizens' complaints, or the ombudsman. In 1995 almost 8,000 complaints were received, and the ombudsman found in 37 percent of the cases completed that the complaint was justified.[22] This was about the same rate as in 1980. In the mid-1970s the percentage of complaints justified out of those decided was almost 50 percent.[23] Israel's public administration, like many of the country's other institutions, has many rules that indicate the intention of the lawmaker was that it be run in a modern, apolitical, and detached fashion. Unfortunately, rules are not enough to determine the outcome. The human element—the kind of people attracted to the civil service, their motivations and professional competence, the satisfaction they have in their jobs—influences the way in which the administration operates. Add to this the political dimension that always must be taken into account in Israel, and the resulting picture is one of an administration that does not live up to the lawmaker's original intention.

COMMISSIONS OF INQUIRY

In Israel's charged political atmosphere, a detached appraisal of a situation is hard to achieve. In 1968, the Knesset passed the commissions of inquiry bill that allowed the government to establish such commissions on vital public matters. Once the government decides to establish such a commission, the law empowers the president of the Supreme Court to appoint the members of the commission. The Supreme Court president also appoints the commission's chair, who must be either a Supreme Court or a district court judge. The usual size of the commission is two members and the chair.[24]

The commission decides on its agenda, its procedure, the witnesses to appear, and the material to subpoena, and it has the power to ensure that these witnesses and evidence be brought before it. If a person might be damaged by the findings of the commission, that person must be notified by the commission of that possibility, and then he has the right to be represented by counsel, to interrogate witnesses, and to bring additional evidence. In principle, the proceedings are public, but sensitive security, foreign policy, or economic matters may be discussed behind closed doors.

The end result of the commission's deliberation is a report to the government, reviewing its findings and making recommendations. The report is to be public, unless sensitive security matters are involved. The government may also decide not to publish part or all of the report of a commission of inquiry. The government is not obliged to accept the recommendations of the commission, but it has always accepted the recommendations made regarding disciplining public servants, either by removing them from office or by limiting the responsibilities they could bear in the future.

Between 1969 and 1996 twelve national commissions of inquiry were established. Their topics included such varied matters as the investigation of the fire in the al-Aksa Mosque in Jerusalem (1969); corrupt practices in the national football (soccer) league (1971); the management of the oil fields in Sinai (1971); conditions in the prison system (1979); the 1933 murder of Chaim Arlozoroff (1982); the health system (1991); the massacre of dozens of Arabs at the Cave of Mahpelah in Hebron (1994); the disappearance of Yemenite babies in the period following independence (1995); and the assassination of Yitzhak Rabin (1995).

Four other commissions have been especially important to the country's political history:

1. The Agranat Commission, established in 1973, was charged with examining the preparedness of the army and the country before the surprise attack of Yom Kippur. This commission was chaired by the president of the Supreme Court, had four other members, including two former chiefs of staff, and held only secret sessions. It recommended relieving Chief of Staff David "Dado" Elazar, the head of the southern command, and the chief of intelligence of their commands. It did not place personal responsibility on Prime Minister Golda Meir or Defense Minister Moshe Dayan.

2. The Kahan Commission of 1982 investigated the massacre at the Palestinian refugee camps of Sabra and Shatilla during the Lebanese war of that year. The massacre was carried out by elements of the Christian Falangists, but the commission determined that Minister of Defense Ariel Sharon, Chief of Staff Rafael "Raful" Eitan, and two other generals were indirectly responsible for the massacre and that they should be relieved of their command positions.

3. The Bejsky Commission of 1985 was established after the publication of the report of the State Controller regarding the bank-shares collapse of 1983. The report concluded that Finance Ministers Yigael Horowitz and Yoram Aridor, the governor of the Bank of Israel, and the directors of the four largest banks bore personal responsibility for the collapse of the shares. The governor of the bank was removed from office; the bank managers were ultimately tried and found guilty. The politicians were untouched.

4. The Landau Commission of 1987 dealt with the methods of investigation used against terrorists by the Shin Bet, Israel's internal security service. The hearings were held behind closed doors, and the most widely cited of its public findings was that it was permissible for the Shin Bet to use "mild physical force" on suspects, especially nonviolent psychological pressure. The commission recommended that the Shin Bet and its activities be more carefully supervised by authorities outside the service because of the instances of perjury in court by service members when interrogated about the methods used.

Commissions of inquiry enjoy a high degree of prestige in the system, and in general their findings are viewed as impartial. What is striking in these cases is that the political leaders are generally left unscathed, while harsh punishment is often meted out to persons acting at the operational level. Yet the commissions' recommendations are taken seriously: When Netanyahu was putting together his government in 1996, it was clear that both Sharon and Eitan would be in it but that neither would be defense minister because of the Kahan Commission report. In the end, Sharon became minister of national resources and Eitan was made minister of agriculture and the environment.

The government and the Knesset each has rules for setting up committees of inquiry made up of ministers and Knesset members, respectively. These committees have lesser powers of forcing witnesses to appear and to present documents and other material on demand. They are suspect because they are peopled by sitting politicians, while the national commissions of inquiry are generated from the Supreme Court.

Local Government

Local government and the quality of the services it provides affect every citizen directly. In Israel local government is highly dependent on the national government ministries, but it would be an inappropriate oversight to ignore local government completely. Local government is important because it was in municipal elections that much-discussed electoral reform was achieved. Local government is important because it has become a major source of recruitment of young and promising leaders. Although the national government is dominant, local government provides services, and the local government budget is a vehicle for redistribution among communities.[25]

The municipal elections of November 1978 were the first to be held using two separate systems: direct election of mayors and proportional election of the council. Until then, the proportional system was used exclusively, and the mayor was elected by the council. The selection of the mayor became political, with coalition maneuvering within the council. More than that, it was not unknown for national parties to take an interest in the selection of the mayor; parties sometimes used coalition negotiations, especially in the bigger cities, to achieve added leverage in the national negotiations for the composition of the coalition.

In addition to being a pawn in national negotiations, local policy sometimes displays acts that may be interpreted as promoting a politician's status. The exploitation of a political situation to further personal goals is not unknown in politics. In Israel it has a special name: Kalanterism. The name comes from a municipal crisis that occurred in the Jerusalem city council in August 1956. A majority of the city council decided to remove Mapai Mayor Gershon Agron from the mayor's seat. At that time mayors were elected by the city council in much the same way that prime ministers were elected by the Knesset. The religious parties were displeased with Mayor Agron's support for establishing an Institute of Archeology and attached chapel affiliated with the Reform movement in Jerusalem. The opposition General Zionists denounced the economic policies of Agron's administration. Rahamim Kalanter, a member of Hapoel Hamizrachi, defected from the anti-Agron group, voted for Agron, and was subsequently appointed deputy mayor in charge of religious affairs and made responsible for the sanitation department. Kalanter's defection was attacked by his political opponents (and former allies) as treason and was defended by his new allies as civic-minded behavior. Kalanter bettered his immediate political fortunes and became immortalized in Israel's political vocabulary.

Political clashes between the council and the mayor occurred in about 10 percent of the municipalities. In the period between 1950 and 1973 the mayor was replaced in mid-term fifty-three times during the five election cycles in the ninety-eight Jewish municipalities.[26] Usually these crises ended with the formation of a new coalition with a different allocation of responsibility, patronage, and offices.

A new law regulating municipal elections was passed in 1976 and is still in effect. The mayor is now elected by direct vote, the winner being the candidate who receives the most votes providing that he achieves at least 40 percent. If no candidate achieves 40 percent, a second round is held two weeks after the first. In the second round the two biggest vote-getters of the first round compete with each other.[27] In the 1993 municipal elections, about a third of the mayoral contests were decided by a second round. The council is still elected using proportional representation and a fixed list; the minimum required for representation is .75 percent.

This new law reflected the growing popular support for electoral reform before the elections to the Knesset of 1977 and would ultimately serve as a precursor to the direct election of the prime minister twenty years later. The structure invites political clashes between the popularly elected mayor and the municipal party activists on the council. Even though the mayor is directly elected and cannot be replaced, council members have many opportunities to hinder the efficient administration of local affairs if the mayor does not have majority support in the council. There is no evidence that it is easier to form a ruling coalition under the new system, nor is it possible to show that the coalition deals made are more benign.[28] Since the Interior Ministry is ultimately responsible for the smooth functioning of local administration, appeals to disband the council are made to authorities in the central government in extreme cases.

Even after the law, conflict between the mayor and the council remained at about the 10 percent level. In the 1978–83 period, 8 of the 110 Jewish municipalities had mayors not supported by the majority of the council, compared with 19 cases in the 1983–89 period, and 14 after the 1989 elections. The parallel figures for the sixty-one Arab and Druze units were five, four, and seven.[29]

Until its ascent to national power in 1977, the major political base of the parties of the Likud was in local government. The General Zionists (later the Liberal Party) controlled major cities such as Tel Aviv, Ramat Gan, and Netanya. Haifa, Holon, and Bat Yam were long considered safely in the Alignment camp. In 1959 the Mapai candidate became the Tel Aviv mayor; the party held the post until 1973. Competitiveness has become the characteristic of local elections, especially since the advent of local lists, which have often shifted the distribution of the vote between the major parties within a locality.[30] The 1989 and 1993 municipal elections witnessed a weakening of power for the Labor Party in an arena that they had long dominated. In 1989, in cities like Holon, Beersheva, and Petach Tikva, Labor mayors were defeated. Even in Haifa, long a bastion of the

Labor Party, the Likud candidate came very close to unseating his Labor Party opponent. The relative success of religious parties among the Jewish voters (and fundamentalist Islamic parties among the Arabs) precluded the conclusion that the 1989 municipal elections represented a clear Likud victory. But it was clear that the elections presented Labor with a resounding political defeat. In 1993, two former Likud ministers who lost their jobs in the Knesset election defeat of 1992 were elected mayors. Ehud Olmert in Jerusalem beat the respected Teddy Kolleck, and Roni Milo was elected mayor of Tel Aviv.

The change in the electoral system captured the spirit of a process that was developing and helped perpetuate it. It would ultimately provide the model for the direct election of the prime minister. Young and ambitious politicians, especially from the development towns, emerged in local politics and used this exposure as a base to enter national politics. The young generation of Sephardi Knesset members, especially in the Likud, is the best example: David Levy of Beit Shean, Maxim Levy of Lod, Meir Shitrit of Yavne, Moshe Katzav of Kiryat Malachi, and David Magen of Kiryat Gat. These politicians have counterparts in Labor, but those in Labor have not reached the levels of visibility and power enjoyed by those in the Likud—partly because Labor has a larger reservoir from which to draw, and partly because there is a feeling that Likud leaders of this type are more "authentic" inasmuch as they have been active and successful in electoral politics for years, whereas many of their opposite numbers in Labor were drafted as pseudo representatives and lack similar roots in local politics. Two Labor leaders who were Sephardi and former mayors did succeed: Amir Peretz of Shderot became a Knesset member and head of the Histadrut, having followed Chaim Ramon in the breakaway group in 1994. Another was Eli Dayan of Ashkelon. There was no clear evidence, however, that their place on the list improved Labor's success among Sephardim.[31]

The pioneering aspect of electoral reform and the generating of political leadership notwithstanding, the proper perspective for understanding Israeli local government is its extreme dependence on the center. The legacy of Ottoman rule, the British Mandate, and Yishuv politics created a heavy bias toward politics from the capital. The politics of independent Israel reinforced this tradition, and the center retains a vital role in the budgeting, planning, and development of local affairs.

It is not that local authorities are unimportant but that government ministries are so dominant in determining what goes on at the local level. Past practices of overt favoritism and postponing money transfers have largely disappeared as the system has become more rationalized and bureaucratized. But the political element has not been eradicated. Local governments succeed when they are adept at the political tasks of bargaining and applying political leverage. For it is the Ministry of the Interior (which is in charge of local authorities) and the Ministry of Finance (which releases the money) that must be penetrated if a municipality or local council is to enjoy a budget for developing beyond the minimum required by law and regulation.

The most important actor in determining local government affairs and the clearest indication of the retention of the forms of the British Mandate is the district field officer. He is appointed by the Interior Ministry and has wide-ranging discretionary power regarding local governments, up to and including dismissal of the elected councilors and the appointment of administrators to run the affairs of the local authority. This power of the district field officer is in the tradition of direct rule as it was practiced in British colonies. That the Israeli system carried over this tradition seemed natural given the pressing problems of the independence period. Subsequently, the system has become an important instrument of central control over local affairs and a symbol of the dominant status of the central government and its Interior Ministry.

The bargaining that can be entered into concerns the size of budget, the programs to be supported, and the timing of program execution. The services the local government provides are varied, and the forms of payments are complex. What determines the success of the local authority, especially the mayor, is access to and influence with bureaucrats, ministers, and party politicians active in the decision-making process regarding local affairs. When it was permitted to be a mayor *and* a Knesset member, special leverage was possible; perhaps these Knesset members were also mayors because of their political traits. Now that Knesset members are not allowed to have another job, this advantage has disappeared. Going beyond the authorized plans demands special approval, which cannot be divorced from the political process.

The functions of local government, including education and health services, are closely monitored and influenced by national rules. The budget and the number of approved job slots are determined by the size of the community and its past activities. Education is a good example of the relation between central and local governments. This is the biggest item for most local authorities, yet most of the important decisions regarding education come from Jerusalem. Teachers are paid by the municipal authority, but the budget to pay them comes from the center. Up to a quarter of the curriculum is permitted to local discretion on the part of parents, but since most communities do not take advantage of this opportunity, curriculum is mostly dictated by the Ministry of Education. Teachers are hired, trained, and licensed by national supervisors. The local government is left with the administration of buildings (which must meet nationally dictated standards), the administration of the payroll, and tasks such as hiring guards and nurses for the schools. Teachers throughout the country are paid according to the same contract.

Between one-half and two-thirds of the budget of a local authority comes from the central government. The amount varies by community and type of service. For example, in Kiryat Shmona, a town close to the Lebanese border and made up of many Sephardi families, as much as 90 percent of the welfare budget comes from central authorities. In Givatayim, a middle-class suburb of Tel Aviv, the figure may be a third that of Kiryat Shmona. Not only are there fewer welfare cases in Givatayim, but the authorities are anxious to bolster the social fabric and morale of the border town, which became the symbol of vulnerability to terrorist shelling before the Lebanese wars of 1982 and 1996. Money channeled to the local authorities plays a redistributive role because block grants are used to encourage poorer local authorities to provide better services, though uniformity of service is not sought.[32]

Local governments finance the rest of their activities by collecting taxes, especially property taxes. Two other methods developed over the years are the special municipal endowment funds, especially for cultural purposes, and Project Renewal. The endowment funds, usually collected from wealthy contributors outside Israel, allow mayors to be more flexible and more creative in handling the affairs of the city. The most successful use of this method has been by Teddy Kolleck, former mayor of Jerusalem, whose initiatives were widely acclaimed. Tel Aviv and Haifa have also been successful. But having mentioned Israel's three biggest and most important cities, as we continue down the list the record of success using this method dwindles. Most local authorities cannot compete with the historical and emotional attraction of Jerusalem or the appeal of large cultural, business, and industrial centers like Tel Aviv and Haifa. Thus the funds at their disposal are relatively smaller.

Project Renewal was an attempt to help local authorities by raising funds from Jewish communities abroad. The funds were earmarked to renew neighborhoods that had deteriorated and were becoming slums. The money was to be spent on housing, ecology, and cultural and educational projects. Despite a slow start occasioned by a complex method of coordinating the desires of the citizens with the plans of the local authority, the various government ministries involved, and the Jewish Agency, Project Renewal has begun to help communities and to give a psychological lift to many of their residents.[33]

The role of local government is relatively weak. This is obvious when one considers the structure of the planning and zoning process in Israel. Local, regional, and national commissions must approve plans. The local level plays an important role because its city council, which is popularly elected, must first approve plans. But the approval of local government is not sufficient; this function is shared with the central government. Plans are then forwarded to the regional commission and in some cases to the national commission. These last two are composed of members who represent government ministries and major local governments. This composition obviously reflects the strength of the political parties in the government, in ministries involved, and in the local councils.

Planning is hindered because of the lag between approval and performance. In the past, well-connected politician-mayors could ignore plans and "create facts." Large projects have at times been approved by various commissions well after the projects were complete. Illegal constructions are widespread; even minor changes in a building often demand a license, and licenses are often not obtained. Enforcing these laws is done sporadically. Rather than force compliance with the plans, fines are usually assessed, and the infraction is not corrected.

The dilemma between lawmaking and law enforcement, on the one hand, and the provision of services, on the other, is nowhere better seen than in regard to parking in the large cities. Business, commerce, and entertainment are encouraged to draw customers, clients, and spectators to the cities, which quickly become snarled because the streets and parking lots are inadequate for the growing number of cars in the country. Parking on the sidewalks spreads. This is a clear violation of city laws and a hindrance to residents of the neighborhoods. The municipality tries to give preference to residents in parking but it still must contend with the problems of traffic congestion and parking by others. It may block sidewalk parking, or use the Denver Boot to punish illegal parkers, while it simultaneously encourages people to come to the city. And the discussions regarding rapid transportation by train and subway creep ahead.

Local government plays an important role in setting the cultural atmosphere of the city or town. The uneven enforcement of laws prohibiting entertainment on the Sabbath provides a good example. In Tel Aviv, movies and theaters operate, but buses do not run. In Haifa some buses run (supposedly because of the Arab population and in accord with the rule of maintaining the status quo), and movies are open. In Jerusalem, there are no buses on the Sabbath. Entertainment was prohibited, but in 1987 the situation changed when a judge dismissed the indictment brought by the Jerusalem municipality against a private club that showed movies on Friday evening. The decision caused an uproar and led to moves by the religious parties in the coalition to overcome the court's decision. The issue heated up again in view of the results of the municipal elections in 1989, in which the religious parties did well, positioning themselves to play pivotal roles in local coalitions. There was no doubt that the religious parties would press for a change in public policy and legislation.

In 1990 a law was passed giving the municipality the authority to regulate activities within its jurisdiction. The competing values in this case are the individual's freedom of religion, on the one hand, and the right of freedom from religion, on the other. Can the majority in a locality regulate behavior that infringes on the rights of individuals? This of course cuts both ways: religious persons want a quiet neighborhood on their days of rest, seculars want direct paths of travel. Should streets be closed along main traffic arteries? The issue becomes acute because the police in Israel is a national force and might be expected to use uniform rules in law enforcement. What is obvious is that the political climate of the city (especially the size and concentration of the religious population and its political power) influences law enforcement. In the power-sharing balance between national and local government, the former is clearly dominant, but the latter is also an actor.

12. Aspects of Political Culture

Every observer, most journalists, and many tourists are alert to differences among countries. Those who research political culture attempt to explore these differences by focusing on the distribution of such factors as norms, attitudes, and behaviors as they relate to government and politics. Political ideology, the left-right continuum, dominant values, democratic norms and political tolerance, communications, and socialization are a few of the many aspects included in the study of political culture.[1]

Political Ideology

An ideology is a system of ideas that is normative in nature in that it depicts and justifies an ideal, is based on assumptions concerning the nature of man and social reality, and is action oriented. Politics, being a normative activity, must be accompanied by guidelines against which the actors gauge their behavior. Political ideology is a set of attitudes employed in answering questions of political priority.[2]

Ideology, much like politics, is a concern of the elite. Members of the elite not only produce ideology but are also its largest distributors and consumers. They distribute it to their constituents in programs and statements; they consume ideological output because, trained in the language of ideological discourse, they tend to communicate with their peers in that idiom and are alert and sensitive to messages that have an ideological cast.

In ideological intercourse the elite tends to be active, the people passive. Since ideology is less than salient to the population at large, deviations from ideological purity by the elite are accepted by the electorate. Ideologues in power invariably find that they must modify and adjust ideological pronouncements to fit policy imperatives. Both phenomena can exist simultaneously: ideology may be modified, yet ideological discourse continues at a high level of intensity.

Two principles to be kept in mind are that ideology is largely an elite affair and that ideology is not necessarily a good predictor of policy. Political communication in Israel tends to be highly ideological, public policy much more pragmatic. Israel has developed an economy with a very high level of government activity and with principles of market forces and profitability ascendant. The previous period featured socialist ideologies but also fostered policies that were centralized while encouraging private investment. This dualistic form has been developed by ministers of the Labor left and augmented by officeholders of the Likud right. The rhetoric of their parties still identifies them as socialist and capitalist, respectively.

Political discourse, and the ideologies and parties associated with it, is generally based on the assumption that political groupings can be ordered on a continuum from left to right. The concepts left and right (or liberal and conservative in the American version) are common terms in politics. Nevertheless, their meaning is multifaceted at best, elusive at worst, and divergent over time and across polities.

Most often in political discourse the left-right continuum has been given economic meaning, referring to equality as opposed to inequality, government intervention as opposed to free enterprise, tolerance of change as opposed to adherence to the status quo. Other issues, such as abortion, foreign aid, and integration, have all been subsumed under these headings in their time. On closer examination, however, it becomes clear that notions of left and right are too simplistic to capture the complexity of reality. It is important to consider the problems related to a left-right continuum.[3]

First, the assumption of unidimensionality is explicitly made in discussing a left-right continuum, yet it is questionable whether so simple a concept is adequate. The test is whether the continuum provides an ordering of parties such that if we know, for example, that a party is on the right of the continuum, we then know its views on the issues of the day. Clearly this is not the case. The positions of Israeli parties on issues raised by the role of religion in the state, for example, are not related to the locations of the party on the continuum when arranged by social welfare policy or foreign policy. The left would be expected to be least amenable to the religious position, the right more so. Yet many Likud leaders and supporters are fervent secularists on these questions, and some Labor people accept religious policy not only because they feel they must do so to maintain coalitions when in power. Different issues are salient for various parties. In Israel at least two, and possibly more, dimensions are needed for making sense of the orderings of political parties.

A second problem relating to the left-right continuum has to do with the meanings of left and right. Broadly, the left represents the socialist values of equality, social justice, and international cooperation and brotherhood. The right has historically been associated with capitalist values such as freedom of opportunity, competition, restricted government activity, and nationalism. In certain senses this description fits Israel, but in other important senses it is incomplete. For many years, and certainly since the Six-Day War, the major Zionist parties have competed in their nationalism. The highest values have been security and Israel as a Jewish state. The Likud argued that these goals could be achieved using a firm, nonconciliatory policy, and Labor favored more flexibility and concession. But the Alignment began the policy of settling the territories, and the Likud ceded the Sinai to the Egyptians. Neither of these government actions could have been anticipated if only the left-right continuum were our guide. Being a party of the "left" did not prevent Ahdut Haavoda in the 1950s from taking a very strong militant line against neighboring Arab states. And it was on this very issue that the party split from Mapam in 1954.

Parties near the center of the continuum tend to differ in ideology and to be more similar in policy. Parties at the extreme edges, rarely tested by the exigencies of power, are generally more consistent in their ideology. During 1967 and 1993, between the Six-Day War and the Oslo accords, it was relatively easy to differentiate between the extreme parties of the left and the right, but harder to do so regarding the parties at the center. The two large parties were in the middle tending toward the right, meaning that the left-right continuum failed to distinguish easily among the parties on this most critical issue. The major parties were close on this issue with the extremes much more spread out.

This phenomenon would hold as well for social and economic issues such as compulsory arbitration in public-sector labor disputes or welfare benefits to the underprivileged. Again, the large parties would cluster toward the center; variation would be evident among extreme, and weaker, political groups. On religious matters, the problem is more complex. Almost all secular parties stress the importance of religious freedom and civil rights, and the religious parties promote the importance of behavior in accordance with Jewish religious law. Secular parties tend to release their Knesset members from the obligation of party discipline on Knesset votes on these issues by referring to such issues as matters of personal conscience. Often, however, the coalition needs of the party in power offset the principle of freedom of conscience and the Knesset member faces the dilemma of choosing between personal views, the party's ideological stand, and the party's political needs.

A third difficulty arises from the lack of a fixed structure in the continuum. The meaning of left and right may change over time. The ranking provided by the continuum today may well be different from that of earlier years. Party positions change. The NRP was much less militant in its foreign policy before the 1967 war than after it. Since then, it has become a prominent advocate for the positions of Israeli settlement in all of Eretz Israel. This stunning change must be understood in terms of the changes in the mood of the times, the ascension of a young generation of leaders in the NRP, and the increased salience of these issues in the public mind.

Labor and Likud also moved in this sense. Labor abandoned its long-held opposition to negotiations with the PLO *after* the 1992 elections and removed the plank opposed to the establishment of a Palestinian state, without supporting its establishment *before* the 1996 elections. The Likud had little choice but reluctantly to follow Labor on the first, and hope it would not be tested regarding the second. Ideology was clearly replaced by the pragmatic political needs of a party seeking to win votes from the center of the continuum.

The difficulty of fixed structure is clearest in the lack of necessary connection between party platform and policy when that party is in power. Power tends to modify extreme positions because responsibility is more keenly felt as problems are confronted. Opposition affords a politician the luxury of being judged by his words and not by his deeds. The economic policies followed by Pinhas Sapir when he was finance minister in the 1960s would not have been anticipated by a student of socialist economic theory. But for a dynamic leader faced with difficult problems, Sapir's program was conceived as an answer to national needs; only then was the question of ideological purity addressed. His socialist party could encourage private investment and even subsidize it to achieve goals thought important. Leaders such as Sapir have no problem with ideology because ideology is never rigid; only some ideologues are.

The surprises that followed Prime Minister Begin's turnabout on the question of the peace negotiations with Egypt in 1978 that culminated in the Camp David agreements, and the change in policy by Prime Minister Rabin regarding recognition of the PLO in 1993, are good examples of the inadequacy of the continuum to provide precise indication of the behavior of the politician in a given situation. Begin had been associated with tough, nationalist stands throughout twenty-nine years of parliamentary opposition. Upon achieving power and after Sadat's visit in November 1977, Begin altered many of his views. Rabin was a leader of the tough Labor Party opposition to negotiating with the PLO because it was a terrorist organization. Feelings were so intense that at one point it was made illegal for an Israeli to have contact with the PLO or any of its members.

A fourth problem of the left-right continuum is the difficulty in determining what a party's position is on a given issue. In the 1970s and for much of the 1980s the larger parties refrained from clearly stating ideological positions in order to include diverse elements. The two biggest groupings, the Likud and the Labor-Mapam Alignment, were composed of separate and autonomous political parties. Often the platforms of the Herut and Liberal parties (or the Labor Party and Mapam) were not identical. There was great pressure to generalize ideological positions and dilute their specific meaning.

A good example of this is the party platforms prior to the 1969 elections, which took place after the Six-Day War. *Alignment:* Until peace comes, our forces will remain on all the cease-fire lines. . . . Israel will never return to the armistice lines used before the Six-Day War. . . . Additional settlements will be established in the border areas. *Gahal:* Our security requirements in peace treaties with Arab states, stemming from our experience, demand our ruling in areas that served as the basis of our enemies' aggression. . . . Large-scale Jewish settlement . . . must be given priority in the development plans of the state. . . . *NRP:* . . . will work for continued large-scale, speedy urban and rural settlements in the liberated areas.

The most striking feature of these excerpts on security policy from the platforms of the country's three strongest parties was their similarity. Both the Alignment and Gahal platforms were straining toward the middle. Within the Labor Party there was considerable difference of opinion regarding security policy, Abba Eban and Pinhas Sapir supposedly being much more dovelike than Moshe Dayan, Yigal Allon, or Golda Meir. As if these differences were not enough, the platform committee had to attend to the demands of Mapam, the group farthest to the left in the Alignment. That the final document turned out as tough as it did caused much ill feeling among Mapam members. The possibility of returning territory (the word "retreat" is never used) is only mentioned in a positive form: "until peace comes, our forces will remain on all the cease-fire lines." But the next sentence, "Israel will never return to the armistice lines used before the Six-Day War" quickly recovers the momentarily lost initiative of the more hawklike.

It used to be that you could tell a person's position by whether he or she talked about the "conquered territories" or the "liberated territories." Both Gahal and the NRP used the phrase "liberated territories." The Alignment talked only of the "territories." When speaking of settlements, it could not bring itself to use the word "territories"; instead, it stated that "additional settlements will be established in the border areas." Gahal, too, strained a bit toward the center, but not nearly as hard. Those looking for the statement "not one inch of land will be returned" will look in vain. Deleting this line was in deference to the more centrist Liberal Party, many of whose leaders became uncomfortable when categoric language was used.

By the 1980s some movement was evident. The Likud government spoke only of Judea and Samaria instead of the West Bank territories, thereby annexing them semantically. The Alignment approved a platform calling for territorial concessions for a true peace, placing themselves in firm opposition to the Likud government. The NRP, after losing half its electoral strength in 1981, attempted to moderate some of its more extreme statements on the territories. This was difficult because the mood of the times shifted, from more militant in the 1980s to more conciliatory in the 1990s.

All these changes indicate the election platform is a compromise among the factions of a party and the constituent parts of a list. On very difficult issues the surest formula is not to mention them. According to an old saying, party platforms are like train platforms—something to get in on, not to stand on. In addition, a party platform does not commit the party in any legal sense. If a party wishes, it may ignore part of its platform entirely. A good example of this is the recurring commitment of the platform of the Democratic Party in the United States to move its embassy to Jerusalem from Tel Aviv. Just as consistently as the platform has promised it, Democratic presidents have ignored it, or even opposed it, as in the case of President Clinton's reaction to a Republican-sponsored decision in the U.S. Senate.

A fifth problem relates to how the continuum is perceived and understood by the electorate. In Israel, as in other countries, only people with high levels of sophistication in conceptualizing politics concern themselves with the left-right continuum. For most people, politics is a matter of parties and leaders. The images of parties and leaders are no less important than ideological issues of left and right. Alternately, some think of politics in terms of specific questions facing the polity or in terms of the ability of a party to satisfy group demands. The left-right continuum in Israel often fills a political function more than an ideological one.

Left-Right and Political Attitudes

The left-right continuum is a useful shorthand for the initiated to understand and order the political scene.[4] But it is misleading to expect the parties on our man-made continuum to conform in their behavior to our expectations. For most people, left and right are political labels used to make sense of the party system. The left-right label is part of one's political vocabulary, of one's political education. It is learned the way one learns about other labels, being Jewish or being Israeli. Behavior reinforces this labeling. The process seems to work this way: having voted Likud and learned that it corresponds with "right," one identifies with that label. Most people do not start by being for a certain policy, identifying that policy with left or right and then searching for the appropriate party. The left-right label seems to be related and probably stems from one's party identification.

The best evidence of this is to consider the distribution of left and right in the Israeli population over the past thirty-five years. Israel is often seen as being evenly split between left and right, and having drifted to the right over the years; the data presented in table 12.1 (p. 358) bear this out. The right increased almost fivefold, from 8 percent in 1962 to 16 percent in

1969 to 39 percent in 1996. Not only has the answer become more legitimate in the system, so too has the word. When the Israel Institute of Applied Social Research ran a pretest before the 1962 study, the "right" political trend was found to be so discredited that it was decided to substitute the political party of the right, Herut, in the questionnaire. The final version of the question had as its extremes "Marxist left" and "Herut" with "moderate left" and "center" as the other two categories. By 1969 this problem had disappeared, and the terms left and right were used for the extreme responses. By 1981, some studies began splitting the "right" response into "right" and "moderate right" because the distribution had so shifted over time.

If the left-right continuum were a representation of ideological differences in Israel, we would expect that as the right grows, so too should the distribution on attitudes identified with a "right" ideology. The fascinating finding is that although the "right" response has become more prevalent and the parties of the right more prominent, there is a stability of attitude over time in the society. For example, 90 percent in 1969 favored returning none of the territories or only a small part, and 92 percent in 1981, after most of Sinai had been returned. Using wording more relevant to the political situation of the 1980s and 1990s, the evidence of a population split down the middle on this issue, and relatively stable, is striking (see table 12.1).

Since the mid-1980s, there is evidence this attitudinal shift has also become more capitalist in economic matters, as might be expected from the "right" label. Almost 60 percent favored socialism in the surveys through 1984; since then the range is 40–45 percent. Government centralization is often decried, and there is much talk of the economy becoming liberalized, and this has begun to be reflected in this response.

What has happened in Israel over the last few decades is a process of political change followed by ideological change. The growth of the Likud and the growth of the right must be understood as a reaction to the years of dominance of the Labor-Mapam Alignment and the left. The terms are important as labels but not necessarily as instructors of ideological content. Likud means not only "right," it also means non-Alignment and hence non-"left." Left-right has a greater importance in its labeling function than in its ability to instruct regarding ideological questions.

Most people do not impute issue meaning to left and right. When asked at the beginning of the 1980s about the meaning of left and right, 70 percent did not respond. Of the 30 percent who did respond, the farther to the right one was, the more likely there was to be a response. This seemed to indicate that the former dominant left was in retreat ideologically as well as politically and that its adherents were less equipped to confront the

TABLE 12.1
LEFT-RIGHT TENDENCY, 1962–96 (IN PERCENTAGES)

	1962	1969	1973	1977	1981	1984	1988	1992	1996
Left-right label[a]									
Left	31	6	3	4	4	5	8	10	12
Moderate left		19	19	14	13	18	18	20	14
Center	23[b]	26[b]	33[b]	29	39	21	11	18	16
Moderate right				28[b]	19	23	24	20	23
Right	8	16	23		14	15	25	22	16
Religious	5	6	7	6	6	2	4	3	3
No interest in politics; no answer	33	27	15	19	6	15	10	7	6
Economy									
Capitalist	7	10	—	11	10	7	21	21	17
More capitalist	19	24	—	18	25	28	32	35	36
More socialist	39	38	—	31	40	50	28	29	34
Socialist	15	19	—	25	20	6	13	11	11
No answer	20	9	—	15	5	9	7	4	2
Return the territories									
None	—	38[c]	31	41	50	41	36	[d]	[e]
A small part	—	52	52	43	42	44	43		
Most	—	5	10	7	4	6	9		
All	—	1	2	7	3	8	10		
No answer	—	4	5	2	1	2	2		
Sample size:	1,170	1,314	1,939	1,372	1,249	1,259	873	1,192	1,168

SOURCES: From 1962 through 1977, the surveys were conducted by the Israel Institute of Applied Social Research; from 1981 through 1992 by the Dahaf Research Institute; in 1996 by Modi'in Ezrachi.

NOTE: — = not asked.

a. The question was "With which political tendency do you identify?" The first responses were suggested to the respondent, the "religious" and "No interest in politics; no answer" responses were not. In 1962, "Left" and "Right" were not used; "Marxist left" and "Herut" were offered in their place.

b. This response category was not offered.

c. The 1969 "return the territories question" was posed in August to a sample of 380 respondents.

d. Between 1984 and 1992 the maximum amount of territory Israel should give up in order to achieve a peace settlement was probed using two questions, the first asking the preference among return of territories for peace, annexation, or status quo, and a follow-up question forcing a choice from those who chose the "status quo" option. The results were as follows, in percentages:

	1984	1988	1992
Annex	23	26	25
Leave as is, but if necessary annex	30	23	16
Leave as is	2	2	2
Leave as is, but if necessary return for peace	10	10	7
Return for peace	35	40	50

e. In 1996, a seven-point agreement-disagreement question asked about returning territories for peace: 43 percent of the answers were in the three "agree" categories, 42 percent were in the three "disagree" categories, and 14 percent were in the middle category.

issues than the more assertive voters of the right. The political pendulum in Israel then was swinging in their favor, and the respondents of the right were more prone to talk about it. These data are similar to findings for the United States, Britain, and other countries regarding the prevalence and function of ideology and the left-right continuum.[5]

That political labels should fill a function of veto by pointing out whom we want to avoid is not surprising to observers who know the nature of political communication in Israel. This function was filled by the left in the period of dominance in the prestate and early state eras when the left was widely considered as the appropriate legitimate authority in the system. As that basic understanding was being reconsidered, the term "right" filled the role of identifying the bad guys (the left) as much as it does of identifying the group with which one might wish to identify (the right). The prime motivation was the identification with one of the political parties; from that flowed identification with one of the political labels.

In a basic sense all politics in Israel are ideological. Messages are packaged in ideological containers; codewords are frequently attached. "Isms" and phrases such as fascism, socialism, Revisionism, and the basic values of the labor movement abounded in the campaigns of the 1980s, yet for many of the voters they were empty sounds. The style of Israeli political communication has overshadowed the importance of the substance.

Ideological differences among the large parties in Israel have been proclaimed regularly, but in reality these differences seemed to have diminished over time. Elections have turned on party image and leader popularity, with ideological themes underscoring these more individualistic features. Attitudes on the future of the territories predict voting behavior well in the 1990s, and they predict left-right labeling. Public opinion in Israel is structured primarily along political lines, and only then along class lines. The appeal of a party or a leadership group could possibly bring about change in the public stand regarding policy. This is more likely, it seems, than the possibility of class or group interests emerging to redefine public policy. This gives the political leaders enormous leverage. They can change policy, if they so decide, secure in the knowledge that they will be able to swing public opinion to their position if they present it properly; in short, if they lead. No less important, they can retain the status quo. They can make a case for that position as well.

At the end of the 1980s, Israeli politicians and public opinion were rather hard-line regarding returning the territories and opposing the establishment of a Palestinian state. After the Rabin-Peres decision to enter negotiations with the Palestine Liberation Organization (PLO), there seemed to be a clear difference between the parties. But when in power after the 1996 elections, the Likud found itself constrained by the policy initiatives undertaken by Labor. There seemed to be no political necessity or ideological will to do otherwise.

For the first decades of Israeli history, with the dominance of the left-of-center party, Israeli public opinion supported a pragmatic policy of military strength and political flexibility. After the 1967 war, policy and public opinion were intransigent regarding the territories (although Sinai was returned to the Egyptians during that period). In these years, a hard-line nationalist platform emerged: Rabbi Meir Kahane was perhaps its most extreme representative, advocating the forcible transfer of Arabs from the territories occupied by Israel. Other parties, such as Tehiya, Tzomet, and Moledet, echoed some of these positions. But support for conciliation and negotiation increased in those years. The 1980s and 1990s saw an almost even division in public opinion and in political power between the two major camps in Israeli politics. When the turn came in Oslo in 1993, it was the political will of the leaders that brought about the shift in policy, bolstered by the split in opinion.

Elites decide as they see fit, with little or no accountability or threat of reprisal from an incensed public. Even with an informed, interested, and articulate citizenry, as in Israel, politicians are free to do as they choose when the distribution of opinion is relatively balanced. Under these conditions, "elections are virtual lotteries because the two sides cancel each other out,"[6] and precisely because of the balanced division of public opinion, the elite can do as it sees fit.

Elections can thus foster experiments in public policy, with no direct relationship to the party platform or the campaign. This has happened in Israeli elections and is the root explanation of why the fit between public opinion and policy is less than good. The vote is the important ingredient in determining who will decide, but not in determining the direction policy will take. Begin, Rabin, and Netanyahu are all examples of this principle. An election is sometimes portrayed as a referendum regarding an important issue; however, that portrayal is almost always inappropriate.

Values

Politics is conflict over what to decide (and who should make the decision) about desirable things that are in short supply, such as power, money, or status. Often we think of politics in terms of competing ideologies. But politics is often more accurately portrayed as competition among cherished values.[7] That is the real stuff of politics.

The concept of right and left is a conflictual way of thinking about politics. Concentrating on various values instead of one overall ideology represents a way of thinking about politics that does not expect or require people to develop an integrated system of beliefs. Instead the focus is on discrete values, which, like ideology, may provide the vehicle to explain reality and to posit standards of desirability. These values serve as shortcuts to guide people's interpretation of a complex and changing world, but they may or may not be connected, integrated, or coherent.

This approach recommends itself because values in political situations often conflict, and tradeoffs are required. Many societal values are consensual, that is, they are supported by almost all members of a society or at least by a large majority. People vary on the way they rank a value when it is in conflict with another cherished value, rather than how much they support that idea in isolation. The order of priorities becomes the bone of contention.

The basic values in conflict in Israeli political culture are (1) Israel as a Jewish state; (2) Eretz (the land of) Israel; (3) democracy; and (4) peace. Each of these may an be end in itself or may be a means to achieve other ends. In principle, for example, most Israeli Jews might support a value if it were cost-free, but in reality tradeoffs must be made. Thus, for many on the right and among religious Jews (but not only them), greater Israel is an end in itself. For others, it is a means for achieving peace and security, or for absorbing more immigrants. Each of the values considered may be instrumental for some, serving as a means for achieving another value, or it may be an ultimate value, an end in itself, for others.

These four values are enunciated in Israel's declaration of independence, which embeds the basic values of Israeli society. While not legally binding, the declaration has great symbolic importance. The right of the Jewish people to its homeland embodies the Zionist justification for the establishment of the State of Israel. This value of Israel as a Jewish state is the most pervasive one in the culture. In a 1988 survey, 97 percent said that it was important or very important that the Jewish character of the state be preserved (that there be a Jewish majority).[8] Eretz Israel is referred to in the opening section of the declaration, thus binding the notion of the national home closely to the land, and is a value deeply ingrained in the Zionist ethos of national revival.

Democracy in the broadest sense of equality of political rights is also generally supported, at least in the abstract, with the courts bolstering these rights in principle and in practice over the years. In the same survey, 82 percent said it was important or very important that the democratic character of the state be maintained (i.e., that every resident have equal rights). Peace is a common aspiration, reiterated by politicians, sung about in popular songs. Being accepted among the nations of the world, and in particular by states of the region, was always one of the major goals of Zionism and of Israeli policy, and an important dimension of Israel's national interest.[9] After almost half a century of independence, peace seemed progressively more feasible.

The issue of the territories is the basic dividing line in Israeli politics because of the tradeoffs it involves. If it were not for the indigenous Palestinian population (the "demographic problem") and international pressure, and if holding on to the territories were not perceived as an obstacle to peace, most Israeli Jews would prefer a greater Israel (the post-1967 war boundaries) to the smaller Israel which was militarily more vulnerable. If Israel could keep these territories with no price attached, just about every Israeli Jew would support that situation.

But to opt for a greater Israel means either to restrict the political rights of the Arabs of the territories or to face the possibility of a country without a Jewish majority, or perhaps to raise the probability of war. To prefer a democratic state with a Jewish majority makes keeping the territories less attractive. To want a greater Israel with a Jewish majority would mean that the demographic imbalance between the Jewish and Arab populations would have to be redressed. Some support the notion of transfer, others think denying civil and political rights to the Arabs of the territories makes the issue unthinkable, while others believe that large Jewish immigration would solve the problem.

Peace would be possible, many on the left argue, only with returning the territories and avoiding the need to deal with the Arabs under Israel's military rule. Activists on the right argue that the strategic depth provided by the territories, coupled with massive Jewish immigration, would strengthen the state, would offset the demographic advantage of the Arabs in the territories, and would be the best recipe for a low probability of hostilities. The permutations are many; the substance of these tradeoffs is the stuff of contemporary Israeli politics.

The tensions and dilemmas around these values are not new; they have accompanied Zionism from the onset.[10] Consider the following value priorities as expressed by Israeli Jews in 1996. Most Israeli Jews would be happy to achieve each one of them, if they did not conflict with achieving other goals. Were they to be observed in a political vacuum, one would learn little; much more will be understood by considering them in terms of competing values in specific contexts.

Respondents were asked the following question: "In thinking about the various paths along which Israel can develop, there seem to be four important values which clash to some extent, and which are important to different degrees to various people: Israel with a Jewish majority, Greater Israel, a democratic state (with equal political rights to all), and peace (that is, a low probability of war). Among these four values, which is the most important to you?" The "Jewish majority" was presented since it seemed closest to the original Zionist idea, as well as to common usage in Israel, although competing specifications of a Jewish state, such as a state where Jewish culture and tradition are dominant, or a theocratic state where the Torah is the law of the land, are also possible. The Hebrew term for "Greater Israel" is commonly recognized and widely used in political discourse. Democracy was conceived of as equal political rights for all, including the franchise to Arabs under Israel's jurisdiction. Peace was explained as a situation in which there was a low probability of war, so as to set it clearly apart from more formal aspects of peace agreements. The respondents were asked to rank all four values, and they had no apparent problem with the task.

Two values—Jewish majority and peace—were ranked high by a vast majority of the population, and the two other values—a greater Israel and democracy—ranked generally low (see figure 12.1).[11] A Jewish majority was mentioned first by 37 percent of the sample, with peace close behind at 34 percent. The other two values, democracy and a greater Israel, were mentioned as the first priority by 18 percent and 11 percent, respectively. The last two values were directly related to the political disposition of the territories—a greater Israel related to the land, democracy related to the citizen rights of the people on the land. Forced to choose among the four goals, neither a greater Israel nor democracy was high on the priority lists of most respondents.

These results accentuate how superficial it is to portray politics in Israel as a struggle between the camp that wants to keep the territories and the camp that is willing to give them up if it would lead to a secure Jewish state. The picture that emerges is of a population firmly supporting a Jewish majority in their state, with a very strong desire for peace. Keeping Israel Jewish by maintaining in it a Jewish majority is a major value of political consensus. Peace is, too, though to a lesser extent. The values of land and democracy are less important. While there is consensus regarding democracy as an abstract principle, and a greater Israel could also be an agreed-upon goal, their collective lower priority and contemporary political circumstances make them the substance of debate and conflict. Indeed, they have been transposed into divisive position issues in Israeli politics.

This picture is made even clearer when considered by vote for the prime minister in 1996 (see figure 12.2). Netanyahu's supporters ranked Jewish majority very high and peace and a greater Israel at a lower level. For Peres's voters, peace was the highest priority by far, followed by Jewish majority and democracy. The sum of these differences (see figure 12.1) meant that both candidates could talk in terms of a Jewish majority and peace, while toning down discussions of democracy and a greater Israel. The consensus issues of Jewish majority and peace could be used in every

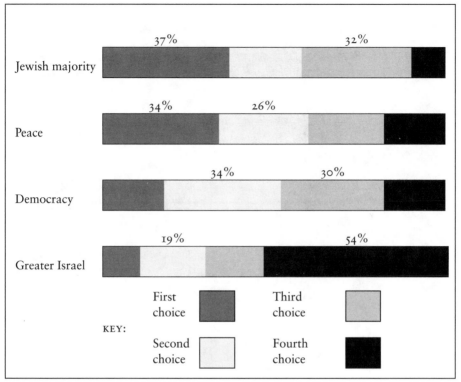

FIGURE 12.1
VALUE CHOICES (ENTIRE POPULATION), 1996

campaign speech, while stressing a greater Israel was good policy for Netanyahu and stressing democracy was good policy for Peres only when they were speaking with loyalists.

Political Communication

A free press is a major prerequisite of a democratic system and Israel's record on this score is a good one. The dilemmas posed by the difficult security problems Israel faces make its tradition of having a lively press even more impressive. Two conflicting sets of priorities lie at the base of the dilemma. On the one hand, there are the values of free speech, freedom of the press, and the right of the people to know. All of these are basic democratic rights. On the other hand, there is the legitimate demand to prevent publication of information that will be of use to the enemy. Some cases are clear-cut: divulging information about troop strength and location may

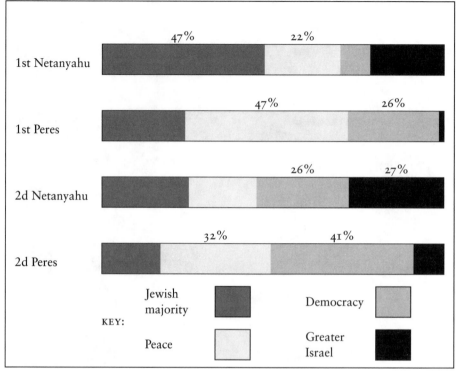

FIGURE 12.2

VALUE PRIORITIES FOR NETANYAHU AND PERES VOTERS, 1996

legitimately be suspended; quoting an opposition politician who thinks the government's policy is wrong must be allowed. The difficulties are at the borderline: should stories that morale is low or that emigration is rising or that a minister says he has no faith in the senior army command be permitted or not?

The answer to the question of a free press in Israel is difficult; its implementation is even more so, since freedom of the press is not safeguarded by constitutional or legal provisions. On the contrary, almost all the legislation enacted enables the prevention of publishing or broadcasting news. In fact, the Israeli press operates freely because the authorities allow it to do so through voluntary arrangements worked out by them and the editors of the largest daily newspapers.

The State Security Ordinance (Emergency Regulations) is the legal basis for the military censorship of news published in Israel or abroad that could "endanger the defense of Israel, or the well-being of the public, or public order." Appeals may be heard by a special committee of three, representing the press, the military, and the general public. While unanimous decisions are final, majority decisions can be appealed to the chief of staff. The Press Ordinance of 1933, issued during the Mandate and still in effect, requires licensing of all newspapers and printing houses by the Interior Ministry. The license may be revoked for incitement "endangering public order."[12]

The agreement between the defense minister and the Committee of Newspaper Editors broke down in 1992 when the editor of *Haaretz* withdrew from the agreement because of the military censor's decisions regarding the paper's coverage of an accident. In 1995 the editor of *Yediot Aharonot* also withdrew from the voluntary agreement. A proposed law regulating newspapers was opposed by the editors, and in 1996 a new voluntary agreement was reached. Under it, the rules would apply to all newspapers, including Arab ones, and editors would be allowed to appeal decisions of the censor to the High Court of Justice.

Israelis consume news at very high rates. More than three-fourths of the Jewish population over the age of fourteen read a newspaper at least one day a week, and about two-thirds read one daily; almost half the population read two or more papers daily.[13] Before the 1996 elections, 8 percent claimed they read more than one paper every day, 45 percent said they read a paper every day, and an additional 20 percent said they did so two or three times a week. Only 6 percent stated that they never read a newspaper.

The Hebrew press is active and competitive. The two largest newspapers are the mass-circulation afternoon tabloids *Yediot Aharonot* and *Maariv.* In 1995, *Yediot* had more than half the market, *Maariv* about a quarter.[14] Both papers are independently owned and present a wide range of opinions in their signed columns. The editorial tone of both papers tends to be right of center. The important Hebrew morning paper is *Haaretz,* with about 7 percent of the market. It is probably the most prestigious of Israel's papers, blending liberal values and pragmatic Zionism in its editorial columns.

Newspapers affiliated with political parties were much more important during the Yishuv and in the early state years.[15] They provided the political line to activists and served as important channels of communication among segments of the party. With statehood, their partisan function was eclipsed by the more general mass-circulation papers. These appealed to the growing market and downplayed political and ideological matters. The most prominent party paper was *Davar,* the Histadrut newspaper, renamed *Davar Rishon* in its last period. *Davar* steadily lost readership, even in Histadrut strongholds such as the kibbutz movement. In the mid-1970s its circulation was 45,000 newspapers, and that fell to 25,000 in the mid-1980s, and to 10,000 in the mid-1990s, less than 1 percent of the public. In recent years, its editorial staff has been increasingly free from political in-terference, but the newspaper was always heavily subsidized by the Hista-drut and was identified with the Labor Party. With Labor's loss of hege-mony in the Histadrut, and the emergence of a leadership dedicated more to labor unionism and the bottom line, *Davar* published its last issue in 1996, some seventy years after its founding.

Newspapers depend on good reporting, and reporters are only as good as their sources. Even reporters for independent newspapers must en-ter tacit agreements with politicians to receive information. The politicians' interest is to have his name in print, preferably with his point of view as well. The reporter wants to know what is really going on. Symbiotic rela-tions are bound to develop. And in Israel, a small country where everyone who counts knows everyone else, and a country with a competitive press and a news-attentive population, these symbiotic relations are useful to both reporter and politician. Information or opinions that it would be in-appropriate to have the minister reveal can be released through the friendly reporter. Such revelations may be designed for public consumption or as part of the intragovernment or intraparty battle taking place at the mo-ment, or for international targets.

Leaks are generated the same way. Reporters do not create leaks from government meetings or secret deliberations; reporters are fed leaks by minis-ters who take part in these consultations and have an interest in having infor-mation that may be helpful to them or harmful to their opponents brought to public attention. Periodically there is a public uproar regarding the secrecy of deliberations and the lack of professional discipline on the part of the news-papers. The real culprit is, of course, the minister who provides the informa-tion. In the debate over the role of the press in the 1982 Lebanese war, for in-stance, it was maintained that the antigovernment position expressed by the Alignment opposition was detrimental to the morale of the troops and the ci-vilian population. Reports of dissent within the government itself were even more harmful to public morale. Note that the source of these reports was not the opposition but members of the government.

Preventing leaks is a matter of concern to all governments. In the 1950s Ben-Gurion resigned the premiership over leaks in his government and returned to the job only after extracting support for legislation making all cabinet proceedings secret. That was not as successful a solution as the arrangement worked out in 1966 in which deliberations of the Cabinet Se-curity Committee were defined as "state secrets," which meant that unau-thorized publication could be punished as severe espionage.[16] In the 1970s, a practice developed of declaring cabinet meetings special sessions of the Security Committee, thus achieving total secrecy. This practice can easily be abused. The Begin government attempted, unsuccessfully, to consider settlement policy under these total blackout rules. The line that protects the government's right to keep its secrets safe is also the line that may infringe on the public's right to know. The balance is a difficult one, but one that is crucial to maintain in a democracy.

Radio and television operated under the Israel Broadcasting Authority, set up in 1965, which was patterned on the British Broadcasting Corporation. Before the law was passed, radio was located in the prime minister's office (television did not yet exist), and political interference in broadcasting was not unknown. The Broadcasting Authority brought much more autonomy to the world of the airwaves but did not divorce programming and news broadcasting from the political sphere. The plenum of the Authority has thirty-one members, the board seven. The plenum meets three times a year; the board weekly. Members are appointed by the government according to a party key that assures coalition control of the Authority, at least at the moment of appointment. The British model calls for nonpolitical appointments based on ability, professional expertise, and independence; the Israeli system clearly deviates from that norm. The director-general is appointed by the government in Israel and by the board in Britain. Again, political rather than professional considerations predominate.

The composition of the Authority and its exposure to the political process meant that the staff had to keep political considerations in mind, even if it was not given clear-cut political dictates. Deliberations within the Authority often reflected the political debate in the country. Members from parties participating in the government coalition were likely to argue that the Authority emphasized negative aspects of life in Israel, while its mandate should call for encouraging the public by emphasizing the positive. Opposition party members were likely to be critical of reporting they perceived as propaganda for the party in power. Who should be interviewed, how much weight should be given to a story, and what is news were not only professional questions of radio or television journalism. In Israel they were very important political questions, and they still are.

The Broadcasting Authority law afforded Israeli television and radio a monopoly on news broadcast in Israel, and then the competition began. The commercial channel was set up by law in 1990 after intense political maneuvering; the law calls for the division of broadcast time among three equal franchise groups, each broadcasting for two days, with joint broadcasts on Saturday and a shared news department. The franchise is for four years; at least 51 percent of the controlling interests must be in the hands of resident Israeli citizens.

The three groups that won the franchises are controlled by three families prominent in newspaper publishing, raising serious issues of overlapping ownership and control. The Moses family of *Yediot,* the Nimrodi family of *Maariv,* and the Schocken family of *Haaretz,* as well as banking interests and other investors, are leaders in the organizations that received the franchises. In addition to commercial and economic interests, political interests are close to the surface. The prime minister, education minister, and minister of communications have formal responsibility for the various public broadcasters, including educational television and the army radio station, the second channel and the cable channels.

The Broadcasting Authority is funded by a user's fee; Channel 2 is funded commercially; cable users pay the companies directly. The authority allows sponsorship of productions, not quite commercials, but close. Cable stations have no commercials—yet. Netanyahu has called for the privatization of public broadcasting partially because this is in tune with his economic view, and partially because of the feeling on the part of leaders of the right that the media are a stronghold of the left. The opponents of privatization fear that having only commercial broadcasting will deprive the minority of higher-quality art and entertainment, to say nothing of more in-depth coverage of worthy topics.[17]

The second channel has been very successful both commercially and in drawing a larger share of the viewing population than the Broadcasting Authority's Channel 1. Politicians are anxious to appear on the popular shows of these channels, and some of them have developed into raucous debating opportunities. The boisterousness and energy of these shows are an accurate reflection of the political debate in Israel—loud, rude, energetic, and unlikely to convince anyone to change a position previously held.

Competition and diversity are now a fact in television and radio, and Israel has undergone a revolution in the last decades in this regard. Where there was one public broadcasting authority, one television channel, and two radio stations (including one run by the IDF), there is now a proliferation of channels and stations.[18] In addition to the public authority's Channel 1, there is commercial Channel 2, an education channel, cable, and regional outlets. The same is true of radio. In the early 1980s, 95 percent of all television viewers watched the evening news on the government authority's channel;[19] in 1994 the parallel figure was 30 percent. It was not that Israelis were less interested or less well informed but that they now had a choice about what and how to consume their news. There was variety in what could be consumed, and there was variety in reports of who watched what. In April 1996, a Channel 2 survey showed that 41 percent of television watchers tuned in to the news on the second channel, 18 percent watched the news on the public authority's Channel 1, and an additional 41 percent were watching nonnews cable shows when the news came on. For the same month, the Channel 1 survey had 31 percent watching the news on its channel, and 15 percent on Channel 2.[20]

Israel is widely covered by foreign journalists; foreign television and radio signals are received in Israel, and foreign publications are distributed without restriction. Other points of view are available, and this can be important in a crisis situation. When the security forces prohibited coverage of the early phases of the 1982 Lebanese war, international coverage originated from the Lebanese side of the battle lines. Inevitably reporters saw the war, and reported it, through the perspective of the Palestinian forces and the Lebanese civilians. No countervailing reporting was permitted at first. This inflicted severe damage on Israel in Western public opinion.

In internal politics Israeli journalists can be as inquisitive and courageous—although few are—as any in the world. In most security areas they are more restrained than foreign journalists. This stems from national loyalty, a desire to maintain good relations with sources, and a self-imposed mechanism of self-censorship. Foreign correspondents usually work without these restraints, sometimes leaving the impression that Israeli journalists are lackeys of the government. In the government's attempt to win the battle of public opinion it must walk the hazardous line between controlling the news and those who report it and respecting the right of the people—and the world—to know. The more controversial the policy that lies at the heart of the story, the harder this dilemma is.

Public opinion is a phantom often worshipped by politicians and the press. Public opinion is of course more than simply a computation of the attitudes of members of the population. Public opinion must be understood in terms of the distribution of opinions within the population, the intensity with which they are held, their stability, and the organizational means used to translate the opinions into actions that will have an impact on policy.[21] Demonstrators outside Mapai Party headquarters in 1967 are said to have had an impact on the decision to appoint Moshe Dayan minister of defense before the Six-Day War. The mass rally of hundreds of thousands in the summer of 1982 preceded the government's decision to reverse itself and set up a commission of inquiry into the events that occurred in the Palestinian refugee camps of Sabra and Shatilla in Beirut. These were expressions of "public opinion" but they were also carefully organized demonstrations in support of ideas frequently expressed in the press.

In the era of individualism, television has become a major focus of the electoral campaign. In the past the mass rally and the visits of politicians to the neighborhood or place of work were ways that the public was exposed to competing politicians. And yet, even in the 1996 campaign, the rule persisted that no candidate's picture could be shown on television during the month preceding the election in order to prevent giving unfair advantage to one party. None of the politicians liked this rule, but they preferred living with it than risking the advantage that the other side might win. But the agreement worked out before the 1996 elections also stipulated that it would not apply in future elections.

Broadcast time for the parties on television and radio during the campaign is provided free of charge and is allocated in proportion to the party's strength in the outgoing Knesset. Each list competing was provided with a base of ten minutes on television, with six additional minutes for each member of the outgoing Knesset. Thus the Likud and Labor had a good deal of free television time, while small and new parties had very little.

The impact of the media on the electorate is not great, if we believe the report of survey respondents. In 1996 about a quarter of the population said they viewed most of the party political broadcasts, compared to about a half in 1977. The variety of programming choices available evidently makes the repetitive political broadcasts not very appealing. Yet, the state continues to provide the parties with free prime time for their political commercials. Only 2 percent said that the broadcasts would help them very much in deciding how to vote, a quarter said somewhat, and 76 percent said not at all. Comparable numbers in 1981 had television helping 7 percent very much and a third somewhat, while 60 percent said that it did not help at all. When similar questions were asked about newspaper and radio commercials, these figures were similar, if a bit more favorable to the impact of television.

Opinion polls have proliferated in the last few decades, and they now dominate much of the campaign. In the 1969 elections, three dailies reported polls, and the total number of reports on polls was sixteen. In 1992, fifteen dailies reported on polls, and there were 421 such reports.[22] More than half the respondents follow the polls, and 42 percent believe them. More than a third believe that people are influenced by the polls in determining how to vote. When asked about the proposal to ban the publication of the polls in the preelection period, only 29 percent agreed.

Newspaper advertising is extensive during the campaign. A major party can limit a paper's income by not advertising or advertising little in it. The Likud never emphasized advertising in *Davar,* the paper identified with the Labor Party. But in the 1981 elections it also advertised very little in *Haaretz* as a protest against that paper's editorial policy, and evidently under the assumption that readers of *Haaretz* were unlikely to vote for the Likud or would be exposed to its campaign in one of the mass-circulation afternoon papers.

Political Socialization

Political socialization refers to the process in which values important to the political system are internalized. The way a person responds to authority, the way he (or she) perceives his responsibility toward the collectivity, whether he sees himself as active or passive in the political system—these are all topics affected by one's political socialization. More party-specific and issue-specific dimensions are also involved: For whom should I vote? What is my attitude regarding the territories?

Political socialization studies place great emphasis on the formative years of childhood, adolescence, and early adulthood in determining one's political outlook and later behavior. Any individual is influenced both by early experiences (the primacy hypothesis) and by current political developments and issues (the recency hypothesis). No thorough research has yet been done in Israel to throw light on the primacy/recency argument.[23] There is no doubt that one's primary reference groups in the formative years influence one's political ideas. Most Israelis report that they vote as their families do, and this is true in other countries as well. The exact rate of congruence between the voter and his or her family is difficult to ascertain because "one's family" may be understood to include only spouse or parents or a much more extended group. In 1981 the question was put whether "your family" votes as you do; 55 percent said yes, 25 percent said no, 18 percent reported that they did not know how their family votes. An interesting aspect of this matter points to the independent temperament of Israelis. When the question was phrased in 1988, "Do you think you are influenced by the way members of your family vote?" a much lower agreement rate was recorded: Only 14 percent gave a definite yes, and 55 percent answered with a definite no. The respondent is the leader, and the family acts as he does, not vice versa.

In a multiparty state such as in Israel, intergenerational transmission is clearest when considering the side in the left-right division, less so when discussing the party group, and least when looking at the actual party voted for. Raphael Ventura found that 81 percent of the respondents voted for the same left or right side as did their father, that 76 percent voted for the same party group (left, center, religious, right), and that only 52 percent voted for the same party. This finding held for mothers too, and for the voting patterns of married respondents with their spouses.[24]

Schools and the youth culture are important sources of influence in political socialization. The inherited wisdom regarding the Israeli polity is that in the prestate period and in the first years of statehood, schools and youth movements were influential agents in the hands of political parties. As such, it is not surprising that much of the curriculum dealt with material that could be used to strengthen identification with Zionism and with the political struggle that the Yishuv had undertaken.[25] After independence and the changes in the school population as the result of mass immigration, the school curriculum began more fully to represent the complexity of

Israeli society. Schools, especially high schools, were no longer treated as sources of elitist education but stressed public and mass education, and achieved almost universal attendance through the age of sixteen. This change is clear in high school civics instruction. Early texts barely mentioned political parties, although the role of the political party was dominant in almost every sphere of life. Over time, issues that were salient in public life were discussed in the schools, and representatives of various points of view were invited to speak.

The decline of the youth movements in the secular neighborhoods paralleled the general decline of party-related activity after the founding of the state. In the religious areas, the investment in education and youth groups expanded just as it was contracting among the seculars. Alternative frameworks within the school system competed with the particularistic youth movements. Nonetheless, peer-group pressure remains strong among Israeli youth in general. One discerns high levels of conformity in dress, entertainment, leisure-time activity, and lifestyle. These are direct carryovers of the more organized pressures of youth movements, even though fewer youths are organized in these political and ideological movements.[26]

The army service of young Israelis coincides with their entrance into active participation in politics by virtue of their right to vote, and with the period in which historical events can have their strongest ongoing impact on the future political behavior of an individual. A good case in point is the vote of the army in 1973. Some two months after the Yom Kippur War, army voters supported the Likud at a higher rate than did the general population. For some time, the young had tended to support the Likud at higher rates, but evidently the war accelerated this phenomenon.[27] Army service is not only important in terms of specific acts of voting. Perhaps more crucially it is in the army that the young citizen receives his first independent taste of the systems of hierarchy and bureaucracy that are such important features of Israel's political culture. As this service becomes more selective (see chapter 10), the structure of the society will likely change.

The agents of socialization—family, friends, schools, army—are usually crucial for relatively set periods of time. The system also acts to reinforce attitudes and predispositions. The most obvious examples are the national pageants associated with events such as Holocaust Day and Independence Day, which tug at the collective memory and attempt to rekindle feelings of collectivity, shared destiny, and patriotism. More subtle are the presentation of Jewish holidays in ways that reinforce national and patriotic feelings. In these efforts the governing system—ministries, television, and radio—play a central role.[28]

Political socialization leads to the internalization of values and attitudes; it does not occur in a vacuum. It is clear that the family and its social environment will be important conditioners of the results of political socialization. In Israel's varied society, different patterns are obviously at work on different parts of the population. Extreme examples are provided by groups that are relatively isolated from general society, such as kibbutz members and the ultra-Orthodox, who live in relatively hermetic quarters. Both groups seem relatively successful in socializing their younger generations politically if we use community perpetuation and voting patterns as indicators. There are many cases of people leaving these groups and out-voting, but compared to the general society, rates of conformity there are high.

As a country of immigration, Israel has had experience with the resocialization of immigrants, usually adults. Adult immigrants arrive after the early phases of their political socialization are over. Their experiences before arriving in Israel may be thought of as important in determining their political predispositions in Israel. For many, especially Europeans, the various Zionist parties were active and exposed the potential immigrants to the ideological differences among them well before their arrival in the country. For many others, Israel was a place of refuge after the displacements experienced before the move. Ideological issues were not really at stake. For many Sephardim who arrived in Israel, religious motivation and messianic vision were more central than earthly divisions among competing political groups. Almost all these groups came from political systems that lacked democratic traditions. Being introduced to a democratic regime was as novel for Russian immigrants in 1991 as it was for Poles or Moroccans in the 1950s. After carefully studying the political resocialization of Soviet and American immigrants to Israel in the early 1970s, Zvi Gitelman concluded that the process "affects attitudes toward specific issues most, abstract political ideas less, and fundamental orientations to politics least."[29] The children of Israel who wandered in the desert for forty years before entering the promised land were a transitional generation, not capable, we are told, of independence. As Israel approached its fiftieth anniversary of independence, the system was dominated by citizens born in Israel. Those born and raised in Israel have known no other, predemocratic or nondemocratic, experience. Unlike their forefathers, they were born to democracy. They have witnessed the institutionalization of democratic processes in the country and the periodic rotation of power in a peaceful manner from one party to another. And this while the system still faced severe challenges.

Democratic Norms and Political Tolerance

Israelis support abstract democratic norms at high rates. The belief in majority rule, in freedom of expression, in the right of the citizen to criticize the government, and in equality before the law is supported by sizable majorities.[30] But when the question becomes less abstract and more salient in the political context, the rate of democratic support falters. Only about 60 percent agreed that minority-opinion groups should be allowed to operate freely to gain majority support for their positions. The disparity between abstract norms and practical tolerance is seen even more clearly when the problem is concretized by referring to the group least liked by the respondent. In Israel in the 1980s the "least liked" groups most often mentioned were on the political left, especially Arab groups, and outside the Zionist consensus. In 1980, 73 percent of the sample mentioned these. In 1984, after Meir Kahane's election to the Knesset and the growing salience of his presence on the public scene, many more named his group as least liked (22 percent compared to 3 percent in 1980). But still most people (52 percent) mentioned groups on the left, and in particular Arab groups (43 percent). About one-sixth of the respondents identified as least liked the ultra-Orthodox anti-Zionist Neturai Karta. When the abstract norm of free speech was applied to the least-liked group, support for these democratic principles shrank by more than half.

Michal Shamir and John Sullivan found that the overall levels of political tolerance in Israel, while not high, are similar to levels found in the United States in the 1980s.[31] Moreover, they found that in Israel crucial variables such as ethnicity, religiosity, and social status relate to the selection of the least-liked group but not to the level of tolerance. More closely related to political tolerance, they find, are such factors as psychological security, political ideology, and the threat that the least-liked group is perceived to pose to the individual and the political system.

POLITICAL EFFICACY

The feeling that you have influence in the political system, or can have if you choose to, is generally considered an important feature of a democratic system. Israelis are interested in politics, discuss it quite a bit, vote in great numbers, change their government from time to time, and believe in the potency of elections to change policy; but they do not have much faith in their own ability to influence policy (see table 12.2). What is more, this rate has consistently dropped from 1969 to 1981 to 1996. In 1969, 51 percent reported that they had little or no power to influence policy; in 1981, 61 percent said so; and by 1996, those pessimistic responses had risen to 68 percent. When asked specifically about influencing security policy in a 1988 survey, 75 percent answered that they and people like them had little or no power to do so.

Based on the 1969 data, it appeared that the *lower* on the social scale

TABLE 12.2

POLITICAL EFFICACY BY PLACE OF BIRTH,

1969, 1981, 1996

"To what extent can you and people like you influence policy?"

	N	Very much and much	Some-what	Little	Not at all
1969					
Asia or Africa	296	19%	26%	23%	32%
Israel (father Asia or Africa)	89	15	23	26	37
Israel (father Israel)	68	5	39	29	26
Israel (father Europe or America)	213	14	43	29	14
Europe or America	629	15	34	27	24
Total	1,295	15	33	26	25
1981					
Asia or Africa	316	22	18	28	33
Israel (father Asia or Africa)	190	18	22	22	38
Israel (father Israel)	127	10	20	28	43
Israel (father Europe or America)	196	12	26	28	35
Europe or America	321	10	24	29	38
Total	1,150	15	24	24	37
1996					
Asia or Africa	170	9	17	37	37
Israel (father Asia or Africa)	324	11	24	39	26
Israel (father Israel)	186	12	27	39	22
Israel (father Europe or America)	208	8	24	39	28
Europe or America	267	6	23	38	28
Total	1,155	9	23	39	29

the Israeli citizen was, the more likely he or she was to feel efficacious. The Asian- or African-born were most efficacious, the European- or American-born least efficacious. Among those who claimed no efficacy, the pattern was even more striking. Those born in Asia or Africa and their Israeli-born children stood out as being least influential, with the Europeans and Americans, and especially their children, having the lowest nonefficacious rate. Place of birth and level of education are related, with the European groups tending to have more years of education. The inverse relationship between efficacy and social status (as measured by place of birth and education) could be explained by greater sophistication in understanding the essentially closed nature of the Israeli political system. With higher levels of education, the Israeli became more realistic and realized that his chances of penetrating the system were slight.

By 1981 changes had taken place. Efficacy on the whole declined, and it fell most dramatically among those European- or American-born groups that evidently perceived most clearly their loss of power with the ascent of the Likud in 1977. This analysis is strengthened by the relatively high levels of efficacy reported by the Asian- or African-born and their children. The data are especially fascinating since no real change of political power in ethnic terms was evident in Israel between the two time periods. But the high rates of low efficacy, especially among the Israeli-born whose fathers were also Israeli-born, is striking.

By 1996, the overall rate of efficacy had fallen even lower, with the least efficacious still the European- or American-born and those born in Israel of a father born there. Low levels of efficacy are reported by the Asian- or African-born and their children. The most change was shown by those born in Israel of an Israeli-born father. They were the most efficacious, or more accurately, the least nonefficacious. These data provide a mixed message. There has been a decrease in feelings of efficacy, although there has been little evidence of alienation from the system. The fact that the second-generation Israelis feel more nonefficacious than in the past is perhaps an encouraging sign for Israeli democracy.

PARTICIPATION

The tension between high rates of support for democratic norms, high rates of voting turnout, and low levels of efficacy is further complicated by high levels of participation in politics. Israelis have been shown to have high levels of political information, with 87 percent knowing the correct answer (compared with 53 percent in a comparable American sample).[32] Almost two-thirds of respondents knew the number of terrorists involved in an exchange of prisoners deal and the size of defense as a percentage of the government budget. Respondents were also asked about the rights of Arabs in the territories; since most Israeli Jews have no meaningful social contact with Arabs, these questions identify those who had made an effort to gain and retain information on subjects of importance. The two questions asked were "Do the Arabs of Judea, Samaria, and the Gaza Strip have the right to apply to the High Court of Justice?" and "Do the Arabs of Judea, Samaria, and the Gaza Strip have the right to vote in Knesset elections?" The correct answers at the time of the question were yes for the first question and no for the second. More than 55 percent answered the first question correctly, and more than three of four answered the second one correctly.[33]

Compare these levels to the 46 percent of Americans who could name their representative in Congress, and to the 30 percent who knew that the term of a U.S. House member is two years. Only 38 percent knew in 1964 that the Soviet Union was not a member of NATO, and only 23 percent in 1979 knew that the United States and the Soviet Union were the two nations involved in the SALT talks. In 1987, at the height of the Iran-*contra* scandal, only half knew that the United States was supporting the rebels rather than the government in Nicaragua.[34]

Israelis live politics, with 57 percent (compared with 33 percent in the United States) reporting that they talk about politics at least once a week. We have already observed the high rates of news media consumption; more than a third of the respondents before the 1981 elections said they read election advertisements in the newspaper "often." In 1996, 27 percent reported watching the television election broadcasts "every day" or "usually."

Participation is high and is less party based and is now often centered in extraparty protest.[35] More than 20 percent of the Israeli public have participated in demonstrations, a high figure by international standards. In the 1996 survey, 12 percent reported having participated in a demonstration regarding the peace process, 10 percent regarding the Rabin assassination.

The major parties are no longer the vehicle of articulating interests, but the political system remains vibrant and dynamic. Protest groups and movements arise and activists find ways of making their demands felt. The responsiveness of the system is another matter. But even here the data are far from conclusive. Groups such as Gush Emunim and Peace Now, which are formally outside the party system, have certainly had an impact on policy since the 1970s.[36] With the direct elections of the prime minister and the primaries, parties become holding companies for party leaders, an atmosphere that does not encourage specific messages. Therefore, extraparty organization proliferates.[37]

RULE OF LAW

In times of security threat, all democracies reveal a tension between upholding the rule of law and pursuing national security interests. Liberal principles demand respect for the rights of individual liberties and of property; this may seem like a luxurious excess to those who feel that the freedom of the country, if not its very existence, is at stake. These issues emerge strongly in cases in which the government seemed to be ignoring the principle that all government actions must be in accord with the law. Implementing the rule of law is often frustrating since what seems right and necessary at the moment must be deferred owing to abstract principle and legal maneuvering. Whether fighting crime or fighting wars, the temptation to suspend the rule of law is always present.

The choice between the two polar extremes—security on the one hand, and the rule of law on the other—was a stark one, and most situations allowed for obfuscation and interpretation so that a clear choice between two extremes was unnecessary. This dilemma characterized the public debate in Israel, especially in the 1980s and 1990s. In the face of the Lebanon campaign in 1982, and then with the onset of the Intifada in 1987, the relations between the political and military spheres, and the manner in which the military operated within the framework of the rule of law, were closely scrutinized by the public.[38]

The issues were especially complex regarding the Intifada, because the defense forces were not designed or trained for the type of police action called for by the low level of hostilities, almost always consisting of stone-throwing demonstrators, that characterized the early stages of the uprising. The tactics used to repress and deter the Arab population called into question the commitment of the army to the rights of the demonstrators and focused attention on the zealousness of certain officers and soldiers in interpreting the orders of commanders and political leaders.

The cover-up of Shin Bet activities by the authorities seemed to ignore these principles. Government officials at the highest levels denied any wrongdoing.[39] The Israeli public comes down on the side of security interests even if the rule of law must be abridged. Two-thirds of a 1988 national sample chose security interests in a hypothetical choice between the two; 15 percent chose rule of law; the remaining 22 percent were in the middle. But the respondents felt that there has been a shift over time in the direction of the rule of law. Sixty percent said that the present political leadership generally preferred security interests over the rule of law. On the other hand, 70 percent of the same respondents felt that the leadership at the time of independence would have preferred security interests to the rule of law.

This ability to give a tough-minded evaluation of the security situation is an important characteristic of Israeli public opinion. And turnabout is fair play. A good example of that was evident regarding a set of questions asked in 1987 about spies and spying. In the period before the survey was conducted, Jonathan Pollard, an American Jew working for the U.S. Navy, had been convicted of spying for Israel. When asked whether it was "justifiable for Israel to spy on the United States in order to procure information vital for Israel's security," 40 percent of the sample thought that this was acceptable. That percentage is almost identical to those who were asked whether it is "justifiable for the United States to spy on Israel in order to procure information vital for America's security."

STRONG LEADERSHIP

A different question generated when the low-efficacy-high-participation dilemma is considered is whether politicians pay attention to the opinions of the ordinary citizen. In 1969 a quarter of the sample thought they did, a third thought that perhaps they did, and 38 percent were convinced that they did not. By 1981 a picture of greater responsiveness on the part of politicians emerged. Forty-two percent of the sample thought that politicians paid attention to the opinions of ordinary citizens, 23 percent thought that perhaps they did, and a third thought they did not.

The data for both time frames seem to indicate that the Israeli citizen is very attentive and interested in politics; both citizen participation and lack of efficacy seem to be rising. Perhaps one is influenced by the other: The more frustrated you are, the more you participate; and the more you participate, the more frustrated you become. In addition, the citizen seems more convinced than before that the politician is attentive to demands.

The consistent result of this skein of conflicting patterns is the desire for assertive political leadership. This pattern was noted in the 1960s, and it persists. In 1969 some 64 percent of a national sample preferred strong leadership to "all the debates and laws"; by 1981 the percentage was 72 percent. In 1984, after Begin's resignation, it was 50 percent, and by 1988 it was up again, this time to 69 percent. Despite the surface support for democratic norms, there is a stubborn respect for the strong personality in Israeli politics. This explains at least in part the overwhelming popularity of leaders such as Ben-Gurion and Begin, and the support for reforms such as the direct election of the prime minister.

Impressive achievements in military and other areas have fashioned a nation that seems to be impressed with doing, creating, action. The élan of a leader is compared very favorably with the humdrum of the cumbersome parliamentary process with its weak personalities and compromising atmosphere. In comparison with magnetic leadership, the political system seems inefficient; politicians appear to lack imagination and resourcefulness. We must seek an explanation for these findings by noting that Israel is a nervous, energetic nation. The doers—pilot, manager, builder, settler—are rewarded heavily both materially and symbolically. Much of this nervous energy is evident in the army or in more anonymous situations, such as on the highways and in buses. There, Mediterranean friendliness merges with this nervousness to produce a fundamental Israeli characteristic. Hemmed in on many sides by bureaucratic regulation and anxious about terror and possible international isolation, Israelis exhibit a jaunty assertiveness in less formal, less structured situations. Yet the need for guidance, for structuring, and for leadership remains strong.

The resulting syndrome appears paradoxical, but its elements actually mesh nicely. On the surface there is a cockiness and self-assurance about running the country—and many less important issues, for that matter. At a more fundamental level there is also a desire for order, for security, and for leadership. The former provides the semblance of the latter: in place of the desired authority comes an assertive dogmatism. Whether this fundamental insecurity has its roots in the individual psyche or the educational system—or in one of any number of other sources—is unclear. At the public level, however, it provides a very fertile soil for cultivating widespread support for positions associated with leaders invested with legitimacy. Public opinion in Israel is malleable and can be brought to support the dominant position of the appropriate leaders when the proper symbols and appeals are applied.

Notes

Chapter 1. Introduction

All voting statistics are from official publications of the Central Bureau of Statistics. *Haaretz, Maariv,* and *Yediot Aharonot* are Hebrew daily newspapers.

1. Giovanni Sartori, *Parties and Party Systems* (Cambridge, England: Cambridge University Press, 1976); Arend Lijphart, *Democracies in Plural Societies* (New Haven: Yale University Press, 1977); Amos Perlmutter, *Military and Politics in Israel* (London: Cass, 1969); Gabriel Ben-Dor, "Politics and the Military in Israel," in *The Elections in Israel — 1973,* ed. A. Arian (Jerusalem: Jerusalem Academic Press, 1975), 119–44; and S.N. Eisenstadt, *Israeli Society* (London: Weidenfeld and Nicolson, 1967).

2. Arend Lijphart, "Israeli Democracy and Democratic Reform in Comparative Perspective," in *Israeli Democracy under Stress,* ed. Ehud Sprinzak and Larry Diamond (Boulder, Colo.: Lynne Rienner, 1993), 107–23; *Israel in Comparative Perspective,* ed. Michael N. Barnett (Albany: SUNY Press, 1996).

3. See the special edition of *Iyunei Mishpat,* in Hebrew, "A Jewish and Democratic State," 19, no. 3 (1995); Baruch Kimmerling, "State-Society Relations in Israel," in *Israeli Society: Critical Perspectives,* ed. Uri Ram, in Hebrew (Tel Aviv: Breirot, 1993), 328–50; and Rebecca Kook, "Between Uniqueness and Exclusion: The Politics of Identity in Israel," in *Israel in Comparative Perspective,* ed. Michael N. Barnett (Albany: SUNY Press, 1996), 199–225.

4. Yair Auron, *Jewish-Israeli Identity* (Tel Aviv: Sifriat Poalim, 1993); Simon N. Herman, *Jewish Identity in the Jewish State* (Beverly Hills: Sage, 1977), 175, 184.

5. Yaron Ezrahi, "Democratic Politics and Culture in Modern Israel: Recent Trends," in Sprinzak and Diamond, *Israeli Democracy under Stress,* 255–72.

6. Yitzhak Samuel and Ephraim Yuchtman-Yaar, "The Status and Situs Dimensions as Determinants of Occupational Attractiveness," *Quality and Quantity* 13 (1979): 485–501.

7. *Haaretz,* 9 March 1983.

8. On the importance of history in political culture, see Robert D. Putnam, *Making Democracy Work: Civic Traditions in Modern Italy* (Princeton: Princeton University Press, 1993).

Chapter 2. People of Israel

1. Joel Migdal, "Society Formation and the Case of Israel," in *Israel in Comparative Perspective,* ed. Michael N. Barnett (Albany: SUNY Press, 1996), 173–98.

2. Data on Israeli and Jewish population are plentiful. An authoritative source, from which most of the data in this chapter are taken, is Dov Friedlander and Calvin Goldscheider, *The Population of Israel* (New York: Columbia University Press, 1979); and Calvin Goldscheider, *Israel's Changing Society: Population, Ethnicity, and Development* (Boulder, Colo.: Westview Press, 1996). For material on world Jewish statistics, see Roberto Bachi, *Population Trends of World Jewry* (Jerusalem: Institute of Contemporary Jewry, Hebrew University, 1976); and for material on Israeli population statistics, see Roberto Bachi, *The Population of Israel* (Jerusalem: Institute of Contemporary Jewry, Hebrew University, 1977); and the annual *Statistical Abstract*.

3. See, for example, Joseph Gorni, "Changes in the Social and Political Structure of the Second Aliyah, 1904–1914," in Hebrew, *Zionism* 1 (1970): 204–46.

4. Cf. Drora Kass and Seymour Martin Lipset, "America's New Wave of Jewish Immigrants," *New York Times Magazine*, 7 December 1980.

5. Good discussions of the Zionist idea are found in Ben Halpern, *The Idea of the Jewish State* (Cambridge: Harvard University Press, 1961); Arthur Herzberg, *The Zionist Idea* (New York: Meridian, 1960); and Shlomo Avineri, *The Making of Modern Zionism: The Intellectual Origins of the Jewish State* (London: Weidenfeld and Nicolson, 1981).

6. Important treatments of the prestate period include S.N. Eisenstadt, *Israeli Society* (London: Weidenfeld and Nicolson, 1967); and Dan Horowitz and Moshe Lissak, *The Origins of the Israeli Polity: Palestine under the Mandate* (Chicago: University of Chicago Press, 1978). For good overall historical treatments, see Walter Laqueur, *A History of Zionism* (London: Weidenfeld and Nicolson, 1972); and Noah Lucas, *The Modern History of Israel* (New York: Praeger, 1974).

7. Anita Shapiro, *The Frustrated Struggle: Jewish Labor*, in Hebrew (Tel Aviv: Hakibbutz Hameuhad, 1977).

8. See Gorni, "Changes in the Structure of the Second Aliyah."

9. Friedlander and Goldscheider, *The Population of Israel*, 16.

10. See Shabtai Tevet's discussion in his *David's Jealousy: The Life of Ben-Gurion*, vol. 1, in Hebrew (Jerusalem: Schocken, 1977).

11. See Dan Giladi, *The Yishuv at the Time of the Fourth Aliyah (1924–29): Economic and Political Aspects*, in Hebrew (Tel Aviv: Am Oved, 1977).

12. Cited in Friedlander and Goldscheider, *The Population of Israel*, 97.

13. For a thorough discussion, see Zvi Gitelman, *Becoming Israelis: Political Resocialization of Soviet and American Immigrants* (New York: Praeger, 1982).

14. Ruth Westheimer and Steven Kaplan, *Surviving Salvation: The Ethiopian Jewish Family in Transition* (New York: New York University Press, 1992).

15. Tamar Horowitz, "The Absorption of Immigrants from the Former Soviet Union in Israel: Integration or Separatism?" *EuroSocial Report* 54 (1995): 75–96.

16. "The Absorption of Immigrants," Ministry of Immigrant Absorption, March 1996.

17. Abe Kay, *Americans "On the Map,"* in Hebrew (Jerusalem: American Jewish Committee, 1996); Nadav Zeevi, "Uncle Sam's Other Contribution," *Haaretz Weekend Supplement*, 12 January 1996, 21.

18. Drora Kass and Seymour Martin Lipset, "Jewish Immigration to the United States from 1967 to the Present: Israelis and Others," in *Understanding American Jewry*, ed. Marshall Sklare (New Brunswick, N.J.: Transaction, 1982); and Dov

Elizur, "Israelis in the United States: Motives, Attitudes, and Intentions," Bar Ilan University Monograph, 1979.

19. Cf. Friedlander and Goldscheider, *The Population of Israel,* 27–28.

20. Salo Wittmayer Baron, *The Social and Religious History of the Jews,* vol. 2, 2d ed. (New York: Columbia University Press, 1952).

21. Figures cited from a poll of the Israel Institute of Applied Social Research, in Kass and Lipset, "America's New Wave of Jewish Immigrants."

22. See Yinon Cohen, "War and Social Integration: The Effects of the Israeli-Arab Conflict on Jewish Emigration from Israel," *American Sociological Review* 53 (1988): 908–18; and Moshe Shokeid, *Children of Circumstances: Israeli Emigrants in New York* (Ithaca, N.Y.: Cornell University Press, 1988).

23. "The Absorption of Immigrants," Ministry of Immigrant Absorption, 57.

24. Michal Shamir and Asher Arian, "Ethnicity in the 1981 Elections in Israel," *Electoral Studies* 1 (1982): 315–32; Sammy Smooha, *Social Research on Jewish Ethnicity in Israel, 1948–1986* (Haifa: University of Haifa Press, 1987); Eliezer Ben-Rafael and Stephen Sharot, *Ethnicity, Religion, and Class in Israeli Society* (Cambridge, England: Cambridge University Press, 1991).

25. For a thorough discussion, see Raphael Patai, *Tents of Jacob* (New York: Prentice-Hall, 1971).

26. *Encyclopedia Judaica,* s.v. "demography." For a broader analysis, see Sammy Smooha, *Israel: Pluralism and Conflict* (Berkeley: University of California Press, 1978).

27. These figures are based on Central Bureau of Statistics data pertaining to the Jewish population over the age of twenty. See *Israel, Demographic Characteristics 1977, 1978,* 14–15; *Statistical Abstract, 1992,* 94–95.

28. *Statistical Abstract, 1995,* 139–40.

29. See Martin Gilbert, *The Arab-Israeli Conflict: Its History in Maps* (London: Weidenfeld and Nicolson, 1974); and Baruch Kimmerling, *Zionism and Territory: The Socio-Territorial Dimensions of Zionist Politics* (Berkeley: University of California Press, 1983).

30. See Benny Morris, *The Birth of the Palestine Refugee Problem, 1947–1949* (New York: Cambridge University Press), 1988.

31. Uzi Benziman and Atallah Mansour, *Subtenants,* in Hebrew (Jerusalem: Keter, 1992).

32. *Statistical Abstract, 1995,* 43, 138.

33. *Haaretz,* 16 July 1996, A5.

34. Nadim Rouhana and As'ad Ghanem, "The Democratization of a Traditional Minority in an Ethnic Democracy: The Palestinians in Israel," in E. Kaufman, S. Abed, and R. Rothestein, *Democracy, Peace, and the Israeli-Palestinian Conflict* (Boulder, Colo.: Lynne Rienner, 1993), 163–84.

35. As'ad Ghanem, "The Palestinians in Israel as Part of the Problem and Not the Solution," *State, Government, and International Relations,* in Hebrew, forthcoming; Baruch Kimmerling and Joel S. Migdal, *Palestinians: The Making of a People* (New York: Free Press, 1993). See also William M. Brinner, "The Arabs of Israel: The Past Twenty Years," *Middle East Review* 20, no. 1 (Fall 1987): 13–21; Nadim Rouhana, "The Collective Identity of Arabs in Israel," *New Outlook,* July/August 1987, 22–23.

36. Yehoshafat Harkabi, *Fateful Decisions*, in Hebrew (Tel Aviv: Am Oved, 1986); Aryeh Shalev, "Unilateral Autonomy in Judea and Samaria: Israel's Option," *Jerusalem Quarterly* 43 (1987): 71–86.

37. Herbert C. Kelman, "The Palestiniazation of the Arab-Israeli Conflict," *Jerusalem Quarterly* 46 (1988): 3–15.

38. See Meron Benvenisti (with Ziad Abu-Zayed and Danny Rubinstein), *The West Bank Handbook: A Political Lexicon* (Jerusalem: Jerusalem Post, 1986, 49–50); and the annual reports of Benvenisti's West Bank Data Base Project published by the American Enterprise Institute and the *Jerusalem Post*.

39. For some sense of developments and mood, see Raja Shehadeh and Jonathan Kuttab, *The West Bank and the Rule of Law* (Geneva: International Commission of Jurists, 1980); and Dov Shinar, "The West Bank Press and Palestinian Nation Building," *Jerusalem Quarterly* 43 (1987): 37–48.

40. Asher Arian, *Security Threatened: Surveying Israeli Opinion on Peace and War* (New York: Cambridge University Press, 1995).

41. Peter Jones, "The Middle East in 1995: The Peace Process Continues," *SIPRI Yearbook 1995*, chap. 4.

42. Khalil Shikaki, "The Peace Process, National Reconstruction, and the Transition to Democracy in Palestine," *Journal of Palestine Studies* 25 (1996): 5–20.

Chapter 3. Political Economy

1. Reviews of Israel's economy can be found in Assaf Razin and Efraim Sadka, *The Economy of Modern Israel: Malaise and Promise* (Chicago: University of Chicago Press, 1993); Michael Shalev, *Labour and the Political Economy in Israel* (Oxford: Oxford University Press, 1992); Yair Aharoni, *The Economy of Israel* (New York: Routledge, 1991); Yakir Plessner, *The Political Economy of Israel: From Ideology to Stagnation* (Albany: SUNY Press, 1994).

2. Zvi Gitelman and David Naveh, "Elite Accommodation and Organization Effectiveness: The Case of Immigrant Absorption in Israel," *Journal of Politics* 38 (1976): 973–79.

3. Background material on the Histadrut can be found in Rachel Tokatli, "Political Patterns in Labor Relations in Israel," Ph.D. dissertation, in Hebrew, Tel Aviv University, 1979; and Dan Horowitz and Moshe Lissak, *The Origins of the Israeli Polity: Palestine under the Mandate* (Chicago: University of Chicago Press, 1978).

4. Amnon Barzilai, *Ramon* (Tel Aviv: Schocken, 1996).

5. Chaim Ramon, "Report of the Chairman of the Histadrut—July 1994 to November 1995," New Histadrut (n.p., n.d.).

6. Arie Shirom, "Changing the Histadrut, 1994," in Hebrew, *Economic Quarterly* 42 (April 1995): 51–52.

7. D.G. Blanchflower and R.B. Freeman, "Unionism in the United States and in Other Advanced OECD Countries," *Industrial Relations* 31 (1993): 56–80.

8. Yitzhak Haberfeld, "Why Do Workers Join Unions? The Case of Israel," *Industrial and Labor Relations Review* 48, no. 4 (1995): 656–70.

9. Michal Shalev, *Labor and the Political Economy of Israel* (New York: Oxford University Press, 1992); Asher Arian and Ilan Talmud, "Electoral Politics and

Economic Control in Israel," in *Labor Parties in Postindustrial Societies,* ed. Frances Fox Piven (London: Polity Press, 1991).

10. Ira Sharkansky, *Wither the State? Politics and Public Enterprise in Three Countries* (Chatham, N.J.: Chatham House, 1979), 75.

11. Lev Grinberg, *Split Corporatism in Israel* (Albany: SUNY Press, 1991).

12. "The Histadrut—Wither?—A Symposium," in Hebrew, *Economic Quarterly* 42 (April 1995): 7–81.

13. Emanuel Sharon and G. Rosenthal, "The Pensions System: Policy Alternatives," in Y. Kopf, *Resource Allocation in Social Services: 1993–1994,* in Hebrew (Jerusalem: Israel Center for Policy and Social Research, 1995), 53–87.

14. Elkana Margalit, *The Trade Union in Israel—Past and Present,* in Hebrew (Tel Aviv: Ramot, 1994).

15. Yair Aharoni, *Structure and Performance in Israeli Economy,* in Hebrew (Tel Aviv: Gomeh, 1976), 222–63.

16. *Report on Government Companies, 1994,* 54.

17. E.S. Savas, *Privatization: The Key to Better Government* (Chatham, N.J.: Chatham House, 1987); Yitzhak Katz, "Privatization in Israel—1962–1987," in Hebrew, *State, Government, and International Relations* 35 (1991): 133–45.

18. Noya Ben-Arieh, "The Merger between Israel Ports Authority and Israel Railways," M.A. in Public Policy, Tel Aviv University, 1995.

19. *Haaretz,* 21 January 1994, 1.

20. See Haim Barkai, "Israel's Attempt at Economic Stabilization," *Jerusalem Quarterly,* Summer 1987, 3–20.

21. Haim Barkai, "The Public Sector, the Histadrut Sector, and the Private Sector in the Israeli Economy," *Sixth Report 1961–63* (Jerusalem: Falk Project for Economic Research in Israel, 1964), 28–30.

22. *Statistical Abstract, 1979,* 292.

23. Assaf Razin and Efraim Sadka, *The Economy of Modern Israel: Malaise and Promise* (Chicago: University of Chicago Press, 1993), 190.

24. *Statistical Statistical Abstract, 1985,* 176.

25. Jaffee Center for Strategic Studies, *Middle East Military Balance,* 1996.

26. *Encyclopedia Britannica Yearbooks.*

27. David Dery and Emanuel Sharon, *Bureaucracy and Democracy in Budgetary Reform* (Tel Aviv: Israel Democracy Institute and Hakibbutz Hameuhad, 1994).

28. *Statistical Abstract, 1981,* 198–99.

29. Ibid., 190.

30. *Bank of Israel Annual Report 1987,* 2.

31. *Statistical Abstract, 1995,* 587.

32. Gabriel Sheffer and Yohanan Manor, "Fundraising: Money Is Not Enough," in *Can Planning Replace Politics? The Israeli Experience,* ed. Raphaella Bilski et al. (The Hague: Martinus Nijhoff, 1980), 283–319; United Jewish Appeal, *Annual Report.*

33. "Israel in the World Economy: Israel as an East Asian State?" in *Israel in Comparative Perspective,* ed. Michael N. Barnett (Albany: SUNY Press, 1996), 107–40.

34. Hanan Sher, "Riding High-Tech," *Jerusalem Report,* 11 July 1996, 36–39.

35. *Statistical Abstract, 1995,* 590.

36. Ibid., 368.

37. *State Comptroller Report* 46 (1996): 475–96.

38. Arie Shirom, "Changing the Histadrut, 1994," in Hebrew, *Economic Quarterly* 42 (April 1995): 58.

39. Yonatan Reshef, "Political Exchange in Israel: Histadrut-State Relations," *Industrial Relations* 25, no. 3 (1986): 303–19.

40. Yoram Ben-Porath, "The Years of Plenty and the Years of Famine—A Political Business Cycle?" *Kyklos* 28 (1975): 401.

41. Gideon Doran and Boaz Tamir, "The Electoral Cycle: A Political Economic Perspective," *Crossroads*, Spring 1983, 27, table 4.

42. Eli Arom, "Economic Motivation for DMC Support," graduate paper, in Hebrew, Political Science Department, Tel Aviv University, 1978.

43. Zvi Zussman, "Poverty and Economic Gaps," *Economic Challenges in the Next Four Years*, Caesaria Conference, Israel Democracy Institute, 16–17 July 1996.

44. *Salaries and Incomes* (Jerusalem: Ministry of Labor, 1987), 43.

45. Chanoch Bartov, "Not to Feel Too Good," *Maariv Sabbath Supplement*, 6 January 1989, 10.

46. M. Semyonov and N. Levin-Epstein, *Hewers of Wood and the Drawers of Water: Noncitizen Arabs in the Israeli Labor Market* (Ithaca, N.Y.: Institute for Labor Relations Press, 1987); E. Yaar-Yuchtman, "Economic Entrepreneurship as a Socioeconomic Mobility Route: Another Aspect of Ethnic Stratification in Israel," in Hebrew, *Megamot* 29 (1986): 393–412.

Chapter 4. The Political Elite

1. Gaetano Mosca, *The Ruling Class* (New York: McGraw-Hill, 1939), 50.

2. See Robert D. Putnam, *The Comparative Study of Political Elites* (Englewood Cliffs, N.J.: Prentice Hall, 1976).

3. Yonathan Shapiro, "Generational Units and Inter-Generational Relations in Israeli Politics," in *Israel—A Developing Society*, ed. A. Arian (Assen: Van Gorcum, 1980), 161–79.

4. Mosca, *The Ruling Class*, 144–45.

5. Asher Arian, "Incumbency in Israel's Knesset," in *The Victorious Incumbent: A Threat to Democracy?* ed. Albert Somit, Rudolf Wildenmann, Bernhard Boll, and Andrea Rommele (Aldershot: Dartmouth, 1994), 71–102; Gideon Doron and Moshe Maor, *Barriers to Entry into Israeli Politics*, in Hebrew (Tel Aviv: Papyrus, 1989).

6. Yael Yishai, *Between the Flag and the Banner: Women in Israeli Politics* (Albany: SUNY Press, 1996).

7. Avraham Brichta and Yael Brichta, "The Extent of the Impact of the Electoral System upon the Representation of Women in the Knesset," in *The Impact of Electoral Systems on Minorities and Women*, ed. Joseph Zimmerman and Wilma Rule (Westport, Conn.: Greenwood Press, 1993).

8. For the judiciary, see Elyakim Rubinstein, *The Judges of the Land*, in Hebrew (Jerusalem: Schocken, 1980), chap. 6; Martin Edelman, *Courts, Politics, and Culture in Israel* (Charlottesville: University Press of Virginia, 1994). For the army, see Yoram Peri, *Between Battles and Ballots* (Cambridge, England: Cambridge Uni-

versity Press, 1983), chap. 5. For the mass media, see Yitzhak Galnoor, *Steering the Polity: Communication and Politics in Israel* (Beverly Hills: Sage, 1982), 250–53; and Dan Caspi and Yehiel Limor, *The Mass Media in Israel 1948–1990,* in Hebrew (Tel Aviv: Am Oved, 1995).

9. Walter Laqueur, *A History of Zionism* (New York: Schocken, 1976), 308–9.

10. Emanuel Gutmann and Jacob Landau, "The Political Elite and National Leadership in Israel," in *Political Elites in the Middle East,* ed. George Lenczowski (Washington, D.C.: American Enterprise Institute, 1975), 166–67.

11. Avraham Brichta, "The Social and Political Characteristics of Members of the Seventh Knesset," in *The Elections of Israel—1969,* ed. A. Arian (Jerusalem: Jerusalem Academic Press, 1972), 109–31.

12. Max Weber, "Politics as a Vocation," in *From Max Weber: Essays in Sociology,* ed. H.H. Gerth and C. Wright Mills (New York: Oxford University Press, 1946), 84.

13. Zbigniew Brzezinski and Samuel Huntington, *Political Power: USA/USSR* (New York: Viking Press, 1963), 150–73.

14. "The Cincinnatus and the Apparatchik: The Israeli Case," *Jerusalem Quarterly,* Winter 1984, 105–12.

15. Dan Horowitz and Moshe Lissak, *The Origins of the Israeli Polity: Palestine under the Mandate* (Chicago: University of Chicago Press, 1978), 159.

16. Emanuel Gutmann and Jacob Landau, "The Israeli Political Elite: Characteristics and Composition," in *The Israeli Political System,* in Hebrew, ed. Moshe Lissak and Emanuel Gutmann (Tel Aviv: Am Oved, 1977), 192–228.

17. Peter Medding, *Mapai in Israel* (Cambridge, England: Cambridge University Press, 1972), 158–60.

18. Shevah Weiss, *Israeli Politicians,* in Hebrew (Tel Aviv: Ahiasaf, 1973), 51.

19. Aharon Lapidot, "Informal Election: Predicting the Results of the Election of the Fifth President," in Hebrew, *State, Government, and International Relations* 13 (1979): 111–13.

Chapter 5. Political Parties

1. Dan Avnon, ed., *The Parties' Law in Israel: Between a Legal Framework and Democratic Norms,* in Hebrew (Jerusalem: Israel Democracy Institute and Kibbutz Hameuhad, 1993).

2. See Jonathan Mendilow, "Party Cluster Formations in Multi-Party Systems," *Political Studies* 30 (1982): 485–503.

3. See the sources listed in chapter 2, note 6, especially Lucas, *Modern History of Israel.*

4. See Zvi Even-Shushan, *The History of the Workers' Movement in Eretz-Israel,* in Hebrew (Tel Aviv: Am Oved, 1963).

5. Michael Bar-Zohar, *Ben-Gurion: A Biography* (London: Weidenfeld and Nicolson, 1979); Peter Medding, *Mapai in Israel* (Cambridge, England: Cambridge University Press, 1972).

6. Natan Yanai, *Split at the Top,* in Hebrew (Tel Aviv: Lewin-Epstein, 1969).

7. Uri Bar-Josef, *Intelligence Intervention and the Politics of Democratic States:*

The United States, Israel, and Britain (University Park: Pennsylvania State University Press, 1995), chap. 7.

8. See Yonathan Shapiro, "The End of a Dominant Party System," in *The Elections in Israel—1977*, ed. A. Arian (Jerusalem: Jerusalem Academic Press, 1980), 23–38; and Ariel Levite and Sidney Tarrow, "The Legitimation of Excluded Parties in Dominant Party Systems: A Comparison of Israel and Italy," *Comparative Politics* 15 (1983): 295–327.

9. Dan Korn, *Time in Gray*, in Hebrew (Tel Aviv: Zmora Bitan, 1994).

10. See Joseph B. Schechtman, *Rebel and Statesman, Vladimir Jabotinsky: The Early Years* (New York: Thomas Yoseloff, 1956); and Menachem Begin, *The Revolt* (London: W.H. Allen, 1951); Rael Jean Isaac, *Israel Divided: Ideological Politics in the Jewish State* (Baltimore: Johns Hopkins University Press, 1976).

11. Nakdimon Rogel, *Tel-Hai*, in Hebrew (Tel Aviv: Yariv, 1979).

12. Miriam Geter, *Chaim Arlozoroff, A Political Biography*, in Hebrew (Tel Aviv: Kibbutz Hameuhad, 1978); Shabtai Tevet, *The Murder of Arlozoroff*, in Hebrew (Jerusalem: Schocken, 1982).

13. Yaacov Shavit, *The Season of the Hunt: The "Season": The Confrontation between the "Organized Yishuv" and the Underground Organizations, 1937–1947*, in Hebrew (Tel Aviv: Hadar, 1976).

14. Shlomo Nakdimon, *Altelena*, in Hebrew (Jerusalem: Idanim, 1978).

15. Efraim Torgovnik, "Likud 1977–81: The Consolidation of Power," in *Israel in the Begin Era*, ed. Robert Freedman (New York: Praeger, 1982), 7–27.

16. For background, see Gerson Shafir and Yoav Peled, " 'Thorns in Your Eyes': The Socioeconomic Basis of the Kahane Vote," in *The Elections in Israel—1984*, ed. Asher Arian and Michal Shamir (New Brunswick, N.J.: Transaction, 1986), 189–206.

17. Gary Schiff, *Tradition and Politics: Religious Parties of Israel* (Detroit: Wayne State University Press, 1977); and Menachem Friedman, *Society and Religion: Non-Zionist Orthodoxy in Eretz Israel, 1918–1936*, in Hebrew (Jerusalem: Ben-Zvi Institute, 1978).

18. Yoram Bilu and Eyal Ben-Ari, "The Making of Modern Saints: Manufactured Charisma and the Abu-Hatseiras of Israel," *American Ethnologist* 19, no. 4 (1992): 672–87.

19. See Ehud Sprinzak, "Gush Emunim: The Tip of the Iceberg," *Jerusalem Quarterly*, Fall 1981, 28–47; and Danny Rubinstein, *Gush Emunim*, in Hebrew (Tel Aviv: Kibbutz Hameuhad, 1982).

20. For a geographical insight into the competition, see Yosseph Shilhav, "Spatial Strategies of the Haredi Population in Jerusalem," *Socio-Economic Planning Science* 18, no. 6 (1986): 411–18.

21. For information on Rafi, see Yanai, *Split at the Top*. For information on the DMC, see Amnon Rubinstein, *A Certain Political Experience*, in Hebrew (Jerusalem: Idanim, 1982); Nachman Orieli and Amnon Barzilai, *The Rise and Fall of the DMC*, in Hebrew (Tel Aviv: Reshafim, 1982); Miri Bitton, "Third Reformist Parties," Ph.D. dissertation, City University of New York, 1995.

22. Avraham Brichta, "Primaries in the Labor Party in Light of the Primaries in the DMC—Lines of Reform," in *The Electoral Revolution*, in Hebrew, ed. Gideon Doron (Tel Aviv: Hakibbutz Hameuhad, 1996), 139–45.

23. Jacob Landau, *The Arabs in Israel* (London: Oxford University Press, 1990).

24. Eli Reches, "Between Communism and Nationalism—Rakah and the Arab Minority in Israel (1965–1973)," Ph.D. dissertation, in Hebrew, Tel Aviv University, 1986.

Chapter 6. Party Organization

1. Maurice Duverger, *Political Parties* (New York: Wiley, 1963), 308.

2. Amitai Etzioni, "Alternative Ways to Democracy: The Example of Israel," *Political Science Quarterly* 74 (1959): 196–214.

3. Ibid., 312.

4. Harry Eckstein, *Division and Cohesion in Democracy* (Princeton: Princeton University Press, 1966).

5. Asher Arian and Michal Shamir, "Two Reversals in Israeli Politics: Why 1992 Was Not 1977," *Electoral Studies* 12 (1993): 315–41.

6. Duverger, *Political Parties;* also Giovanni Sartori, *Parties and Party Systems* (Cambridge, England: Cambridge University Press, 1976).

7. Peter Medding, *Mapai in Israel* (Cambridge, England: Cambridge University Press, 1972), 88.

8. Yaacov Shavit, *From Majority to State—The Revisionist Movement: The Settlement Program and the Social Idea, 1925–35,* in Hebrew (Tel Aviv: Yariv, 1978), 101–3.

9. Otto Kirchheimer, "The Transformation of West European Party Systems," in *Political Parties and Political Development,* ed. Joseph LaPalombara and Myron Weiner (Princeton: Princeton University Press, 1996), 177–200.

10. Morris Fiorina, *Retrospective Voting in American National Elections* (New Haven: Yale University Press, 1981).

11. Richard S. Katz and Peter Mair, "Changing Models of Party Organization and Party Democracy," *Political Parties* 1 (1995): 5–27.

12. Robert Michels, *Political Parties* (New York: Hearst, 1915).

13. Ibid., 391.

14. Ibid., 56.

15. Ibid., 228.

16. Medding, *Mapai in Israel.* The quotations are from 301–5.

17. Aliza Bar, *Primaries and Other Methods of Candidate Selection,* in Hebrew (Jerusalem: Israel Democracy Institute and Kibbutz Hameuhad, 1996).

18. Menahem Hofnung, *Party Funding and Campaign Funding in Israel,* in Hebrew (Tel Aviv: Israel Democracy Institute and Kibbutz Hameuhad, 1993).

19. Dan Avnon, ed., *The Parties' Law in Israel,* in Hebrew (Tel Aviv: Israel Democracy Institute and Kibbutz Hameuhad, 1993).

20. Duverger, *Political Parties.* The quotations are from 140–41.

21. Ibid.

22. Most of the examples are from Natan Yanai, *Party Leadership in Israel* (Ramat Gan: Turtledove, 1981).

23. Shevah Weiss, *Politicians in Israel,* in Hebrew (Tel Aviv: Ahiasaf, 1973).

24. Myron J. Aronoff, *Power and Ritual in the Israeli Labor Party* (Assen: Van Gorcum, 1977), chaps. 2 and 6.

25. Gary Schiff, *Tradition and Politics: Religious Parties of Israel* (Detroit: Wayne State University Press, 1977), 81.

26. Gloria Goldberg and Steven Hoffmann, "Nominations in Israel: Politics of Institutionalization," in *The Elections of Israel—1981,* ed. A. Arian (Tel Aviv: Ramot, 1983).

27. Medding, *Mapai in Israel.* Quotations are from 122–24.

28. Michels, *Political Parties,* 407–8.

Chapter 7. The Electoral System

1. Avraham Brichta and Yair Zalmanovitch, "The Proposals for Presidential Government in Israel: A Case Study in the Possibility of Institutional Transference," *Comparative Politics* 19 (1986): 1.

2. Raphael Cohen-Almagor, *The Boundaries of Liberty and Tolerance: The Struggle against Kahanism in Israel* (Gainesville: University of Florida Press, 1994).

3. Shlomo Deshen, *Immigrant Voters in Israel* (Manchester, England: Manchester University Press, 1970).

4. Moshe Atias, *Knesset Israel in Eretz Israel,* in Hebrew (Jerusalem: National Committee, 1944), 20–21.

5. Avraham Brichta, "1977 Elections and the Future of Electoral Reform in Israel," in *Israel at the Polls: The Knesset Election of 1977,* ed. Howard R. Penniman (Washington, D.C.: American Enterprise Institute, 1979), 39–57.

6. Arend Lijphart, *Electoral Systems and Party Systems* (Oxford: Oxford University Press, 1994), 134–35.

7. Dana Arieli-Horowitz, *The Labyrinth of Legitimacy: Referendum in Israel,* in Hebrew (Jerusalem: Israel Democracy Institute and Kibbutz Hameuhad, 1993).

8. Harry Eckstein, "The Impact of Electoral Systems on Representative Government," in *Comparative Politics—A Reader,* ed. Harry Eckstein and David E. Apter (Glencoe, Ill.: Free Press, 1963), 247–54.

9. Douglas Rae, *The Political Consequences of Electoral Laws* (New Haven: Yale University Press, 1967); Rein Taagepera and Matthew Soberg Shugart, *Seats and Votes: The Effects and Determinants of Electoral Systems* (New Haven: Yale University Press, 1989).

10. Maurice Duverger, "A New Political System Model: Semi-Presidential Government," *European Journal of Political Research* 8 (1980).

11. Avraham Brichta, *Democracy and Elections,* in Hebrew (Tel Aviv: Am Oved, 1977), chap. 4.

12. Stanley Waterman and Eliahu Zefadia, "Israeli Electoral Reforms in Action," *Political Geography* 11, no. 6 (November 1992): 563–78.

13. U. Reichman, B. Bracha, A. Rosen-Zvi, A. Shapira, D. Friedman, B. Susser, K. Mann, A. Maoz, and A. Klagsveld, *A Proposal for a Constitution for the State of Israel* (Tel Aviv: A Constitution for Israel, 1987).

14. Guy Bechor, *A Constitution for Israel,* in Hebrew (Or Yehuda: Maariv, 1996); Tamar Hermann, "The Rise of Instrumental Voting: The Campaign for Politi-

cal Reform," 275–97; and Gideon Doron and Barry Kay, "Reforming Israel's Voting Schemes," 299–320, both in *The Elections in Israel—1992,* ed. Asher Arian and Michal Shamir (Albany: SUNY Press, 1995).

15. Gideon Alon, *Direct Election* (Tel Aviv: Meidan, 1995).

Chapter 8. Electoral Behavior

1. All voting statistics are from official publications of the Central Bureau of Statistics.

2. Uri Avner, "Non-Voting in the Elections for the Tenth Knesset (1981) and Its Causes," *Statistical Monthly of Israel,* appendix 5, in Hebrew, 1982, 79–101.

3. A. Arian, *The Choosing People: Voting Behavior in Israel* (Cleveland: Press of Case Western Reserve University, 1973), chap. 6.

4. The literature on voting is extensive. Among the important contributions are Bernard Berelson, Paul E. Lazarsfeld, and William N. McPhee, *Voting* (Chicago: University of Chicago Press, 1954); David Butler and Donald E. Stokes, *Political Change in Britain* (London: Macmillan, 1969); Angus Campbell, Gerald Gurin, and Warren E. Miller, *The Voter Decides* (Evanston, Ill.: Row Peterson, 1954); Angus Campbell, Philip E. Converse, Warren E. Miller, and Donald E. Stokes, *The American Voter* (New York: Wiley, 1964); Morris P. Fiorina, *Retrospective Voting in American National Elections* (New Haven: Yale University Press, 1981); Norman G.H. Nie, Sidney Verba, and John R. Petrocik, *The Changing American Voter* (Cambridge: Harvard University Press, 1976).

5. Russell J. Dalton, *Citizen Politics: Public Opinion and Political Parties in Advanced Industrial Democracies* (Chatham, N.J.: Chatham House, 1996); Stefano Bartolini and Peter Mair, *Identity, Competition, and Electoral Availability: The Stabilisation of European Electorates 1885–1985* (Cambridge, England: Cambridge University Press, 1990); Mark N. Franklin, Thomas T. Mackie, and Henry Valen, *Electoral Change: Responses to Evolving Social and Attitudinal Structures in Western Countries* (Cambridge, England: Cambridge University Press, 1992).

6. Michal Shamir, "Realignment in the Israeli Party System," in *The Elections in Israel—1984,* ed. Asher Arian and Michal Shamir (New Brunswick, N.J.: Transaction, 1986), 272–75.

7. Paul Abramson, "Generational Replacement, Ethnic Change, and Partisan Support in Israel," *Journal of Politics* 51 (1989).

8. These figures are based on the Central Bureau of Statistics data pertaining to the Jewish population over the age of twenty. See *Israel, Demographic Characteristics 1977, 1978,* 14–15; *Israel, Statistical Abstract—1992,* 94–95; *Israel, Statistical Abstract—1995,* 98.

9. Charles Liebman and Eliezer Don-Yehiya, *Civil Religion in Israel: Traditional Judaism and Political Culture in the Jewish State* (Berkeley: University of California Press, 1983).

10. Michal Shamir and Asher Arian, "The Ethnic Vote in Israel's 1981 Elections," *Electoral Studies* 1 (1982): 315–31.

11. Franklin et al., *Electoral Change,* 403.

12. Butler and Stokes, *Political Change in Britain,* 293.

13. See H. Smith, "Analysis of Voting," in *The Elections of Israel — 1969,* ed. A. Arian (Jerusalem: Jerusalem Academic Press, 1972), 63–80.

14. V.O. Key Jr., "A Theory of Critical Elections," *Journal of Politics* 17 (1955): 4. See also V.O. Key Jr., *The Responsible Electorate* (Cambridge: Harvard University Press, 1966); and Angus Campbell, "A Classification of Presidential Elections," in *Elections and the Political Order,* ed. Angus Campbell, Philip E. Converse, Warren E. Miller, and Donald E. Stokes (New York: Wiley, 1966), 63–77.

15. Maurice Duverger, *Political Parties* (New York: Wiley, 1963), 307.

16. Morris Fiorina, *Retrospective Voting in American National Elections* (New Haven: Yale University Press, 1981); Arthur H. Miller and Martin P. Wattenberg, "Throwing the Rascals Out: Policy and Performance Evaluations of Presidential Candidates, 1952–1980," *American Political Science Review* 79 (1985): 359–72.

17. Michal Shamir and Asher Arian, "The Intifada and Israeli Voters: Policy Preferences and Performance Evaluations," in *The Elections in Israel — 1988,* ed. Asher Arian and Michal Shamir (Boulder, Colo.: Westview Press, 1990), 77–92; Roni Shachar and Michal Shamir, "Modelling Victory: The 1992 Elections in Israel," in *The Elections in Israel — 1992,* ed. Asher Arian and Michal Shamir (Albany: SUNY Press, 1995).

Chapter 9. The Knesset, the Government, and the Judiciary

1. Walter Bagehot, *The English Constitution* (London: Watts, 1964); and Ivor Jennings, *The British Constitution* (Cambridge, England: Cambridge University Press, 1966).

2. Material for this section is from Basic Law: Knesset. Other sources are Shevah Weiss, *The House of the Elected,* in Hebrew (Tel Aviv: Ahiasaf, 1977); Asher Zidon, *Knesset* (New York: Herzl Press, 1967); and Amnon Rubinstein, *The Constitutional Law of Israel,* 4th ed., 2 vols., in Hebrew (Tel Aviv: Schocken, 1991).

3. Rubinstein, *Constitutional Law,* 343.

4. Reuven Y. Hazan, "Presidential Parliamentarism: Direct Popular Election of the Prime Minister, Israel's New Electoral and Political System," *Electoral Studies* 15 (1996): 21–37.

5. Gideon Doron, ed., *The Electoral Revolution: Primaries and Direct Election of the Prime Minister,* in Hebrew (Tel Aviv: Kibbutz Hameuhad, 1996).

6. William H. Riker, *The Theory of Political Coalitions* (New Haven: Yale University Press, 1962); and David Nachmias, "Coalition Politics in Israel," *Comparative Political Studies* 7 (1974): 316–33.

7. Yehuda Ben Meir, *Civil-Military Relations in Israel* (New York: Columbia University Press, 1995), 31–32.

8. R.T. McKenzie, *British Political Parties* (New York: Praeger, 1963).

9. Rubinstein, *Constitutional Law,* 437, n. 56.

10. Philippa Strum, "The Road Not Taken: Constitutional Non-Decision Making in 1948–1950 and Its Impact on Civil Liberties in the Israeli Political Culture," in *Israel: The First Decade of Independence,* ed. S. Ilan Troen and Noah Lucas (Albany: SUNY Press, 1995), 83–104.

11. Knesset Proceedings 5, in Hebrew, 1721–22.

12. Rubinstein, *Constitutional Law,* 449.

13. Menachem Elon, "The Way of Law in the Constitution: The Values of a Jewish and Democratic State in Light of the Basic Law: Human Dignity and Freedom," in Hebrew, *Tel Aviv University Law Review* 17, no. 3 (1993).

14. *Bergman* v. *Minister of Treasury,* Israeli Supreme Court 23 (1) 693.

15. Menachem Hofnung, "The Unintended Consequences of Unplanned Legislative Reform: Constitutional Politics in Israel," *American Journal of Comparative Law,* forthcoming.

16. Clauses 49 and 50 of the Basic Law: Government. See Rubinstein, *Constitutional Law,* 616–18. See also Baruch Bracha, "Restriction of Personal Freedom without Due Process of Law According to the Defense (Emergency) Regulations, 1945," in *Israel Yearbook of Human Rights, 1978,* 296–323.

17. See J.E. Baker, *Legal System of Israel* (Jerusalem: Israel Universities Press, 1968).

18. Martin Edelman, *Courts, Politics, and Culture in Israel* (Charlottesville: University Press of Virginia, 1994), 36–37; Rubinstein, *Judges of the Land,* chap. 5.

19. Pnina Lahav, "Foundations of Rights Jurisprudence in Israel: Chief Agranat's Legacy," *Israel Law Review* 24 (1990): 211–69.

20. Ian Lustick, "Israel and the West Bank after Elon Moreh: The Mechanics of De Facto Annexation," *Middle East Journal* 35 (1981): 557–77.

21. Pnina Lahav, "Rights and Democracy: The Court's Performance," in *Israeli Democracy under Stress,* ed. Ehud Sprinzak and Larry Diamond (Boulder, Colo.: Lynne Rienner, 1993), 125–52.

22. Rubinstein, *Constitutional Law,* chaps. 28, 29.

23. Aharon Barak, *Judicial Interpretation,* in Hebrew (Jerusalem: Nevo, 1992); Aharon Barak, "The Constitutional Revolution: Human Rights Protected," in Hebrew, *Law and Government in Israel* 1, no. 1 (August 1992): 9–35.

24. Aharon Barak, *Judicial Discretion* (New Haven: Yale University Press, 1989); Aharon Barak, *Interpretation of Law,* in Hebrew (Jerusalem: Nevo, 1993).

25. Menachem Mautner, *The Decline of Formalism and the Rise of Values in Israel Law* (Tel Aviv: Ma'agalay Da'at, 1993), 34–35.

26. Moshe Negbi, *Above the Law,* in Hebrew (Tel Aviv: Am Oved, 1987); Menachem Hofnung, *Israel — Security Needs vs. the Rule of Law,* in Hebrew (Jerusalem: Nevo, 1991).

27. David Kretzmer, *The Legal Status of Arabs in Israel* (Boulder, Colo.: Westview Press, 1990).

28. Ian Lustick, *Unsettled States, Disputed Lands: Britain and Ireland, France and Algeria, Israel and the West Bank-Gaza* (Ithaca, N.Y.: Cornell University Press, 1993).

29. Shalev Ginossar, "Access to Justice in Israel," in *Access to Justice,* ed. Mauro Cappelletti and Brian Garth (Milan: Giuffre, 1978), 1: 627–48.

Chapter 10. Interest Groups and Public Policy

1. David Truman, *The Governmental Process* (New York: Knopf, 1951). A good summary of the field is to be found in "Interest Groups," by Robert H. Salis-

bury, in *Nongovernmental Politics*, vol. 4, *Handbook of Political Science*, ed. Fred I. Greenstein and Nelson W. Polsby (Reading, Mass.: Addison-Wesley, 1975), 171–228.

2. The term is developed in Brian Chapman, *The Profession of Government* (London: Allen and Unwin, 1959); and by H. Gordon Skilling, "Groups in Soviet Politics: Some Hypotheses," in *Interest Groups in Soviet Politics*, ed. H. Gordon Skilling and Franklin Griffiths (Princeton: Princeton University Press, 1971), 19–45.

3. Clive Thomas, ed., *First World Interest Groups: A Comparative Perspective* (Westport, Conn.: Greenwood Press, 1993).

4. Sam Lehman-Wilzig, "Public Protests against Central and Local Government in Israel, 1950–1979," *Jewish Journal of Sociology* 14 (1982): 99–116; Gadi Wolfsfeld, *The Politics of Provocation: Participation and Protest in Israel* (Albany: SUNY Press, 1988); Sam N. Lehman-Wilzig, *Wildfire: Grassroots Revolts in Israel in the Post-Socialist Era* (Albany: SUNY Press, 1992).

5. See Suzanne D. Berger, *Organizing Interests in Western Europe: Pluralism, Corporatism, and the Transformation of Politics* (Cambridge, England: Cambridge University Press, 1981); and Alan Cawson, *Corporatism and Political Theory* (Oxford: Basil Blackwell, 1986).

6. Yael Yishai, "Interest Groups in Israel," *Jerusalem Quarterly*, Spring 1979, 130; Yael Yishai, *Interest Groups in Israel: The Test of Democracy*, in Hebrew (Tel Aviv: Am Oved, 1988); and Elihu Katz and Michael Gurevich, *The Secularization of Leisure: Culture and Communication in Israel* (London: Faber and Faber, 1976), 135.

7. Gabriel Almond and James Coleman, eds., *The Politics of Developing Areas* (Princeton: Princeton University Press, 1960).

8. Gabriel Almond and G. Bingham Powell, *Comparative Politics: A Developmental Approach* (Boston: Little, Brown, 1966).

9. E.E. Schattschneider, *Party Government* (New York: Farrar and Rinehart, 1942); and L. Harmon Ziegler, *Interest Groups in American Society* (Englewood Cliffs, N.J.: Prentice Hall, 1964); Yael Yishai, "Interest Parties: The Thin Line between Groups and Parties in the Israeli Electoral Process," in *How Political Parties Work: Perspectives from Within* (Westport, Conn.: Praeger, 1994), 197–225; Marcia Drezon-Tepler, *Interest Groups and Political Changes in Israel* (Albany: SUNY Press, 1990).

10. Samuel Finer, *Anonymous Empire: A Study of the Lobby in Great Britain* (London: Pall Mall Press, 1966).

11. Yoram Peri, *Between Battles and Ballots* (Cambridge, England: Cambridge University Press, 1983), chap. 5; and Dani Zamir, "Generals in Politics," *Jerusalem Quarterly*, Summer 1981, 17–35.

12. Asher Arian, Ilan Talmud, and Tamar Hermann, *National Security and Public Opinion in Israel* (Boulder, Colo.: Westview Press, 1988), chap. 5; Asher Arian, *Security Threatened: Surveying Israeli Opinion on Peace and War* (New York: Cambridge University Press, 1995), chap. 3.

13. Uri Ben-Eliezer, " 'In Uniform'/'Without a Uniform': Militarism as an Ideology in the Decade Preceding Statehood," *Studies in Zionism* 9 (1988): 173–96; Baruch Kimmerling, *The Interrupted System: Israeli Citizens in War and Routine Times* (New Brunswick, N.J.: Transaction, 1985); Uri Ben-Eliezer, *Through the Target-Sights, Derech Hakavenet*, in Hebrew (Tel Aviv: Dvir, 1995).

14. Peri, *Between Battles and Ballots,* chap. 2; Yehuda Ben Meir, *Civil-Military*

Relations in Israel (New York: Columbia University Press, 1995).

15. Peri, *Between Battles and Ballots,* 50–51.

16. Daniel Shimshoni, *Israeli Democracy* (New York: Free Press, 1982); Ben Meir, *Civil-Military Relations,* chap. 6.

17. Gabriel Ben-Dor, "Politics and the Military in Israel: The 1973 Election Campaign and Its Aftermath," in *The Elections in Israel—1973,* ed. A. Arian (Jerusalem: Jerusalem Academic Press, 1975), 119–44.

18. Avner Yaniv, *Dilemmas in Security: Politics, Strategy, and the Israeli Experience in Lebanon* (New York: Oxford University Press, 1987).

19. Zeev Schiff, "The New Man in the Defense Ministry," *Haaretz,* 27 May 1977, 13.

20. Shimshoni, *Israeli Democracy,* 189; and Peri, *Between Battles and Ballots,* chap. 9.

21. Dina Goren, *Secrecy, Defense, and Freedom of the Press,* in Hebrew (Jerusalem: Magnes Press, 1976), 203–6, cited by Peri, *Between Battles and Ballots,* 200.

22. Amnon Barzilai, *Ramon* (Tel Aviv: Schocken, 1996).

23. Shlomo Bahat, "Structural Relations between Trade Unions and Labor Parties—A Comparative Study," in Hebrew, M.A. thesis, Department of Labor Studies, Tel Aviv University, 1979.

24. See Yonatan Reshef, "Political Exchange in Israel: Histadrut-State Relations," *Industrial Relations* 25 (1986): 303–19; Efraim Kleiman, "The Histadrut Economy of Israel," *Jerusalem Quarterly,* 1987, 77–94.

25. Yosef Sapir Institute, *Yosef Sapir,* in Hebrew (Tel Aviv: Yosef Sapir Institute, 1977), 125.

26. Arian, *Ideological Change,* 81–82.

27. Dan Horowitz and Moshe Lissak, *The Origins of the Israeli Polity: Palestine under the Mandate* (Chicago: University of Chicago Press, 1978). For later developments, see Jay Abarbanel, *The Cooperative Farmer and the Welfare State: Economic Change in an Israeli Moshav* (Manchester, England: Manchester University Press, 1974); and Alex Weingrod, *Reluctant Pioneers* (Ithaca, N.Y.: Cornell University Press, 1966).

28. A. Arian, *Ideological Change in Israel* (Cleveland: Press of Case Western Reserve University, 1968), 87; and Neal Sherman, "The Agricultural Sector and the 1977 Knesset Elections," in *The Elections in Israel—1977,* ed. A. Arian (Jerusalem: Jerusalem Academic Press, 1980), 149–70.

29. Moshe Dayan, *Pathmakers,* in Hebrew (Tel Aviv: Idanim, 1976), 379.

30. Yair Aharoni, *State-Owned Enterprises in Israel and Abroad,* in Hebrew (Tel Aviv: Gomeh, 1979), 24.

31. Differing viewpoints may be found in Charles Liebman and Eliezer Don Yehiya, "Israel's Civil Religion," *Jerusalem Quarterly,* Spring 1982; Gershon Weiler, *Jewish Theocracy,* in Hebrew (Tel Aviv: Ofakim, 1975); Yeshayahu Leibowitz, *Judaism, the Jewish People, and the State of Israel,* in Hebrew (Jerusalem: Schocken, 1976); Amnon Rubinstein, "State and Religion in Israel," *Journal of Contemporary History,* October 1967, 107–21; Charles Liebman, "Religion and Democracy in Israel," in *Israeli Democracy under Stress,* ed. Ehud Sprinzak and Larry Diamond (Boulder, Colo.: Lynne Rienner, 1993), 255–72.

32. Menachem Friedman, "The Structural Foundation for Religio-Political Ac-

commodation in Israel: Fallacy and Reality," in *Israel: The First Decade of Independence,* ed. S. Ilan Troen and Noah Lucas (Albany: SUNY Press, 1995), 51–81.

33. Shlomit Levy, Hanna Levinsohn, and Elihu Katz, *Beliefs, Observances, and Social Integration among Israeli Jews* (Jerusalem: Louis Guttman Institute of Applied Social Research, 1993).

34. Martin Edelman, *Courts, Politics, and Culture in Israel* (Charlottesville: University Press of Virginia, 1994).

35. *Rufheisen* v. *Minister of Interior,* High Court of Justice 62/72, decision xv 2428.

36. *Shalit* v. *Minister of Interior,* High Court of Justice 68/58, decision xxiii (2) 477; and *Shalit* v. *Minister of Interior 72/18,* decision xxvi (1) 334.

37. Gary Schiff, *Tradition and Politics: Religious Parties of Israel* (Detroit: Wayne State University Press, 1977).

Chapter 11. Public Administration and Local Government

1. David Ben-Gurion, *Eighth Histadrut Convention,* in Hebrew (Tel Aviv: Histadrut Executive, 1956).

2. *Statistical Abstract, 1995,* 668.

3. A. Shmaltz, ed., *Educational and Cultural Statistics,* in Hebrew (Tel Aviv: Histadrut Executive, 1956).

4. *Haaretz,* 4 October 1996.

5. On the establishment of the Labor Fund for Israel and the political debate that followed, see Giora Goldberg, "The Labor Exchanges as a Political Instrument in a Developing Society," in Hebrew, M.A. thesis, Tel Aviv University, 114–17.

6. Louis Avraham, "The Government Employment Services—Changing Roles," M.A. thesis in Public Policy, Tel Aviv University, 1993.

7. *Statistical Abstract, 1995,* 709; Yael Yishai, *Doctors and the State: Creating Hospital Trusts in Israel* (Jerusalem: Jerusalem Institute for Israel Studies, 1994).

8. David Chinitz, "Hiding in the Market Place: Technocracy and Politics in Israeli Health Policy," in *Comparative Health Policy,* ed. James Bjorkman and Christa Altenstetter (London: Macmillan, 1996).

9. *Statistical Abstract, 1995,* 714; Yishai, *Doctors and the State.*

10. Amnon Barzilai, *Ramon* (Tel Aviv: Schocken, 1996), 304–6.

11. See Yair Zalmanovitch, *Policy Making from the Margins of Government: The Case of the Israeli Health System,* forthcoming. See also Yair Zalmanovitch, "Public Policy Decision Making in the Light of Government and Public Administration in Israel," Ph.D. dissertation, Hebrew University of Jerusalem, 1991.

12. Yael Yishai, *The Power of Expertise: The Israel Medical Association* (Jerusalem: Jerusalem Institute for Israel Studies, 1990).

13. A. Arian, "Health Care in Israel: Political and Administrative Aspects," *International Political Science Review* 2 (1981): 43–56.

14. Ministry of Health, "Principles for a National Health Insurance Law," in Hebrew, 1978.

15. Brenda Danet, *Pulling Strings: Biculturalism in Israeli Bureaucracy* (Albany: SUNY Press, 1988).

16. Gerald E. Caiden, *Israel's Administrative Culture* (Berkeley: Institute of Governmental Studies, 1970), 18–19.

17. Jacob Reuveny, *The Israel Civil Service* (Ramat Gan: Massada, 1974); and David Nachmias and David H. Rosenbloom, *Bureaucratic Culture: Citizens and Administrators in Israel* (New York: St. Martin's Press, 1978).

18. David Dery, *Political Appointments in Israel* (Jerusalem: Israel Democracy Institute and Kibbutz Hameuhad, 1993).

19. Michael Brecher, *Decisions in Crisis: Israel, 1967 and 1973* (Berkeley: University of California Press, 1980), 239.

20. Benjamin Akzin and Yehezkel Dror, *Israel: High Pressure Planning* (Syracuse: Syracuse University Press, 1966).

21. Yitzhak Galnoor, "Water Planning: Who Gets the Last Drop?" in *Can Planning Replace Politics? The Israeli Experience,* ed. Raphaella Bilski et al. (The Hague: Martinus Nijhoff, 1980), 137–215.

22. *Haaretz,* 10 July 1996, A6.

23. *Statistical Abstract, 1981,* 599.

24. Rachel Gruman and Moshe Peleg, *Democracy in Israel,* in Hebrew (Jerusalem: Carmel, 1995).

25. See David Dery and Binat Schwarz-Milner, *Who Governs Local Government?* in Hebrew (Jerusalem: Israel Democracy Institute and Hakibbutz Hameuhad, 1994); Efraim Ben-Zadok, ed., *Local Communities and the Israeli Polity* (Albany: SUNY Press, 1993); Daniel Elazar and Chaim Kalchheim, eds., *Local Government in Israel* (Lanham, Md.: University Press of America, 1988).

26. Arye Hecht, "Municipal Councils Opposed to the Mayors in Israel's Local Government," Jerusalem Center for Public and National Issues, August 1993, 4.

27. Mordecai Ben-Porat, "The Election System for the Local Authorities," in Hebrew (Jerusalem: Ministry of the Interior, 1978). Mimeographed.

28. Hecht, "Municipal Councils," 9.

29. Ibid., 26–27.

30. Shevah Weiss, *Local Government in Israel,* in Hebrew (Tel Aviv: Am Oved, 1972).

31. Hanna Herzog, *Realistic Women: Women in Local Politics,* in Hebrew (Jerusalem: Jerusalem Institute for Israel Studies, 1994).

32. Efraim Torgovnik and Yeshayahu Barzel, "Block Grant Allocation: Relationship between Self-Government and Redistribution," *Public Administration* 57 (1979): 87–102.

33. Fred Lazin, *Politics and Policy Implementation: Project Renewal in Israel* (Albany: SUNY Press, 1994).

Chapter 12. Aspects of Political Culture

1. Gabriel Almond and Sidney Verba, *The Civic Culture* (Princeton: Princeton University Press, 1966); Mary Douglas and Aaron Wildavsky, *Risk and Culture: An Essay on the Selection of Technological and Environmental Dangers* (Berkeley: Uni-

versity of California Press, 1982); Robert D. Putnam, *Making Democracy Work: Civic Traditions in Modern Italy* (Princeton: Princeton University Press, 1993).

2. A. Arian, *Ideological Change in Israel* (Cleveland: Press of Case Western Reserve University, 1968).

3. Donald E. Stokes, "Spatial Models of Party Competition," *American Political Science Review* 57 (June 1963): 368–77.

4. This section is based largely on A. Arian and Michal Shamir, "The Primarily Political Functions of the Left-Right Continuum," *Comparative Politics*, January 1983, 139–58.

5. Philip E. Converse, "The Nature of Belief Systems in Mass Publics," in *Ideology and Discontent*, ed. David E. Apter (New York: Free Press, 1964), 206–61; David Butler and Donald E. Stokes, *Political Change in Britain* (London: Macmillan, 1969); Ronald Inglehart and Hans D. Klingemann, "Party Identification, Ideological Preference, and the Left-Right Dimension among Western Mass Publics," in *Party Identification and Beyond*, ed. Ian Budge, Ivor Crewe, and Dennis Farlie (London: Wiley, 1976), 243–73.

6. George Rabinowitz and Stuart E. MacDonald, "A Directional Theory of Issue Voting," *American Political Science Review* 83 (1989): 115.

7. This section is based largely on Michal Shamir and Asher Arian, "Competing Values and Policy Choices: Israeli Public Opinion on Foreign and Security Affairs," *British Journal of Political Science* 24 (1994): 111–33.

8. Elihu Katz, "Forty-nine Percent Lean towards 'Transfer' of Arabs," *Jerusalem Post International Edition*, 20 August 1988; Charles Liebman and Eliezer Don-Yehiya, *Civil Religion in Israel: Traditional Judaism and Political Culture in the Jewish State* (Berkeley: University of California Press, 1983).

9. Yehoshafat Harkabi, *Israel's Fateful Decisions* (London: I.B. Tauris, 1988).

10. Dan Horowitz and Moshe Lissak, *Origins of the Israeli Polity: Palestine under the Mandate* (Chicago: University of Chicago Press, 1978); Baruch Kimmerling, *Zionism and Territory* (Berkeley: University of California Press, 1983); Dan Horowitz and Moshe Lissak, *Trouble in Utopia: The Overburdened Polity of Israel* (Albany: SUNY Press, 1989).

11. Asher Arian, *Security Threatened: Surveying Israeli Opinion on Peace and War* (New York: Cambridge University Press, 1995), chap. 8.

12. Daniel Shimshoni, *Israeli Democracy* (New York: Free Press, 1982), 83–84.

13. The former figure is from *Statistical Abstract, 1982*, 72.0; the latter, based on 1970 data, is from Elihu Katz and Michael Gurevich, *The Secularization of Leisure: Culture and Communication in Israel* (London: Faber and Faber, 1976).

14. Israel Advertising Association, "Survey of Exposure 1995," 1995, 17.

15. Dan Caspi and Yehiel Limor, *The Mass Media in Israel 1948–1990*, in Hebrew (Tel Aviv: Am Oved, 1995).

16. William Frankel, *Israel Observed* (London: Thames and Hudson, 1980), 138.

17. Caspi and Limor, *Mass Media in Israel*, 122–33.

18. Rachel Lael, ed., *Channel 2 — The First Year*, in Hebrew (Jerusalem: Israeli Democracy Institute, 1994).

19. Of those who watched television on the Sabbath, almost 80 percent viewed the news. Sabbath television watchers were 87 percent of the total television audi-

ence. These data are from *Statistical Monthly of Israel, 1981,* in Hebrew, appendix 3, 30; and *Statistical Abstract, 1982,* 722–23. For a detailed report on television viewing, see mimeographed report, in Hebrew, of Israel Institute of Applied Social Research, March 1983.

20.*Haaretz,* 7 May 1996, C4.

21. V.O. Key Jr., *Public Opinion and American Democracy* (New York: Knopf, 1961); Benjamin I. Page and Robert Y. Shapiro, *The Rational Public: Fifty Years of Trends in Americans' Policy Preferences* (Chicago: University of Chicago Press, 1992); James A. Stimson, *Public Opinion in America: Moods, Cycles, & Swings* (Boulder, Colo.: Westview Press, 1991); John R. Zaller, *The Nature and Origins of Mass Opinion* (Cambridge, England: Cambridge University Press, 1992).

22. Gabriel Weimann, "*Caveat Populi Quaestor:* The 1992 Pre-Elections Polls in the Israeli Press," in *The Elections in Israel—1992,* ed. Asher Arian and Michal Shamir (Albany: SUNY Press, 1995), 258.

23. David O. Sears, "Political Behavior," in *The Handbook of Social Psychology,* vol. 5, ed. Gardner Lindzey et al., 2d ed. (Reading, Mass.: Addison-Wesley, 1969), 315–45; David Nachmias, "A Temporal Sequence of Adolescent Political Participation: Some Israeli Data," *British Journal of Political Science* 7 (1977): 71–83; Orit Ichilov and Nissan Naveh, "The Perception of the 'Good Citizen' by Israeli Adolescents," *Comparative Politics* 13 (1981); 361–76; and Eva Etzioni-Halevy with Rina Shapira, *Political Culture in Israel* (New York: Praeger, 1977).

24. Raphael Ventura, "The Influence of the Close Family Circle on the Voting Patterns of the Individual in Israel," Ph.D. dissertation, Tel Aviv University, 1997.

25. Yonathan Shapiro, *An Elite without Successors,* in Hebrew (Tel Aviv: Sifriat Hapoalim, 1984).

26. Rina Shapira, *Blue Shirt and White Collar,* in Hebrew (Tel Aviv: Am Oved, 1979).

27. A. Arian, "Were the 1973 Elections in Israel Critical?" *Comparative Politics,* October 1975, 152–65.

28. On this and related topics of culture, see Nurith Gertz, *Captive of a Dream: National Myths in Israeli Culture,* in Hebrew (Tel Aviv: Am Oved, 1995); Tamar Katriel, *Communal Webs: Community and Culture in Contemporary Israel* (Albany: SUNY Press, 1991); Tamar Katriel, *Talking Straight: "Dugri" Speech in Israeli Sabra Culture* (Cambridge, England: Cambridge University Press, 1986); Charles Liebman and Eliezer Don Yehiya, *The Civil Religion of Israel* (Berkeley: University of California Press, 1983).

29. Zvi Gitelman, *Becoming Israelis: Political Resocialization of Soviet and American Immigrants* (New York: Praeger, 1982).

30. Michal Shamir, "The Lack of Political Tolerance," *Haaretz,* 22 February 1983; Ephraim Yuchtman-Yaar and Yochanan Peres, "Trends in the Commitment to Democracy, 1987–1990," in *Israeli Democracy under Stress,* ed. Ehud Sprinzak and Larry Diamond (Boulder, Colo.: Lynne Rienner, 1993), 221–34.

31. Michal Shamir and John Sullivan, "The Political Context of Tolerance: A Cross-National Perspective from Israel and the United States," *American Political Science Review* 77 (1983): 911–28.

32. Ibid.

33. Asher Arian, *The Peace Process and Terror: Conflicting Trends in Israeli*

Public Opinion in 1995, memorandum #45 (Tel Aviv: Jaffee Center for Strategic Studies), February 1995, 23–24.

34. Page and Shapiro, *The Rational Public,* 9–11.

35. Gadi Wolfsfeld, "The Politics of Provocation Revisited: Participation and Protest in Israel," in *Israeli Democracy under Stress,* ed. Ehud Sprinzak and Larry Diamond (Boulder, Colo.: Lynne Rienner, 1993), 199–220.

36. Yael Yishai, *Land or Peace: Whither Israel?* (Stanford: Hoover Institution, 1987).

37. Gadi Wolfsfeld, *The Politics of Provocation: Participation and Protest in Israel* (Albany: SUNY Press, 1988); Sam N. Lehman-Wilzig, *Wildfire: Grassroots Revolts in Israel in the Post-Socialist Era* (Albany: SUNY Press, 1992).

38. Ehud Sprinzak, *Political Violence in Israel* (Jerusalem: Jerusalem Institute for Israel Studies, 1995); Ehud Sprinzak, *The Ascendance of Israel's Radical Right* (New York: Oxford University Press, 1991); Moshe Negbi, *Above the Law,* in Hebrew (Tel Aviv: Am Oved, 1987).

39. Uri Bar-Joseph, "State-Intelligence Relations in Israel—1948–1996," *Journal of Conflict Studies,* Fall 1997, forthcoming.

Glossary

AGUDAT ISRAEL (also AGUDA). Ultra-Orthodox Ashkenazi religious political party with a non-Zionist ideology.

AHDUT HAAVODA. *(a)* Political organization founded in 1919 and dominant in the politics of the Yishuv; *(b)* left-wing party that joined Mapai and Rafi in 1968 to form the Israel Labor Party.

ALIGNMENT. *(a)* Name of election list in 1965 composed of Mapai and Ahdut Haavoda; *(b)* name of election list between 1969 and 1984 composed of Labor and Mapam.

ALIYAH (plural ALIYOT). Waves of mass immigration to Israel. Literally, going up.

ASHKENAZIM. Jews whose background is generally the countries of Europe.

BADER-OFER AMENDMENT. Law that sets the method of distributing the last seats to be allocated in Knesset elections.

BALFOUR DECLARATION. Statement by British secretary of state for foreign affairs in 1917 supporting the establishment of a Jewish national home in Palestine.

BASIC LAW. Legislation of constitutional stature. Collection of Basic Laws to form the Israeli constitution.

BEITAR. The youth group of the Revisionist movement and later of the Herut movement.

BLACK PANTHERS. Jewish protest movement to better social and economic status of Sephardim. Affiliated in electoral list with Rakah.

CITIZENS RIGHTS MOVEMENT (CRM). Left-wing party now part of Meretz.

COUNCIL OF TORAH SAGES. Committees of rabbis of ultra-Orthodox parties (Agudat Israel, Degel Hatorah, and Shas) that provide political and religious decisions for those parties.

DEGEL HATORAH. Ultra-Orthodox non-Zionist party, which split from Agudat Israel.

DEMOCRATIC FRONT FOR PEACE AND EQUALITY (DFPE). Arab communist and nationalist list, dominated by Rakah (q.v.).

DEMOCRATIC MOVEMENT FOR CHANGE (DMC). Party headed by Yigael Yadin; ran only in 1977 and won 15 seats.

D'HONDT SYSTEM. Allocation of seats in parliament taking into consideration the relative strength of the competing lists.

DMC. *See* Democratic Movement for Change.

DOMINANT PARTY. A political party in power for some time with spiritual and wide-ranging dominance.

EDA HAHRIDIT. Ultra-Orthodox group that rejects Zionism.

EL AL. National airline of Israel.

ELECTORS' COUNCIL (ASEFAT NIVHARIM). Elected assembly of the Yishuv.

ERETZ ISRAEL. Land of Israel, denoting the biblical Promised Land.

ETZEL. *See* Irgun.

FREE CENTER. A splinter group from Herut in 1967, a part of the Likud between 1973 to 1977, and a component of the DMC in 1977. Headed by Shmuel Tamir.

GAHAL. Originally, an acronym for the Herut-Liberal bloc. Established as a joint list in 1965; expanded in 1973 and called the Likud.

GENERAL ZIONISTS. Right-of-center bourgeois party that joined with the Progressives between 1961 and 1965 and was known as the Liberal Party.

GESHER. List headed by David Levy after leaving the Likud before 1996 election. Eventually formed a joint list with Likud and Tzomet.

GREATER ISRAEL. Notion of completeness and indivisibility of Eretz Israel.

GUSH EMUNIM. Settlement movement, largely religious, active in the territories acquired after the 1967 war and staunchly opposed to any territorial compromise.

HAGANAH. The defense force of the Yishuv.

HALACHA. Jewish religious law.

HAPOEL HAMIZRACHI. Religious workers' movement and a major component of the National Religious Party.

HAPOEL HATZAIR. A political party in the Yishuv period representing labor.

HAREDIM (singular haredi). Ultra-Orthodox non-Zionists. Literally awe-inspired, fearful of God's majesty.

HASHOMER HATZAIR. The settlement movement and youth group of Mapam.

HERUT. A political party with nationalist ideology and a major component of the Likud.

HEVRAT OVDIM. Former holding company for Histadrut enterprises.

HISTADRUT. The General Federation of Labor, formerly a key economic and political force; since 1994 restyled to focus on trade-union matters.

HOVEVEI ZION. First organized national Jewish groups that encouraged immigration to Eretz Israel at the end of the nineteenth century.

IDF. Israel Defense Force. Israel's army.

INDEPENDENT LIBERAL PARTY. Formerly the Progressive Party. Part of the Liberal Party between 1961 and 1965. In 1984, part of the Alignment.

INTIFADA. The uprising by Palestinians in the West Bank and Gaza that began in December 1987.

IRGUN. Also known as the Etzel, the Irgun Zva Leumi, National Military Organization. A pre-independence military organization associated with the Revisionist movement.

ISRAEL LABOR PARTY. *See* Labor-Mapam Alignment.

JEWISH AGENCY. Executive body of the World Zionist Organization.

KACH. List of the Jewish Defense League founded by Rabbi Meir Kahane. Not permitted to run in Knesset elections since 1988 because of its racist ideology.

KALANTERISM. The exploitation of a political situation to further personal goals, in particular switching support from one party to another, thereby determining the party that will be able to form the governing coalition.

KEREN HAYESOD/MAGBIT. An institution of the World Zionist Organization charged with raising funds for the movement.

KEREN KAYEMET. Institution of the World Zionist Organization charged with purchasing and reclaiming land in Eretz Israel.

KIBBUTZ. Communal settlement sharing production and consumption.

KIPAH. Skullcap, worn for religious purposes.

KNESSET. Israel's parliament, with 120 members.

KNESSET ISRAEL. Communal organization of Jews in the Yishuv in which membership was voluntary.

KUPAT HOLIM. The sick fund that provides health insurance and treatment.

LA'AM. A political party that developed from the Rafi faction of Mapai; in 1968 it refused to support the Labor Party, then joined the Likud.

LABOR ALIGNMENT. *See* Labor-Mapam Alignment.

LABOR-MAPAM ALIGNMENT. List that included the Labor Party and Mapam; 1969–84.

LABOR PARTY. One of Israel's major political parties. A socialist party dominant in the pre-state era and during the first three decades of independence.

LADINO. Language combining Spanish and Hebrew; spoken by many Sephardim.

LAVON AFFAIR. Political conflict in Mapai with far-reaching implications within the party. Conflict began as a question regarding the role Defense Minister Lavon played in a security mishap in 1954.

LAW OF RETURN. Law passed in 1950 by the Knesset granting to every Jew in the world the right to immigrate to Israel.

LEHI. Extreme rightist pre-state underground organization opposed to co-operation with the British.

LIBERAL PARTY. Middle-class party; a member of Gahal and Likud. Formerly the General Zionists.

LIKUD (UNITY). One of Israel's major parties. Right-of-center party historically opposed to the return of territories taken in 1967 war.

MANDATE. The British administration of Palestine by a decision of the League of Nations after World War I, lasting until 1948.

MAPAI. Originally, an acronym for Israel Workers' Party. Created in 1930, it was the dominant party in Israel until its merger in 1968 with Ahdut Haavoda and Rafi to form the Israel Labor Party.

MAPAM. Originally, an acronym for the United Workers' Party. A left-wing socialist-Zionist party, Mapam was part of the Alignment between 1969 and 1984.

MERETZ. Left-wing party formed by Mapam, the Citizens Rights Movement, and Shinui.

MIZRACHI. A major component of the National Religious Party.

MOLEDET. Party led by Rehavam "Gandhi" Ze'evi, calling for the voluntary transfer of Arabs from Israel.

MOSHAV. Cooperative settlement in which production (but usually not consumption) is collective.

MOSHAVOT. Small agricultural towns.

NAAMAT. Women's branch of Histadrut labor federation. Formerly Pioneer Women.

NATIONAL COMMITTEE (VAAD LEUMI). Executive committee of the Yishuv.

NATIONAL RELIGIOUS PARTY (NRP). Zionist and Orthodox religious party, active in settlements in territories.

NATURAI KARTA. Anti-Zionist ultra-Orthodox Jewish religious group.

NEW HISTADRUT. Formed in 1994.

NEW ZIONIST ORGANIZATION. Established in 1935 by Revisionist movement led by Jabotinsky after splitting with the World Zionist Organization.

PALMACH. Elite striking force of the Yishuv's military arm, the Haganah.

PEACE NOW. Movement formed after the 1973 Yom Kippur War urging conciliation and moderation toward Arabs and Arab states. Opposes most settlement in the territories.

POALEI AGUDAT ISRAEL. Ultra-Orthodox religious party with a workers' orientation. In 1984, a component of Morasha.

POALEI ZION. A major socialist political party in the Yishuv period.

POGROM. Organized massacre, especially of Jews.

PROGRESSIVE LIST FOR PEACE (PLP). Established in 1984 as a joint Arab-Jewish list supporting the creation of a Palestinian state alongside Israel.

PROGRESSIVES. Political party originally supported and dominated by German immigrants. In 1961, merged with General Zionists to form the Liberal Party. This party split in 1965 and the Progressives took the name Independent Liberals. In 1984, part of the Alignment.

PROTEKTZIA. Political pull; favoritism shown or access achieved because of informal connections with an official or clerk.

RAFI. Party founded by David Ben-Gurion and others who split from Mapai. Ran once in 1965 and won 10 seats. In 1968, most of the activists (excluding Ben-Gurion) returned and formed the Labor Party along with Mapai and Ahdut Haavoda.

RAKAH (New Communist List). Broke off from the Israel Communist Party in 1965, based primarily on Arab support. In 1977, formed the Democratic Front for Peace and Equality as a joint list with the Black Panthers.

SEPHARDIM. Jews of African and Asian ethnicity. Also called Eastern Jews and Oriental Jews.

SHAS. Ultra-Orthodox religious party established in 1984 with special appeal to Sephardim. Split from Agudat Israel.

SHINUI (CHANGE). Centrist party established as a protest movement after the 1973 Yom Kippur War. Part of the Democratic Movement for Change in 1977, and of Meretz in 1992 and 1996.

SIX-DAY WAR. 1967 war between Israel and Arab states resulting in Israeli capture of East Jerusalem, West Bank of Jordan, Gaza Strip, Sinai Peninsula, and Golan Heights.

SMDS. The single-member district system of electoral representation.

STATE OF ISRAEL. Founded in 1948.

STATE LIST. A political party made up originally of Rafi members who refused to reunite with Mapai in 1968.

STATUS QUO. Regarding the role of the Jewish religious law in Israel, perpetuating the arrangements that existed in the Yishuv period.

TEHIYA. Extreme nationalist party, which claimed Israel's right to the Land of Israel and opposed the peace treaty with Egypt. Last elected in 1988.

TZOMET. Right-wing party established in 1988 by "Raful" Eitan, former IDF chief of staff, splitting from Tehiya. In 1996 formed a joint list with Likud and Gesher.

UNITED TORAH JEWRY (YAHADUT HATORAH). Joint list of ultra-Orthodox non-Zionist parties, Agudat Israel and Degel Hatorah.

WESTERN WALL. Sometimes known as Wailing Wall. Remnant of outer wall of the Second Temple in Jerusalem. Considered the most holy site in Judaism.

WHITE PAPER. Policy statement of the British government. Used during the Mandate period to announce restrictions on Jewish immigration.

WORLD ZIONIST ORGANIZATION (WZO). Established by Theodor Herzl in 1897 to promote plans of Jewish nationalism.

YAHADUT HATORAH. *See* United Torah Jewry.

YERIDA. Out-migration from Israel. Literally, going down.

YESHIVA (plural YESHIVOT). Seminars of higher learning of Jewish religious law and ritual.

YIDDISH. Language combining German and Hebrew; spoken by many Ashkenazim.

YISHUV. Jewish settlement and communal organizations in the pre-state period.

ZIONIST CONGRESS. Governing body of the World Zionist Organization.

Index of Names

Index of Subjects

About the Author

Asher Arian was born in Cleveland, Ohio, in 1938. He received an A.B. degree from Western Reserve University and earned his doctorate in political science at Michigan State University in 1965.

Since 1966 he has been teaching and researching in Israel, most recently with the University of Haifa and the Israel Democracy Institute. Since 1986 he has been at the Graduate Center of the City University of New York, where he holds the rank of Distinguished Professor. At Tel Aviv University he served as chairman of the political science department and as dean of the Faculty of Social Sciences, and he was the Romulo Betancourt Professor of Political Science.

Arian's professional writing has concentrated on elections, public opinion, and political parties, and most of it has been concerned with Israeli politics. He is the author of many books, including *Security Threatened: Surveying Israeli Opinion on Peace and War; The Choosing People: Voting Behavior in Israel; Ideological Change in Israel;* and (with others) *Changing New York City Politics.* Since the 1969 elections Arian has edited the series entitled The Elections in Israel. His articles have appeared in such journals such as the *British Journal of Political Science, Public Opinion Quarterly,* the *Journal of Conflict Resolution, Comparative Politics,* the *Journal of Politics,* the *Western Political Science Quarterly,* and *Electoral Politics.*

Arian has served as president of the Israel Political Science Association and was twice elected to the Executive Committee of the International Political Science Association. He is currently editor of the International Political Science Asssociation's book series.